Sir Robert Falconer: A Biography

Sir Robert
FALCONER

A Biography

JAMES G. GREENLEE

UNIVERSITY OF TORONTO PRESS

Toronto Buffalo London

© University of Toronto Press 1988
Toronto Buffalo London
Printed in Canada

ISBN 0-8020-2655-9

Printed on acid-free paper

Canadian Cataloguing in Publication Data

Greenlee, James Grant Christopher.
Sir Robert Falconer

Includes index.
ISBN 0-8020-2655-9

1. Falconer, Robert, Sir, 1867–1943.
2. Education, Higher – Canada – History.
3. College presidents – Ontario – Biography.
4. Scholars – Canada – Biography.
5. University of Toronto – Presidents – Biography.
I. Title.

LE3.T517 1907.G73 1987   378'.111   C87-095203-X

All photographs are from the collection of
the University of Toronto Archives.
This book has been published with the help of a grant
from the Social Science Federation of Canada,
using funds provided by the Social Sciences and
Humanities Research Council of Canada.

Contents

Acknowledgments

Inevitably, in the course of sustained scholarly endeavour, one accumulates a staggering burden of debt, largely moral but sometimes all too tangible in nature. To thank adequately all those who helped encourage, guide, and maintain me as I pursued Sir Robert Falconer would require rather more wit and ink than I have at my disposal. Even so, let all those, named or unnamed, who rendered assistance rest assured that, long after the pages of this book have yellowed, my memory of their gifts will linger, forever green.

In this regard, none has a stronger claim to my gratitude than that phalanx of archivists and librarians upon whose goodwill and knowledge I so liberally drew. At Dalhousie, McGill, Queen's, UBC, Balliol, the Bodleian, and Edinburgh they smoothed my way and laid their treasuries open to an eager pillager. Guardians of public repositories in Toronto and Ottawa were no less open-handed. From the University of Saskatchewan Archives came priceless copies of Falconer's correspondence with his life-long friend W.C. Murray. Emmanuel and Knox colleges at Toronto gave me access to their splendid collections. To the east, the Atlantic School of Theology made it possible to trace Falconer's early life and that of his peripatetic sire. Closer to home, Elizabeth Behrens, librarian of Grenfell College, displayed on my behalf all the resourcefulness and ingenuity one could ask from a fellow scholar. By her and all these others I was generously and professionally served.

In the end, however, my most enduring debt is owed to Dr David Rutkin and the staff of the University of Toronto Archives. Despite shortages of manpower and financial support, he went out of his way to ensure that I wasted not a moment of my time. Never was I made to feel an intruder. Never was I hampered in my work. And above all else, I had the aid of Harold Averill. Master of the sources, this scholar guided me unfailingly as I burrowed deeper and deeper into Falconer's life. He also compiled the photographs reproduced in this book. Beyond this, his cheefulness helped make the work a daily pleasure. May his tribe increase!

Sympathetic ears and discriminating eyes helped make this book better than it might have been. Professor Robin Harris was particularly generous with insightful advice, as was Professor John Moir of Scarborough College. Not for the first time, C.M. Johnston of McMaster endured endless hours of conversation with a former graduate student who has continued to be inspired by his sterling example. And Olaf Janzen, one of the finest critics I know, wore out several blue pencils on my behalf. Other helpful readers included Tom Willey of McMaster and Georgina Quick and Michael Newton of Grenfell College. Nor can I forget the members of our faculty colloquium who provided sharp interdisciplinary criticism. As for Gerry Hallowell of the University of Toronto Press, I can only wish that all authors had so sympathetic and professional an editor. To all these patient readers and especially Catherine Frost I extend my thanks for inanities weeded out and my apologies for any that remain.

On the all too vital material side, I take pleasure in thanking Drs Niall Gogan and 'Mac' Macleod of Memorial's Office of Research. Without their advice and generous financial support this work could never have been undertaken. Drs C.F. Poole and James K. Hiller also played an important role in this regard. In Hamilton, the Swans of Province Street and the charming proprietors of the Hotel Watts made my long association with Robert Falconer more memorable and rewarding in a dozen different ways.

For her part, Joanne knows how much I depended on the help of my live-in research assistant, typist, and editor.

Preface

Joseph Flavelle and Robert Falconer were good friends. Neighbours on Queen's Park Crescent, they were also bridge partners and sympathetic colleagues on the governing board of the University of Toronto. As ardent champions of empire and devout but liberal Protestants they had even more in common. Indeed, the similarity extended to the point that both men dismissed suggestions that their lives might one day provide fodder for biographers. On this score, however, as well as on many others, the parallel disintegrates, because Falconer meant what he said, whereas Flavelle was merely being coy. Thus, the pork baron carefully saved much of his personal correspondence, while the university leader assiduously destroyed most of his. To a point, therefore, Sir Robert continues successfully to hold the biographer at arm's length.

For all his resolve, however, Falconer could not wholly isolate himself from the prying of a stubborn meddler. One of the best published Canadians of his era, he also left a mass of official papers in which the public man lies well preserved in plain view. Together these sources reveal the mind and actions of a man who, by the common assent of contemporaries, stood as the very personification of Canadian higher education in his own day. A thoughtful academic leader, Falconer made significant contributions to redefining the nature of the university as it moved into the twentieth century. He also fought a sustained battle against rising American influence and in the process helped mould graduate studies in a fledgling nation. Just as doggedly, he struggled to enhance the autonomy of the university in the face of popular and at times political pressures from without. Along the way he became embroiled in some of the period's most celebrated controversies concerning academic freedom.

In the midst of all this activity, Falconer wielded a potent and productive pen. From youth to old age he poured out his thoughts in a tide of books, articles, and speeches which embraced a galaxy of subjects. Ranging freely over religion, philosophy, history, literature, and scores of contemporary issues, he displayed an eclectic and mediating cast of mind during an era of intellectual turmoil. If one thread served to unify the whole, for him that thread was a Christian idealism that was flexible enough to accommodate other strands of truth.

Academic and author, Sir Robert was also very much a public man. In this regard, he won his spurs as a young professor in Halifax, who bitingly criticized the evils of unrestrained individualism. Anxious to refurbish society, he nevertheless rejected many of the panaceas then on offer. Die-hard conservatism, unreconstructed liberalism, and the socialist as well as the social gospel were eschewed in favour of a 'progressive yet conservative' approach to reform. As events transpired, his would be a voice for moderation and gradualism. Over time Falconer sponsored many specific causes ranging from church union to conscription; from imperial co-operation to a deeper internationalism. In the end he won a national and an international reputation in his many fields of endeavour. Altogether, despite his rejection of the suggestion, he seems to merit a biography and one, moreover, that ranges well beyond the confines of local or university history. Therefore, in begging Sir Robert's posthumous indulgence, one can only hope that he would not fail to recognize himself in the pages that follow.

J.G.G.
Sir Wilfred Grenfell College
Memorial University of Newfoundland

At New College, Edinburgh, c. 1890:
(standing) Robert Falconer, second from left; James Falconer, far right;
(seated) Clarence McKinnon, second from left

Pine Hill, c. 1900

Convocation Hall is packed for Falconer's inauguration in 1907.
Laurier and Borden, in white-faced robes, flank the podium.

President Falconer in 1908,   Robert Falconer at forty-six.
forty-one years old   This portrait, dated 24 October 1913,
      was a gift to Edmund Walker.

Sir Robert Falconer, official portrait, 1926

Showing the strain of office: Sir Robert Falconer in 1926

On board ship with Sophie, en route to South Africa, 1929

Lady Falconer on the evening of Sir Robert's retirement dinner, 1932

Profile in charcoal: sketch for a bust of Sir Robert Falconer
that now stands in the University of Toronto Archives

The University Commission of 1905–6:
(left to right) the Rev. D. Bruce Macdonald, the Rev. Canon H.J. Cody,
Sir W.R. Meredith, J.W. Flavelle (chairman), A.H.U. Colquhoun (secretary),
Goldwin Smith, Sir Edmund Walker

The Rev. Henry John Cody, c. 1920:
a powerful member of the Board of Governors,
he succeeded Falconer as president of the university in 1932.

The pup tents of a 'mortarboard army' were an eloquent riposte
to those who charged Falconer and the university
with slackness in the early days of the First World War.
Pictured here is an OTC camp on the lawns of Victoria College in early 1915.

Sir Byron Edmund Walker,
long-time chairman of the Board of Governors and
later chancellor of the University of Toronto

The setting for so many dramatic moments in Falconer's life,
Convocation Hall, shown here as it appeared in 1918

Winter 1918: Convocation Hall and Knox College

Hart House, a gift from the Massey family, photographed shortly after its completion in 1919. The building was thought by Falconer to be the greatest single contribution to the corporate life of the student body.

Soldier's Tower, 5 June 1924. Half of the funds raised by the Alumni Association to commemorate the university's fallen were allotted to the construction of the tower and the remainder provided scholarships for returned soldiers.

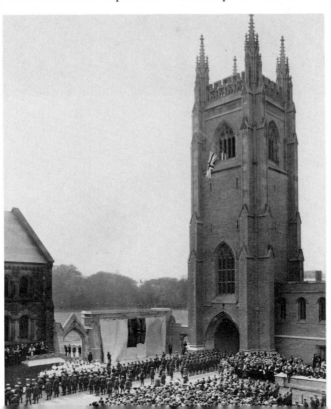

University College, illuminated for centenary celebrations, 6 October 1927

Sir Robert Falconer: A Biography

CHAPTER I

Cold Baths and Classics

Conflicts of tribal identity were alien to the Falconers of Pictou County. They were transplanted Scots and rugged Presbyterians. It was as simple as that. The passage of a few generations in the New World did nothing to dim their ancestral memory. There was, of course, no reason why it should. Alexander Falconer of Inverness left Scotland in 1784 only to settle among kinfolk who had departed in the storied brig *Hector* a decade earlier.[1] Following the American Revolution the Pictou settlements grew with an infusion of former highland soldiers and some loyalists. Privation may have been general but a sense of community flourished. In 1786 it was bolstered by the arrival of the Reverend James MacGregor, the result of an appeal to Scotland for a Gaelic-speaking minister capable of off-setting the influence of American-born preachers. In time this tireless 'coureur de bois of the Kingdom of Heaven' was followed by a growing number of Scottish missionaries, who, while representing variant strains of Presbyterianism, collectively helped confirm the ethnic and religious consciousness of their colonial charges.[2] Later a native ministry flourished, and it was as influential members of that ardent band that the Falconers registered their first significant impress upon history.

Alexander Falconer, grandson of the pioneer, was the first of his clan to ascend the pulpit. A future moderator of the Presbyterian church in Canada, his beginnings were humble enough. He was born in Riverton, a community of some 300, to James, a mason and farmer, and Elizabeth, a woman of loyalist stock. Beyond that, so little is known of his early life that speculation about it is fruitless. That he was a sober and serious young fellow may be assumed. By the mid-1850s his sense of vocation was apparently strong enough to lead him to the door of the Reverend James Ross, principal of the West River Seminary. That institution was an offshoot of the Pictou Academy, founded in 1817 by one of the fathers of Maritime higher education, the Reverend Thomas McCulloch.[3] Quite literally beginning with a log cabin, McCulloch sought to provide for the education of a local Presbyterian ministry. By 1820 the academy had attained the status of a theological college. A classical education formed the backbone of its curriculum, although the natural sciences were not neglected.[4] Theological studies supplemented the program offered to those destined for the church. Sectarian squabbles and government parsimony, however, led McCulloch to despair of the experiment. In 1839 he accepted the post of president of Dalhousie University. The idea of the Academy, none the less, lived on. Thus in the 1840s Dr John Keir revived the divinity hall in his own house on Prince Edward Island. By 1848 the mantle of leadership fell on James Ross, who brought the hall back to its original home in Pictou County. It was, therefore, to West River that the aspiring Alexander Falconer ventured in search of an education.

Although formally designated a 'seminary,' the hall at West River was a less than impressive structure. The reality was 'a dingy and ill-ventilated room above a little country schoolhouse.'[5] Each of the dozen or more students in turn chopped wood, kindled the fire, and swept the floor. It is unlikely, of course, that Nova Scotian farmboys, accustomed to hard work and imbued with religious fervour, looked upon these simple chores as onerous tasks. On the contrary, the shared efforts of something like a common life undoubtedly fostered a spirit of brotherhood in the school. Youthful idealism, after all, frequently feeds on hardships, real or imagined. Ross, for his part, bore the burden of instruction alone until 1850, when he was joined by Keir, now home from Prince Edward Island, and Dr James Smith. Under these men, Alex was introduced to the classics and theology. Purposeful and intelligent, he prospered. A classmate later recalled that as a student, Falconer was 'diligent, eager and successful.'[6] When the seminary moved to a more central location in Truro, in 1858, he followed.

At Truro the precise nature of his vocation came into clearer focus. There Alex was instrumental in founding a student organization dedicated to promoting Presbyterian missions abroad.[7] In time, missionary work would become the abiding passion of his life. For the moment, however, he was content to address the ills of his own society and could be heard from time to time delivering temperance lectures by torchlight in local barns.[8] After graduating in 1860, Alex sought to extend and refine his theological knowledge and perhaps to satisfy an inherent wanderlust.

Accordingly, he applied for and was granted admission to New College, Edinburgh, then the foremost seat of Presbyterian learning. After a year of graduate studies, he returned to Nova Scotia eager to take up his vocation.

Eager he may have been but Presbyterian ministers were never guaranteed a congregation as a matter of right. In a decentralized and democratic church they had to await a 'call.' For the better part of 1862 Alex, although licensed by the Presbytery of Pictou, was forced to bide his time. At last, however, word came of an opening at the newly constructed Zion Church in Charlottetown, and Falconer's name was mentioned. For some reason his candidacy met with a degree of opposition within the presbytery, but in the end he was selected for the post.[9] Voted a salary of £150 per year, he was ordained on 14 October 1862. Any misgivings about his installation were soon dispelled. Indeed, he proved a popular minister. It was later recalled that he was 'diligent and painstaking' and that his sermons were 'thoroughly evangelical, full of thought and always carefully prepared.'[10] Within a few years Alex was appointed clerk of the presbytery. Apparently, he had proved himself not only in the minds of his parishioners but also in those of his colleagues.

Meanwhile, as the fathers of Confederation met in solemn conclave, Falconer was preoccupied with courtship, the happy issue of which was a marriage to Susan C. Douglas on 14 November 1865.[11] His choice was appropriate and predictable. The bride's father, the Reverend Robert Douglas, had been born in Jedburgh, Scotland, and, like Alex, educated at New College. In a sense, therefore, the union helped reaffirm the Falconer inheritance. Obedient to the injunctions of scripture, the young couple were fruitful and multiplied. Three new Presbyterians were added to the fold. James and Jean would make their marks but it was the eldest, Robert Alexander, born 10 February 1867, who would become a national and an international figure.

From the outset the Falconer children were imbued with a spirit of sober devotion and a love of learning by their strong-willed but kindly father. Alex imparted to them the faith, values, and prejudices of that Presbyterianism he himself typified. Assessing his father years later, Robert recalled a man who was 'an unusually good preacher, well-educated and thoughtful, clear and direct in speech, logical but by nature tolerant. He rarely exhibited emotion, was reserved as to his inner life, and was suspicious of overwrought sentiment.'[12] The religion to which Alex introduced the children, while prayerful and warm, was not dogmatic or shrill. Simple truths were digested gradually and formed a familiar element in the rhythm of their lives. Daily readings round the family hearth, palatable doses of the Westminster Catechism and Sunday services blended with the routine of life. 'There was,' wrote Robert, 'no harshness in our home, nor any marked inconsistency between what my parents professed and the way they lived.' The atmosphere was reverent, but the commonsensical Falconers eschewed mysticism and emotional extremes. Consequently, young Robert never underwent 'periods of religious exaltation, nor any such momentous experience as some have gone through in definite conversion.' As far as he could recall in later life, his boyhood thoughts were undisturbed by doubt. 'I had not,' he said, 'a rebellious mind.'

The moral tone of the Falconer home was strongly puritanical, and the values preached were typically Victorian. Restraint in all things was urged. Sexual contemplation or expression was, of course, taboo, and 'total abstinence was a primary virtue.' Honesty, thrift, industry, kindness, and charity all were deemed fundamental to the flowering of a Christian character. Wealth and luxury were regarded suspiciously. Stalwart representatives of lower-middle-class morality, this clergyman's family wondered 'whether there was not some lurking sting in the pride and display of which [they] knew nothing.' As he came to know men of means at first hand, Robert gradually lost much of this prejudice against wealth per se. His career would bring him into contact with some of the weightiest pocketbooks in the world. Slowly he learned to discriminate between those people who indulged in vainglorious ostentation and those who preserved a moral conscience. In making his adjustment to a larger world than that inhabited by his father, Robert maintained a code of personal puritanism. He learned, however, to tolerate at least minor differences in others. He was, for example, a life-long, non-smoking teetotaller, but guests in his home were permitted wine and tobacco. Even in his personal life, moderation was the key. Puritanism was never confused with asceticism by the Falconers. Alex, for one, delighted in a good table and was particularly fond of West Indian food.[13] Robert later condemned asceticism as 'neither mature nor virile.'[14] It represented to him an excessive and unwarranted reaction to the world which, for all its corruption, was not absolutely evil.

On the negative side, there was a certain insular smugness, almost a snobbishness about Alexander and his brood. Some have argued that Canadian Presbyterianism as a whole suffered from a superiority complex.[15] Robert came to recognize that 'particles of social and even political self-esteem clouded the draft in our cup.' Alex in particular was prone to entertain and propagate stereotypes of other groups in society. Anglicans were viewed as closet Catholics: far too easy-going and wont to exalt the ecclesiastical above the spiritual. They were indelibly scarred by the tradition of church establishment against which dread practice Alex railed wherever he saw it exemplified.[16] In contrast, Presbyterians were portrayed as the friends of 'sturdy voluntaries' everywhere who preached the doctrine of the separation of church and state.[17] As for the Church of Rome, it was regarded with thinly veiled distrust. 'Popery' was described by Alex as the natural handmaiden of 'intolerance and persecution.'[18] Sinister motives were imputed to incessant Catholic demands for separate schools. The language applied to describe Catholicism would have been familiar in sixteenth-century Geneva. Anglicans and Catholics, of course, were natural targets for the heirs of Calvin, but Methodists and Baptists did not escape unscathed. Emotionally reserved and prizing the intellectual content in religion, some Presbyterians, Alex among them, found the enthusiasms of the more evangelical sects distasteful and crude. 'We suspected,' said Robert, 'that in their effervescence some of their morality might evaporate.'

Much of the sense of caste displayed by Alex and other Presbyterians is traceable to their self-image as an intellectual élite. Among themselves it was believed that a tradition of excellence in the ministry was part of their Scottish heritage. A story is told of a Scottish professor who, when asked about the qualifications required of a Presbyterian minister, once replied: 'Brains and the grace of God.' He added that 'if you lack the grace, the Lord may help you; but if you lack the brains, the Lord help you!'[19] Education, Robert was taught, was 'a prize to be pursued at all costs.' The intellect, properly attuned, was regarded as a necessary helpmate and buttress of faith. Belief founded on raw emotion was held to be a fragile and vulnerable thing. Hence the deeply ingrained suspicion of Methodist 'effervescence.' Wandering evangelists were regarded as disturbing and dangerous. How, it was asked, could assent to doctrine be given unless the tenets were clearly defined and understood? Worse still, what remained when the initial glow of enthusiasm engendered by the transient evangelist inevitably dimmed? It was feared that religion and morality could collapse in ruins were they not grounded securely on a firm intellectual foundation. This, it should be noted, is not to assume that faith proceeded from reason but merely to assert that faith should be reasonable and that reason guided by faith was unlikely to err. In many ways this attitude to the intellect was a Presbyterian equivalent of the Thomistic notion of 'right reason.' In any event, Presbyterians and the Falconers in particular were ardent champions of education.

As to the vehicles for promoting learning, a distinction was drawn between religious and general education. It was assumed that religious education was the province of the family and the church, not the state. Consequently, while assiduously developing their own Sunday schools and theological colleges, Presbyterians emerged as champions of the common school and the secular university. They were unmoved by the fear of 'godless colleges' which haunted Anglicans such as John Strachan. Indeed, in mid-century Nova Scotia, Thomas McCulloch and other Presbyterians led the fight for an all-embracing, non-sectarian university. This was in line with Scottish tradition which in principle held that higher education should be democratic in form and spirit.[20] As Robert came to realize, this enthusiasm for secular education 'was not to be attributed to any especially broad and tolerant conviction that Truth is great and will prevail.' Instead, it was founded on the then reasonable assumption that the task of religious education was seriously pursued in the home. Beyond that, it was sensed that there was little to be feared from common education in small, homogeneous communities dominated by broadly shared Protestant values.

This intellectual tradition, then, perhaps bred a degree of hauteur in some Presbyterians. It also, however, made them somewhat less fearful of novel ideas than many of their fellow Protestants. It has been argued, for example, that Canadian Presbyterians adapted more smoothly to new interpretations of the Bible than did Methodists or Baptists.[21] Alex Falconer, for one, made the adjustment. Perhaps he was influenced to do so by his friends in the ministry. These included no less a figure than George Munro Grant, future principal of Queen's University. As early as 1866 Grant criticized all who clung narrow-mindedly to biblical literalism.[22] In the 1870s Alex was a member of a Halifax study group that met regularly to discuss current ideas. Its members included the likes of John Forrest, later president of Dalhousie University and Allan McKnight, principal of Pine Hill Theological College.[23] At the General Assembly of 1876 it was McKnight in company with Grant who defended the Reverend D.J. Macdonnell in a celebrated heresy trial.[24] Macdonnell had preached a sermon which, in the light of recent study, called into question traditional interpretations of the doctrine of eternal punishment. While his interpretation was rejected by the gathering, Macdonnell was not forced to recant. Instead he was merely asked to sign a statement of faith purposely worded in conciliatory terms to encourage harmony and protect freedom of inquiry. If a man can be judged by the company he keeps, Alex Falconer was to be numbered among those hospitable to reasonable change.

He was not, however, a straw tumbling in whichever direction the winds of current opinion might blow. New ideas were to be assessed cautiously.

Alex once observed that 'rationalistic or liberal Christianity may accomplish certain things, but nothing is more manifest than its weakness as an instrument for the soul's salvation.'[25] He urged people to 'ignore the cries that the intelligence of the age has outrun the old gospel.'[26] Evidently, therefore, he rejected the more extreme claims of those who challenged the faith of his fathers. Equally, however, he reacted strongly against those who would have stifled the new learning. For himself, he did not fear the critical movement. Properly understood, he maintained, it had a significant role to play in the continuing mission of the church.[27] Indeed, he felt that it would ultimately produce a more intelligent grasp of scripture. Although the intricacies of theology and criticism were rarely to be dealt with in the pulpit, a minister true to his calling was not at liberty to wallow in unresolved doubt or retreat to a comfortable but arid dogmatism. On the contrary, counselled Alex, if he would be a man he must learn to confront all theological difficulties with fortitude and integrity. He must, indeed, cultivate 'a masculine intelligence.'[28]

Altogether the domestic conditions of Robert's youth encouraged a sense of clear-cut identity, emotional security, and intellectual confidence. These were valuable, stabilizing assets in the son of a man who was by nature peripatetic. In September 1869 the family was on the move. The congregation of St James's Church, Dartmouth required a new pastor, and Alex eagerly responded. For the children this was a stroke of good luck, since the Halifax region boasted far better educational facilities than those available on Prince Edward Island. When the time came the boys were enrolled in an academy run by Alexander Howard MacKay, where they were introduced to the classics. No mean scholar, MacKay was a noted classicist. In addition to an MA degree he boasted a B SC degree and was later elected a fellow of the Royal Society of Canada.[29]

Alex meanwhile threw himself into parochial work. Some pleasant hours were also spent in the stimulating atmosphere of McKnight's ministerial association. Furthermore, the continuing battle against drink provided yet another outlet for his abundant energies. Recognition was soon afforded him. In 1873 Alex was made clerk of the Synod of the Presbyterian Church of the Lower Provinces, the youngest man in Canada to hold such a position at the time.[30] He came to this post at a historic moment in the life of Canadian Presbyterianism. Talk of reuniting the fragments of Knox's kirk was in the air. Alex, in company with his moderator, P.G. McGregor, contributed to the lengthy but successful negotiations. Finally, in June 1875 he joined the moderators and clerks of the four uniting synods on the platform at Victoria Hall, Montreal to celebrate the birth of the Presbyterian Church in Canada. At that point, had he been content to settle down, Alex would no doubt have carved out a worthy place for himself in the annals of the new church. He was, however, growing restless. He once confided to G.M. Grant that 'long pastorates and citizenship may have advantages but I think that on the whole, occasional changes do good both to the ministers and congregations.' Critical of the complacent, he added that 'I think I know some ministers in Nova Scotia to whom a change would be beneficial.'[31] But the root of his restlessness lay deeper. Indeed, he still yearned to carry the cross to foreign parts.

In the fall of 1876 it happened that the Reverend George Brodie, missionary pastor of Greyfriars Church in Trinidad, died creating a vacancy in the local presbytery. As luck would have it, a friend and former schoolmate of Alex, Kenneth J. Grant of Merigomish, was labouring in the same missionary field. Aware of Falconer's interest in missions, Grant wrote to inform him of the opening.[32] Alex rushed to apply.[33] His own merits and Grant's considerable influence won him local endorsement. Final approval rested with the Mission Board of the United Presbyterian Church of Scotland under whose wing Greyfriars fell. The board, it appeared, was sufficiently impressed to offer Alex the post. His lineage and his studies at New College no doubt stood him in good stead. Light of heart, the Falconers took ship for Trinidad late in December 1876.

One of the many things Robert inherited from his father was a zest for travel. His experiences over the next fifteen years bred in him a taste for the cosmopolitan, a spirit of adaptability, and a sense of the physical reality of the British empire, whose champion he would become. The outward voyage to Trinidad, tinged as it was with a spirit of adventure, undoubtedly helped to kindle these enthusiasms. Alex, after all, was fairly bubbling with anticipation and for once took no pains to disguise it. A mood of exuberance coloured the flood of letters that streamed from his eager pen.[34] Not even the gales of an Atlantic winter could dampen his spirits. After 'an average amount of storm-tossing,' 'cribbed, cabined and confined,' the family reached its first port of call, St Thomas in the Virgin Islands. Clearly stimulated by the change of scene, Alex exulted in the cosmopolitan atmosphere of that 'cozy little town.' The harbour was crowded with over seventy sail, and the red-roofed houses amid swaying palms gave the whole settlement 'a novel and somewhat romantic aspect.' To cap everything, his first sabbath in the tropics seems to have offered Alex all the hope a young missionary could crave.

That Sunday began well with services at eight o'clock in the morning, a time, he noted, when northern sabbath-keepers were customarily abed. This token of enthusiasm was heartening, but the principal highlight of that memorable day was the family's attendance at a 'love-feast' arranged by the local Moravian mission. The church hall, marvelled Alex, was crowded with over 300 negroes, all singing lustily at one moment; all reverent and attentive the next. When the collection plate was passed round, these mere labourers donated something in excess of $400. Alex was staggered! Such liberality, he observed, was all but unheard of even in the richest parishes of Nova Scotia. The love-feast itself was movingly simple, consisting of the ritual consumption of a bun and beverage. Following the service, he was inspired to learn that since 1732 over sixty-one Moravian missionaries had died at their posts on this tiny island. As he stood by their graves, a wave of romantic resolve flooded his heart. Here, he reflected, were 'servants of the Lord Jesus Christ who were prepared to enter upon the path of self-denial at the Master's bidding, surrender the comforts of home and even life itself, without repining, and endure hardship, as good soldiers of Jesus Christ.'[35]

By early January, in a buoyant mood, the Falconers disembarked in Trinidad. This particular crown colony offered as lush a field as any missionary could desire. It boasted a population of well over 100,000 souls drawn from the four corners of the earth. Fundamentally, the inhabitants of this immigrant society were distinguishable as Creole and non-Creole in origin.[36] The term 'Creole' identified anyone born in Trinidad who was of European or African descent or a mixture of the two. All others constituted groups apart. These non-Creoles included a significant Chinese minority and an even larger Indian population, known locally as 'Coolies,' who had settled down in Trinidad after a period of indentured service. When added to the mass of now-free black Creoles, they provided ample scope for even the most assiduous proselytizer.[37]

The Falconers were greeted warmly at dockside. A delegation from Greyfriars conducted them immediately to their new home. The manse might have been constructed to Alex's own design, so well did it please him at first sight. It was a perfect combination of the spartan and the spacious. A wooden structure, it fronted on Brunswick Square, an area of some five or six acres planted with magnificent flowering trees. A grape vine twined round the front door through which one entered a large parlour of some sixteen by twenty-four feet. Even the sparse furnishings delighted Alex's puritanical soul. 'The lover of an elegantly furnished house may well grow sad, as she sees only a few yards of grass matting upon the floor, a table or two and a few cane-seated chairs, with two or three inevitable rockers.' The missionary, however, 'goes into ecstasies that that tyrant fashion does not demand that anything more than what comfort necessitates shall be required.' A dining room, a study, and the bedrooms were grouped around the parlour. The beds, of course, were draped in mosquito netting in order to fend off that ever-present 'little admirer of humanity.' A large bathtub was a special blessing. In order to combat the debilitating effects of the tropical sun, the Falconers rose daily at six and in turn 'plunged and floundered' in the chilly waters of the outsized tub.[38] Meals were prepared by a Creole cook over a charcoal pit in the yard. The family dined well. 'There is' wrote Alex, 'no lack of good vegetables that may be cultivated here. And with beef imported from the Main ... fowls in abundance, and a good supply of fair fish, plenty of edible vegetables and excellent fruits, no man need wish for a more wholesome or agreeable diet.'[39] He further recorded that he found the climate hot but tolerable. Indeed, after a few months he rejoiced that he had never enjoyed better health.

The backbone of the congregation of Greyfriars was the small but highly influential Scottish community of Port of Spain. Scots dominated the dry goods trade. In 1883 a petition signed by twenty-five of the most powerful local businessmen featured the names of no less than ten Scottish merchants.[40] Nearly all were Presbyterians, and most struggled to preserve their sense of ethnic identity in this corner of the empire. In 1880 a St Andrew's Society was formed. The birthday of Robert Burns was regularly celebrated. No doubt the Falconers joined in the festivities. Robert made life-long friends among the ranks of these merchant families. In particular, he kept in touch with the Grants, who had built one of the greatest merchant houses on the island. These Scottish connections, of course, helped maintain an element of continuity in the Falconers' lives. But Alex had not ventured forth merely to take up a comfortable sinecure among like-minded men. He had come to win converts, and his real inspiration was found on the streets and in the countryside. There he personally encountered the uncovenanted masses.

Alex once criticized Charles Kingsley for having viewed Trinidad solely through 'Government House spectacles.'[41] The blinkered canon, said Falconer, had painted too rosy a picture and overlooked too many problems. While this was a rather shrewd observation, it is perhaps ironic that it emerged from the lips of a man who was to a great degree a prisoner of the racial assumptions of his generation and profession. It has been argued that 'industry' was the favourite Victorian yardstick for assessing the qualities of various races.[42] In Falconer's case this was certainly true, but like other missionaries he was also prone to evaluate a race according to its capacity for Christianization. As he surveyed the Trinidadian scene, he quickly devised a thumbnail sketch of the local racial hierarchy. At the bottom of the scale one found the negro.

Accepting planter mythology at face value, Alex argued that the black man was the author of his own misfortune. Following emancipation in the 1830s the negro, through some flaw in his character, had proved himself 'naturally indolent.' Thus did Falconer explain the large number of idle blacks who loitered about Port of Spain. 'Singularly improvident' and having fruit readily available, the negro gave little thought to the future. Even when assessing the black's positive features, the standard note of colonial paternalism rang in Alex's words. The negro, after all, was 'a jolly, cheerful, happy looking fellow. He appears strong, lusty, and healthy. Seldom do you meet with a prematurely wrinkled haggard countenance among them.' These, essentially, were children in need of guidance. That need, moreover, was urgent. The moral condition of the negro was described as 'low and loose.' Altogether, Falconer's general impression was that several decades of missionary effort had produced little change in this heathen mass.[43]

The Indian 'Coolie,' in contrast, struck Alex as belonging to 'a higher order of manhood.' The Indian worked the fields and often settled down on a small piece of land once his indenture was fulfilled. In short, he displayed 'industry.' The coolies also were proving themselves amenable, if not to Christianity, then at least to some measure of westernization. It has been noted, for example, that by 1892 over 80 per cent of Indian children were being educated in the Canadian mission schools.[44] This success has been ascribed to the fact that Canadian missionaries, such as Grant, unlike their European counterparts, chose not to berate Hinduism but merely to preach Christ in a positive and unusually tolerant way.[45] Alex, at any rate, came to focus more and more of his attention on the Indian community as time went by.

Among the immigrant population, however, no element ranked higher in his estimation than the Chinese. He had no doubt that 'once Christianized, the Chinese must take a leading position among the nationalities of the world.' He was impressed by their sobriety and economic acumen. 'The Chinaman,' he wrote, 'is a sober, indeed somewhat demure looking character, for it is said that [he] seldom smiles. He looks as if someone had sat upon his nose, as soon as he was born and he had been bitterly weeping over the calamity ever since. But be this as it may, the Chinaman is capable of becoming a good citizen. He is active, diligent and persevering, fond of money yet not afraid to spend it.'[46] In contrast to the open libertinism of the negro, Alex applauded the public modesty of these orientals. Indeed, the men and women dressed so alike that as a stranger he had 'some difficulty in distinguishing the sex.' Since the Chinese at the time were rapidly merging with the local community and adapting European ways, he came to regard them as the group most likely to be fully Christianized one day.[47]

In the light of these assessments it is tempting to describe Alex as a 'racist' and leave it at that. To do so without qualification, however, would be to indulge in the very practice for which he may justly be criticized, that is, fostering a stereotype. All too often in a post-colonial age, terms such as 'racist' and 'imperialist' have been employed indiscriminately as oversimplified labels to characterize what in reality were complex and variegated ideas. Falconer, for example, never subscribed to some of the cruder and more vicious forms of Victorian racial thought. The lust to dominate, so singularly exemplified in Carlyle's 1849 pamphlet, *The Nigger Question*, was foreign to his make-up. The 'struggle for mastery' which bulked so large in social Darwinist theory found no echo in his heart.[48] Alex never prophesied an inevitable 'great war of the races.' Neither did he preach the permanent inferiority of coloured peoples. Biological determinism was not for him. At first glance, his view of the Trinidadian negro may seem to contradict this assessment. He did, after all, describe him as 'naturally indolent.' Against this, however, must be set his optimism concerning the black Moravians of St Thomas. Apparently, for him some negroes were more readily 'improved' than others. Unfortunately, he never speculated on the factors that helped condition these different responses. His comments about the Chinese, on the other hand, would seem to rule out any systematic biological basis in his general approach to the question of race. Instead, he appears to have exemplified a milder school of racial thinking which focused its attention on culture rather than blood.

That Alex was ethnocentric is beyond dispute. Just as he regarded other Christian sects as inferior to Presbyterianism, so also he viewed alien civilizations as deficient in some respects. In company with the English Creoles, he maintained that British civilization, inspired by a fervid Protestantism, represented all that was best and most enlightened in human society.[49] In his opinion, however, this lofty position had not been conferred upon the British peoples that they might exploit or tyrannize others. Privilege and responsibility, power and a providential mission went hand in hand. Indeed, his thoughts on empire, which were inseparable from his racial attitudes, echoed the note of trusteeship that had tempered imperial thinking since at least the time of Burke. Some, of course, regarded such notions as the purest humbug. But Alex embraced them in deadly earnest. 'Influence and supremacy,' he wrote, 'have been bestowed for some higher purpose than to echo forth national glory.' Indeed, providence had declared that it was the special task of the

English-speaking peoples 'to diffuse the light of Divine life and love over the darkened nations and tribes of the earth.' Britain and America, he argued, had become great precisely because they had shouldered that burden. Prefiguring the caveat in Kipling's 'Recessional,' Alex warned that 'if we shirk, God will use other agencies.' Ancient monarchies, past empires, and once-powerful churches had all suffered decline as soon as they had demonstrated 'faithlessness of stewardship.'[50] Clearly, in his mind British supremacy was conditional, not absolute, in nature. Furthermore, even in his ethnocentricity, Alex was not wholly insensitive to the feelings of those he sought to convert. Recognizing, for example, the Indian as 'a noble specimen of humanity, a gentleman in his bearings' he followed the lead of Kenneth Grant in avoiding denunciations of Hindu culture.[51] In this spirit in 1879 he drafted a scheme for the education of local Indians who would aid in tutoring their brothers. The proposed curriculum included not only English, but also the reading and writing of Hindustani.[52] Alex was not bent on stamping out all vestiges of alien culture. His attitude to the Indian contrasted sharply with that of most whites on the island. John Morton, the first Canadian missionary, saw little but immorality and degradation in his Hindu charges.[53] Alex saw more. Indeed, while his racial statements inevitably grate upon the modern ear, he must be judged a moderate among his contemporaries.

The degree to which Robert was influenced by this atmosphere is difficult to gauge precisely. He became an altogether more sophisticated thinker than his father and drew his inspiration from a variety of sources. Still, some general affinities with Alexander's thought are fairly apparent. Most obviously, Robert developed a broad Anglocentric streak. He too used British yardsticks to categorize and evaluate other peoples. Even more than Alex, however, he perceived racial and national differences as the outcome of historical and geographical rather than biological factors. It followed, therefore, that the values preached by more advanced nations were communicable to others. He too held that Britons in particular had a global mission to perform. In time he emerged as one of Canada's most eloquent proponents of an empire envisioned chiefly as an agent of moral betterment. Concerning blacks and Indians, Robert wrote and said little. The Chinese, however, captivated his imagination as fully as they had that of his father. Indeed, he became convinced they would play a more dynamic and perhaps decisive role in the world's affairs as time went by. Accordingly, at several points in his life he laboured earnestly to increase educational links between China and the west.[54] Altogether, Robert's thoughts on race were optimistic in tone. That he struck such a note, having grown up on an island where bigotry and prejudice flourished, says much perhaps for the moderating influence of Alex.

The ethnocentric tendencies inspired by his father were stoutly reinforced by Robert's education in Trinidad. Queen's Royal College, where he and James were enrolled, was British to the core. Founded in 1859, the college had been intended to help heal religious and cultural divisions on the island by offering a common secular education to the Protestant and Catholic élite.[55] In practice, French Creoles had almost immediately condemned it as a 'godless college' and set up their own rival Catholic institutions.[56] Consequently, the Royal College had emerged as a largely Protestant and British preserve. The coloured boys whom Robert encountered there were either sons of prosperous Creoles or holders of the few free places that existed. In either case, all were well on the road to assimilation and did not disturb the essentially British atmosphere of the school. A bastion of the well-to-do, the college charged fees in excess of £9 per year. On his clergyman's salary, Alex found this sum a considerable burden. He earned more than his Canadian-sponsored colleagues, but even so, as he complained to G.M. Grant, he found it 'impossible to do anything more than live on it.'[57] Even so, the money was found, and the Falconer boys were treated to an English public school education in the tropics.

From its inception the college had been envisioned as an Eton or Harrow overseas. Horace Deighton, a Cambridge man and first headmaster, had set the tone. Under his leadership the college, if anything, placed greater emphasis on scholastic achievement than did many of its British prototypes. The staff were all Oxbridge graduates fully conversant with British education. As such they were well equipped to prepare their students to compete for places in the ancient universities. A commitment to excellence soon achieved the desired results. In 1862 the Cambridge Local Examiners declared that the college's candidates were quite capable of holding their own with British matriculants.[58] This was encouraging, but there was real rejoicing when in 1868 the college tied for first place in the Cambridge pass list.[59] Small wonder, then, that Alex, with his Presbyterian respect for education, was willing to sacrifice that his sons might benefit from such training. And benefit they did. Robert, indeed, excelled. With an abiding love of the classics, a talent for languages, and a penchant for sustained work, he emerged as the premier student of his day. His teachers, he recalled, were 'all excellent,' but the strongest impression was made by the headmaster, William Miles, formerly of Oriel College, Oxford. Miles has been severely censured for his criticism of free places which opened the door to blacks. He considered these students 'injurious to the moral tone of the school.'[60] Prejudiced he may have been, but he was also a brilliant teacher who instilled a respect for patient, careful scholarship. Robert once reminisced that he was 'a first class scholar and I owe him more than I can say. He taught me to seek accuracy, and to try never to miss the main point. He never allowed the main point to be lost in the mass of detail, but recognized that accuracy in detail is necessary to grasp the meaning of anything.'[61] Under the influence of Miles and his colleagues, Robert acquired not only good study habits but reinforcement for his father's view that the British universities represented the pinnacle of the educational world. This assumption would persist throughout his life.

In most ways Robert was very much a typical public schoolboy. Cold baths and the classics formed his daily round. One aspect of the life, however, remained forever foreign to his nature. Of above average height and sturdily built, he was, nevertheless, unmoved by the cult of games. By his own admission he had neither the talent nor a taste for the more robust sports that others relished. An occasional round of golf in later years seems to have satisfied whatever competitive urges may have lurked unsatisfied in his less than savage spirit. Even then, as his favourite partner, Archibald MacMechan, observed, when one strode the links with Falconer, challenging conversation was the only stimulation to be had.[62] What then, besides omnivorous reading, served to occupy his island days? Rambles in the surf and in the countryside with James toughened his adolescent form. Police band concerts in the botanical gardens were pleasant enough. His chief amusement, however, was derived from stamp collecting.

A historical summary appended to the album developed by Robert and his brother records that the collection was formally launched on Christmas day 1879.[63] A nucleus of a few hundred stamps given them by a local gentleman provided the necessary encouragement. Never one to take even hobbies lightly, Robert saw in his collection 'a stimulus to geography.' Through those colourful paper patches he felt himself drawn into closer contact with a larger world he had yet to see. Trinidad, he found, with its cosmopolitan community and far-flung trade was an excellent centre for acquiring stamps. English, French, Dutch, and German steamers called regularly on their way to a hundred ports of call and all of them generated correspondence. For young lads with plenty of contacts in the business community the opportunities were endless. 'We plied our own commerce,' wrote Robert, 'as small boys do, visiting shops and offices, accosting people as they got their letters, exchanging with other collectors, and doubtless making ourselves more or less a nuisance.'[64]

The fathers of their schoolmates proved obliging and the collection blossomed. The day would come, of course, when Robert became expert at wheedling a good deal more than stamps out of the men of commerce. These early experiences may well have provided some rudimentary promotional training. In any case, the stamp collection remained for him a source of fascination well into old age.

Heartier diversions were not wanting in Trinidad. Alex, family in tow, delighted in excursions into the interior and visits to coastal settlements. A typical family holiday saw the Falconers off to meet the Mortons on nearby Gasparillo. Forty minutes by steam yacht from Port of Spain, the island lay in the Gulf of Paria. A waterfall plunging some 600 feet was the foremost local attraction. Determined to see it, Alex led his brood through miles of vegetation so lush that it had to be hacked away with cutlasses. The prize, however, was worth the labour, and, as they munched from a picnic basket, all marvelled at the spectacular cascade. 'Oh what a paradise for the enthusiastic naturalist,' rhapsodized Alex.[65] On the Queen's birthday, 1877, another outing took them to the pitch lake at La Brea across which Alex was carried by 'two very obliging negroes.' The most memorable of these family trips took the Falconers in August 1882 up the Orinoco River and into the interior of Venezuela.[66] Alex had long denounced the government of Guzman Blanco as corrupt. Furthermore, he thundered, in Venezuela 'popery and infidelity hold sway: and the natural fruits of such systems everywhere abound.'[67] Such experiences must have increased young Robert's sense of venturing into the exotic. The river itself proved impressive, carving as it did a path through dense jungles. A week in Ciudad Bolivar did little to temper Alex's opinion either of President Blanco or of Catholicism. For the next few years he lamented bitterly that Britain did not govern Venezuela, and he unavailingly sponsored schemes to salt the country with Presbyterian missionaries.[68] By that time, however, the Falconers' days in Trinidad were numbered.

Among other things, the climate, which Alex had initially found so congenial, was beginning to take its toll. As early as December 1877 he noted that his wife was beginning to feel the strain of life in the tropics.[69] By 1882 even he admitted to a growing debilitation. 'It is impossible,' he wrote, 'to work continuously with any degree of vigor in this land where there is so much to enervate, without occasional change to a cooler clime to tone up mind and body.'[70] In addition, there are also hints that the romantic fires dimmed in Alex as he encountered some disillusioning realities. He came to find the moral atmosphere of Port of Spain depressing. The town was in places squalid, overcrowded, plagued by petty crime, and hospitable to prostitution.[71] To make matters worse, the white community had adopted disturbingly casual ways and Alex was doubtless offended by the large number who kept black mistresses. Confiding his thoughts to G.M. Grant, he confessed that he found his congregation generous enough. Greyfriars, under his care, more than balanced its books. He regretted, however, that 'the spiritual prosperity of the congregation does not keep pace with its financial growth.' To be sure, people attended church, but, he lamented, 'tropical Christianity is not such a heated article as the thermometer would indicate the atmosphere to be.'[72]

Thus, in April 1884 Alex resigned his charge at Greyfriars.[73] He agreed to remain while a replacement was sought, but nothing could shake his resolve 'to return to a more bracing climate.'[74] Over the next few months he contemplated an uncertain future. Any anxieties that may have plagued him, however, were soon dramatically resolved. Robert, it was announced, had quietly scored a resounding triumph. In the recent London Matriculation Examinations he had placed at the head of over 1,000 British and colonial candidates.[75] At a stroke his future was assured. He was awarded one of the four scholarships for study in Britain granted annually by the government of Trinidad. More significantly, he won the prestigious Gilchrist scholarship for the Caribbean region. Spirits in the Falconer household soared. The terms of the Gilchrist award specified that the recipient had to attend University College, London, or Edinburgh University. Family tradition, of course, made this decision simple. With one son provided for, Alex scraped together sufficient funds to enrol James with his brother. Anxious to accompany them, if only for a little while, he wrote feverishly to colleagues in Britain and was rewarded with offers of temporary postings at churches in Edinburgh, Chester, and Cambridge. Confident again of the future, on 23 May 1885 Alex and his sons set sail for the Firth of Forth.

CHAPTER II

Of Tools and Their Wielders

In those days a trip to Scotland was no trifling matter for a colonial Presbyterian. Clarence Mackinnon, a contemporary and classmate of Falconer, once likened the experience to a sojourn in the Holy Land.[1] Understandably then, as he drew nearer to Edinburgh, Robert's habitual emotional reserve deserted him. Here, after all, was the 'ecclesiastical hearth of Presbyterianism.'[2] Here was the fabled city so often described to him as his 'intellectual capital.' At eighteen the excitement was difficult to contain. Half a century later that well-remembered glow still warmed him. 'Few moments of my life.' he once recalled, 'have been charged with more eagerness than that on a beautiful afternoon in late June, 1885, when my father pointed to us, as we came from Falkirk, the Castle of Edinburgh on its Rock in the distance, which he had not seen since he was a student.'[3] If first impressions bred enthusiasm, deepening acquaintance fostered security. The ennui which so often haunts the freshman far from home never plagued Robert. It might well have been otherwise. For all his travels, he had led a rather sheltered life. Under the close tutelage of Alex and in the rarefied atmosphere of Queen's Royal College he had been insulated against threats to his faith and values. As he later confessed, 'my puritan mind was naturally disposed to react negatively to strange phases of life, and felt that its safest course was to avoid the ways of the world of which it was suspicious.'[4] It was, accordingly, undoubtedly significant for his personal and intellectual development that Robert was not to be confronted by an alien or threatening environment in Presbyterian Edinburgh. On the contrary, he was conscious only of continuity with his past.

Far from inciting an intellectual crisis, his formal undergraduate education tended to reinforce Falconer's traditional values. The Scottish universities as a whole leaned towards conservatism. Struggling to resist English assimilation in the nineteenth century, many Scots had come to view their universities as fortresses of national culture.[5] In consequence, curricular or pedagogical modification was often seen as a concession to the anglicizers. Complicating the situation, sectarian quarrels, such as the Great Disruption of 1843 which had produced the Free Church, also served to sap vitality by encouraging internecine strife. To be sure, in Falconer's day some signs of change were in the wind. At Glasgow, for example, the philosopher Edward Caird was one of the leading exponents of the Idealism that was sweeping Britain. Aberdeen boasted Alexander Bain whose teaching expanded on the psychology and ethics preached by John Stuart Mill and Herbert Spencer. Edinburgh, however, as Falconer later realized, 'was not a provocative centre of new ideas.'[6]

As a candidate in arts, Robert followed a curriculum that had not been seriously altered since 1708.[7] Seven traditional subjects, mirroring the medieval trivium and quadrivium, formed its compulsory core. Electives were eschewed in favour of a synoptic approach that emphasized the wholeness of knowledge and the inherent value of mental discipline. The object was to provide a sound general education. Latin, Greek, and mathematics were studied in the first two years. Logic, moral philosophy, natural philosophy, and rhetoric, which included English literature, occupied the student's remaining sessions. In addition an interested and gifted person could elect to take an extra course, but many found this option burdensome. Criticism of the curriculum was mounting while Robert was an undergraduate. There were those who complained of its failure to include vital modern studies such as history, political economy, and current European languages.[8] Similarly, complaints were heard from students concerning university pedagogical practice which emphasized formal lecturing to the virtual exclusion of all other methods of instruction. They pointed to the German seminar as a better vehicle and called for its introduction, protesting that Edinburgh's professors tended 'to dictate paragraphs rather than suggest criticism.'[9] Many changes would ensue in the 1890s. Legislation passed in 1889 allowed for the broadening of the curriculum and the introduction of tutorial instruction. These modifications, however, came too late to affect Falconer. Indeed, he was among the last to be educated completely under the unreformed system. Although later critical of the conservatism of his alma mater, at the time of his admission Robert was largely content to absorb what he was offered. 'What its pundits of orthodoxy decreed,' as he put it, 'I had neither the desire nor the ability to challenge.'[10]

Edinburgh was a non-residential university. Consequently, Robert and James moved into 'digs' some distance from Old College. The daily trek through blustery streets was long remembered. 'How cold that walk was; how we bent close-buttoned against the driving rain, sleet or snow, a long line hurrying to class, threading the dingy streets down to the South Bridge when we turned through massive, high-vaulted portals into the Quadrangle of the Old University.'[11] Chilled by the weather, only the truly puritanical soul would have warmed to the sight of Old College. Blending perfectly with the somber classicism of the city's architecture, 'the severity of the cold grey structure was relieved by no grass, no flowers, not a tree and seldom by sunshine.'[12] Crossing a quadrangle spread only with gravel, one entered cheerless classrooms into which icy drafts wafted from under the doors. And yet, within this spartan shell there was life. The place, in fact, was 'packed like a beehive' as something in excess of 3,000 students took classes there or in the medical building.[13] The halls swarmed with young men who 'kept themselves warm by tramping, wrestling, or shouting indifferently a psalm-tune or a snatch of the latest music-hall song.'[14] Moreover, whatever its limitations, the atmosphere of the university was far from listless. Discipline and hard work alone paved the road to the Edinburgh MA (there was no BA). A Greek motto inscribed on the wall of one lecture hall captured perfectly the spirit of the institution. 'The gods' it read, 'sell us all our blessings in return for toil.' The point was not lost on Falconer. 'Our undergraduate society,' he wrote, 'was one in which "men" (not boys) worked hard at intellectual pursuits, one in which if there was much that was commonplace there was also an abundance of sheer ability.'[15] Falconer, for one, bent to his labours with a will.

With a firm grounding in classics, he breezed through the entrance examinations. Thus, he was admitted directly to the second year of the obligatory pass course. Thriving on hard work, he regularly undertook extra study in order to qualify for the honour list. The competition was fierce, far more so that he had ever faced before. There were no more first-place finishes. Still, he did well enough. In his first year he won a bursary and also managed to place eighth in the Latin competition.[16] In 1886 he stood sixth on the honour list, a ranking that he maintained at his graduation three years later.[17] As a further outlet for his native industry, Falconer added fine arts to his portfolio of compulsory courses. It was a decision he never regretted. Under the kindly tutelage of G. Baldwin Brown, he came to appreciate and cherish great art. The aesthetic interests aroused by Brown endured for a lifetime. In later years Falconer made frequent pilgrimages to the artistic shrines of Europe. Occasionally, although not posing as an expert, he would lecture on Greek sculpture or write about the religious significance of early Christian painting.[18] In time, mutual respect between professor and student blossomed into a warm friendship which flourished until Brown's death in 1930. Indeed, it would be fair to say that while Falconer respected most of his under-graduate professors, it was Brown alone who truly stimulated his imagination. Towards the others he had mixed feelings.

It was with the classicists that Falconer had most contact. His decision to take an honours degree in classics brought him frequently to their classrooms. Among them S.H. Butcher, who held the Greek chair, was once described as 'the pet professor of the discriminating Freshman.'[19] Not one to employ such maudlin language, Robert nevertheless admired this 'handsome young man, with dark flashing eyes, black hair and moustache, [who was] graceful after the best manners of English society.'[20] Falconer, in youth and maturity, was always easily impressed by the polish of the English upper classes. The aristocratic Butcher, a son and son-in-law of bishops, certainly charmed him. Although well-connected with the cream of British society, there was no trace of hauteur in the affable professor of Greek. Many a student, including Robert, was flattered by invitations to his home where introductions to various political and literary luminaries were not uncommon. A social success with his students, Butcher was also an accomplished, if conservative, scholar and a gifted teacher. Under him Robert was introduced to the elements of literary criticism. He thus acquired the basic tools of his future trade. Butcher, he later recalled with gratitude, 'taught me how to approach a Greek author.'[21]

William Young Sellar, on the other hand, struck Falconer as a man well past his prime. Whereas Butcher was demanding and exact, Sellar was 'not a very precise scholar.'[22] In his honours class, Robert read selections from Tacitus, Martial, and Horace but was disappointed to find that 'he took slight interest in our Latin versions.' Already in failing health, Sellar died in the early 1890s and appears to have had very little influence on Falconer's thinking. Indeed while his experience in classics sharpened his technical abilities as a linguist and textual critic, it did nothing to alter his view of the world. 'Though we read Plato and Aristotle,' he recalled, 'they did not stir me to philosophise overmuch; nor did the Greek tragedians move me to ponder the problems of existence as they saw them; the irreligion of Lucretius did not affect me; Horace and especially Virgil charmed me, but I did not then penetrate beyond the melancholy beauty of Virgil's poetry to the wistful religion which it enshrined.'[23]

If Falconer found classics 'an ample demesne for conservatism and tradition,' he found philosophy as it was espoused at Edinburgh even more so. In company with Sellar, A. Campbell Fraser and Henry Calderwood stood in the van of those who resisted proposals to modify the curriculum.[24] The great issues and movements of the day, such as evolution and idealism, were glossed over or left untouched in their teaching. Fraser, the professor of logic and metaphysics, was by then an old man from whom Falconer received 'some formal logic of old vintage, a few glimpses into philosophical questions, but no recent psychology.'[25] Calderwood, who lectured in moral philosophy was, if anything, even more conservative. A former Presbyterian minister, he recoiled against anything that smacked of the unorthodox. 'Gossip had it,' wrote Clarence Mackinnon, 'that Scottish piety was chiefly responsible for his appointment as a bulwark against disintegrating German theories.'[26] If the implications of the higher criticism provoked his ire, so did the utilitarianism of Mill. His overriding concern was to demonstrate the concordance between philosophy and the received truths of religion. This he attempted to do in a particularly rigid and dogmatic manner. His lectures, as J.M. Barrie recalled, were simply dictated for verbatim reproduction.[27] As Falconer remembered him, Calderwood was 'an excellent teacher of the theory and maxims of his own wooden text-book.'[28] The cumulative effect, as Mackinnon put it, was to give the worthy professor 'the aspect of a reactionary.'[29] More generously, Falconer conceded that, if nothing else, Calderwood at least 'gave us average students a framework into which to fit our conventional morals.' The professor, however, failed to induce in students a passionate interest in philosophical pursuits.

A more positive impression was made by Andrew Seth, later known as A.S. Pringle-Pattison, who succeeded Fraser in 1891. During his last year, Falconer took Seth's honours course. Here he finally came into direct contact with one of the major intellectual currents of his generation, philosophic idealism. As Seth reviewed philosophy from Descartes to Hegel, Falconer came more clearly to understand the possibilities that confront the man who would explain the nature of existence. One could adopt the 'naturalist' position. In this case ultimate reality was said to lie in observable phenomena or to be essentially unknowable. Thus the door was opened to scepticism and agnosticism. Alternatively, one could espouse 'idealism,' whose adherents contended that genuine reality lay beyond mere phenomena in the realm of ideas that were absolute yet knowable. As Maurice Mandelbaum has put it, 'metaphysical idealism holds that within natural human experience one can find a clue to an understanding of the ultimate nature of reality, and this clue is revealed through those traits which distinguish man as a spiritual being.'[30] Apart from theoretical niceties, idealism appealed to men of Falconer's generation because it afforded some philosophical comfort to those alarmed by the religious and moral implications of naturalism.[31] So it was that thanks in part to Seth's influence, Falconer came to conclude that 'the Christian religion requires an idealistic philosophy.'[32]

Nineteenth-century idealism, however, was not at all monolithic. Some of its prophets, such as T.H. Green, were far from orthodox Christians. That Balliol don, after all, had written that 'A spiritual principle exists, indeed, [it] is the condition of our knowledge, morality, citizenship. This is what can reasonably be meant by the conception of God. There is no need to believe in revelation or authority.'[33] This conclusion, it seems, was too much for Robert's more conventional mind to absorb. His belief in a personal God was too deeply ingrained for him to venture as far afield as Green. Similarly, he had little sympathy with those, such as the American Josiah Royce, who submerged the human personality in a vague 'universal self.' An essay on Emerson, written in 1891, reflected Falconer's effort to come to terms with these ideas. As he saw it, Emerson was to be thanked for having underscored the dignity of the individual. 'The individual soul,' wrote Falconer, 'is of supreme worth and each has a call to do something unique.' The great American transcendentalist also had helped reinforce belief in the spirituality of man. His audiences 'could not go away from his lectures without learning ... that they had a spiritual nature beyond and above the material, which indeed gives the material its worth.' With these sentiments Falconer heartily agreed. But he could not embrace Emerson's pantheism or his notion that the religious experience was 'a mere "emotion"; a thrill at the presence of a universal soul.' He asked, somewhat dismayed, how it was 'that a man of Emerson's genius and purity of character misunderstands and will not accept what is to the average mind the all-sufficient and only solution of the problems of life?' Why, indeed, he went on, did so many other great thinkers reject Christianity?[34] At the time he offered no elaborate answer but simply identified extravagance and extremism as the sources of confusion. Later he came to feel that religious truth was simple but not wholly accessible to the purely philosophical mind, bound as it was by reason's categories. In any event, bored by Calderwood and suspicious of the more elaborate formulations of idealism, Falconer never developed a systematic philosophical position. To be sure, he gravitated towards idealism but, as a colleague once observed, 'he lived more in the Platonic atmosphere than by the Platonic system.'[35] From this early experience, however, he did distil one lesson. 'In my Arts course,' he later wrote, 'I began to discover the function of philosophy and how it differs from religion: that it is necessary for a complete religion, but is only the temple within which there must be an altar at which to worship.'[36]

Although Falconer was introduced to idealism, at no point in his undergraduate studies did he encounter science in its full strength. To be sure, the professor of natural philosophy, Peter Guthrie Tait, was a physicist and mathematician of note. A friend and collaborator of the future Lord Kelvin, he was once offered a fellowship in the Royal Society. An accomplished scholar, Tait also was acknowledged to be the finest lecturer in the university.[37] In class, however, he stuck to physics and avoided raising metaphysical and moral questions that lurked at the fringes of his subject.[38] This attitude, perhaps, was natural enough. The real controversies swirled around biology. Unfortunately, however, the biological sciences were not offered to arts candidates. Some, like Clarence Mackinnon, availed themselves of the opportunity to hear J.G. Romanes lecture on evolution when he visited the city in the early 1890s.[39] If Falconer accompanied his friend on these occasions, he never recorded the fact. He was, of course, not unaware of the major hypotheses of evolution and their general significance. Calderwood, for one, had at least touched on the subject but only, said Falconer, in the process of setting up a straw man for rapid demolition.[40] Earnestly beavering away at the traditional curriculum under learned but largely conservative professors, Falconer was not made to realize the degree to which science was seriously disturbing long-established doctrine. As he later wrote, 'though I could see storm signals swaying in the wind, I was not conscious of the violence of the gale outside.'[41]

As so often happens, it was beyond the classroom in the company of his fellow students that Robert first met with significant challenges to his inherited ideas. In moments snatched from the remorseless grind for examinations, they gathered to discuss eagerly devoured private reading. Falconer indicates that the authors scanned included Browning, Tennyson, Wordsworth, Carlyle, Emerson, Matthew Arnold, Ruskin, Eliot, Meredith, and Stevenson.[42] It is significant, perhaps, that figures such as Mill, Spencer, and Huxley are not mentioned. Clearly, his friends' tastes ran to the literary and the aesthetic. In any event, there was apparently plenty of material to stimulate awakening minds. Compared with the lecture hall, indeed, the atmosphere was electric. 'We were constantly arguing; we baulked at nothing. Acute companions challenged the value of my beliefs and practices. As a rule I defended my puritan heritage which was strong within me; but after discussion I was not the same as before, as over and over I had to ask myself, What is the essential value of this faith of mine and of my way of life?'[43] Significantly, Falconer did not retreat into a dogmatic shell but reacted to these debates in a positive manner. At no point in his various recollections does he indicate that he felt threatened or harassed. The discussions, one suspects, were co-operative rather than personal or competitive in tone. Thus, among friends, he began to measure old and new ideas in an honest search for truth. The experience was invigorating.

In this time of reassessment, Falconer derived much solace from the weekly lectures of Henry Drummond. Every Sunday night without fail, Robert and hundreds of his fellow students crowded into the Odd Fellows Hall on Forest Road to hear the man Mackinnon once described as a 'modern scientific saint.'[44] Tumultuous cheering invariably greeted the professor of natural science from the Free Church College of Glasgow. As he was led to the podium by Edinburgh's principal, Sir William Muir, or other members of the faculty, a hush gradually fell over the assemblage. When he spoke, Drummond held his audience spellbound. Originally trained as a scientist, Drummond had later turned to theology. With a foot in both camps he was ideally placed to expand on the religious implications of Darwin's discoveries. This he did most winningly in both print and speech. His several published works, including *Natural Law in the Spiritual World, The Ascent of Man*, and *The Greatest Thing in the World*, won scant praise from philosophers, so confused was the use of terms.[45] Among the general public, however, they proved immensely popular, and his Sunday sermons at Edinburgh regularly drew 500 to 600 eager listeners.[46] Chadwick has described Drummond as a 'revivalist preacher.'[47] Falconer, however, recalled a man who 'set forth the Christian life in chaste and sincere English without undue emotional appeal.'[48] The substance of his message was that Christianity and evolutionary theory were perfectly compatible. The evidence of an ordered evolution, he contended, merely confirmed the existence of a creator. More important-ly, he averred, this observable unfolding of God's plan offered tangible clues to the nature of the spiritual realm itself. Thus, challenging Huxley and other scientific agnostics, Drummond affirmed that the infinite was knowable. 'In time,' wrote Falconer, 'one asked for more than the simple reiterated talks of Drummond, but I must always revere his memory because he did not a little, at a stage when I needed it, to clarify my conception of essential Christianity.'[49]

His mind was being opened, albeit gently, to problems and possibilities once beyond his ken. Inspired perhaps by Seth, certainly by Drummond, and undoubtedly by his friends, Falconer began to reach a conclusion in line with some aspects of his Presbyterian heritage. The man of faith, he discovered, ignored the claims of reason only at his peril. A constant sifting of ideas, he found, served not to undermine but to clarify his religion and his morals. 'The more intellectually secure I became,' he records, 'the more consistent was my inner life.'[50] Gradually it came to him that a healthy religion drew on two major roots for sustenance. The strongest root was grounded in the life-giving earth of faith informed by insight and intuition. The other nestled in 'the pure soil of reasonable knowledge.' His father, of course, had always counselled him to be suspicious of 'over-wrought' sentiment as a force in religion. Now his own experience led Robert to affirm that 'one who cannot find some basis in reason for his religious intuitions will be a double-minded man unstable in his ways. It is to be remembered that Jesus taught that the first and greatest commandment was to love the Lord thy God with all thy heart, and with all thy soul and with all thy *mind* and with all thy strength. He taught that intellectual love is a primary quality in religion.'[51] A 'masculine intelligence' was being formed. Unlike some who recoiled in the face of change and new ideas, Falconer in maturity became an adaptable, optimistic, and a highly eclectic thinker. Sophisticated answers to complex and more clearly perceived problems lay in the future. But a life-long search for the essential roots of a purified Christianity had begun.

Like all undergraduates, even the earnest Falconer took time from his intellectual pursuits to nurture other interests. Edinburgh might not have been London, but compared with Nova Scotia or Trinidad it offered a brilliant array of distractions. The recently completed Royal Lyceum Theatre provided a splendid forum for the dramatic arts. Here Robert was to be found, whenever his purse allowed, ensconced among 'the gods' to cheer the likes of Henry Irving and Ellen Terry as they interpreted the plays of Shakespeare. His appreciation of music grew as he frequented the fortnightly organ recitals of Sir Herbert Oakeley and the regular round of chamber concerts offered in the city. Always keenly interested in the latest news, he delighted in having ready access to a variety of well-informed newspapers. From time to time spasms of political excitement captured his attention. As the Home Rule controversy raged, Falconer joined a massive throng in the Corn Market to hear Joseph Chamberlain pour scorn on an idea that was not unpopular in Scotland. He was impressed by the man from Birmingham, whose histrionic flare fascinated and tamed the normally raucous Edinburgh crowd. Ultimately, however, he preferred the more restrained Lord Rosebery. 'He was,' wrote Falconer, 'not the equal of Chamberlain in appeal to the masses, but was his superior in polished, urbane, indeed at times nobly eloquent speech.'[52]

There was time as well for travel. His first excursion in June 1886 made a particularly deep and lasting impression on Falconer. Throughout the preceding winter Alex had served as a locum tenens in Chester. With the spring he moved to Cambridge as a replacement for a minister vacationing abroad. Eager to see his father and to catch a glimpse of that storied seat of learning, Robert joined him for a fortnight. The ancient university quickly worked its magic on both father and son. Alex waxed eloquent on the tradition of scholarship enshrined in its stately colleges.[53] Robert was enthralled by the shapely trees, the ivy-covered quads and the sequestered gardens. His reaction, it might be suggested, was rather like that of an awe-struck colonial rustic. 'The sufficiency of ease,' he recalled, 'made one understand that the young England which went to Cambridge was well-established in the art of cultured living.' That June he was touched with 'more than a passing regret' that his scholarship was tenable only at Edinburgh or London.[54] As a wistful observer it was easy for him to romanticize that in which he could never directly share. In any event, his outsider's enchantment with Oxbridge only increased as time wore on. Those colleges by the Isis and the Cam would one day become yardsticks against which he would measure all similar institutions.

Perhaps equally significant was a summer spent in Germany in 1888. Traces of evidence indicate that most of his days were passed at the University of Leipzig. As to what he did there, however, he was maddeningly silent. One suspects that part of his purpose was to familiarize himself with the language of a people who then stood in scholarship's advance guard. Whatever his motives, Falconer found that summer exhilarating. In a rare burst of athletic zeal he and three unidentified companions trudged through Thuringia seeking out the places where Goethe, Schiller, and Luther had worked. He thrilled to the scenery of rural Germany and took the place to his heart, comparing it to his native Nova Scotia. At one point the happy wanderers covered 106 miles in four days of steady tramping. Impressed with his own herculean qualities, the breathless Falconer wrote home excitedly urging other sluggards to don hiking boots in the name of health and pleasure.[55] Altogether, he greatly enjoyed this German interlude. The positive nature of the experience no doubt played a role in his decision to return later in order to indulge more serious tastes.

In 1889 Falconer reaped the reward of four years' sustained effort. Having completed the program in classical honours, he graduated sixth in his class. While others looked forward to careers in law, journalism, or business, Robert and James enrolled directly in the Divinity College of the Free Church at Edinburgh. There appears to have been no agonizing over the decision. Indeed, there is nothing to indicate that any other course of action was ever contemplated. Family tradition no doubt played a crucial role. Personal piety must also have come into play. In Robert's case, particularly, a growing interest in the sources of Christian belief may well have sharpened an older sense of purpose. In any event, the move from Old to New College came so naturally that the motives for it occasioned no comment then or later.

Founded by the Free Church following the Great Disruption of 1843, New College occupied a choice site atop the Mound a few paces from the castle's forecourt. The grey stones of 'that severely ecclesiastical pile' struck Falconer as 'handsome but rather cold' in comparison with the softness and antiquity of Cambridge.[56] Even so, he was anxious to begin his studies. His appetite was whetted by a controversy that was gripping the Church of England and had spilled over into the public press. In 1889 there appeared *Lux Mundi: a Series of Studies in the Religion of the Incarnation*, a collection of essays written by eleven Anglicans most of whom were teachers at Oxford. In essence, the tome represented the effort of devout but liberal churchmen to come to terms with evolutionary theory and advances in biblical criticism.[57] Falconer sympathized with these scholars in whose work he found echoes of his own concerns. The plea for Christians to face squarely the intellectual challenges of the day was not lost on him. When Aubrey Moore, in an essay entitled 'Christian Doctrine of God,' refused to accept Spencer's division between the realms of faith and reason, Falconer could not help but applaud.[58] When the volume's editor, Charles Gore of Trinity College, argued that, inspired though it was, the Old Testament was not an infallible guide to history, Robert saw the force of common sense. Conservatives attacked Gore, but liberals and moderates such as Samuel Driver sprang to his defence.[59] There had been nothing like it since the storm aroused by *Essays and Reviews* in the 1860s. As it happened, Falconer was witnessing the last great public controversy in England over the new learning. In the end, Gore and his supporters would play a vital role in reconciling the Anglican church with modern thought. For the moment, the debate probably helped Falconer identify more clearly the major issues affecting the studies he was beginning.

The young man of twenty-two who entered New College was very different from the stripling freshman of 1885. His once incurious mind was now on the prowl for new ideas. An instinctive respect for authority was giving way before an aroused critical sense. There were momentous changes taking place in religious thought, and he yearned to grapple with them face to face. He was keenly disappointed therefore, when, at first blush, New College seemed even more conservative than the university he had just left. Some of the professors, it appeared, refused to acknowledge that the world was changing. John Laidlaw, who conducted classes in systematic theology, clung to a traditional approach. Dr William Garden Blaikie was best known for a pious biography of Livingston. Dr John Duns went to great lengths to confute evolution only to be branded a reactionary by his students. The principal, Robert Rainy, was engrossed in contemporary ecclesiastical affairs. Mackinnon recalled that his lectures on church history were 'read in so listless a manner, that one wondered whether he was listening to them himself or not.'[60] In lecture after dreary lecture Falconer 'listened to a dry analysis of "the body of divinity."' All received doctrines were held to be intellectually true. Theology was presented as a philosophy to be deduced from scripture in accordance with Christian tradition. The Bible was viewed as a repository of dogma, and in consequence its interpretation was treated as 'a process of discovering a system adumbrated or fully laid down.' All too often, lamented Falconer, scant attention was paid to the original meaning of words or to the historical environment in which they had been framed. Instead, resort was had to allegory or to 'the analogy of faith' in order to make conflicting passages agree. Furthermore, Robert and his classmates were surprised to find so many of their teachers ardently defending the shop-worn concept of verbal inspiration. To do so, it seemed, was to ignore the case put by Gore and scores of critics before him.[61]

Disenchanted, Falconer came to sympathize with a group of outspoken students who for some time had been criticizing the traditional views embraced by some at New College. Occasionally these complaints found their way into print. In 1889 an article in the *Student* slammed the Free church for 'doggedly pinning its faith to exploded fallacies which are now only laughed at by all thinking men who are not paid theologians.' The anonymous author went on to ridicule all those who sought to bar the door to free inquiry. With the vitriolic self-righteousness of youth he ladled out his cup of abuse. 'In the undisguised truth,' he howled, 'they have no faith; they think it needs the support of their paltry myths and fables, of their cowardly subterfuges and soul corroding casuistry.'[62] Such hysterical blasts, of course, could achieve little beyond reinforcing conservative fears. Fortunately, however, not all student spokesmen were so unconstructive.

In February 1889 a more responsible critic voiced the misgivings of his peers in the same journal. He was unimpressed by a theological college that taught its candidates to 'gerund grind' but left them without sophisticated guidance in dealing with the complex moral issues confronting modern society. While conceding that a few professors stimulated the zealous to transcend the curriculum, the author argued that more was needed. Comparing Scottish schools with their German counterparts, he noted that 'grave differences at once appear.' In German theological colleges, he pointed out, one often found rival courses in Christian ethics under the same roof. In Scotland the subject was virtually ignored. The comparison, he continued, was even less flattering in the area of specialized study. Here the Germans excelled. Their schools offered a wide range of special programs which the student was encouraged to undertake. At New College, he lamented, concentrated specialization was only informally available thanks to a few enlightened professors who offered private help. The Germanic seminar was applauded, as was the encouragement of original thinking in the form of thesis writing. These features contrasted with Scotland's emphasis on rote learning and cramming for examinations, which tested only memory.[63] If Falconer read this piece, he most certainly would have agreed with its thrust. He also found confining an institution in which 'exposition and defence were the dominant notes, not free and untrammelled inquiry.'[64]

The reluctance of some professors to plumb the depths of the higher criticism is understandable. One of their colleagues had recently suffered for expounding modern views. In 1881 William Robertson Smith had been summarily removed from his chair at the Free Church Theological College in Aberdeen. A leading semitic scholar, Smith had been in close touch with higher critics in Germany and had sought to apply their methods in his own teaching. Hounded out of Aberdeen, he was welcomed by Cambridge, but the precedent of his dismissal was long remembered. As Mackinnon, who joined Falconer at New College, recalled, the after-effects of the case 'hung like a heavy pall, especially over the Highland Glens.'[65] Congregational tremors were registered in the Assembly of the Free Church, where appointments to the theological colleges were made. There it became habitual to consider safety first in the selection of professors. In time, however, said Falconer, it was these 'safe but dull' men who created a restless spirit among his more able classmates.[66] On their own these students absorbed a good deal of the most recent literature. A focus for this activity was provided by the Theological Society. Meeting on Friday nights from eight to midnight over penny cups of coffee, earnest students 'fearlessly faced every new question of philosophy and criticism.'[67] Some, Falconer recalled, came to adopt 'far more extreme views than they would have accepted under the direction of genuine scholars and thinkers.'[68]

Much of this student criticism was no doubt deserved, but there was inevitably, as Falconer indicates, some overstatement. His own initial misgivings were soon partially offset. In his last years at New College he came into closer contact with two professors who would exercise a powerful influence on his mind. Andrew Bruce Davidson and Marcus Dods were for him 'the first rays of a new dawn' in the otherwise conservative theological world of Scotland.[69] The Free church, he slowly discovered, was not quite as unbending as he once suspected. The ghost of Robertson Smith was retreating into the shades and not all Presbyterians lived in dread of German ideas. Davidson, in fact, had been Smith's teacher and friend. A man of tact and transparent piety, he had survived the icy blasts that swept his unlucky pupil away. Meanwhile he continued quietly to teach similar views. It was late in 1890 that Falconer first encountered the man whose portrait would later adorn his study wall.[70] Knowing of Davidson's connection with Robertson Smith, many students in his Old Testament course expected to hear a controversial presentation of the latest critical theories. In this they were disappointed. Davidson in class 'was caution itself.'[71] There was to be no immediate plunge into the method, history, and results of the higher criticism. Indeed, as Falconer came to appreciate, Davidson, though a master of technique, was not primarily concerned with method at all. Instead, he was anxious chiefly to bring the Hebrew world vividly alive for his students in order to illustrate what to him were some enduring religious truths. Ultimately, he sought to demonstrate that God was a living force in history. All the minutiae of criticism were subordinated to this higher purpose.

'Behind the physical world,' he told his students, 'is God, the immediateness of whose operations is found throughout the Old Testament.' While this was a form of idealism that Robert found easy to embrace, it was hardly a revolutionary position. In many ways, Davidson was very much a man of conventional faith. There was never in his teaching any question about the existence of a personal God. Similarly, he considered the principle that man's moral life had to be in harmony with the will of the deity quite beyond any critical questions. Where he did depart from accepted wisdom, however, was in his approach to scripture. The doctrine of verbal inspiration was not for him. Revelation, he taught, was never cut and dried. It was not a simple disclosure of objective truth easily recognized by all men. The Old Testament was used to clarify the point. Conditions of life in Israel, argued Davidson, were similar to those in any age. 'The Hebrews,' he said, 'believed that there was a divine voice, but it spoke through men, and there was room to doubt which was Jehovah's.'[72] Consequently, he continued, then as now, men had to use their moral judgment to decide which was the true prophet. It was here that critical analysis guided by faith had a role to play.

Davidson never presented the higher criticism to his students as a systematic body of theoretical canons. His approach, instead, was practical and he taught slowly by example. In him Falconer came to recognize a 'consummate teacher.' 'He was not,' wrote an admiring Robert, 'the venturesome pioneer careless of those who had to follow. He did not choose a path to show his courage and exploring skill; he brought his students along unfamiliar ways, but he was a considerate guide; he pointed out the unsuspected beauties of the path, and every now and again led them after a somewhat stiff climb to an eminence to enjoy with himself a vision of the Divine over an expanse of human life or history.' Outlining the development of Old Testament criticism briefly, Davidson simply adopted the newer methods as the best vehicles for bringing most fully to life the remote world of historical Israel. An exacting scholar, he demanded a knowledge of Hebrew. His exegesis was minute but 'sane and temperate' as he stuck close to historical facts. In the end his object was achieved. 'He left on my mind,' says Falconer, 'an ineffaceable impression of his faith in the reality of the Divine in the facts of the daily life of the Hebrew people.' For Robert, as never before, the scriptures came alive. Davidson had fired his historical imagination. Never again could he regard biblical scholarship as a cold, intellectual discipline. Indeed, the impress of Davidson's teaching is clearly visible in Falconer's later works which throb with the same pulse of historical immediacy.

Apart from introducing them to critical methods, Davidson also helped his students reach an accommodation with the claims of science. The Hebrews, he pointed out, had no great interest in the subject. The prophets did not concern themselves with secondary causes. Consequently, scripture was not careful of the order of things. That, said Davidson, could be left to science. 'The theism of Scripture,' he argued, 'is all that is important, and it can never come into conflict with science until it is atheistic.' Fresh from Romane's lectures, Mackinnon, in particular, found this point of view congenial.[73] In Davidson's hands Revelation itself was shown to have evolved over time as 'a stream of life and ideas broadening as it advances.' Since he also taught that the physical was merely a manifestation of the moral, it was natural for many of his listeners to conclude that evolution in the natural world was but a part of God's overall plan. Such was the normal position of those who conceived of Revelation as 'development.'

Altogether, the hours spent with Davidson were among the most formative in Falconer's early life. He noted pointedly that for once there was intense discussion in the dining hall after lectures. 'It was a time,' he recollected, 'when one had the sense of adding to one's mental and spiritual stature.' Under Davidson he first clearly perceived how constructive a tool modern criticism could be when wielded expertly by a man of faith. Like him, Falconer would adopt a largely historical approach to the study of the Bible rather than concentrating, for example, on systematic theology or apologetics. Unlike Davidson, however, Falconer would focus his attention on the New Testament. It was in shaping this decision that Marcus Dods was of help.

To the excitable editors of the student newspaper, Dods was something of a hero.[74] He was no bolder in approach than Davidson. If anything, he was more circumspect than his older colleague. Nevertheless, he was admired chiefly because he dared, however cautiously, to apply new principles of interpretation to his subject. For many this was a sensitive point. The New Testament, after all, was the very ark of the Christian covenant. It was one thing to challenge the reliability of this or that Hebrew prophet. It was quite another to assail the validity of an Epistle or a Gospel. Most ordinary churchgoers and not a few clergymen had been reared in the tradition of biblical literalism. If Old Testament critics such as Smith and Gore could rouse their ire, those who seemingly trifled with the cardinal documents of Christianity left them fearful and incensed. As Frederick Harrison so bluntly put it, churchmen who were not fundamentalists were not considered Christian.[75] Very few were brave enough to maintain publicly that if the New Testament were truly inspired it would only gleam all the brighter in the light of criticism.[76] Dods, it appears, was one of the few. He had, however, paid a price for his views.

Preferment in the church had come slowly. Graduating from New College in 1854, Dods had not been licensed to preach until 1858.[77] For the next six years he sought in vain for a pulpit. Industrious to a fault, he passed his days in study and writing, editing, for example, the complete works of Augustine. Finally in 1864 he was called to a church in Glasgow. There he preached for twenty-five years, exercising considerable influence on young men such as Henry Drummond. From time to time, however, his liberal views drew the fire of an older generation. In 1878, for example, he came close to being tried as a heretic. Local conservatives were up in arms over a sermon in which Dods questioned the doctrine of verbal inspiration. Luckily, the General Assembly declined to intervene. Perhaps this was because they had bigger fish to fry.

The Robertson Smith controversy was on in earnest at that time. As the conflict raged, the able Smith defended his views so deftly that his trial was never concluded. Instead, he was ousted from his chair on the pretext of a want of confidence. Throughout, the church had winced occasionally as liberals charged it with obscurantism. In the long run the affair appears to have exercised a gradual liberalizing influence.[78] Certainly, Dods's appointment to the faculty of New College in 1889 was greeted as a sign that the Free church was at last prepared cautiously to receive new light in theological matters.[79] But the door had been opened only a crack. No sooner was Dods installed than in 1890 he was hauled before the Assembly yet again. As before, his unorthodox views concerning inspiration had touched an exposed nerve. A protracted debate gripped the conclave. In the end, Dods was spared the anxieties of a formal trial. Instead he was simply admonished to keep his teaching in tune with the faith. It was another near-miss. Apparently the church was starting to mellow, but discretion was still a watchword for champions of the new learning.

All this was transpiring at the very moment that Dods was introducing Falconer to the basic problems raised by nineteenth-century New Testament scholarship. Foremost among them were questions concerning the authenticity of sources and others that touched on the very nature of Christ himself. Regarding sources, the thorniest issues involved matters of dating and authorship. Together, the Gospels, Epistles and allied material had for centuries been viewed as a repository of doctrine that faithfully reflected apostolic teaching. Many, therefore, were alarmed when some modern critics tried to demonstrate that large portions of the New Testament had been authored long after Christ and his apostles had departed the scene. Some argued that the farther in time these documents were removed from the first pulse of Christianity, the less reliable they were as guides to the original message of Jesus. Suggestions of late authorship, it was feared, would undermine the church and much of traditional dogma, which could be portrayed as the all too human creations of fallible secondary writers.

The fears of the orthodox were not groundless. By mid-century some of the most influential scholars in Germany were assigning much of the New Testament to the post-apostolic age. In this movement Ferdinand Christian Baur and his so-called Tübingen School took a leading part.[80] Borrowing from Hegel, Baur applied the dialectic model to his subject. He posited a struggle between Jewish or Petrine Christianity and its antithetical Gentile or Pauline form. The upshot, supposedly, was the Catholic synthesis of the second century. If Baur and his disciples were correct, then great portions of the New Testament had been written after 130 AD. Quite apart from the specifics of the 'tendency' theory, Tübingen gave biblical historicism a tremendous boost.[81] In Britain near panic ensued in 1860 when Benjamin Jowett and other admirers of Baur published their thoughts in a volume entitled *Essays and Reviews*. A student of German literature, Jowett demanded that the Bible as a whole be read 'like any other book.'[82] Another contributor, Mark Pattison, startled contemporaries by suggesting that if religious ideas changed with the times then, in all likelihood Victorian beliefs reflected nineteenth-century concerns more than they did original Christian concepts.[83] During the 1860s and 1870s Baur's works were translated into English, just as they began to pass out of fashion on the continent. In Europe, more moderate scholars such as Albrecht Ritschl, Bernhard Weiss, and Theodor Zahn continued to use the critical method but rejected Baur's dialectics. They began to place many of the disputed sources back in the apostolic age.[84]

Across the channel, a few British scholars quietly pursued a similar approach. It was a delicate task in the wake of *Essays and Reviews*. Ultimately, however, Joseph Barber Lightfoot, John Anthony Hort, and Brooke Foss Westcott succeeded in establishing a credible school of English criticism. These Cambridge scholars approached the New Testament in a rigorous academic spirit but without the philosophical presuppositions favoured by earlier German masters.[85] Controversy was eschewed. By the mid-1880s Lightfoot in his *Apostolic Fathers* and other publications had demolished the Tübingen thesis. To his own satisfaction and to the delight of the British churches he demonstrated that the major Christian sources were products of the first century. For their part, Westcott and Hort, after twenty years of patient labour, published in 1882 a purified text of the New Testament in Greek. The introduction to this work included a thoroughgoing exposition of the theory of textual criticism which would guide British investigators for generations to come.[86] Of course, disputes about authorship and chronology did not end at this point. Falconer himself would later take up arms against those who continued to question the dependability of various texts. For many, however, the Cambridge trio had pointed the way to a reconciliation with the new learning.

If documentary debates caused consternation, novel assessments of Christ also created uneasiness. The conventional saviour, divine, yet anchored in history, himself became a subject of dispute. Clouds gathered in 1835 when David Friedrich Strauss, a pupil of Baur, penned his *Life of Jesus*. Scanning the sources with Tübingen spectacles, Strauss contended that the Christ of history was essentially unknowable. The facts of his life, it was argued, had been transformed and enlarged upon by imaginative early Christian writers. In the end, said Strauss, what the Gospels transmitted was a mythical rather than the real Jesus.[87] These startling assertions raised an outcry even in Germany. Discomfort was not relieved when the first substantial biography was published in 1863 by the Frenchman Ernest Renan. The Christ described here was all too historical for many conservative tastes. The note of divinity was left unsounded. Renan's Jesus was a genius, a great soul, a moralist of profound insight but not recognizably the Son of God.[88] Less controversial was *Ecce Homo*, published anonymously in 1865. The author, John Seeley, did not present the study as a biography of Jesus but merely as an investigation of the foundations of Christian morality.[89] Theological issues were avoided, and no claim to have furnished a definitive portrait was made. Consequently, no violent storm of protest was evoked. Nevertheless there persisted, as Falconer noted, 'a widespread suspicion that, under mere historical scrutiny, the human element in Jesus might be magnified to the detriment of the Divine.'[90]

By the time Falconer entered New College, moderate criticism of the type spawned by Lightfoot had won considerable quiet support in British academic circles. But even here there was opposition. The redoubtable Canon Gore, in a tour de force of inconsistency, failed to rally to the defence of his New Testament colleagues. The church, he counselled, should continue to insist on the factual character of the Gospels.[91] The latitude he craved in his study of the Old Testament he denied to investigators of the New. Beyond the groves of academe, the new learning encountered even greater resistance. Accordingly, many scholars refused to broach uncomfortable questions. Others feared to publish at all.[92] Still, as an Edinburgh student put it at the time, 'let a new idea get loose in the world, and if it is worth spreading, no power on earth will stop its progress.'[93] Thus, scholars such as Dods continued to work, albeit with caution.

In him Falconer met a typical representative of the moderate British school. Dods employed the same critical principles as Davidson 'though with greater reserve.'[94] His lectures were characterized by a calm and chastened eloquence, occasionally laced with humour.[95] Although a champion of the historical approach, he persistently warned against focusing too much attention on method for its own sake. 'The danger of criticism,' he once wrote, 'is not in what it discovers but in turning the mind aside to details and externals.'[96] Thus the lessons of Davidson were reinforced. The purpose of inquiry into the Bible, said Dods, was to perceive as clearly as possible God's ultimate revelation in Christ. From this one ought not to be distracted by an inordinate concern with technical problems. He did, however, consistently maintain that errors flowing from the abuse of critical tools could be corrected only by a sane application of those very instruments. There was no room in his teaching for a retreat to verbal inspiration.

As he introduced his students to the New Testament, Dods never hesitated to point out incongruities or inaccuracies embedded in the Gospels. These were, after all, records compiled by men, however inspired they might have been. On the whole, however, he held that the mistakes in scripture were trifling and did not detract from its general reliability as a witness to Christ's teaching.[97] Furthermore, as Falconer recalled, Dods voiced no startling opinions concerning the dating or authorship of the sources.[98] In dealing with the synoptic problem, he maintained that the Gospels involved emanated from the first century and were in the main historically reliable.[99] Indeed, he later wrote that 'there is no doubt that the bulk of the books of the New Testament come to us so accredited that to reject them is equivalent to rejecting the authority of Christ.'[100] In Dods's mind Jesus was not a myth but a real and knowable historical person. He was, moreover, no simple ethical teacher, but the focal point of Revelation; a living spirit whose voice continued to speak to men through nature, history, and their own experience. In keeping with many nineteenth-century critics, Dods's emphasis was Christocentric rather than bibliocentric. The true Protestant order, he said, was first faith in Christ and then faith in scripture.[101] Christ, not the Bible, was the normative authority for him as he had been for Schleiermacher and would be for Falconer.[102]

All told, Falconer spent two years with Dods. He thought with affection of that professor whose home at 23 Great King Street was a familiar student haunt. Personally, the man was irresistible. Whether in the guise of instructor or as boon companion on the hiking trail, he treated his students as adults and as friends. However, Robert came to recognize that as a scholar Dods had some limitations. He certainly never accorded him the same unqualified accolades he later bestowed on Davidson. Years afterwards he described Dods as 'a tolerant, devout, and courageous scholar up to the limit of the knowledge at his disposal.'[103] Was this the result of a trick of memory? Had later experience made Falconer critical after the event? Probably not. Even the columnists of The *Student* who lionized his courage recognized that Dods was not a 'creative genius.'[104] He was, instead, a man of wide reading who had a particular gift for popularization.[105] In comparison with the titans Robert encountered elsewhere, Dods could not but suffer. Nevertheless, he presented the fundamental problems of the age clearly to his students, and for this

Falconer was thankful. 'I owe him,' he acknowledged, 'a debt of gratitude for having put me on the right track.'[106]

In those days, of course, Germany was the most bustling station abreast the 'right track.' Inevitably, Falconer was drawn to its fabled universities like a sailor to the Lorelei. The questions raised by Dods had both troubled and intrigued him. In particular, he longed to discover whether there was any sure foundation for the body of doctrine he had so long taken for granted. It was a fine thing to applaud the champions of intellectual liberty from the sidelines. Youth has ever favoured the heroic posture. But face to face with the deeper implications of the higher criticism, Robert found that his traditional mind was still inclined to baulk.[107] By the spring of 1891, perhaps for the first time in his life, he was feeling mildly insecure. To his credit, he determined to slake his growing curiosity and to confront his problems directly. Accordingly, he passed the next two summers in Germany drinking thirstily of the new knowledge at its source.

In April 1891, fresh from examinations at New College, Falconer arrived in Berlin. With him were brother James and Walter Murray, his closest, life-long friend. The three Canadians were anxious to cram as much as was humanly possible into the next few months. Time was short and there was so much to see and do. As if by order, the state provided a lavish military spectacle the day after their arrival. The great von Moltke was dead, and all Berlin, or so it seemed, turned out to bid him farewell. Falconer, still weary with travel, joined the throng lining the streets. He saw the emperor pass by on foot accompanied by kings, grand dukes, and ambassadors. He regretted only that the legendary Bismarck, sulking in forced retirement, was nowhere to be seen.[108] Reconnoitering the imperial capital, he found to his delight that it boasted an array of cultural attractions that made Edinburgh seem provincial. There was time, in the weeks before classes began, to sample the theatres, museums, and art treasures that abounded. The heady strains of Wagner became familiar. Above all, he never forgot an evening when he saw Brahms accept an enthusiastic ovation after a performance of his latest concerto. These, however, were but casual diversions. Falconer's real interests, after all, centred on the universities, not the concert halls.

His experience in Berlin and in Marburg the following summer formed a unity in Falconer's mind. Indeed, throughout the country he encountered an atmosphere strikingly different from that which reigned in Edinburgh. As he saw it, if Scotland were more devout, Germany was more confident, ambitious, and energetic. Wealth accumulated rapidly as commerce expanded and science was applied to industry. In tune with society, German universities seemed to exude the scientific spirit. In fact, within their walls, said Falconer, that spirit 'brooked no caveat.'[109] It was assumed, he observed, 'that the new scientific method could give entry even to spiritual mysteries; that it could unlock rooms into which the educated person might glance without awe or dread, confident that those who opened them had in their method the master-key to all knowledge.'[110] Without surprise, he found that even the theological faculties had felt 'the full throb of the modern mind.' For good or ill, he was at the centre of things at last. There was much to learn and much to ponder. Accordingly, Falconer wasted not a moment of these visits. The views of the great were sought out, listened to, and evaluated.

His appetite was insatiable as he ran from classroom to classroom. At first, Falconer confessed, he was awed and 'almost oppressed' by Germany's intellectual prestige.[111] However, recovering his composure quickly, he soon learned to view his teachers with a discriminating eye. Of the various luminaries under whom he studied, some attracted and some repelled him. He thought Otto Pffeiderer, one of the last followers of Baur, an excellent speaker but considered his dialectical views passé.[112] The ageing Bernhard Weiss simply bored him, so dull were his lectures.[113] Graf von Baudissin, a Marburg Old Testament scholar, was congenial enough but did not bear comparison with Davidson. The dapper German count, said Falconer, lacked the insight, saintliness, and literary acumen of his old Scottish master.[114] A stronger impression was made by Adolf Jülicher. To Falconer this young man seemed to embody the very spirit of science in its fullest and most rigorous sense.[115] Jülicher, he said, appeared at times 'almost ruthless' in his rejection of interpretations that had even the slightest hint of a dogmatic flavour. 'History, comparative religion, psychology were all bound to have their say before he would allow that there might be some new contribution from the Christian faith itself to account for a hallowed passage.'[116] Here was a man, he suspected, who had become too deeply engrossed in methodological concerns. Nevertheless, exposure to this severe brand of scholarship helped Robert hone his critical skills.[117] Indeed, his German experience as a whole undoubtedly served to round and polish him as a scholar. It would have been less than decisive, however, had he not in that first brilliant summer of 1891 encountered the compelling Adolf Harnack. To Falconer, in the shadow of that giant all others seemed lilliputian.

Barely forty at the time, Harnack had already established himself as the foremost New Testament scholar of the age. Born in 1851, he came from the Russian province of Livonia. Following in the footsteps of his professorial father, Harnack was educated at the universities of Erlangen,

Dorpat, and Leipzig. In 1888 he was appointed to the theological faculty at Berlin on the strength of a successful early career at Marburg and other leading schools. A prolific author, he was best known for his massive *History of Dogma* published in three volumes between 1886 and 1889. He was by no means a radical in the context of German scholarship, but his Berlin appointment had been challenged by the powerful Supreme Council of the Evangelical Church. Publicly, clerical officials focused their attack on Harnack's open disavowal of miracles and his insistence that baptism had never been sanctioned by Christ. Privately they nurtured a more basic fear of the man who argued that ecclesiastical organizations were foreign to the true nature of Christianity.[118] Fortunately, the university, more liberal than the church, insisted on the appointment. In the end, Wilhelm II overruled the clerics, but Harnack thereafter lived under something of a cloud.

Whatever the misgivings of the church, among his peers Harnack was regarded as a moderate. He stood in the tradition of Friedrich Schleiermacher and Albrecht Ritschl. Despite their many differences, the representatives of this so-called 'mediating' school were as one in minimizing the role of dogma. Instead they identified the historical Jesus as the fountainhead of Christianity.[119] Basic religious truth, they argued, was to be found through personal inner experience rather than in external conformity with any given doctrinal or theological position.[120] Christ spoke to the individual through the gospel. When apprehended with faith, his message transformed the hearts of men. The Christian faith, said Schleiermacher in the 1820s, was not a body of doctrine but a condition of man.[121] It was not to be confused with philosophy or theology. The intellect, he counselled, could not be called on to pass judgment on the truth of Christianity but only to interpret it.[122] Ritschl had clarified this position by insisting on the divorce of theology and metaphysics. He rejected, for example, the Hegelianism of Baur because it 'tried to squeeze all life into the limited categories of logic.'[123] Yet even theology he considered secondary to personal experience; for it was this experience that provided insight, and insight was the key to understanding. Altogether, it was a plea for a simplified religion; a call to strip away the gloss accumulated over centuries of speculation and rationalization. It represented a desire, keenly shared by Falconer, as it happened, to get down to bedrock. Harnack's special contribution in this regard was to illustrate copiously how, through the use of historical tools, this might be done. His synthesis was perhaps the highest expression achieved by the Ritschlian school.

'Dogma,' said Harnack, 'must be purified by history.'[124] His life's work was a commentary on that statement. The gospel of Jesus, he contended, contained all that the human mind could ever know of God. Like Baur, however, Harnack felt that the pristine message had been obscured by later commentators. There was, therefore, a marked difference between the historical Jesus and the Christ of the church. Only by peeling away a veneer applied over centuries could the essence of Christianity be revealed. Thus far did he travel the path charted by Tübingen. But he rejected the notion that the church and its dogma were products of a Pauline-Petrine conflict internal to Christianity. Instead, he contended that an adequate explanation had to include external influences exerted on the growing Christian community. In particular, he isolated the force of Hellenistic civilization. Dogma and ecclesiasticism, said Harnack, had formed no part of Jesus' original teaching. Rather, they had originated in the effort of early Christians to render the gospel comprehensible to a Hellenized world. Later, as the world changed, so did the forms and emphases applied to Christianity. Over time, however, doctrine and ecclesiastical organization solidified to the point where authority took precedence even over the gospel itself.[125] Sixteenth-century reformers had done much to weaken the claims of the church, but they had not gone far enough. Luther, said Harnack, had failed to cut himself loose from dogma. He had not fully recognized that scripture itself was a product of history.[126] Accordingly, Harnack sought to complete the work of the Reformation by liberating the gospel from dogmatic influences in his own age.

The task was urgent. Surveying the contemporary scene, Harnack perceived tendencies pointing towards the re-Catholicization of Christianity. The indifference of the masses and the timidity of those who sought external authority for their faith were undermining spiritual liberty.[127] Continuing sectarian division only reinforced a concern with the unessential elements of religion. These developments merely heightened his desire to clarify the fundamentals of faith. In this endeavour he turned to history for an answer. 'The Christian religion,' he wrote, 'includes a particular *knowledge* of God ... ; so far, however, as this religion teaches that God can be truly known only in Jesus Christ, it is inseparable from historical knowledge.'[128] Speculative methods could not penetrate to the heart of a religion that had evolved over time. Only history could accomplish this by separating the enduring from the ephemeral. Harnack set about his labours optimistically; for he believed that, despite changing perceptions, the gospel contained 'something which, under differing historical forms, is of permanent validity.'[129] Those permanent elements could be isolated by careful historical scrutiny. Thus, he was drawn to study the history of dogma.

A sketch of his method was outlined for popular consumption in his *What Is Christianity?*.[130] Published in 1900, it was a summary of his earlier teaching. Using modern critical techniques he attempted to show that the proper approach was to proceed from the gospel of Jesus. Then one could estimate his impact on the first generation of disciples. Next, he advised, one should follow the leading changes which Christianity had undergone in the course of history trying to recognize its principal forms. In the end, argued Harnack, a sound historical synthesis would emerge. 'What is common,' he wrote, 'to all the forms which it has taken, corrected by reference to the Gospel, and, conversely, the chief features of the Gospel, connected by reference to history, will, we may be allowed to hope, bring us to the kernel of the matter.' He never defined the essence of Christianity precisely. This, he said, was impossible given that 'our wavering knowledge of nature and history' was relative.[131] Absolute judgments were beyond the competence of the historian. This message he drove home in a passage more than vaguely reminiscent of conclusions reached by contemporaries such as Croce.[132] Historical judgments, he observed, 'are the creation only of feeling and of will. They are a subjective act.'[133] Nevertheless, whatever its limits, the study of history could achieve solid results. In an oft-quoted passage from his *Outlines of the History of Dogma*, Harnack summed up his findings and his program. 'The history of dogma,' he wrote, 'in that it sets forth the process of the origin and development of the dogma, offers the very best means and methods of freeing the Church from dogmatic Christianity.'[134] In addition, he prophesied, such history offered some hope for an end to sectarian rivalry because it testified to 'the unity and continuity of the Christian faith.'[135]

It was Harnack's tolerance, breadth of vision, and capacity for synthesis that captivated Falconer. Here was an 'inspiring' religious personality who preserved his faith while doing justice to scientific truth.[136] At one and the same time, Robert was consoled and stimulated. Decades later every detail of his months with Harnack remained graven on his memory. He lived in digs above a fencing school where every Friday young bloods sharpened their deadly skills in anticipation of weekend bouts. Falconer, needless to say, was not amused. Still, the place had its attractions. It was cheap but more importantly, it was near the university. Proximity was vital: the great man lectured six days a week at seven in the morning! Scrambling out of bed, Falconer had time only to shave, choke down a roll, snatch a sip of coffee, and bolt for the door. Trundling along Dorotheenstrasse, he occasionally had to force the pace after catching a glimpse of Harnack atop the tram-car rolling in from his home in

Charlottenburg. Aesthetically, the university itself was scarcely worth the hurry. Rumour had it that the main buildings had once housed the royal stables. The ventilation was notoriously poor. Fortunately, in summer some fresh air wafted in through open windows, but a certain mustiness was ever-present. None of these discomforts, however, bothered Falconer in the slightest as he hung on Harnack's every word.[137]

In his devotion he was not alone. Each day, precisely as a gong sounded, Harnack 'walked with a brisk step to his desk, an erect, lithe figure, with dark hair brushed high from his forehead, a slight moustache, and a keen eye giving kindly recognition through his spectacles to an enthusiastic and eagerly waiting roomful of hero-worshippers.'[138] Something in excess of 250 students were packed into the hall; for Harnack was not only a gifted scholar but also a lecturer of brilliance.[139] That term he was offering his famous course on the history of dogma down to the Reformation. As Falconer recalled, Harnack threw himself with abandon into his subject.[140] He spoke ex tempore but with force and clarity. Humour mingled with precise analysis and sweeping generalization. 'As he got into his subject,' says Falconer, 'he moved away from the desk, walked backwards and forwards with his thumbs in the arm-holes of his vest; then would sit upon his desk, bend forward intensely with flashing eye and point a finger emphasizing some remark. Perhaps he would pick up a quill pen, tear it to pieces and throw the bits about him.'[141] Harnack, however, never gave Falconer the impression of putting on a show or playing to his audience. This was merely the outward manifestation of a mind utterly absorbed in its argument. Even so, intentional or not, it was good theatre. Although he would never have admitted it, Robert was no doubt enthralled by the master's flare, as well as by his scholarship.

Many elements in his previous experience had prepared Falconer to embrace Harnack's ideas. His desire to establish an intellectual foundation for his religious instincts had not been satisfied by philosophical speculation. Historical criticism, especially that moderate form developed by Davidson, seemed to offer more hope. The notion, preached by Drummond and others, that Christianity was 'developmental' had made its appeal. Dods's emphasis on New Testament problems had helped Falconer find a focus for his interests. But it was Harnack who provided a majestic overview, a longed-for synthesis. He wove together the varied strands of faith and scholarship in a fashion so pleasing that Falconer himself felt whole again. More than any other, Harnack had shown him how religion and historical inquiry might comfortably live together. Throughout his life, he acknowledged a tremendous debt to that German scholar: Harnack, said Falconer, 'planted my feet on solid ground on which my faith could maintain itself amidst ... an all powerful science.'[142]

What he took from Harnack was a general disposition to religion and scholarship rather than specific solutions to this or that individual problem. Falconer was nobody' s slave. He never, for example, sought to remove the Old Testament from the canon of holy scripture as Harnack had advised.[143] Nor did he question the sacramental nature of baptism. In later years he disagreed substantially with the Berlin professor's views concerning the fourth Gospel's authorship.[144] In fact, if anything, he proved more lenient than Harnack in estimating the reliability of various New Testament writings.[145] In these and other matters of detail he was very much his own man. On the broader plane of assumption, however, the Ritschlian impress would be unmistakable. Most notably, he came to share in the Christocentric vision of the school. Similarly, he would draw attention to the crucial significance of inner experience and insight in religious life. Moreover, in company with Harnack, he would subordinate arguments over detail to an emphasis on the total impression received from the New Testament. Finally, as a practising scholar, Falconer would make full use of the tools of criticism without forgetting how tentative and subjective the historian's findings remained. It is impossible, of course, to determine precisely how much of Falconer's mature thought is traceable directly to Harnack's influence. None the less, it surely bears mentioning that of all his teachers Harnack alone is described by Falconer as a 'genius.'[146] For his part, had he lived to read it, Harnack would surely have been proud of this Canadian student who wrote that 'no spiritual experience can ever be defined adequately in a formula.'[147]

On 14 April 1892 Falconer was granted the degree Bachelor of Divinity by New College. The long process begun some six years earlier had reached its successful conclusion. Along the way, the boy had evolved into a gentleman. Among other things, he had acquired the polish and urbanity of the well-read and seasoned traveller. Proud of his Canadian roots, he had, nevertheless, become a citizen of the larger world, equally at home in the tropics, Europe, Britain, and North America. An array of lauguages, spoken or read, included English, Greek, Latin, German, French, and a smattering of Hebrew. These gave him access to the mind of an international scholarly community. The broadening of his interests and identity was not the least important result of his student years. It would serve him well when he later took his place as an academic statesman and university leader. For the moment, he came from his schooling as well equipped as any Canadian of his generation to interpret the New Testament in the light of recent scholarship. His had been a long progress from conventional belief to a more refined and liberal approach to religion. In this gradual awakening, Falconer had experienced some moments of confusion and discomfort, but there had been no profound shocks or transforming crises. In consequence, his native optimism had not been shattered, and with confidence he had tested and absorbed some new ideas. Emotionally conservative, he was becoming intellectually more liberal. In the long run he would emerge something of a Burkean in his attitude to change. At the time, at least, he was learning to distinguish between tools and their wielders. Historical criticism, science, and reason itself were, after all, only implements in the hands of men. Harnack and Davidson had demonstrated that men of faith and character had little to fear in casting about for new and better instruments. Falconer, in 1892, was still a long way from pulling together the various threads of his newly acquired learning, but he had the confidence and the energy to try. All that was wanting was an opportunity.

CHAPTER III

Pine Hill

Fortune smiled on Robert Falconer. Unlike many of his fellow graduates, he did not have to endure long years of apprenticeship in a rural pulpit. A scholar by inclination, he yearned to teach and write. As it happened, his wish was swiftly realized. In the autumn of 1892 he was appointed lecturer at the Presbyterian College, Halifax, an institution popularly known as Pine Hill. From his point of view this was the happy issue of a process, at times stormy, which had begun some years earlier. The college had evolved out of the old Pictou Academy. After decades of incessant wandering, it had finally settled in Halifax in 1860 following the union of the Free and Secession churches. Prosperity, however, remained elusive. The 1870s had been lean to say the least. For a time there was talk of closing the school. Competition from American theological colleges was fierce.[1] At one point enrolment plummeted to a mere five students.[2] The Presbyterian reconciliation of 1875, however, provided a new and timely impetus. By the late 1880s health and vigour had been restored. Attendance climbed and thirty candidates a year became the norm. In some minds the time had come to consolidate recent gains and look to the future. Falconer's appointment was the outcome.

Initiative in this venture came from Daniel M. Gordon, himself a graduate of the Pictou Academy and since 1889 a member of Pine Hill's governing board. At a meeting of that body on 2 October 1890 he recommended hiring a fourth professor 'in whatever field might require fuller treatment.'[3] The phrasing of the proposal would suggest that expansion, rather than the fulfilment of any specific curricular need, was Gordon's chief concern. The bald minutes of the board omit the reasons advanced in favour of the idea. Perhaps there was a mood of optimism fostered by recent improvements in the fortunes of the college, but such confidence would hardly have been unbounded, since Pine Hill still staggered under the weight of a $12,000 debt.[4] The addition of even one professor was a major undertaking for such a small institution in the best of times. As it stood, when the board finally decided to go ahead, it had to sell off some valuable property in order to finance the scheme.[5] High spirits, then, would not seem to account for this serious step. Instead, its leaders might well have been concerned to widen the range of studies so that Pine Hill could compete with larger schools abroad. A desire to inject new blood into a rapidly aging faculty may also have coloured their thinking. Of the three professors then on staff not one had been born after 1830. Finally, since their choice of Falconer was unanimous, one suspects that the college was anxious to draft someone in touch with the latest currents of scholarship.

Whatever their motives, by October 1891 the board stood four-square behind Gordon's proposal. But there agreement ended. United in their desire for expansion, the members fell out over the direction it should take. Some called for an academic chair focusing on New Testament Greek and exegesis. Others insisted that the new professor devote his time to 'practical' studies. This group urged the funding of a 'pastoral' chair. Here, in part perhaps, was an early and microcosmic symptom of a division that would later plague Canadian Presbyterianism as a whole. As the 1890s progressed, there would be increasing talk in Protestant circles of the importance of 'evangelism and social service.' Methodists in particular took up the 'social gospel' with enthusiasm. Presbyterians, however, were of two minds. Some, such as D.H. MacVicar and George Pidgeon, called on the church to take a direct and active role in solving social problems. Others, including the venerable G.M. Grant, opposed turning the church into a political pressure group and preferred to emphasize its indirect, spiritual role as a force for betterment.[6] The degree to which these contrary opinions influenced the Pine Hill board is unclear. At any rate, the members were sufficiently at odds to require external mediation. The upshot was an appeal to synod, which in turn sent the matter down to presbyteries for discussion in November 1891. Now the debate was conducted in earnest.

The premier contention of those favouring a pastoral chair was that Pine Hill had become isolated from the congregations it ultimately served. It was pointed out, then and later, that the professors were reluctant to stray far from Halifax. Accordingly, in some remote rural areas the college seemed an abode of the aloof and the privileged.[7] To farmers and fishermen alike the salaries drawn at Pine Hill appeared extravagant. Professors, it was assumed, enjoyed perpetual ease amid pleasant academic groves remote from the problems of ordinary life. For a college dependent on congregational generosity, such neglect of popular opinion was suicidal. As late as 1897 sixty-five churches within the Maritime Synod donated nothing to the divinity hall, despite the fact that its graduates were ministers in twenty-two of them.[8] In the winter of 1892 this pent-up resentment surfaced in many quarters. It was sharpened, no doubt, by the onset of a particularly harsh influenza epidemic. One observer argued that institutions such as Pine Hill ought to be regarded as 'schools of applied theology.'[9] So viewed, he contended, they would inevitably attract a type of student more sympathetic to common perceptions than those exalted beings who dabbled in Greek exegesis. The Presbytery of Halifax, in part, echoed this concern. Its prolonged discussions, in the opinion of the local press, demonstrated that the people wanted to see more of their professors and that any new lecturer would have to be 'more than a book-worm.'[10]

The case for an academic chair was supported by the principal and staff of the college as well as by many former graduates. Not least among these was the redoubtable Alexander Falconer. In an impassioned letter to the college journal, he denounced those who pleaded for a 'simple gospel.' 'One fears,' he observed, 'that there is a growing desire for a superficial, sentimental, anecdotal kind of preaching.' This, warned Alex, threatened to produce 'a narrow and shallow type of Christianity.' The only antidote was a well-educated ministry, a body of 'wise scribes' familiar with the deeper and more substantial aspects of religion. Healthy preaching, he advised, was the product of 'sound and accurate' sermon preparations, not ill-informed sentiment. Consequently he called for an exegetical chair whose occupant would set a sober and scholarly example to his youthful charges.[11] Alex and others who supported him were not indifferent to the problems of society. Similarly, those who preferred a pastoral chair were not the foes of scholarship. It was a question of emphasis, and in the end the issue was settled through compromise.

In October 1892 the board, with the support of a majority of the presbyteries, resolved that the new professor should hold an academic chair. Acknowledging the force of minority arguments, it further stipulated that in future more attention would be paid to the practical training of its students.[12] Finally, with very little discussion, Robert Falconer was unanimously nominated for the new post. With synod's approval he was appointed lecturer in New Testament Greek and exegesis for an initial three-year probationary period. In addition to his academic duties, he was made dean of residence, an office that would ease the strain on his pocketbook and give him some valuable administrative experience. A salary of $1,500 per year was provided. While not lavish, this stipend was roughly equivalent to those received by men of his rank in Canadian universities of the era. Altogether, the offer from Pine Hill was everything Robert could have hoped for, and he jumped at the chance.

In many ways Falconer was the obvious and logical candidate for the post. He was, for one thing, a far from unknown quantity. Following his Leipzig visit, he had spent the rest of the summer of 1889 as a student missionary in Pictou County. Before returning to Edinburgh, he had stayed on for part of the fall term to study at Pine Hill. During that brief period he helped found the *Theologue*, a journal edited by students of the college. In selecting Falconer the board were, in a limited sense, turning to one of their own. Beyond this, of course, his credentials were sterling. A prizeman several times over, he came to the college, as the *Theologue* observed, 'literally with honours thick upon him.'[13] These honours, furthermore, had been won 'at the highest seats of learning in the world.'[14] Moreover, any fears that he had been tainted with radicalism while abroad were probably quelled by his essay on Emerson which appeared in the *Theologue* in 1891.

Thus, his scholarship and demonstrated moderation recommended him. But so did his youth. It was frequently remarked that, until well into middle age, Falconer projected a boyish quality. That was Archibald MacMechan's initial impression of the new professor, who at their first meeting 'seemed no more than a boy, a typical undergraduate – a slim figure – a pleasant beardless face – flannels – straw hat – a tennis racket in his hand.'[15] At twenty-five Robert promised to bring new life to the college. Indeed, he may have been looked to as a bridge between his aged colleagues and a student body which, as the 1890s progressed, took an ever-deepening interest in contemporary issues and events.[16] The new dean of residence shared their concerns and quickly developed a rapport with his pupils. Student alienation would not plague Pine Hill as it had New College in Falconer's day. Indeed, he would play a vital role in keeping the lines of communication open between faculty and students. If the board had envisaged such a role for Robert, he more than justified their choice.

Apart from these considerations, the absence of any viable contenders also worked in his favour. Clarence Mackinnon might have been scouted, for example, but he had decided to do an extra term of postgraduate work at Edinburgh and was not available. James Falconer was deemed a worthy young fellow but was said to lack the exceptional ability and force of his elder brother.[17] Robert, therefore, had the field pretty well to himself. Finally, the influence of Alex in the Maritime church cannot be lightly dismissed. In a province where the missionary was a hero, Alex's stock was high. He was a power in the synod, a graduate of the Pictou Academy, and convenor of the mission board. No able son of his would be quickly passed over. Altogether, it would seem, circumstance, ability, and perhaps some measure of influence combined to bring Robert to Pine Hill.

News of the appointment generated considerable interest in the Halifax press. If the columns of the local newspapers were any guide to public interest, then it must be said that the devout Haligonians of the period were obsessed with the comings and goings of the local clergy. Notable sermons were reported in full. Missionaries in particular were lionized. On more than one occasion the *Halifax Herald* thumped its chest, proudly boasting that 'no part of Canada has given so many missionaries to convert the heathen as Nova Scotia.'[18] Religion in the 1890s was still a powerful current in the lifeblood of this community of 38,000. At the same time, fierce pride was invested in the institutions of higher learning that abounded in Halifax and the province. Small wonder then that Falconer's appointment rated front-page coverage, competing for attention with reports of a cholera outbreak in England, an attempted patricide in Kentville, and a crushing victory by the French over yet another remote African tribe.[19] Whether he liked it or not, it must have quickly dawned on Robert that he would be something of a public figure. As it happened, he would grow to like it very much. For the moment, however, he might have been slightly disturbed by other articles in the press that reflected a mounting popular debate about the implications of the higher criticism. Throughout the autumn of 1892 and the following winter, the newspapers were crowded with letters and editorials for and against the newer methods of biblical study. Many denounced them as inimical to the faith.[20] A few brave souls offered defence. One individual, discreetly identifying himself as a 'student,' pointed out that the higher criticism was merely a tool.[21] Another writer agreed, stating that it need be feared only in the hands of lesser lights.[22] And so the argument went. It had been heard before and would be raked over again. This time, however, it was of immediate personal concern to Falconer; for he was an exponent of criticism who was about to take up residence in a goldfish bowl.

Fortunately for him, the atmosphere at Pine Hill itself was decidedly tolerant. The tone was set by its three professors, Allan McKnight, Allan Pollok, and John Currie. 'They were,' said one acquaintance, 'reverent and venerable, far removed from the blatant modern spirit.'[23] Venerable they may have been, but they were definitely not fossilized. As Clarence

Mackinnon later recalled, Falconer brought 'a breath of the new learning and it is much to the credit of the older men that they gave him every opportunity.'[24] McKnight, of course, was well known as the defender of D.J. Macdonnell in the heresy trial of 1875. As principal of Pine Hill after 1878 he had supported Caven at Knox College and Grant at Queen's in their pleas for a less than literal reading of scripture.[25] John Currie was the only native Canadian among the three. Born in Tatamagouche, he had been educated at West River and New College, Edinburgh. After fifteen years of parochial work he had joined the college faculty in 1871 as professor of Hebrew and Old Testament exegesis. Like McKnight, he had no fears of modern scholarship. Currie, in fact, argued that Pine Hill should welcome all forms of genuine learning whether they emanated from Britain or Germany. Theologically, he contended, the school should be 'conservative yet progressive.'[26] The most dynamic and engaging member of this triumvirate, Allan Pollok, shared his colleagues' outlook. A Scot like McKnight, he had been educated in Glasgow in the late 1840s and had even spent time studying in Germany. Emigrating to Canada in 1853, he had served as professor of church history at Pine Hill since 1875. In that year his liberal sympathies had come to the fore as Presbyterians negotiated union among themselves. Always outspoken, Pollok objected to the use of the word 'infallible' to describe scripture in the new basis. Infallibility, he argued, was 'applicable to a person, not to a document.'[27] None of these men was a scholar in the sense that Davidson or Harnack was, but time had not entirely passed them by and they were open to new ideas. They treated Falconer as a favourite son, and he responded in kind with warm filial respect. No unbridgeable 'generation gap' yawned between them.

The liberal sympathies of the established faculty were pointedly displayed on the evening of Falconer's ordination. The services were held on 2 November in Chalmers Church. McKnight was in the chair, and Pollok took the podium for the opening address. He wasted no time and went straight to the heart of the matter. Heresies, he acknowledged, sometimes cropped up in theological colleges, let alone universities; but there was no reason to impose dogmatic chains on them. To do so would be to frustrate the untrammelled investigation that supplied their very raison d'être. 'Occasional error,' said Pollok, 'is the price that must be paid for freedom of enquiry.' Theological schools, in particular, had a special duty to keep up to date even with new errors, if only to combat them more effectively. Fresh attacks on the faith had always necessitated the development of new lines of defence. While admitting that the higher criticism had sometimes been carried to a length 'sufficiently absurd,'

Pollok warned of the dangers of neglecting its more reasonable claims. The mistake of Scottish colleges had lain in trying to insulate their students from the ferment on the continent. That error, he implied, would not be repeated at Pine Hill.[28] Clearly, Falconer was being given a mandate to bring the college into the modern era. Seated in the congregation, a proud Alex no doubt inwardly beamed as his eldest son stepped forward to be ordained. Robert himself, however, was conscious primarily of the heavy responsibility that accompanied the trust reposed in him.

Thus far, Falconer's quest for a secure intellectual foundation on which to rest his faith had been a compelling but unfinished personal odyssey. Now, however, it took on a new dimension. Fresh from college himself, he was being asked to interpret the New Testament to impressionable students preparing for the ministry. The task, therefore, of sorting out and clarifying his thoughts assumed a new urgency. 'It would,' he later wrote, 'have been dishonest of me to take the position and proceed to tear away light-heartedly the props on which the faith of these men of my own age clustered without substituting a better support.'[29] To a degree, however, he was still groping his way through 'broken lights.' From Germany he had returned with 'the uneasy suspicion that extreme scholars might be more scientific in spirit and in method than those who upheld the authenticity of Christian tradition.'[30] He had instinctively mistrusted, for example, Jülicher's claims to scientific objectivity but at the time found it difficult to respond effectively. Even the comparatively moderate Harnack, in whom he found so much to admire, favoured a greatly reduced canon. At Marburg in 1892 Robert had read Carl Weizsäcker's *Apostolic Age*, in which searching questions about the reliability of the synoptic Gospels had once again surfaced.[31] Inevitably when he assumed his new post, Falconer was driven to ask how much of the New Testament could be relied on to yield a historically accurate picture of Jesus and primitive Christianity. The question was vital, since he was already committed to the idea that only historical understanding could supply the intellectual security he and others craved. Over the next several years he worked patiently through the books of the New Testament, focusing particularly on the Gospels and the major Pauline Epistles. The result was a stream of addresses and articles in which he carved out his own position and through which he established himself as a scholar of note.

As Falconer sought to order and refine his thoughts, he was guided by some fundamental principles which gave him confidence in facing the task ahead. Mulling things over for a year, he chose the anniversary of his

ordination to make public these basic concepts. In keeping with established custom, a large congregation assembled in Chalmers Church to
celebrate the start of a new session at Pine Hill. Interest was keener than
usual, because the new professor, still on probation, was to be the keynote
speaker. Memories of the debate over the 'academic' or 'pastoral' nature
of the new chair were still fresh. Arguments about the beneficial or
deleterious effects of the higher criticism had yet to cool. Falconer would
be judged on the strength of this first address. It was an important début
and he knew it. It is tempting, therefore, to interpret his remarks as
having been tailored to the moment. Perhaps in some minor respects they
were. In broad outline, however, they faithfully anticipated the main
themes of all his future pronouncements. As such, they provide a clear
indication of the assumptions he entertained at the outset of his career.

Significantly, his address was entitled 'Christ: The Personal Source of
Religion and Theology.' With an eye, perhaps, to comforting those who
had favoured a pastoral chair, Falconer began by outlining his notion of a
well-rounded theological education. The object of a divinity college, he
asserted, was not so much to impart specific knowledge as general
'theological culture.' Intellectual training, of course, was essential. It
heightened the student's mental agility and thereby his ability to cope with
his forthcoming moral and spiritual mission. But practical training could
not be neglected. Nothing, said Falconer, should be alien to a seminarian
which could contribute to a deeper and more perfect understanding of
his own religious experience. Only the fully aware could hope to lead
others. In truth, he continued, the intellectual and the spiritual could not
be separated. 'The fully developed man,' he argued, 'is he in whom the
intellect pays homage to the spirit.' Thus, there were in his estimation two
sides to a complete education, the theological and the religious. 'The great
danger,' he warned, 'is that the seductive value of theological study, which
in itself is purely intellectual, should blunt the keenness of our spiritual
life.'

Elaborating on this theme, Falconer proceeded to consider theology
itself. It was, he stated, in many respects, a science. The material studied,
of course, differed from that of other sciences, but the exegete, the critic,
and the historian used investigative methods comparable to those
employed in all other fields of inquiry. There was, however, as he
carefully pointed out, one very significant difference. The theologian
could not stand apart from his material in the rigidly objective way that,
for example, the physicist did. In theology, as in any of the humanities, a
subjective factor inevitably came into play. The theologian, said Falconer,
required insight gained from personal religious experience in order to

interpret his subject properly. Thus, the deeper his religious life, the more trustworthy was his theology. In this manner, then, did the intellect pay homage to the spirit.

Rising to a higher plateau, Falconer announced his central theme. It was an idea to which he would return time and again throughout his life. Theology and religion, the intellect and the spirit, he proclaimed, had but one ultimate source and standard: 'Everything revolves around the person of Christ.' A historical religion founded on recorded facts, Christianity, argued Falconer, was more than a philosophy, more than the product of mere speculation. Instead, it could be traced to a definite person whose life and thoughts were enshrined in the Gospels. By and large, he averred, that gospel record had withstood the test of criticism and proved itself historically reliable. Consequently, amid the swirl of critical debate, Christ remained 'the most certain thing in our lives.' This is what made him the pivotal point of Christianity. Here also, said Falconer, was the rationale for a historical as well as a devotional approach to the New Testament. Thus, he described the Jesus of scripture as at once the source of both faith and intellectual assurance.

The Gospels, Falconer further observed, demonstrated a perfect relation between God and man as exemplified in the life of Christ. In his mind, it followed that a genuine Christian life must be lived in accordance with the teachings of Jesus and the church. Christianity, after all, was a religion, not a mere sentiment or code of morals. 'Deviation to any large extent from the creed of the church must be due,' he argued, 'either to defective experience, or to defective intellectual training.' On this score, Falconer stressed the historical continuity of Christian development. 'This,' he said, 'is the paradox of our religion. Use every historical means that the best methods of interpretation can provide to understand Christ as He is portrayed for us in the New Testament, as He is shown to us in the gospels and the epistles. Having made this start, our systems and creeds must and will arise in much the same form as now, but with a fuller context.' Doctrines and ecclesiastical organization, it appeared, could not be removed from Christianity. Having said this, however, Falconer immediately made it clear that he was no stubborn dogmatist. There was, he said, a limit to theologizing; many important points were open to question. 'If our own nature is so abysmal,' he asked, 'who can search the Almighty to perfection?' Given the limited nature of the intellect, one frequently had to be content with provisional theories about scores of religious mysteries such as the Trinity. Moreover, he contended, it was the duty of educated Christians to indulge in constructive debate. So long as in their search for truth they referred all to Christ and the gospels, it was unlikely that men of genuine faith would greatly err. Circular logic such as this, of course, was unlikely to satisfy the philosopher. Falconer, however, was not looking for philosophical solutions. He was a man of faith and a historian addressing men who, like himself, never seriously questioned the existence of God or the divinity of Christ.

In closing, Falconer moved from doctrine back to theology. Genuine religious experience, he declared, involved a 'living union with a living God.' Theology did not create religion but sprang from it. Thus, he advised that theology should be more 'biblical' than speculative. By this he meant that it should aim at recapturing that concrete historical moment when primitive Christians responded with intensity to a Christ who had so recently walked among them. To sense, to feel Christ as Peter had was to know and understand him better. Thanks, moreover, to the scriptural record, that moment was repeatable. Nowhere, he exclaimed, could Jesus be more directly encountered than in the New Testament. And here, said Falconer, lay the key to a full, personal, Christian experience. The more one knows Christ, he rhapsodized, the more one knows God and lives entirely in his presence. 'The Holy Spirit,' he mused, 'seems to live in that Book and brings me into contact with a living Christ and a living God now.' Properly undertaken, the study of scripture involved an exercise of historical imagination guided by faith. Approached in that manner, one need have no fear of criticism, 'for criticism,' as he put it, 'when intellectual, can never shatter that which is itself our very life.'[32]

The speech was a resounding success. 'It was,' said one observer, 'a masterly effort and [was] listened to with marked attention.'[33] If there was nothing in it to which anyone was likely to take sharp exception, this was not because it had been shaped to please particular groups. Falconer was no Trimmer then or later. He almost invariably spoke his mind, or he did not speak at all. A blend of the progressive and the conservative came naturally to him. It was a genuine position, not the calculated outcome of expedient compromise. In this outlook, it might be suggested, was the key to much of his later success as a public figure. Falconer, in the broadest sense, became one of the great moderates of his generation. Many Canadians would respond sympathetically to this man who strode the middle ground with utter conviction and transparent honesty. So it was that night at Chalmers Church. The new professor distinguished himself as a scholar who understood the pastoral side of the ministry and as a critic who approached his subject with caution and reverence. Not for the last time in his life, Falconer was the right man in the right place at the right time.

The address illustrated how far he had gone in that first year at Pine

Hill towards rationalizing his beliefs. No temporary construct, the framework of thought aired that evening would serve as the lasting foundation upon which a life of scholarship would be built. Indeed, Falconer's later religious writing was a commentary on these initial concepts. Clearly, he had drunk deeply at Harnack's well. A Ritschlian flavour was dominant in his thinking. All the major elements of the 'mediating' school were present, including an emphasis on inner experience, a christocentric vision, historicism, and a mistrust of unaided reason. For another half-century and more he elaborated on these notions and added a few twists of his own.

Faith, Falconer once wrote, 'is a matter for the individual.'[34] Essentially personal in origin, it was the response, he contended, 'of the living person to the living God in Christ Jesus – mind, thought, soul and affection.'[35] It was, in short, an act of the whole man. It arose, he argued, not from conformity with doctrine or ethical codes, but as the result of an inner transformation wrought by direct contact with Christ.[36] With Harnack, he held that dogma and ecclesiasticism were the secondary creations of men, not the very wellsprings of religion. He rejected the notion that Jesus had sought to establish a new law. That, he said, was a misconceived but 'persistent idea which can only be dissipated by faith at a white heat.'[37] Christ, wrote Falconer, had not come as a dictator to impose statutory conduct on his followers.[38] The moral impulse in primitive Christianity had not been imposed from without: instead, it had been generated within the souls of men quickened by faith.[39] 'Men,' he believed, 'are good or bad not as they conform outwardly to the human standards of their society, but as they act from a renewed conscience.'[40] Thus sin was to be understood not as a transgression of law but as an act of antagonism to a personal God. Its meaning, he wrote, 'is understood only by the soul of a man when he stands in the presence of the Holy God against whom he has sinned.'[41] Everything, therefore, that was essential in religious experience was personal in nature.

On the functions of the church and its doctrines, Falconer was less negative in tone than most Ritschlians. Indeed, he envisaged for that institution and its creeds a more positive role in a complete Christian life than Harnack, for example, was normally willing to concede. To be sure, in 1893 he appeared to argue a very orthodox position in stating that deviation from the credo of the church to any great extent was the result either of defective experience or defective training. At first glance, this would seem to be at odds with his emphasis on the seminal role of personal experience in religion. It must be recalled, however, that even Harnack sought not to destroy dogma but to purify it. He recognized that the urge to rationalize faith was instinctive in man.[42] He also allowed that, historical distortions notwithstanding, the basic elements of gospel truth were to be found in the formulations of every Christian era. The Berlin professor merely warned contemporaries not to seek salvation primarily in these imperfect creations of the human mind. In the entire corpus of his writing, Falconer's message was not dissimilar. Even in Chalmers Church he had been quick to point out that, doctrinally speaking, much would always be open to question. He too recognized that human attempts to express ineffable experience were inevitably incomplete.[43] Still, as this early speech indicates, he was less critical of transmitted doctrine than was Harnack. While acknowledging that men erred, he appears to have held that established doctrine represented the wisdom distilled from untold generations of personal experience. Since the message of Christ was the same for all, he was willing to grant that Christians of every age were likely to agree on essentials. Here he seemed to imply that the range of fundamental doctrine was quite small. Unfortunately, however, he never systematically set forth what he thought the faithful were required to believe. This aspect of his thought, therefore, remained rather vague.

As for the church itself, he conceded that an organized institution had formed no part of original Christianity. The unity displayed by early Christians, he wrote, 'was not constituted by an ecclesiastical hierarchy but in the possession of a common Spirit and love for a common Head.'[44] The silence of scripture he contended, illustrated that little weight was attached to the form of church government.[45] Consequently he vigorously denied the theory of apostolic succession. The Twelve, he stated, were not appointed to be official directors of an organized church.[46] In fact, he pointed out, there was no evidence to indicate that ministerial functions were invested exclusively in the Apostles. They came as witnesses not as organizers. Ordination, said Falconer, conferred no special virtue, grace, or power on the minister. Rather, it constituted a simple recognition by the Christian brotherhood of special talents in an individual for preaching the Word.[47] This said, however, Falconer did not view the church as an unnatural imposition on Christianity. Indeed, he maintained that an itinerant, charismatic ministry, such as that favoured by the Pauline churches, had blossomed naturally in the earliest times.[48] Eventually a regular teaching eldership developed within established congregations, and a church slowly evolved.[49] Properly understood, he maintained, the organized church was a valuable aid to faith. Collective worship was a healthy thing. 'As practised in the Church,' he wrote, 'it is the creation of the Christian mind and spirit down the centuries.'[50] Like-minded worshippers, he continued, could assist one another in blotting out 'the urgent world' and focusing attention on the things of the spirit. Ultimately, however, prayer, like conscience, remained private. Thus the church, like doctrine, was a useful but always ancilliary aspect of Christian experience. This general disposition came to the fore when Falconer at the turn of the century took up the cudgels on behalf of church union. In that crusade he would prove himself tolerant and flexible in dealing with the representatives of other Protestant sects. At heart, he remained a true disciple of Harnack.

Like all Ritschlians, Falconer was intensely Christocentric. While conceding that the church and its doctrines could be aids to faith, he steadfastly maintained that the individual came into contact with God through Christ alone.[51] For him Jesus was the only source of faith and guarantee of salvation. A fervent devotional glow that illuminated even some of Falconer's most technical writings was kindled by his sense of the immediacy and reality of Christ. To Falconer Jesus was not a platonic concept or mythical figure but a real person captured, albeit imperfectly, in the Gospels. He was, however, far from the 'ideal man' of modern liberal scholarship.[52] Falconer's studies convinced him from the first that the religious revolution inspired by Christ was so profound that it could never be adequately explained by the 'tame' Jesus of Renan and others like him.[53] He was struck by the fact that 'those who had been Jews, inheriting intense national pride, were willing to transfer the promises of Israel to the Gentiles.'[54] What, he asked himself, could account for a faith so novel and transforming that it overrode deeply ingrained racial and patriotic prejudices? Certainly not the injunctions of a mere philosopher or ethical teacher! Recalling the 1890s, he later wrote, 'I was thus brought back to consider the Founder of this colossal religious and moral phenomenon.'[55] Riveting his attention on the experience of early Christians, he strove to perceive Christ as they had done and in the end came to share their vision.

Absolute devotion to a personal Jesus, he discovered, had been the source of that ancient metamorphosis.[56] Elation suffused primitive Christians as the promise of personal salvation 'drove out fear for the first time from the multitudes of ordinary people.'[57] Not only the ordinary, but the extraordinary were affected. The conversion of Paul, 'an act of loving grace entirely unmerited,' dramatically illustrated the transforming power of the immanent Christ.[58] Joy, peace, and love were conferred by a messiah whose presence was sensed to be immediate. 'The risen Christ,' wrote Falconer, 'brooded over that early Church.'[59] Even after the ascension Jesus remained for his primitive followers not a vague wandering spirit but a real, almost tangible person. He was at once the font of inspiration and the bond of unity for these first-century men. That unity, argued Falconer, was not an invention of historians. It was, instead, a fact of overwhelming significance to believers welded together by loyalty to a person of transcendent worth.[60]

It was of immense significance to Falconer that the experience of Paul and his contemporaries was endlessly repeatable. Indeed, he declared, it had been duplicated in the lives of Christians down the ages. Augustine, Luther, Pascal, Wesley: all had known the touch of Jesus.[61] So too, it seems, had Falconer. It was in the spirit of the first Christian generation that he confessed his own faith in Christ. 'I respond to Him,' he wrote, 'as my supreme Leader, authoritative by His own inherent personality, giving me the fullest comprehension of God of which I am capable, assuring me that in the end God, as I see Him in Jesus, will cause His Kingdom to come.'[62] A figure of such majesty, he proclaimed, while intimately knowable, escaped definition and was beyond mere biography.[63] Consequently Falconer took little interest in philosophical, psychological, or even theological investigations of Jesus. He did, however, feel that the scholar and the historian in particular had an important contribution to make in efforts to define the fundamentals of religion.

Echoing Harnack, Falconer held that the task of the historian was to distinguish between the transient forms and the enduring substance of religion.[64] Criticism, he confidently believed, could cut away 'the local and the secular' and allow simple universal truths to emerge more clearly.[65] A patient and sincere investigation of the New Testament, he felt, would inevitably 'release a purer flow of loyalty to the Gospel,' which, he dared hope, might one day lead to a reconstruction of Christianity wherein a greater measure of harmony could be achieved.[66] In pursuing his studies, Falconer differed from Harnack in that he evinced very little interest in the post-apostolic age or the history of dogma. Instead, he seems to have taken his cue from Davidson. His focus of attention was different from that of the Old Testament scholar, but his approach was uncannily similar. Thus he sought, above all else, to recapture the inner life of early Christians and brought to his writings the vivid imagination and sense of historical immediacy that he had found in Davidson's work. Reflecting in 1900 on the apostolic period, Falconer obviously yearned to recommend its spirit, its simplicity, and its unity to his contemporaries. It had been, he thought, an idyllic era. Believers, he exclaimed, were still exultant. Christ was held to be very near. Truly, he ventured, those brethren had enjoyed a togetherness such as had never been repeated in history. If there were any hope for this world in days to come, he counselled, surely it was to be sought in those far-off hours when Christian life was young.[67] Accordingly, he set out to distil the essence of that early experience from the major books of the New Testament.

Falconer entertained no illusions about the capacity of the historian to recreate the past in all its fullness. Rankean claims to scientific objectivity he dismissed as 'an ideal to which only an approximation can be made.'[68] The subjective historian working with an always incomplete record inevitably dealt in probabilities rather than in certainties. His early suspicions that radical scholars were more scientific than those who spoke for tradition were quickly dispelled. As he laboured through the sources for himself and applied all the latest vehicles of criticism, he came to understand better their uses and their limitations. What, he asked himself, is the scientific spirit? 'It is,' he replied, 'a spirit which searches for facts and evidence in the most impartial manner, and then by the use of the best available judgment assigns values to such facts and evidence.'[69] Interpretation, then, was unavoidable no matter how scientifically a man collected and tested his evidence. Furthermore, he recognized that interpretation could never be entirely free of subjective factors. 'Every historian,' he commented in 1897, 'writes with "tendency."'[70] By this he meant that every man to one degree or another reflects the ethos of his generation, however impartial he might strive to be in assessing the past. Moreover, Falconer acknowledged that each man entertained some assumptions of which he was only partly conscious. Accordingly, he wrote that the scholar 'must be warned to make allowance for a probable refraction of the path of light in the deeper strata of his convictions which have not hitherto been disturbed.'[71] These observations, of course, would become the commonplaces of twentieth-century historical thought. In the 1890s, however, they represented a rebellion on the part of men like Falconer against the claims of a positivism that had overreached itself. Neo-Kantians, Nietzscheans, Freudians, and idealists alike contributed to the assault. Falconer, as he would have been the first to admit, displayed the 'tendency' of his time. In all likelihood, he had acquired some of his appreciation of the subjective from Harnack. Whatever the case, he was acutely aware of the tentative aspects of biblical study and historical explanation. It advanced, he contended, 'by the formulation of hypotheses and by their overthrow.'[72] Hence his insistence that, while the meaning of Revelation became ever clearer, 'we can never expect to have a complete system of theology elaborated in the minutest detail.'[73]

Unfortunately, the assumptions that underlay these conclusions were never fully clarified by Falconer. Close psychological and epistemological analyses were not for him. In 1893 he seemed vaguely to suggest a mind composed of a reasoning faculty, intuition, and will when he said that in a complete man the intellect paid homage to the spirit. A few years later he rather casually distinguished between the 'mechanical or scientific' part of the mind and its 'spiritual or religious' component.[74] Later still, he recalled that, in his youth, knowledge meant 'more than intellectual truth; it included an intuitive apprehension of spiritual ideals.'[75] There was, he wrote, a principle or a power which laid hold of the intellect and through it moulded the entire personality to produce virtue. While these scattered fragments can hardly be said to constitute a philosophy of mind, they do indicate that Falconer subordinated reason to intuition in his quest for a fuller understanding of scripture. That he was no enemy of reason or science he later made plain.[76] Indeed, he had great confidence in the intellect when it was applied to its own proper sphere, the realm of phenomena. In the end, however, he believed that 'all natural causation works toward spiritual ends.'[77] This being the case, he felt that he who would explain the 'why' of existence, rather than the simpler 'how,' was obliged to rely on the insight spawned in religious experience. This is what he meant when he argued that the deeper a theologian's religious life, the more trustworthy was his theology.

Such, then, in broad outline, were the various assumptions Falconer brought to his study of the New Testament. In many ways he trod a path charted by Harnack. But, when it came to assessing the authenticity and breadth of scripture's canon, the two often parted company. In the twilight of the nineteenth century, many came to fear a progressive atomization, shrinkage, and despiritualization of the Bible.[78] Liberal, let alone radical, criticism had emphasized the differences among its books. As well, many hitherto hallowed texts were viewed with suspicion. Some, such as Albert Schweitzer and Karl Barth, would react sharply against these trends. After 1900 there was a increasing demand for a less historical and more theological, almost mystical, reading of scripture. Prophets of 'neo-orthodoxy' would dethrone the ethical Jesus of history in favour of a transcendant, eschatological Christ.[79] Falconer, suspicious of mysticism and convinced of the utility of history, never went so far. None the less, he was not totally unmoved by the concerns that produced a Schweitzer and a Barth. Thus, while employing critical methods, he sought consistently to defend the traditional canon and to illustrate its spiritual unity. Although he never actually said as much, that tendency is patent in the tide of articles and reviews that issued from his ready pen.

Falconer the reviewer exhibited a marked fondness for authors who displayed spiritual awareness as well as technical virtuosity.[80] He announced a general preference for English over German scholarship. The heirs of Lightfoot, he felt, were less obsessed with method. Furthermore, their works were more popularly accessible than the ponderous and recondite studies favoured in Germany. Beyond these broad considerations, he disliked overly clever and intentionally controversial writing wherever he found it. Reviewing Theodor Zahn's *Introduction to the New Testament* in 1898, Falconer commented that 'one cannot help feeling that he is at times too ingenious, too dogmatic and rests a position too exclusively on an opinion of his own.'[82] Reasonable revision he was happy to embrace, but he always reacted sharply whenever he saw a man bending over backwards to challenge traditional views. Not even the revered Harnack was exempt. The latter, for example, advanced the thesis that Priscilla had authored the Epistle to the Hebrews. Falconer retorted tartly that 'a good deal more is required than the clever reasoning of the brilliant Berlin historian to render such a *prima facie* unlikely theory, utterly unsupported by tradition, in any degree plausible.'[83] His most heavily charged bolts, however, were reserved for those who approached scripture in a bloodless and strictly technical way. In 1900 something very like anger throbbed in his reply to a provocative entry in the recently published *Encyclopaedia Biblica*. The 'scientific' criteria laid down by Herr Professor P.W. Schmiedel, if applied, would have reduced to mere fragments the authentic elements of the New Testament. Picking up the gauntlet, Falconer inveighed against a purely 'mechanical' evaluation of the sources.[84]

Concerning his own studies, Falconer once denied that issues of authorship and dating were primary for him as he examined the New Testament. Instead, he insisted that his object was to investigate the historical and religious phenomena recorded in these 'consentient writings.'[85] Inevitably, however, questions raised by Weizsäcker, Schmiedel, and others compelled him to consider the reliability of the evidence he perused. Thus, perforcedly and perhaps ironically, he was drawn into the documentary debates of the era. Here he quickly established himself as a champion of tradition. An accomplished player of the game, Falconer brought to bear all the usual tools of historical and linguistic analysis. At no point in his extensive publications, however, did he pause to discuss systematically his major principles of criticism. Nevertheless, a few hints were occasionally dropped.

Falconer's use of the term 'consentient writings' affords an important clue to his general approach. In genuine scripture, he said, there was a detectable unity which transcended differences of style and authorship. 'With all their diversity,' he observed, 'the writers of the Bible have no seriously discrepant views of God and man.'[86] Above all else, he looked for this 'congruity' in estimating the authenticity of a text.[87] The Gospels in particular, he noted, were marked by a similarity of tone, outlook, and purpose. They moved forward, he asserted, 'with the sure tread of grand simplicity.'[88] They also were characterized by a 'severe objectivity.' The writers, he continued, never obtruded themselves on their work but stuck close to their central purpose, which was to display Christ and his teachings. As a general rule, Falconer seemed willing to give the benefit of the doubt to any source that did not seriously violate his sense of congruity. He was, of course, no simple-minded dupe. Under his eye the evidence was subjected to exacting scrutiny. Nor was he an inflexible special pleader. His conclusions were advanced as probabilities, not as certainties. In the end, however, he relied, as he advised others to do, on judgment as much as science. The 'acid tests' and rigid formulae of a Schmiedel were not for him.

During his first five years at Pine Hill, he pored over the major books of the New Testament. Thereafter, he began, slowly at first and then with increasing frequency, to publish his findings. In 'The Prologue to the Gospel of John' (1897) Falconer crossed swords with the redoubtable Harnack. The latter had contended that the first eighteen verses of the fourth Gospel should be stricken from the canon. They constituted, he argued, an introduction imposed at a late date by a hand other than that of the original author. The purpose, said Harnack, had been to recast the contents of the gospel in a form intelligible to Hellenized readers. In the process, he averred, the message had been altered. Falconer rejected these claims. The Hellenic influence, he maintained, was at best superficial. The fundamental thought was Hebraic. The 'Logos' of the prologue, he said, referred not to 'Reason' or some nebulous first principle, but to 'a Divine Being who lives.' Furthermore, he continued, the author disavowed metaphysics altogether. 'John,' wrote Falconer, 'a Jew of the Jews, follows in the lead of his nation's effort and success, telling his readers that the riddle of all existence can be solved only in religion.' Analysing the language and the historical conditions reflected in the prologue, he drove towards his conclusion. In style and approach it was pure Falconer. 'If the foregoing interpretation is correct, it will be seen that the prologue is neither designed particularly for Greek readers, nor can it be regarded as an addition by a later hand to accommodate the Gospel to a new environment. Its nerve and tissue are those of the body of the Gospel. Its connections are too subtle, its harmony too delicate, its spirit too indefinitely similar, to be the work of another than the author of the Gospel.'

In 1900 Falconer leapt to the defence of the Book of Acts whose authenticity Schmiedel had challenged. The German had charged that the text was so coloured by a Paulinist 'tendency' that it could not be regarded as a useful source for the early apostolic age. Falconer admitted that the book was a product of the late first century but refused to consign it to the second as Schmiedel had done. Moreover, he attempted to demonstrate that the author of Acts, although a Paulinist, was a reliable commentator on the nature of primitive Christianity. This he did by focusing on the evolving concept of the Holy Spirit. Christ, said Falconer, had introduced his followers to the idea while he was still alive. These early Christians, he continued, had embraced the notion in an unsophisticated and imaginative sense. In time, however, the concept was given a deeper spiritual interpretation by Paul and others like him. In appraising Acts, Falconer was therefore impressed to find that its author took account of the difference between these early generations. Although aware of a fully developed Pauline doctrine of the Holy Spirit, he had not read it back into the minds of primitive brethren. Accordingly Falconer was forced to conclude that the author was not only a good historian but was drawing on early and reliable sources. Thus, in his mind, Acts remained a legitimate and important part of the New Testament.[89]

Falconer's boldest early venture came with the publication of a series of linked articles concerning the Second Epistle of Peter. They appeared in the prestigious English journal, the *Expositor* in 1901 and 1902.[90] No other text had been questioned more vigorously; its supporters among Falconer's generation were few. But he was undeterred. In the course of a lengthy and minute analysis he suggested that the epistle might have been a circular letter to the churches of Samaria composed around 60 AD. He compared it with the more widely accepted First Epistle of Peter and judged it similar. Differences in style and language were a problem. These Falconer accounted for by arguing that two secretaries had transcribed the separate letters. Concerning the contents of these Epistles, he held that since they were addressed to different audiences, some alterations of thrust and emphasis were only to be expected. On the whole, however, he held that 'their teaching is fundamentally of the same type and distinct within the New Testament.' Second Peter, in other words, displayed the required congruity.[91] Most scholars none the less have remained sceptical of this Epistle. Indeed, Falconer himself was not unyielding on the matter. In 1909, in Hastings's *Dictionary of the Bible*, he conceded frankly that his hypothesis had not met with much favour.[92] Retreating from the theory of direct Petrine authorship, Falconer went on to suggest that the Epistle probably came from the hand of a disciple who later reproduced the master's teaching. In the final analysis, he submitted that the issue was probably indeterminable. Nevertheless, in typical fashion, he maintained that the Epistle struck 'a pure Christian note' and on that basis was still worthy of attention.

Falconer's efforts to untangle some of the Gordian knots of New Testament scholarship soon won him recognition. Just after the turn of the century he was invited to contribute to several of the great biblical dictionaries then being compiled.[93] These mammoth undertakings included articles from leading scholars throughout the western world; Falconer was one of the few Canadians whose participation was solicited.[94] In addition, academic honours came his way. In 1902 he joined the handful of men who held an LL D degree from the University of Edinburgh. Four years later Knox College in Toronto honoured him with a DD degree. Meanwhile, his services as a lecturer were increasingly sought. For example, on various occasions he spoke at the Hartford Theological Seminary, the Presbyterian College of Winnipeg, and other such institutions. He had come a long way since the evening of his ordination when he had worried about the problems of instructing young seminarians. Life had been good. It had also been full. After all, the youthful professor had a great deal more than his own studies to occupy his time.

A mood of quiet optimism reigned at Pine Hill throughout most of the 1890s. Enrolment climbed steadily. By 1896 an unprecedented fifty-four students stalked the halls in search of theological enlightenment. As early as April 1893 Professor Pollok was moved to exclaim that the 'wilderness journey' was over.[95] For the first time in decades, he noted, the college was out of debt. Equally heartening was the fact that two-thirds of the Maritime clergy had passed through its classrooms. Indeed, said Pollok warming to his theme, there was never any trouble placing graduates, and he speculated that the region could absorb three times the number the college turned out. Spirits were momentarily dampened when in 1894 the fatherly McKnight passed away. Continuity and confidence, however, were preserved when the affable and liberal Pollok assumed the principalship in his stead. Similarly, the atmosphere of the place was little changed when D.M. Gordon was co-opted from the governing board to fill McKnight's chair of systematic theology and apologetics. Altogether, these were halcyon days in the life of Pine Hill. However, they were not uneventful.

Comparing the twenty-four hours of class work a week demanded of a student at Pine Hill with the fourteen required in most American theological colleges, the editor of the *Theologue* was once moved to comment on behalf of his fellows, 'we are not grumbling – at least not very much; but it is hard all the same.'[96] Yet, if students were busy, the faculty were more so. In a small but growing college there was no room for time-servers. Falconer, for one, shouldered his fair share of the collective load and more. For several years, in addition to his regular teaching duties, he offered a course in biblical literature at Dalhousie University. Wasting not a moment, Sunday afternoons were devoted to Bible classes. These informal sessions soon led him to take a leading role in efforts to promote the Sunday school movement which blossomed in the 1890s. Falconer also sought to add fullness to the extra-curricular life of the college. Recalling, perhaps, the insight and pleasure he had derived from long nights of student conversation at Edinburgh, in 1892 he founded the Theological and Literary Society. Guest speakers were invited to stimulate discussion on topics as varied as the poetry of Wordsworth, the art of Rossetti, and the nature of Hinduism. In this capacity Walter Murray, now professor of philosophy at Dalhousie, was a popular visitor. Clarence Mackinnon, after his return to Nova Scotia in 1894, also lent a willing hand. Typically, however, it was Falconer who cheerfully bore the principal burden. Down the years he opened youthful minds to ideas not normally scanned in the classroom. Still young himself, he revelled in companionship with students and shared many of their concerns. For example, he gave early notice of his sympathy with their mounting desire for practical training, when he sponsored regular hospital visits by his budding charges.[97] In later years, when power rested in his hands, he would make far greater efforts to bring these seminarians into touch with a changing world outside. But a good start had been made, and students responded appreciatively to Falconer's firm yet kindly touch.

Everyone, indeed, seemed pleased by the new man's performance. Local churches were soon after him to preach. The Halifax press, ever watchful, remarked approvingly on these public sermons, coloured as they were by 'deep devotional feeling.'[98] Many, no doubt, heaved a sigh of relief as Falconer, his German experience notwithstanding, proved to be a sane and trustworthy Christian. No group, however, was more enthusiastic in its praise than the student body. The fourth professor, they noted, did not slavishly bind himself to the church's traditional views. Moreover they were impressed that Falconer advanced new ideas without flouting established doctrinal standards or upsetting the harmony of the school. 'He had,' said the Theologue's editor, 'stimulated his students in the exercise of thought, training them to be careful thinkers, cautious thinkers, but withal to be thinkers, the greatest benefit an instructor can confer.'[99] The board and his colleagues evidently shared in the general satisfaction. When his probationary period came to an end in 1895, he was confirmed in the rank of professor by unanimous agreement.[100] At the same time his salary was raised to $1,800 per year. In 1898 it reached $2,000. These were far from princely sums, but Falconer was comfortable enough. As dean of residence he lived in the college and had very few expenses. Whatever spare cash he had was apparently tucked away each year. Some of it went to finance summer travels in Europe and Canada. But even then there was always a bit left over. A note, for example, in the papers of D.M. Gordon records that between 1898 and 1900 Falconer donated over $300 to the college library fund.[101] Clearly, he was not suffering financially.

If Falconer proved successful in handling his own affairs, he also acquired at Pine Hill invaluable practical experience in college management. Besides administering the residence, he was responsible for the college grounds. As the site, though beautiful, was only ten acres, its maintenance posed no serious problems. Still, he was obliged to deal with the household staff and to balance a small budget. As a result, some rudimentary lessons were undoubtedly learned. More significant skills were developed during the annual funding drives. At the best of times, Pine Hill subsisted on a very narrow financial margin. Fees formed an inconsiderable proportion of its income. Consequently, the growth of enrolment was often as much a burden as a blessing, placing as it did an increasing strain on existing facilities. Interest from endowments covered little more than half of operating expenses. The difference, normally about $4,000, had to be elicited from congregations on a voluntary basis.[102] When in 1893 Pollok boasted that the college was out of debt, he neglected to add that solvency had been accomplished only by the sale of some endowment lands and through a special donation from the faithful.[103] This windfall afforded a welcome but all too brief respite from financial pressures which would intensify as expenses rose in the later 1890s.

In these circumstances, yearly appeals to the Presbyterian rank and file remained crucial to the well-being of the college. Every spring Pine Hill designated official agents in each of the Maritime presbyteries whose function it was to stir the consciences and loosen the pocketbooks of true believers. Most congregations proved responsive to this indirect prod, but an alarming number in areas remote from Halifax clung tenaciously to their brass. Rural suspicions about big city colleges died hard. In a few regions confusion reigned concerning the nature and function of Pine Hill. One editor of a country newspaper identified it, in all sincerity, as 'an institution in which young ladies received the finishing touches to their education.'[104] Such delusions and misinformation could not be allowed to persist. Friends of the college called on its professors to take a more active role in public relations and fund raising.[105] The wisdom of this advice was underlined in 1898, when the board, wringing its hands, pleaded for an increase of 25 per cent in subscriptions from the hinterland.[106]

Thus it was that Falconer, personable, young, and energetic, found himself increasingly far from Pine Hill's cloister on the stump for cash. Nobody had mentioned this subject at New College. Harnack had not touched on the subject of theological solicitation. But the wily stamp collector from Trinidad dipped into the side pockets of his character and found some hitherto hidden resources. He discovered, indeed, a positive gift for dealing with people and for separating them from their money with a dignified flourish. Tangible proof came in the summer of 1899, when his swing through Prince Edward Island was so successful that a general canvass planned for the fall was happily cancelled.[107] One suspects that, as Falconer toured the Maritimes palm upward, he came more fully to understand just how vulnerable institutions like Pine Hill were to public criticism. If this experience, indeed, is where he learned that lesson, he certainly never forgot it. In any event, increased attention to popular opinion did not immediately solve the college's financial problems. It should be noted, however, that in 1897 fully sixty-five congregations had given nothing, whereas by 1904 the number of non-contributors was reduced to thirty-seven.[108] The efforts of Falconer and others had not been in vain. Some progress, at least, had been made toward extracting the most from existing sources.

Throughout this period the level of alumni support was frequently disappointing. It had always rankled that many graduates seemed unable or unwilling to move their flocks to largesse. Accordingly, in addition to professorial sorties through the outback, efforts were made to draw old boys into closer association with their alma mater. Once again, the resourceful Gordon supplied early initiative. Why not, he suggested in 1894, rekindle the loyalty of graduates by inviting them to a summer school?[109] The board approved the scheme and handed it over to Falconer for implementation. Planning went ahead through the winter. Lustre was added to the coming event when Principal Grant of Queen's University and Professor McCurdy of the University of Toronto agreed to attend as lecturers. All boded well and high hopes flowered as winter yielded to spring. If the faculty seemed a trifle anxious at times, that was because they had agreed to bear the total financial burden of the venture themselves. More than college pride had been staked on this experiment.

Those who gathered at Pine Hill that summer appear to have enjoyed themselves. One participant gratefully recalled the convivial fellowship that characterized the session. The group, he reminisced, was 'in the rarified but electric atmosphere of Higher Criticism one hour, and ransacking cherry trees or tumbling like a family of porpoises in the waters of the Arm the next.'[110] Falconer made a more than favourable impression. Thrust into a 'fiery crucible before the higher and lower critics of our church,' he emerged unscathed.[111] Yet, for all the high spirits and higher criticism, the results of the summer school were discouraging. Barely enough graduates attended to make ends meet.[112] The effort was renewed in 1896 only to be dropped thereafter when attendance failed to rise. Changing tactics, the college in 1897 turned to the *Theologue* for assistance. Through its pages a 'Guild of Theological Study' was launched. The idea was to encourage ministers to keep up with current ideas and to draw them into regular contact with Pine Hill.[113] Falconer, Currie, and Gordon agreed to write articles and edit replies. Clarence Mackinnon signed up immediately. But few others did, and the guild, like the summer school, was quickly given up.[114] The importance of maintaining a healthy alumni association was thus made painfully clear to a disappointed Falconer.

Hip-deep in scripture or immersed in collegiate duties, Falconer was a very busy man. But there was always time for friendship. With the poetic Archibald MacMechan he enjoyed long afternoons rowing on the Northwest Arm or rambling along its strand. An occasional round of golf and the odd set of tennis served to mellow the bond between them. In some ways, of course, they were an unlikely pair. MacMechan, fanciful, introspective, and romantic, at times lapsed into bouts of pessimism.[115] Falconer, in contrast, was not given to brooding self-examination and was by nature adaptable and optimistic. These two Presbyterians, however, shared a world view in which the ideal took precedence over the empirical and religion coloured all.[116] Similarly, both men were charmed by Halifax and the solid rural values of the Maritimes as a whole. Whatever the basis of their friendship, it endured until MacMechan's passing in 1933. Old schoolmates from Edinburgh also provided genial companionship. In 1894 at a synod in New Glasgow, Falconer, with a group of his former classmates and a few others, united to form a club. In an exuberant frame of mind they styled themselves the 'Round Table.'[117] The stated purpose of the association was that of encouraging the intellectual life of its members, but social pleasures were also to bulk large.

As fate would have it, the individuals who comprised this little group would soon come to exercise an exceptional degree of influence in Canadian higher education. D.M. Gordon was the senior member and held the chair as 'King Arthur.' When he left in 1903 it was to take up the principalship of Queen's. Prominent among the 'knights' was Walter Murray, destined after 1908 to be the first president of the University of

Saskatchewan. Alfred Gandier, who since 1893 had been pastor of Fort Massey Church in Halifax, was an eager recruit. Born in Ontario, Gandier had been educated at Queen's and New College, Edinburgh. A bachelor and a new boy, he no doubt longed for companionship and in any event meshed well with the others in the new association. Later he would become the principal first of Knox College, then of Emmanuel College, in Toronto. Clarence Mackinnon was a moving force behind the Round Table. After a succession of pastorates in Nova Scotia and a brief stint in Winnipeg, he was appointed principal of Pine Hill in 1909, a position he held for twenty-eight years. It is interesting that Mackinnon accepted the principalship only after a long conversation with Murray, 'the family mentor.'[118] In like manner, a year earlier, Falconer had helped open the door for Murray at Saskatoon.[119] He could scarcely have done otherwise for his children's 'Uncle Walt.' For his part, Falconer would rise to be the most influential of them all. When the close association of this group with Dalhousie is also taken into account, an extraordinary picture emerges.

The role of Nova Scotia in shaping nineteenth-century Canadian higher education has long been understood.[120] G.M. Grant and William Dawson were legendary figures. Less fully appreciated, however, is the degree to which that tradition was maintained and broadened in the first decades of the new century. Similarly, the disproportionate impact of Scots Presbyterians on Canadian intellectual life has been well documented.[121] But the extent to which this influence achieved institutional expression at the highest levels of academic leadership needs also to be recognized. The community of outlook and experience shared by the Round Tablers was remarkable. When as presidents and principals these men later met to discuss their own and the country's academic problems, they did so as old friends and kindred spirits. For them, the Canadian academic world was a small one, particularly between 1907 and the end of the First World War, while Gordon was at Queen's and the links with Dalhousie were still fresh. All these developments, however, lay in the future. For the moment, the Round Tablers merely gloried in the delights of their floating seminar.

Throughout the 1890s, the group met three or four times a year in each other's homes. In this talented assembly everyone had something to contribute. Falconer, of course, was a veritable lexicon of recent biblical scholarship. His brother James, now comfortably settled in a church at Newport, shared these interests. Murray added a philosophical element to the discussion. Another member, Arthur Silver Morton, could hold forth with authority on the subject of church history. A son of the missionary John Morton, he had grown up with the Falconers in Trinidad and like them had been educated at New College and Berlin. He later made his mark in the study of western Canadian history as a professor at the University of Saskatchewan.[122] The intense Clarence Mackinnon was emerging as a leading social activist within the church and brought this perspective to the sessions.[123] But, with the exception of Gordon, these men were just out of college and it was more than clever debate that drew them together. Their sombre clerical blacks clothed still youthful spirits, and they revelled in reliving experiences so recently shared in Edinburgh. Normally an almost adolescent enthusiasm marked their gatherings. Mackinnon well recalled the gaiety of just such an occasion in 1895. One thoughtful member, he tells us, proposed that the lavish turkey dinners that inevitably kicked off the evening should be dispensed with as an unwarranted imposition on the ladies. The suggestion, says Mackinnon, was 'received with a cold politeness on the part of the juvenile band who had not yet attained the more mature ideal of "plain living and high thinking."'[124] That issue dispensed with, the happy crew adjourned for a day's fishing during which nothing sporting a gill was spotted, let alone snared. All returned, however, sunburnt, refreshed and eager to turn in on the borrowed mattresses strewn across Mackinnon's floor. Surely, before dropping off to sleep, one of them must have muttered, 'Ah now, this is the life!.'

His association with the Round Table enhanced Falconer's personal life in more ways than one. Alfred Gandier had a sister and Robert was definitely interested. Ever guarded about his private concerns, Falconer tells us nothing concerning his courtship of the tall and willowy Sophie. One imagines, nevertheless, that she caught his eye swiftly in the close-knit clerical community they both inhabited. Miss Gandier had journeyed east to tend house for her unmarried brother when he took up his call at Fort Massey. Children of the manse, they were offspring of the Reverend J. Gandier of Newburgh, Ontario. Born in 1870, Sophie was still in her twenties when Robert first spied her. Closer acquaintance probably developed when Alfred took his turn as host of the Round Table. Robert, boyishly handsome, earnest, and successful, undoubtedly had much to recommend him. In any event, the two were married in Toronto on 12 May 1897. A few days later they embarked in the steamer *Parisian* for a three-month tour of Britain and the continent. As time went by they matured as a well-matched pair. Intelligent and well read, Sophie came to serve as a sounding board for Falconer. In so far as women were then permitted, she took an active role in various church matters, charity functions, and the like.[125] Above all, she was an accomplished hostess and had a flare for putting both students and visiting dignitaries at their ease.[126] She would, in this capacity, prove to be an invaluable asset to Falconer. Nevertheless, for the most part she was content to remain in the background, and Robert did not thrust her forward. That he valued and relied on her quiet support, however, is beyond question. In later life, he likened her to a fellow paddler in a canoe, noting that 'her stroke was strong and steady and never faltered.'[127] It was well that the bond was strong between them; for it was quickly tested by two stillbirths. Some of the sting was taken out of these tragedies, however, when later two children, Gilbert and Bobby, survived.

Sophie, although a poor sailor, enjoyed travel. This was all to the good, since much of her married life was spent tagging after the light-footed Robert. The two, for example, were familiar figures at the Northfield student conferences in the United States. Falconer's frequent addresses at these gatherings were an expression of his interest in the work of the Young Men's Christian Association. From his earliest days in Halifax he had taken a hand in promoting the YMCA, which he interpreted as an effort further to entrench Christianity among the young.[128] In later years, the Student Christian Movement also benefited from his considerable support. Northfield had its charms, but the Falconers also saw a good deal of Canada during this period. The summer of 1898 found them off to Winnipeg, where Robert was to offer a course at the local Presbyterian college. Three months of lectures went well enough. Falconer enjoyed Winnipeg which he described as 'a distinctively Canadian city.'[129] The surrounding countryside, however, he found much too flat and monotonous for his taste. Consequently, when the term concluded, with Sophie in tow, he bid his farewells hastily and boarded a train for British Columbia. As he journeyed through the west, Falconer was struck by the immense difficulties facing missionaries in the region. Vast expanses created obvious difficulties, but so did the nature of the population. Rough-hewn loggers in British Columbia, he said, presented a considerable challenge, although he never doubted that their hard exteriors could be penetrated by the Word.[130] The foreign races settling on the prairies, however, posed an urgent problem. These alien elements, he wrote, needed the gospel just as much as Anglo-Saxons and he urged his church to send forth its best young people as missionaries.[131] At the time he addressed himself only to his Presbyterian colleagues. Shortly, however, he and many other churchmen would call for greater measures of co-operation among all the Protestant sects labouring on the prairies. This western trip had been revealing.

Back at Pine Hill circumstances were slowly beginning to change. In 1899 the Falconers moved into one of the four new faculty cottages erected on campus. They were, no doubt, mightily pleased to be so comfortably housed in a structure replete with all the latest conveniences. The failure of the furnace in 1902 probably did little to cool their love of the place. When all the shingles flew away one stormy night in 1903, their spirits may have been slightly dampened. But when the ceiling collapsed, they were undoubtedly driven to assume that there had been some minor flaws in the education of local craftsmen. Ensconced in the mounting rubble that was his home, Falconer bade farewell to some old colleagues and welcomed their replacements. In 1902 D.M. Gordon was called to the principalship of Queen's, G.M. Grant having died in harness. And so 'King Arthur' sallied forth, but not, as it transpired, to any latter-day Camelot.[132] Alfred Gandier was nominated to replace him but declined, having only just settled down in a parish back in Toronto. In the end, the board's choice fell on Robert Magill lately of Maghera, Ireland. Events began to move quickly. In 1903 the aging Pollok gave up teaching to concentrate on the principalship. To Falconer's delight, A.S. Morton was appointed to the vacancy. On the administrative side, Walter Murray and Clarence Mackinnon joined the board and brought fresh perspectives with them.[133] Arthur might have flown, but his knights, it seems, now held the keep. Finally, in April 1904, with the years weighing heavily upon him, Pollok resigned as principal. Much, it was understood, would hang on the selection of his successor. A freshening breeze blew down the Arm as Pine Hill stood on the verge of a new era in its history.

CHAPTER IV

No Sabbath Droner

No squabbling, no unseemly bickering marred the selection of a new principal. Pollok no sooner resigned than all eyes turned to Falconer. Without hesitation, his nomination was unanimously endorsed.[1] Circumstances, after all, conspired to recommend him. For one thing, there was a natural desire to preserve continuity at Pine Hill. In the space of a few years the old guard had melted away and new men crowded the stage. A decade earlier Currie might have been the obvious choice. But in 1904 he was well past his prime and destined soon to retire. That left Falconer, the next senior man. With twelve years of yeoman service to his credit, he was a well-known and trusted servant of the college. His scholarship, furthermore, was unquestioned. Nor, one suspects, did his talents as a fund raiser go unnoticed. Over the years he had established warm contacts with the business community in the region and could be relied on to put them to good use. Underscoring the point, he had recently landed a donation of $2,000 from the estate of a local dignitary in order to finance a travelling scholarship.[2] It was also significant that Falconer had always enjoyed the most cordial relationships with students. The *Theologue*, indeed, responded enthusiastically to the news of his appointment.[3] All these considerations, no doubt, weighed heavily in his favour. There was, however, an even more significant factor on his side: Falconer, it was coming to be realized, was a born leader. Throughout his life the adjective most commonly used to describe him was 'manly.'[4] He seems to have projected strength, optimism, and virtue with a totally unaffected sincerity which impressed all who met him. The local press, commenting on his speech to a YMCA convention only weeks after his appointment, acknowledged these qualities. 'The students,' it was said, 'felt the power of earnest words coming from an earnest man.' Indeed, observed the *Herald*, Falconer was emerging as 'one of Canada's strong men.'[5]

That Pine Hill required strong leadership was patent. The moderate financial problems of the 1890s gave way to real dearth as the twentieth century dawned. To a menacing degree, expenditures began to climb. During the previous decade $10,000–12,000 per year was enough to keep the college afloat. By 1904 that figure had risen to $14,000.[6] In 1906 it would soar to an alarming $17,000.[7] Hard pressed, Pine Hill pleaded with congregations for increasing amounts of money. More ominous, however, was a dramatic decline in enrolment. Slipping imperceptibly at first, it plummeted disastrously after 1900. In 1902 a nadir was reached when it fell to half the level it had attained five years earlier.[8] Inevitably, these combined misfortunes provoked considerable soul-searching. The *Theologue* speculated that modern education was 'materializing' the young and thereby drying up wells that had once fed the college.[9] One observer spoke for many when he noted that 'the spirit of the age is not devotional ... it is practical.'[10] Indeed, there was a general sense that the reverses suffered by Pine Hill were linked to a change in social moods. Society, it seemed, was in a state of flux, and some feared that the college and even the church stood in danger of being shunted to its fringes.

There was no need to venture far afield in order to glimpse the forces of change at work. Haligonians and Maritimers generally found plenty of startling evidence on their own doorsteps. The lure of mammon was all too apparent as easterners moved west to the gold fields of the Klondike or the industrial centres of Ontario.[11] At home, Sydney's rapid development as a steel town came to symbolize for many the ferment and dislocation that attended industrial urbanization. As pastor of St Andrew's Church after 1902, Clarence Mackinnon observed Sydney's metamorphosis at first hand. The whole character of that once pastoral and God-fearing town was being altered. 'There was now,' he commented, 'no limit to the dreams that disturbed its contentment.' Americans, with their materialistic ways, thronged the streets. Above all, said Mackinnon, 'the religious life was tense.'[12] Traditional values, it seemed, were at a severe discount. Nor, many feared, were they likely to be reinforced by the large-scale immigration of the era. Veritable legions of newcomers, representing all the myriad creeds and cultures of Europe, tramped yearly through Halifax. En route to 'the last, best West,' few of them stayed. Still, many townsmen wondered what these passersby carried in their baggage. Of one thing they were certain. Those contents were not

British or Protestant in nature. On several counts, therefore, anxieties about the future were raised.

To some the mounting evidence of social and moral change was a matter for resigned lamentation. Thus, Archibald MacMechan slipped deeper and deeper into a nostalgic pessimism.[13] To others, however, it represented a spur to the broader diffusion of a Christian message cast in terms appropriate to the moment. The younger men at Pine Hill numbered themselves among the latter group. Mackinnon, for example, had plunged into pastoral work at Sydney. Challenged by the social upheaval he encountered, he developed an intense concern for the daily problems of his working-class parishioners. When labour disputes erupted, he took their side.[14] An active supporter of the YMCA, he also led the local temperance campaign. With these experiences fresh in his mind, Mackinnon, as a member of the board, made plain his vision of Pine Hill's future. The search for truth, he said in 1904, had to take precedence over concern with orthodoxy, and students should be more than mere theologues.[15] Fellow board member Walter Murray shared these views. A charter member of the Halifax Children's Aid Society and a school board trustee, Murray also envisaged an active role for the church and the college in society. Among the faculty, Robert Magill would soon make valiant efforts to acquaint students with the major issues affecting a changing world outside. Evidently, therefore, by 1904 many had concluded that if Pine Hill, let alone the church, were to survive, its leaders and graduates would have to demonstrate a livelier interest in the community they served.

Falconer was not least among those who voiced this opinion. Long before skies darkened at Pine Hill he had shown a keen interest in the pastoral side of his calling. As early as 1893 in his address at Chalmers Church he had called for increased emphasis on practical training. Granted, he could probably have done no less in the light of the controversy on that point that had preceded his appointment. None the less, his conduct over the next decade indicated that his statements that night were sincere. Throughout the 1890s his vigorous support of the YMCA and similar causes testified to his growing concern with the problems of society. Travel, particularly to the west, had opened his eyes. At the same time, he applauded the development of an informal coalition among Presbyterians, Methodists, and Congregationalists who sought to address themselves to the ills of the moment. As opportunities presented themselves, Falconer was quick to join these like-minded men. Thus, his voice was added to the chorus inveighing against drink, political corruption, and injustice in the workplace. When this vague coalition matured into a movement for church union, Falconer became one of its foremost Maritime champions, along with the other knights of the Round Table.

As for Pine Hill, he was convinced that it had to move with the times. Scottish theological schools, he maintained, had once made a fundamental error in this regard.[16] The training they had offered in his day, he maintained, had been too exclusively intellectual in orientation. Students had not been equipped to deal with practical concerns. 'If the Scotch colleges turned out any preachers or pastors,' he recalled, 'it was by chance, rather than design.'[17] Fortunately, he added, there was a strong trend away from that approach in Scotland, and he urged his colleagues to take heed of such hard-won experience. In 1902 he spoke out bluntly and drew attention to the importance of 'preaching to the times.' Reacting sharply to defeatist sentiments, he denied that the pulpit had outlived its usefulness. There was nothing lacking in the gospel message, he proclaimed. It was as relevant as ever. The problem lay in its presentation. The task of the church was to adapt its forms of worship and methods of work to changing tastes and circumstances. 'A good minister,' he advised, 'must be both progressive and conservative.' He must, indeed, said Falconer, be a student of his age in the fullest sense. The supreme goal was to catch the ear of 'the reading, thoughtful young.' Difficult theological and moral issues had to be faced openly for the church no longer ministered to an ill-informed and docile flock. Striking an optimistic note, he argued that the principles of the gospel, if applied to social, political, and commercial questions, would leaven the whole lump, driving out strife and extremism to the benefit of all.[18]

No cloistered academic, by 1904 Falconer had earned a reputation as a public figure. As a citizen, according to one newspaper, he had always taken a 'keen part' in everything that pertained to the general welfare and was 'ever heard on the side of truth and righteousness.'[19] He was, moreover, becoming a polished and effective speaker. Archibald Mac-Mechan testified to his power as an orator. In the pulpit or on the platform, the right word never failed him. 'No Sabbath droner of old saws,' he was 'powerful, earnest and above all, masculine.' There was, said MacMechan, 'something almost combative, menacing, in the set brow and the deep voice' which at times took on 'a rougher grating note.'[20] Throughout his long career others would acknowledge Falconer's oratorical prowess. He was, said the *Halifax Herald* in 1904, a 'splendid speaker.'[21] In 1912 *Maclean's* commented on his 'remarkably clear, carrying voice' and his ability 'to think on his feet,' all of which left him splendidly equipped for the public stage.[22] Indeed, the sterling quality of that resonant voice was such that he rarely used a microphone, even in the largest halls.[23] No mean wordsmith himself, Sir Wilfrid Laurier once observed that parliament had not produced Falconer's superior as an orator.[24] Altogether, it would seem, the leaders of a troubled college saw in him a man appropriate to their needs. Scholar, teacher, public man, and kindred spirit, Falconer offered all they could hope for in a principal and they looked no farther. With a clear mandate in his hip pocket he set about 'preaching to the times.'

That the new principal would be an active one bent on refurbishing Pine Hill and the church it served was swiftly made plain. In his inaugural address Falconer staked out the high ground, choosing as his theme 'The Functions of the Church in the National Life of Canada.' Before a packed assembly, which included all the Presbyterian clergy of the city, he waxed eloquent on the duties of the church in contemporary society. Repeating the words of James Bryce, and perhaps recalling his father's vision, he began by striking an imperial note. 'It is,' he proclaimed, 'the moral mission which Providence has given to the British race which constitutes the greatness of the empire.' What, he then proceeded to ask, was Canada's share in this mission? A great opportunity lay before its people, he argued, because the nation was still young and its ideals had not yet solidified with age. It was important, therefore, to choose directions wisely. The civilization of any people, he contended, consisted of two elements, material development and moral development. Here the latent idealist in Falconer spoke. Sometimes, he continued, those elements were interlaced. Normally, however, in his view the church, as society's moral guardian, had little to do with material concerns. It could never, none the less, ignore the moral implications flowing from the daily life of its people. What then should the church do for Canada at that moment, he inquired.

Its first task, he responded, was to supply cohesion to national life. Immigration, said Falconer, posed a challenge to the moral unity of the nation. Foreign elements were competing for dominance with inherited British ideals. Many newcomers, he observed, were prejudiced against organized religion. There was therefore an urgent need to develop 'a more binding religion' to which all could happily subscribe. Clearly, the spectre of a polyglot and religiously chaotic west haunted him fully as much as it did many other churchmen of the era. Like them, he called for a massive effort to ensure the triumph of Protestantism in the region. The church, he declared, had to supply a new loyalty for the immigrant. 'If Jesus Christ becomes the religious ideal of Canada, the finest instincts and affections of different races will gather around Him and will smooth the sharp, irritating edges of race. Marriage, the home, the duty of religious training of children, the worth of man, justice between the strong and the weak, the rich and the poor, responsibility – these average but essential duties imposed by the Christian Church will weld the nation together.'

The disintegrating force of immigration, in Falconer's opinion, was not the only problem to which the church had to address itself. Unrestrained materialism was, if anything, a more fundamental cancer which needed to be excised. Political corruption, unregulated financial speculation and other evils were but symptoms, in his mind, of mammon's continuing influence. That influence, moreover, was not restricted to the cities. There was, he warned, 'no more desperate problem than a mammonized farmer who sees nothing but profit in fields of grain under a clear blue sky.' It was the function of the church to provide spiritual illumination. As a nation, said Falconer, Canada had benefited immeasurably from the intellectual and technological advances of the era. But what the country most required was to bring 'all public life, all commercial life, all school life and all home life under the clear light of the eternal principles of the King-dom of God.' The need was immediate, he exclaimed, because nations were not like individuals. God did not pardon them. Thus, in his view, the formation of national character was a sacred trust. 'A nation,' he averred, 'corrupted at the start carries the taint in its blood.'

According to Falconer, it followed that the church had a prophetic duty to the country. It had to proclaim that the Canadian people were accountable to God. He conceded that it would be a sad day were the church to use its power to dictate to the state on matters of public policy. Falconer was an heir of Calvin, but he was no theocrat. Still, he argued, it was sometimes necessary and proper for religious bodies to mobilize public opinion on moral issues. Hence, his own vigorous support of the temperance campaign and the Lord's Day Alliance. At no point in this address, however, did he indicate precisely when it was appropriate for the church to step into the public arena. Nor did he outline the methods it should adopt or the lengths to which it should go. He did, none the less, make it clear that individual sects were unlikely to accomplish much on their own. The task, after all, was immense. For example, he said, there were many who laboured to produce a 'pure Canadian manhood' but for one reason or another belonged to no particular church. These, he charged, had to be attracted back to the fold. Similarly, the young who trekked westward had to be infused with moral zeal. Indeed, society as a whole stood in need of spiritual quickening. No dead or divided organization, he counselled, could achieve this end. Only 'a living prophetic voice' would suffice. Thus he urged his listeners to recognize that 'the body of saints whose prayers bind our country with golden chains around the feet of God, has its members in all the churches of the land.'[25]

The speech, which was well received, was a manifesto upon which Falconer would act as principal. Three basic priorities were defined or implied. Most obviously, it signalled his deepening interest in the quest to christianize society. In his new office, Falconer felt free to speak out with increasing frequency on pressing public issues. Along the way he would foster many worthy causes but ultimately would reject the theory and practice of those who promulgated a thoroughgoing 'social gospel.' Furthermore, his growing concern with the future of the west and society in general would be linked to an older ecumenical stream in his thought. As principal of its largest theological college, he automatically inherited a degree of influence in the councils of the Presbyterian church. This he would use to further the drive towards union with compatible sects. Finally, and not least of all, he would wield his authority to make Pine Hill more responsive to the needs of the hour. In so doing, he hoped to revive its sagging fortunes.

Falconer shared a good deal of common ground with other socially conscious people when it came to identifying the specific evils of the day. The dangers inherent, for example, in drink, monopolism, and rapid urbanization were readily apparent. On a broader plane, he also concurred in the growing opinion that individualism had gone to extremes as men forgot that liberty implied not licence but responsibility.[26] With many, therefore, he noted that the utopia prophesied by the high priests of Victorian laissez-faire had not come to pass.[27] In going farther to single out creeping materialism as the villain of the piece, he was not alone.[28] To him as to others, it was an insidious force which was polluting moral values, fastening attention on the secular, and calling forth an acquisitive, mindless individualism. Disaffection, alienation, and tension were the frightening results. In broad outline, Falconer's diagnosis of society's ills was a familiar one, particularly in evangelical circles. However, in labouring to define a cure he ruled out two avenues of approach that were then attracting some attention. For a variety of reasons he rejected both socialism and the emerging 'social Gospel' as viable solutions to the difficulties of the hour.

It is not surprising that Falconer found the premises of socialism distasteful. The excesses of the moment notwithstanding, he was and would remain an individualist. His thoughts on the matter had nothing to do with the shibboleths of social Darwinism. Falconer was no latter-day Samuel Smiles. A powerful humanitarian impulse ran too deeply in him. Nor, it should be mentioned, was his individualism unqualified. His views were far from atomistic. On the contrary, in drawing attention to the importance of a collective national character he signalled his belief in the organic nature of society. No passing whim, this theme would be returned to again and again.[29] Even so, in the final accounting he believed that the roots of all social progress were hidden in 'the elevation of personal character, in aspiration which has carried men out of themselves, in faith usually of religious quality.'[30] Thus, he held that the first step in solving the problems of the time lay in the moulding of the 'individual mind and character.'[31]

This conclusion flowed chiefly from his religious assumptions and to a lesser degree from his native idealism and his reading of history. Falconer's notion that genuine Christian experience was fundamentally personal in nature served as the fountainhead of his individualism. This belief in turn was amplified by his contention that 'what really matters to a person is whether he believes that he possesses an eternal life of such intrinsic value that it will endure beyond the years which he may spend on earth.'[32] Salvation, then, was the primary goal of each man and was to be attained through inner renewal made possible by direct contact with Christ. All else was subordinate. Downplaying the collective, the material, and the institutional in religion, he was not prone to accentuate them in other aspects of his thought. Obviously, he was not prepared to write off the unreformed terrestrial world as a vale of tears and leave it at that. Never for a moment did he counsel Christians blithely to endure worldly injustice or material distress. Life on earth, he observed, was 'a momentous fact' which had to be made 'as far as possible a manifestation of the Divine Rule, or the Kingdom of God.'[33] Thus, temporal improvement was a positive good actively to be sought. It was however, argued Falconer, of secondary importance compared with man's spiritual concerns. There was a question of emphasis involved.

Secular progress, he advised, was not an end in itself. Indeed, properly understood, he maintained, it was inseparable from moral and spiritual factors. Falconer never subscribed unreservedly to the Victorian cult of progress. Civilizations, in his opinion, regularly encountered both peaks and valleys in the course of their development. However, in so far as progress was made, he was convinced that material advancement never occurred first but followed in the wake of ethical or religious enthusiasm. This, he felt, was the unmistakable lesson of British history which had been a 'struggle for liberty throughout.'[34] Modern amelioration in general was traced by him to roots in the desire for political, intellectual or religious freedom.[35] Accordingly he declared in 1907 that 'the real value of life is determined by our ideals.'[36] A moral and religious renaissance was required to purge society of its evils. That this had to begin in individual hearts he had no doubt. Just as, in his estimation, Christian experience was essentially personal, so also, he maintained, ethical renewal was the result of an internal awakening. It was Falconer the idealist who wrote that 'behind each man's soul ... there is a window that opens upon the unseen through which he contemplates the primal virtues that shine aloft like stars.'[37] That window, he concluded, was the gateway to social reform.

Judged by these standards, Falconer was certain that socialism veered in the wrong direction. At best, he thought, it was a mere palliative. At worst, it intensified existing maladies. In February 1905 he held forth on the subject before a sympathetic crowd at the Halifax YMCA. Wasting no time, he tabled his most basic objection immediately. Socialists such as Lasalle and Marx, he declared, had misconceived the essential nature of the problems they sought to solve. They had, said Falconer, 'looked on man as God.' For them, everything was subordinated to the best interests of man. Those interests, however, were mistakenly defined in purely material terms. Human society was viewed as a machine whose structure need only be altered for all to be set right. Such an analysis, he implied, by rejecting the spiritual dimension of life, could offer only superficial reform. It could not attack the moral roots of social distress. Meanwhile, it did incalculable damage in tightening mechanism's icy grip on the hearts of men.[38] Locked as he was into a religious and idealistic mode of thought, Falconer could never accept the world view of this antithetical creed.

Apart from its materialism, socialism troubled Falconer for a number of other reasons. He conceded that its champions had done much to expose the inequities of modern society. With them he was suspicious of accumulated wealth, and like them he denounced examples of exploitation in the workplace. But the appeal by extremists to revolution and violence repelled him. In this his personality as well as his Christian principles came into play. Falconer, throughout his life, demonstrated a marked aversion to controversy. He also disliked aggressive people, demagogues, and all those who played to the crowd. Hence, his early preference for Rosebery over Chamberlain. Not surprisingly, therefore, he found the 'fiery agitations' of revolutionary socialists 'debasing.'[39] Accordingly, he tended to be less critical of the British movement than of some other socialist groups, since the former accepted parliament as the vehicle of reform. Rejecting appeals to violence, Falconer also denied that any one class had a monopoly on virtue or vice. Immoral speculation, he pointed out, was practised, albeit on varying scales, at all levels of society. Similarly, he noted that if some politicians were corrupt, there were also plenty of venal electors who kept them in office.

As a moderate thinker, of course, Falconer could never agree that collective interests invariably took precedence over individual concerns. What he appears to have sought was a balance between freedom and order. 'Liberty has responsibilities and individualism may run mad, this,' he said, 'is the lesson the century has to learn.'[40] To sway from rampant individualism all the way to full-blown collectivism would do little, he thought, to foster that equilibrium whose finest fruit was social harmony. He could not, therefore, recommend to his contemporaries a massive extension of state power. To do so, he implied, would be to deny rather that to fulfil the British tradition of liberty chastened by restraint. Falconer was not inflexible on the question of state regulation. It seems for him to have been a grey area in which fine judgment was required. In any event, he never made any systematic pronouncements on the matter. He did, however, in a somewhat facile reading of socialism's message, reject what he saw as an effort to create equality by legislative fiat. Men, in his estimation, were not equal, except before God, the law, and the ballot box. 'Equality,' he exclaimed, 'is not possible and to make it possible is not within the power of legislatures, because legislation cannot regulate the system of the universe.'

Ever the eclectic, however, Falconer did see considerable merit in some suggestions emanating from the left. Consequently, he selectively weeded the socialist garden to suit his own taste. Noxious growths, such as land nationalization, were uprooted and cast aside. But more promising shoots, such as public insurance, were recommended for cultivation. While holding that every person should support himself, Falconer admitted that this was not always possible. When, therefore, a 'deserving' workman fell on hard times, he argued that the state should guarantee him the means of survival. This view, of course, smacked more of Victorian philanthropy than of socialism. There was, for example, no assertion here of the 'right to work.' A similar ambivalence was evident in his attitude to profit-sharing. Falconer applauded the idea in principle. Yet he did not see how the state could compel employers to adopt the scheme. To do so, he said, would be to infringe on the principle of liberty. Altogether, he spoke on behalf of gradual reform through existing institutions and put little stock in plans for the wholesale reconstruction of society.

Spurning socialism, Falconer also criticized those who appealed to the Gospels as a blueprint for reform. Prior to the First World War his distaste for the 'social gospel' had little to do with his firm belief in the necessary separation of church and state. While at Pine Hill, he appears to have sensed no major threat to that cherished concept. Thus, he happily supported numerous broadly based evangelical assaults on specific social problems. Only later, when militants sought to marry Christianity with socialism and to interfere noisily in the affairs of the state would Falconer attack them remorselessly on that score. For the moment, his misgivings sprang from another source and were less stridently voiced. Fundamentally, he objected to the growing tendency to regard the Bible as a repository of social prescriptions. In particular, he chided those who equated the establishment of the Kingdom of God with the reform of the existing world. This, said Falconer, was a misinterpretation and even an abuse of Scripture. In speaking out on this issue, he was reacting in the first instance to a controversy that had developed in academic circles during the 1890s.

Liberal scholarship had favoured an ethical interpretation of Christ and his teachings. Harnack, Jülicher, and others had increasingly rejected an apocalyptic view of Jesus, preferring to present him as the messiah of moral and spiritual renewal.[41] The Kingdom of God on this earth, they argued, was to be found in the internal regeneration of each individual soul. It could not be fostered by external compulsion. Thus, Harnack emphasized that the divine element in Christ was best appreciated in the light of an intense moral struggle within the individual on a human plane.[42] Falconer, in large measure, agreed with his old master on this point. In 1892, however, Johannes Weiss signalled a mounting reaction against this ethical aproach in his *Preaching of Jesus Concerning the Kingdom of God.* Here he outlined ideas which Schweitzer would popularize just after the turn of the century. Christ, said Weiss, was best understood as an eschatologist who preached the impending end of the world. His pronouncements regarding the Kingdom referred not to the terrestrial sphere but to a post-apocalyptic spiritual domain. In so far as Jesus dealt with the world of men, said Weiss, he had at best outlined a temporary way of life for those who awaited the end. Consequently, Christ's moral teachings constituted no more than what Schweitzer would later term 'an interim ethic.' Liberals reacted sharply to this eschatological thesis. A few went so far as to suggest that the gospels spelled out a program of social reform directly applicable to contemporary society. Some even argued that the Kingdom of God could be forged on this earth. The social gospel, of course, arose from many different strands. In a sense it was an extension of the teaching of Ritschl and the evangelical currents of the era.[43] Viewed in another light, it was an understandable response to the growing social distress of the moment. But the eschatological controversy undoubtedly helped encourage its sharper definition.

Moderate liberals had no more sympathy with the social gospellers than they did with the eschatologists. In particular, the men who had exercised the strongest early influence on Falconer ranged themselves against efforts to use the Bible as a guide to social legislation. Dods, for example, had devoted considerable class time to the nature of the Kingdom. Christ, he taught, had brought forth a new order in which true observance of the Law was inward.[44] Where Jesus was with his disciples, said Dods, there the Kingdom was already present, though not yet in full power. The gospel, he continued, was not a new Law. The message of Christ was deeper and more transforming than that. In 1905 he stated bluntly that the church should look to the living spirit of God for guidance and 'not be referred back to the first century for all its light and inspiration.'[45] Harnack's reaction, if anything, was even more pointed. In his *What Is Christianity?* he denounced those who were 'crying up religion as though it were a job-lot at a sale, or a universal remedy for all social ills.'[46] To do so, he argued, was to abuse religion itself. In one of the most celebrated passages in the book, he made his position explicit. 'The Christian religion,' he wrote,

is something simple and sublime; it means one thing and one thing only: eternal life in the midst of time, by the strength and under the eyes of God. It is no ethical or social arcanum *for the preservation or improvement of things generally. To make what it has done for civilization and human progress the main question, and to determine its value by the answer, is to do it violence at the start. Goethe once said, 'Mankind is always advancing, and man always remains the same.' It is to man that religion pertains, to man, as one who in the midst of all change and progress never changes.*[47]

Clearly, in Harnack's mind, the social gospel represented an unwarranted and extreme reaction to the apocalyptic interpretation. Falconer, whose view of religion was fundamentally the same, reached a similar conclusion.

As early as 1899 he took note of the debate in an article entitled 'The Future of the Kingdom.' Examining the sources, he was unable to agree wholeheartedly with either the eschatologists or the social gospellers. Neither side, he thought, offered a complete or correct interpretation of the gospels. He acknowledged an apocalyptic element in Christ's teaching. Nevertheless, he maintained that Jesus had foreseen a long future for the world as it was at present constituted. Furthermore, he noted that the messiah's description of the age to follow the second coming formed a relatively small part of his overall teaching. On balance, said Falconer, Christ's statements about the Kingdom were devoted primarily to 'the progress of the Gospel in this world.' The weight of evidence, in other words, inclined him to reject a purely eschatological interpretation. This said, however, Falconer did not then concede the argument of those who looked for the perfection of earthly society. Although sparse, he said, there was sufficient prophesy concerning the future world age to indicate that it would not be 'in any way a development from the present.' On the contrary, he contended, scripture made it perfectly clear that the ideal future condition would be spiritual in nature and would come to pass only as the result of a divine act. Christ, wrote Falconer, 'never indicates that in this present order of things His gospel will so captivate the hearts of men, that by the ordinary development of moral life this world in which we live will be transformed into the final Kingdom of God.'

A full understanding of the Kingdom, said Falconer, involved recognizing that it implied 'a condition of life partly present, but ideally complete only in the future.' This interpretation, he contended, reconciled Christ's comments on the subject which ranged over three broad areas. In the Gospels, he argued, there were injunctions directed at the individual, instructions aimed at the church, and statements pertaining to the second coming and its aftermath. The messiah's teaching about the future, in other words, was not all of a piece but manifold and many-tiered. Accordingly, concluded Falconer, considerable discrimination was required in interpreting these pronouncements.[48]

In later years Falconer came to recognize that the eschatological content of the gospel was far greater than he imagined in 1899.[49] But he never retreated from his position concerning the inappropriateness of the social gospel. Indeed, his attitudes to those who plumbed scripture in search of worldly perfection hardened over time. In the last public address of his life he affirmed that the church could not go back to the Gospels in order to discover a new social order. The will of God, he admitted, remained constant but, he added, 'what justice and love demand of us today must be expressed in the human experience of today.'[50] Society, in short, was for him a temporal and a changing thing at best peripheral to the core and purpose of the gospels.

Not content merely to criticize the views of others, Falconer sketched out his own approach to reform in response to what he viewed as an impending general crisis. Although always active, he was particularly vocal on public questions during the eight months following November 1906. Two problems above all preyed on his mind. He found the continued emigration of Nova Scotians deeply disturbing. Similarly, he was appalled by the evidence of intensifying friction between employers and labour. As winter approached, the local newspapers fairly bulged with disquieting news. In November came word that a prolonged strike by coal miners in Lethbridge, Alberta, was souring by the moment. Wages were not the sore point. The Alberta Railway and Irrigation Company had offered a 10 per cent raise. It had absolutely refused to afford recognition to the union, however, and on this issue battle was joined. So bitter was the confrontation that the Mounted Police were called in to quell a rising tide of violence. And still that tide rolled on, while in neighbouring Saskatchewan people shivered in anticipation of a coal famine.

This western clamour, alarming enough in itself, was equalled and surpassed by events transpiring in central Canada. Passions flared as unionists, with considerable popular support, confronted the Hamilton Street Railway Company and the power of civic government. In an atmosphere charged with tension, the mayor forbade public assemblies. Ignoring the warning, hundreds took to the streets in protest. The Riot Act was read and police, backed by dragoons and infantry with drawn bayonets, rushed the crowd. Over a hundred in that throng were later treated for baton-inflicted wounds. Frustrated and anxious for revenge, a few extremists later attempted, unsuccessfully, to blow up the company's car barns on Sanford Avenue. By December a general sigh of relief was audible when the matter was settled with the dismissal of all non-union men. But the events of November hung in the air as a chilling reminder of how near the surface of society violence lurked.

Closer to home there were growing complaints about the oppressive effects of monopolism in the coal industry of Nova Scotia.[51] Throughout the last months of 1906 the two giants, Dominion Iron and Steel and Dominion Coal, were locked in a dispute over the price at which the one sold coal to the other. Unable to come to terms, both companies decided on a partial shut-down rather than yield. The result was devastating to the general economy of Cape Breton. Miners in particular began to feel the bite of privation. Critical of both parties in the struggle, the *Halifax Herald* recalled that only a few years earlier troops had been called out to put down a strike in the region. Where, it asked, were the soldiers when monopolists were wreaking hardship on the community?[52] The world, it seemed, was going mad. To make matters worse, people were leaving the Maritimes for points west in numbers sufficiently large to attract considerable comment from a worried press.[53] In some minds industrial strife and depopulation bid fair to run the entire region into the ground. Surveying the scene from his perch at Pine Hill, Falconer was moved to speak out.

His views were aired before bodies such as the North British Society and the Canadian Club, as well as in the papers. Denouncing violence, he nevertheless made clear his sympathy with the working-class victims of

Lethbridge, Hamilton, and Sydney. Falconer had long held that monopolism in particular was a scourge which only drove men to socialism. Now, he cried, it was provoking them to resort to force. Without recommending government interference, he warned employers that something had to be done soon to remove the cause of workers' desperation. He was already on record as favouring trade unions, profit-sharing, and public insurance. Clearly, however, in the light of recent events he considered the implementation of such schemes an urgent priority.[54] As he told one audience of business and professional men: 'We as Canadians must see that in our industry the people have a chance.'[55] The only alternative, he implied, was ever escalating conflict.

If employers drew his fire, so did politicians who battened on these controversies for their own advancement. Extreme party spirit, he thought, threatened to submerge nobler impulses in a vicious scramble for office.[56] All too often, leaders fed off and aggravated strife. Mutual abuse, said Falconer, had become the debased common coin of the political arena. As a result, he asserted, genuine leadership and truthfulness were sacrificed as corruption was ushered in. There was, he told one audience, 'too much acrimony in public life; too much false speaking.' 'We have overtalked,' he scolded. There was a danger that society would drift into an 'accredited mendacity.' Falconer was a democrat, but he saw little hope for democracy without clear moral leadership. Too many people, he lamented, did not appreciate the value of the vote and would 'sell it without a twinge of conscience.' This, he continued, left the door wide open to party machines and 'secret caucuses' which plundered the body politic. Still, he did not despair. 'I am inclined to believe,' he said, 'that ignorance rather than depravity, lies at the root of a great deal of our corruption.' Thus, without naming individuals, he called on people to support men who sought to tutor society in loftier political ideals.[57]

The mention of ideals usually brought Falconer to expound on another favourite theme. With Canada in the midst of what he considered essentially a moral crisis, he thought it tragic that emigration from the Maritimes went unchecked. The continued vitality of the region, he insisted, was crucial to the dominion as a whole. Its importance, he argued, lay not in any material benefits it might confer. Rather, he told the Canadian Club, 'the maritime provinces serve their highest function according to the quality of manhood they contribute to the commonwealth.' They acted, he maintained, as a moral and intellectual reservoir, a steadying influence, and a model for the nation. In part, he explained, geography and inheritance were responsible for this. The Maritimes jutted out 'like hands that reach across the ocean to grasp the hand of the mother country.' All that was best in Britain was preserved in the local way of life. In consequence, said Falconer, the Maritimes acted as a healthy counterweight to American influence in the west. In making this point Falconer's puritanism and rural values came to the fore. It was, he asserted, easier to foster a pure manhood where the comforts of life were few. 'I believe,' he went on in words reminiscent of his father's teaching, 'that the very fact that the people of these provinces, though prosperous, are not wealthy, is in their favour.' In an atmosphere free of enervating luxury, men toiled to master themselves and their environment. 'The abiding worth of a people,' declared Falconer, 'will be discovered in those simple, honest lives devoted to duties performed, it may be, far from the eyes of the world.' Suspicious of urbanization, he went on to state that the region was undoubtedly fortunate to boast no great cities. Mass urban culture, he averred, tended to sap sturdy individuality. Luckily, however, there was still room in the Maritimes for 'the culture of the few' to have an impact.[58] Never a dyed-in-the-wool physiocrat like Andrew Macphail, Falconer confidently looked forward to a reform of city life. But at heart he remained a champion of the rural values he thought were enshrined in arcadian Nova Scotia.

It was with dismay, therefore, that he observed the departure of the region's most energetic elements. At the request of the Halifax *Chronicle*, he offered an analysis of the problem in a review of the events of 1906. At one level, said Falconer, the exodus was merely a stage in one of those periodic migrations that swept continents from east to west. As such, he counselled, it must be expected to continue for some time. Offering some comfort, he pointed out that it was far better that these migrants went west rather than south. They were, at least, not lost to the dominion. Nevertheless, he cautioned that the Maritimes were increasingly weakened as their best and brightest citizens decamped. The seepage, moreover, could not go on much longer before all vitality was drained away. What, he asked, urged men forth? Unoccupied land and the promise of economic gain could not be discounted. Infectious excitement also contributed to the momentum. But, warned Falconer, everything could not be laid at the door of external forces. Discontent with a decaying quality of life at home also inspired flight. Just as the west had no monopoly on progress, so also it was not the exclusive home of vice. Linking his criticism of industrial injustice and political corruption with the spectre of migration, Falconer called on Maritimers to reclaim their historic role as moral tutors to the nation in sponsoring a general reform in their own backyard.[59]

In this context it seemed to him that significant social betterment could be achieved largely on a voluntary basis through the elevation of personal and public morality. In this effort, said Falconer, both church and state had a positive role to play in their respective spheres. The principal task of each was fundamentally educative. Thus, the duty of the state was to stimulate young people, not just give to them. To achieve this end a complete educational system was required; one in which not only the intellect but the character was honed. Stating a theme common enough in his generation, in 1904 Falconer advised that the ultimate purpose of education was 'to gain control over mental power.'[60] Mere knowwledge was insufficient to equip a man for life. Intellectual training, of course, was valuable. After all, he argued, 'men who know the essential rights and duties of manhood are intelligent men.'[61] Similarly, he applauded moves toward the development of technical education in Nova Scotia. On the whole, said Falconer, 'a higher skill among all who work with their hands or their head, would go far to relieve our discontent.'[62] Nevertheless, he firmly held that all education had to be coupled with the inculcation of simple human virtues if it were to be of lasting benefit. In later years this concept of moral education would be spelled out in lavish detail. For the moment, he was content to state that character building remained the chief function of the teacher. Indeed, he declared that character was 'the supreme commodity' that would always 'serve as the rate of exchange in human life because it cannot be counterfeited.'[63] Thus, on several occasions, he roundly condemned an indifferent public and parsimonious trustees who starved the educational system of funds.[64] In the long run, he warned, the fate of the common school in Cape Breton was of far greater lasting significance than any struggle between local monopolists.[65]

As for the church, its complementary burden, in Falconer's opinion, was to infuse the community with pure religious ideals. If this meant speaking out where social injustice was perceived, so be it. To him, this role did not imply church dictation to the state or direct institutional involvement in politics. Indeed, he felt that such intervention would be unnecessary in a society truly leavened by the gospel. It was a fine point which might well have been lost on many contemporaries. In truth, he fully clarified it only much later, when he wrote that the true mission of the church was to 'the Nation, as distinguished from the State.'[66] At the time, however, Principal Falconer was less concerned with nice distinctions than with prompting churchmen to adapt their preaching to the ears of a changing audience. Properly presented, he argued, nothing was more likely than an invigorated faith to weld Canadians together as a harmonious and just people.[67] Indeed, he implied that, working in tandem, the two arms of Christian society could effect a moral revolution from which all manner of practical reform would automatically flow. Cities would be cleansed, politics purified, and the workplace made humane. Throughout, he proclaimed, the motto should be 'Intelligence, Industry, Integrity.'[68] But everything, he contended, turned in the first instance on inspiring the individual.

To some it must have seemed that Richard Cobden had risen from the grave, donned a preacher's habit, altered his terms of reference, and announced the gospel of 'cumulative morality.'[69] It is misleading, however, to suggest that Falconer was merely yesterday's liberal. He took quite seriously his injunction to others that a minister should be both 'progressive and conservative.' In the eyes of a later generation, more accustomed to state intervention, he might appear to have emphasized the conservative side in this equation. In his own day, however, and in his own circle, he must have seemed at least moderately progressive. That, in any event, was how he viewed himself. After all, in rejecting socialism and the social gospel he did not then embrace a totally unreconstructed doctrine of laissez-faire. Cobden, it should be remembered, was no friend of unionism, profit-sharing, or public insurance!

Seeking as he did a moral and religious rejuvenation of society, Falconer was quick to support those who fostered church union. A definite movement in that direction took shape in 1902. In that fateful year both the Presbyterian General Assembly and the Methodist General Conference selected Winnipeg as the site of their annual conclaves. As the separate but concurrent meetings went on, the Presbyterian body, in a simple gesture of good will, delegated a few of its members to bear fraternal greetings to their evangelical brothers. Acting impulsively, Principal Patrick of the Manitoba Presbyterian College surprised everyone by delivering an impassioned call for organic union. Fellow delegate C.W. Gordon, better known as 'Ralph Connor,' took the cue and seconded Patrick's plea. It was a daring gamble. The issue had hung in the air for some time. Now it was forced dramatically into the open. Caught unawares, Methodist leaders none the less responded with unalloyed enthusiasm. A 'union committee' was struck without much delay, and a hand was extended to other demonimations. Congregationalists acted with dispatch. Although decentralized, they were relatively few in number and could consult among themselves quickly. Thus, in 1903 the Congregational Union of Ontario and Quebec formed its own committee to negotiate a merger. In the same year a formal invitation from Methodists to discuss the matter was presented to the Presbyterian General Assembly in Vancouver. Patrick's spontaneous suggestion seemed about to bear fruit.

Impulsive it may have been, but Patrick's proposition was not without precedent. Thoughts of union had been stirring in ecumenical breasts for over twenty-five years.[70] Some tentative proposals had even been made. In the 1880s Anglicans probed for a response from Presbyterians and Methodists, but the historic episcopate had proved a sticking point. Methodists and Congregationalists in turn sent out feelers in the early 1890s. For their part, Presbyterians seemed ready to listen.[71] At this point, however, there was no sense of urgency sufficient to galvanize the various parties into definite action. The missing spark, nevertheless, was soon provided. Massive immigration, growing urbanization, and social strife combined in the later 1890s to create a series of problems which roused churchmen like Falconer. The west, in particular, with its vast distances and mixed population posed a serious challenge. Taxed to the limit of their resources, individual sects turned inceasingly to informal methods of co-operation. Something like a 'free church consensus' was emerging at the turn of the century, as leaders of the various evangelical bodies met with increasing frequency at temperance rallies, Sunday school conventions and similar gatherings.[72] As expediency matured into habit, co-operative ventures became ever more common, especially on the prairies. In the end, many concluded that only union offered a viable long-term solution to shared difficulties. The timing of Patrick's proposal, therefore, may have come as a surprise, but the substance of it did not. Hence, the rapid response of Methodists and Congregationalists to the Manitoban's arguments. With these two sects proclaiming enthusiasm, all eyes turned to the Presbyterians. The heirs of Calvin, however, seemed to dawdle. In fact, a cumbersome, if democratic, machinery of church government was specifically designed to prevent hasty decisions from being imposed on the fiercely independent rank and file. It was taken for granted that considerable discussion at the parish level would precede even a tentative commitment to negotiate. Accordingly, the Methodist invitation of 1903 was received but not acted on by the General Assembly. Instead, the matter was set aside for the next annual gathering scheduled for June the following year in Saint John, New Brunswick. Meanwhile, the lobbying began in earnest.

The men of Pine Hill were quick off the mark. In a twinkling, professors, trustees, and students alike rallied behind the unionist banner. Throughout the months preceding the crucial assembly of 1904, the college linked hands with like-minded churchmen in the Halifax area to further the cause. Students had long since made their sympathies plain. In 1901 the *Theologue* had condemned wasteful sectarian rivalry and duplication. As a cure, the church was urged to reach an accommodation with other sects whereby fields could be more rationally parcelled out.[73] In March 1904, with full amalgamation in the offing, students registered their wholehearted support for 'a great step in the advancement of God's Kingdom among men.'[74] As other items in the *Theologue* indicate, these would-be ministers were deeply concerned about the inability of an overstretched church to pay its servants a living wage.[75] Thus, in a timely article the editors trumpeted approval of a scheme they thought would ease material strain as well as bestow spiritual blessings on the church.[76]

While students were active, the staff and trustees were anything but idle. In March Principal Pollok restated his already loudly proclaimed allegiance to union for the benefit of the press.[77] Meanwhile Mackinnon, Murray, and Falconer sounded out opinion among the faithful of the city. James Falconer, now pastor of Fort Massey Church in Halifax, assisted. In glowing terms he spoke of 'the spell of that imperial Christianity which St Paul advocated,' which seemed so appropriate to a Canadian environment whose 'expansiveness [forbade] narrowness of vision.'[78] Early April witnessed something like an ecclesiastical pep rally as local Methodist and Presbyterian churchmen gathered to promote union. Pollok read the opening prayer. Murray acted as secretary, and Professor Falconer sat on the platform as his father, Alex, gave a rousing address.[79] A few weeks later Principal-Designate Falconer made pointed references to union in bidding farewell to his predecessor. Praising Pollok's liberal approach as a church historian, he denounced those who clung to 'a one-sided reading of the past.' The latter, he argued, merely catered to sectarian self-conceit. A true scholar, he continued, strove 'to be just to all sides and to remove as far as possible inherited prejudices against others who love the Lord Jesus.'[80]

As he became more vocal, Falconer was increasingly identified as a leading Maritimes proponent of union. Thus, the influential newsman, J.S. Willison, wrote to him while canvassing opinion on the subject. Falconer replied that he was hopeful but did not elaborate.[81] He was more forthcoming, however, in an article for the *Toronto News*. With the General Assembly just over a month away, he was apparently determined to leave no stone unturned in championing the cause. He pointed to the narrow range of doctrinal differences separating the evangelical churches. Thanks, he said, to the tolerant and patient work of scholars, theology had become 'a large commonwealth of many provinces.' Appealing to history, he noted that minor distinctions in Paul's day had not impaired Christian unity. Moving to the present, he trotted out the by then familiar injunctions against economic waste and overlapping. Finally, he charged that sectarianism bordered on the immoral in that it seriously hampered those who sought to do Christ's work.[82] Having done what he could, Falconer then awaited the convening of the assembly in June.

As it transpired, he and scores of others had done their work well. While some among the laity were uneasy about the scheme, church officials were generally very well disposed towards it. At the time, even those who later came out strongly against union were willing to listen to suggestions, so long as no irrevocable steps were taken without the full consent of the people.[83] Those expressing some misgivings were assured that negotiation implied no binding commitments. Indeed, it was argued that a refusal to confer would seem churlish. Accordingly, the assembly appointed a union committee. Falconer was asked, appropriately enough, to sit on the doctrinal and ministerial subcommittees. Murray was to chair the group studying church polity. Other familiar participants included D.M. Gordon and John Forrest, the heads, respectively, of Queen's and Dalhousie Universities. A beginning had been made. The next task was to prepare for the first joint meeting with other churches scheduled for Toronto in December.

Falconer later confessed that as the Toronto session loomed, he was filled with 'grave doubts' about the likelihood of success. Word had filtered back to Halifax that the laity in many regions, especially in Toronto, were opposed to union. Disheartened, he feared that 'all that was left was to let the matter drop out of sight.'[84] Filled with apprehension, his mood must have been as bleak as the December countryside through which his train rolled en route to Ontario. What he found at his destination, however, quickly restored his spirits. The doleful reports, he was assured, had been greatly exaggerated. To be sure, some Presbyterians, fiercely conscious of their Scottish heritage, feared ethnic submersion in a united church. Others, prizing a tradition of local independence, were suspicious of Methodist centralizing tendencies. Similarly, many sober Calvinists found the bubbly evangelism of Wesley's sons distasteful. More substantially, there were misgivings about the Methodist emphasis on a socially, and some feared politically, active church. Finally, deeply ingrained sectarian and social prejudices were not easily overcome.[85] Even so, what opposition existed within the Presbyterian camp was at this stage poorly organized and sporadic.

More importantly in Falconer's eyes, the joint meetings at Knox Church were more successful than he had anticipated even in his most sanguine moments. In an interview granted to the *Halifax Herald,* he advised advocates of union to be 'glad at heart.' Left to themselves, he said, church leaders had proved to be tolerant, co-operative and anxious to reach an accord. Particular praise was lavished on Nathaniel Burwash, President of Victoria University, who, said Falconer, had delivered a 'quiet yet powerful' exposition of the doctrinal tenets held in common. Difficulties, he admitted, existed. But he was happy to report that they had been faced squarely and had paled in comparison with the shared ground discovered. All told, he concluded, the chief obstacle was likely to be the attitude of the laity, particularly within the Presbyterian church. Thus, he counselled that there be no haste, since it was axiomatic that there could be no union until the people were ready.[86]

Others shared Falconer's views. The General Assembly of 1905, in fact, passed a resolution to the effect that no pledge to unite would be given without the consent of 'the entire membership.'[87] It was later argued that this assurance constituted a fatal error.[88] The insistence on near unanimous approval, it was said, only encouraged endless delay which gave an effective opposition time to mobilize. Unquestionably, the choice of the words 'entire membership' was unfortunate, perhaps even naïve. Yet, given Presbyterian tradition, it is difficult to see how significant general consultation could have been avoided. The truly surprising element is the degree to which the moulding of lay opinion was neglected. Here a certain euphoria or perhaps preoccupation came into play. Unionists were inspired by early successes at the bargaining table. As they talked among themselves, rather than with the rank and file, church leaders may well have assumed that union would recommend itself in time, so obvious were its merits. With justice they have been criticized for paying more attention to negotiation than to propagation during this crucial early stage.[89]

Over the next few years Falconer's commitment to the unionist position deepened. For the most part, his energies were poured into efforts to hammer out a formal agreement among the three churches. Thus he kept a seat warm on the train that rolled back and forth between Halifax and central Canada. Doctrinal issues proved less troublesome than had at first been expected. Under the patient chairmanship of Burwash, simplicity was sought, and difficult technical points were generally left open to individual conscience. Accordingly, as early as 1905 the joint committee was able to report substantial progress and 'virtual unanimity' on essentials.[90] This was music to the ears of Falconer. Craving simplicity himself, Harnack's disciple rejoiced. What, he asked, was the use of a complex theology seldom heard from the pulpit?[91] Obviously, he was not advocating that genuine difficulties be swept under the carpet. He was, however, applauding in Ritschlian fashion what he interpreted as a healthy effort to de-emphasize metaphysical elements in the new confession.[92] Accordingly, he was pleased by the progress shown in doctrinal discussions. On matters affecting the ministry, however, some measure of disagreement did surface. Methodists favoured appointment by a central board. Presbyterians preferred a decentralized method whereby each congregation 'called' its own minister. The difference of opinion was real, but the will to achieve a compromise was strong. Altogether, on this and other points, the talks went ahead smoothly between 1904 and 1908 as the Basis of Union was prepared.

Meanwhile, Falconer attempted more carefully to define the case for union. His clearest pronouncements, published in 1905, returned to a theme that coloured much of his ecumenical thinking. He dwelt on the historical precedent set by early Christians, and he argued that union, while unfeasible in Europe, was appropriate in the Canadian environment. In his view, the country was a natural melting pot. Almost as ethnocentric as his father, his cultural goals were primarily assimilative. When he thought about it for a moment, he was usually prepared to exempt the French in his quest for a homogeneous nation. Indeed, as he grew older he came to value quite highly the unique contributions of French-Canadians. For the moment, however, he was chiefly concerned about the central Europeans and others who flocked to the prairies. He professed a belief that Canada had to be more than a mere agglomeration of distinct cultures. Similarly, in religious terms, he argued that the country could be more than a careless mixture of Lutherans, Anglicans, Methodists, and so forth. 'We can,' he declared, 'become a new church as well as a new people.' Just as Canada could and should develop as an organic whole, so also he contended that a 'national Evangelical Church' would be the appropriate 'organism of all the Protestant Christians of this Dominion.' All that stood in the way, he continued, was a penchant for sectarian politics which bred 'eagerness for the prosperity of the church as an institution, rather than love for it as the Body of the living Christ.'[93] This, of course, was a less than generous appraisal of the motives of those who questioned union. Statements of this nature may well have done as much to inflame as to quell opposition.

If the opponents of union were poorly organized in this early period, it was nevertheless occasionally necessary to deal with them. Ephraim Scott, for example, had voiced serious doubts about the project. As editor of the *Presbyterian Record,* he was a man of considerable influence. In 1905, with full pomp and circumstance, Pine Hill conferred upon him the degree Doctor of Divinity. One wonders what Falconer and his colleagues had in mind. Were they rewarding perceived merit or were they trying to mollify the reverend gentleman? In the absence of any clear evidence of their intentions it is impossible to say. If, however, subtle persuasion was their goal, they failed utterly. Scott's opposition would gradually harden into implacability. Whatever the case, more direct action was required the following year. The General Assembly of 1906, which met in London, began well enough. There was, in fact, celebration in the Falconer clan, since Alex was elected national moderator. A few days later, however, the peace of the conclave was shattered as the Reverend John Mackay delivered a blistering attack on unionists who sought to proceed too quickly. In stating his case, he put forward a motion that if adopted would have led to a moratorium on the issue. Speaker after speaker rose to counter the suggestion. When Falconer's turn came, he diplomatically pointed out that any firm commitments were still a long way off. But he insisted that Presbyterians could not stand pat. The past, he exclaimed, ought not to be taken as the index of the future. Simple co-operation such as Mackay proposed was 'a hopeless alternative to organic union.' Finally, he warned that to turn back at that point was to invite even greater sectarian rivalry than had existed before.[94] This last assertion was veritable salt in the wounds of dissenters. It reflected a line of reasoning they had rejected all along. From the outset many had insisted that an agreement to negotiate in no way bound the church to union. Now Falconer and others implied that it did, in the light of the bitter alternative. A few, like Scott, felt betrayed. In their view, a promise had been give in 1904 'only to confer.'[95] Doubters, however, were but a small minority at the London assembly. Consequently, Mackay's resolution went down to a crushing defeat. For his part, Falconer was well pleased. Indeed, by 1907 he was confident that union was at last visible on the horizon.

Falconer's vision of a morally rejuvenated society inspired by a reunited Protestant church provided the broad context within which he laboured to revivify Pine Hill. The task of a theological school, he felt, was to produce spiritual leaders. An appropriately educated ministry, in his opinion, could show the way to secular and religous renewal by moulding the ideals of the nation.[96] It was with deep concern, therefore, that he surveyed the misfortunes of the institution he had been called to lead in 1904. As attendance fell and new debts accumulated, Pine Hill appeared to flag just as unbounded vitality was most sorely needed. That his college should wallow in the doldrums while great changes were afoot in the outside world was intolerable to Falconer. Thus, he put a firm hand on the tiller, planted a reformer's cap on his already balding head, and set a new course. In doing so, he was prepared to alter the nature of the college substantially as he adjusted its trim. Accordingly, a new emphasis was placed on pastoral training: efforts were made to encourage graduate work, alumni were more vigorously courted, and the problem of debt was assailed.

Personally wedded to the idea of an activist ministry, Falconer was anxious to communicate this notion to others. The good of the church and society as a whole was at stake. But so, he thought, was the survival of Pine Hill. From the outset he realized that if the college were to attract greater numbers, an appeal would have to be made to the idealism of youth caught up in a rapidly changing world. Potential candidates had to be persuaded that the modern church could move with the times; that it stood at the centre, rather than on the fringes, of contemporary life. Thus, for a variety of reasons, he sponsored efforts to increase the level of practical instruction offered. Throughout his principalship he strove to deflate the concept that the minister was a man who stood apart from secular concerns. The true pastor, he told one gathering of students, was 'a man among men, ... a friend and comrade for any who would share his friendship, a director of youth, an adviser for the tempted, a comforter for the sorrowing, weeping with those who weep, rejoicing with those who rejoice.'[97] Clerics, he argued, must not stick together but should get out in the world and be humanized; they should, indeed, be 'alien from nothing that is truly human.'[98] This role implied breaking down artificial barriers between the clergyman and his flock. Here, even apparently minor details, such as dress, were important. Accordingly, he was critical of ministers who, armoured in 'official blacks,' kept others at arm's length.[99] Similarly, he stressed that not only intellectual attainment, but personality, had to be considered when candidates were selected for God's service.[100] Pine Hill, he contended, could not afford to be exclusively academic.[101]

In sounding this note, the new principal won the hearts of students who had been thinking along the same lines. Aware, no doubt, of Falconer's sympathies, they made so bold as to offer a suggestion. In January 1905 the *Theologue* featured a plea for the college to break out of its 'sacredotal shell.' The editors complained in somewhat inelegant prose that they were 'not intelligent on modern social and economic questions.' Great virtues were seen in the standard curriculum. 'But,' the item continued, 'would it not seem strange if the sweeping revolutions in social and commercial life which have marked the past fifty years, should call only for more Classics, more History [and] more Theology?' Clearly, changes were called for. In order for the minister to play an effective role in the world, it was argued, he must first learn something of it. Striking out against 'formalism' in all its guises, students went on to recommend the introduction of sociological studies.[102]

The wisdom of this timely proposal was not lost on Falconer. Consulting the staff and trustees, he recruited Robert Magill to study the matter. Keenly interested in such issues, the young Irishman took up the assignment with relish. By October 1906 all was in readiness and the new course was launched. Its success was immediate. Students packed Magill's classroom where they rejoiced to find that things were 'called by their right names.'[103] In a frank and probing fashion, he investigated issues such as drink, housing, unionism, and the condition of modern democracy. The *Theologue* roared approval. 'It goes to show,' ran one of its editorials, 'that Pine Hill has caught the spirit of the age, and is in the very van of those who aim at giving their men the best possible practical equipment for the ministry.'[104] If nothing else, it seemed, this experiment had done much to rekindle esprit de corps at the college. It also attracted attention from outside. In March 1907 Methodist leader S.D. Chown made a special trip to Halifax to view the innovation at first hand. What he found cheered the ardent social gospeller, and he congratulated Pine Hill on being the first Canadian theological school to undertake such a program.[105] With the problems of the day being confronted in the lecture hall and the principal cutting a figure on the public stage, there were no more complaints about 'formalism' during Falconer's regime.

An interest in pastoral training was never allowed to overshadow traditional academic pursuits. Falconer, indeed, was emphatic in urging measures to promote graduate studies. In this regard he made his feelings evident well before assuming the principal's chair. As early as 1899 he had called on the alumni to finance a travelling scholarship for postgraduate work abroad. Significantly perhaps, he suggested that it be tenable in either Britain or Europe, but he failed to mention the United States. The scheme, he argued, offered several advantages. A secure supply of native sons, thoroughly trained in different departments, would be available to Canadian theological schools. Locally, the tone of the college would be elevated, as those who ventured overseas returned to inspire their fellows. Finally, the alumni would take a lively interest in the fate of such scholars and thereby be bound more closely to the college.[106] Over the next few years, Falconer sought support for this scheme in several quarters. His greatest triumph came in 1904, when $2,000 was donated by the family of the late Senator W.J. Carmichael.[107] This bequest and other gifts enabled him to channel a steady flow of Pine Hill's brightest to the theological fountains of Scotland and Germany. Acknowledging Falconer's singular contributions in this area, the *Theologue* later praised a man who had awakened a 'wanderlust' in his students.[108]

Study in foreign parts was always beneficial, but Falconer also nursed a desire to provide for those who were unable to travel abroad. Thus, while cognizant of the limitations on Pine Hill, he was determined that the college should develop at least an elementary graduate program, one on which later generations could build. Accordingly, Falconer set about whipping up interest in a course of advanced studies to be offered in the autumn of 1905. A constituency was sought among senior students and the scores of old boys scattered throughout the Maritimes. In its conception, the scheme was reminiscent of the summer schools convened in the late 1890s. The pitch, however, was noticeably different, as were the circumstances. No longer a sleepy academic enclave, Falconer's college was already being identified as a hive of action. With talk of church union and social reform in the air, many ministers were now anxious to listen when Pine Hill offered to inform them not only of the latest academic finds, but also about public issues of immediate significance. In these conditions, Falconer practically guaranteed a full house in announcing that the theme of his own lectures would be the New Testment position on the ideal of Christian unity. But the attractions did not end there. Dr A.F. Kirkpatrick, Master of Selwyn College, Cambridge, added prestige to the session by agreeing to teach. The Reverend J.A. Macdonald, influential editor of the Toronto *Globe* and ardent proponent of church union, volunteered his services. Rounding out the field, local men such as Murray, Magill, and Morton promised to combine academic prowess with contemporary insights. All told, the tempo was decidedly upbeat, the timing impeccable and the results deeply satisfying. Every presbytery in the Maritime synod was represented by several of its ministers, with the sole exception of Prince Edward Island.[109]

Building on initial success, Falconer repeated the experiment the following spring. Once again an appealing general theme was carefully chosen. In 1905 church union had held the stage. In 1906 social and economic questions were brought to the fore. The unquestioned highlight was a series of lectures by Adam Shortt of Queen's University concerning economic conditions in contemporary Canada.[110] Many, however, were also interested to hear the views of W.P. Archibald on 'The Treatment and Care of the Criminal Classes.' Just back from the far east, Dr R. Grierson lectured on the politics of Korea and Japan, a timely enough topic given the latter's recent and popular victory over Tsarist Russia. Discoursing on nineteenth-century religious thought, Robert Magill drew attention to the triumph of ethical over dogmatic considerations. This, he declared, was the 'bright star of hope' which guided the church in an age of doubt.[111] For his part, Falconer restricted himself to some academic observations on the Lord's Supper. The sessions, though modest, must have given him great confidence as he looked to the future. While lasting only a week they had, for a time at least, left Pine Hill 'full to overflowing.'[112]

In the midst of these events the college was treated to something of a windfall. As activity increased, so did expenses. The synod was generous, as were private donors, in helping Pine Hill meet rising costs, but deficits had become common again after 1900. There was as yet no cause for panic. The total debt in 1905 was only $2,300. Nevertheless, Falconer was concerned that it should go no higher; he desired no repetition of the situation of the early 1890s, when college property had to be sold to settle skyrocketing arrears. A few thousand dollars, as he well knew, could become several thousand all too quickly. The problem, of course, was to remove this still manageable burden while simultaneously attempting to cure stagnation through moderate expansion and innovation. In the end, the difficulty was overcome as the result of an unforeseen chain of events.

In April 1905 Falconer was invited by Knox College in Toronto to take up its chair in New Testament literature and exegesis. He was flattered by the offer, particularly since it included the prospect of succession to the principalship within a few years.[113] Having only just assumed office at Pine Hill, however, he felt obliged to decline. Meanwhile, Robert Magill was approached by the Manitoba Presbyterian College, he but also signalled his intention to remain in Halifax. Falconer's decision in particular was greeted with numerous expressions of relief which were noted in the press.[114] Rejoicing, the *Theologue* and the *Herald* suggested that a vote of appreciation by the community would not be out of order.[115] Cash was mentioned as an appropriate token of esteem.

At this point, the picture becomes cloudy. It is unclear whether Falconer took canny advantage of the situation to lobby among townsfolk, or whether a spontaneous gesture slowly took shape. Whatever the case, in December 1906 the *Theologue* reported that local business interests had retired the college debt.[116] The passage of more than a year between first hints and final action would seem to indicate that some prodding was required. If so, Falconer was well placed to cajole the men of commerce. Although critical of contemporary society, he was a perceived moderate, who numbered among his friends prominent businessmen such as the banker, Dougald Macgillivary. 'Brother to a prince, brother to a beggar': that is how MacMechan once described the principal of Pine Hill.[117] At home with men from many walks of life, Falconer mixed as easily with business and professional people as he did with academics or fellow clerics. It was all part of the job. A charter member of the Halifax Children's Aid Society, he was also a founder and vice-president of the local Canadian Club. At a guess, one suspects that he played no small part in the process whereby Pine Hill was, if only for a while, freed of debt.

By 1907 the prospects of the college looked bright indeed. Of all the advances that had been made, none offered greater encouragement than the steady increase in enrolment. Having fallen to between twenty and twenty-five candidates in 1902, it rose to a total of thirty-one in 1905 and forty-one in 1906.[118] The following year Pine Hill rejoiced to report that the numbers applying for admission 'were considerably larger than for several years past.'[119] Health, it seemed, had been restored. Creative leadership had worked wonders. Backed by like-minded trustees, Falconer looked forward to building gradually on a now solid foundation. Light of heart, he and Sophie eagerly anticipated the spring and a well-earned tour of the Mediterranean region. Little did they realize that Robert's hour as principal was drawing rapidly to a close. Pine Hill and the Northwest Arm would soon be left far behind.

CHAPTER V

Loudon's Ghost

Locked in a struggle to resuscitate Pine Hill, Falconer had known his share of problems. Yet things could have been much worse. Given free rein, he had fostered reconstruction in a positive atmosphere, unimpeded by internal division or outside interference. Finances, of course, imposed a ceiling on ambition. But even here a measure of relief had been found. Altogether, he must have counted himself fortunate if ever he paused to compare his lot with that of others at larger institutions. D.M. Gordon, for example, was finding Queen's University a trying burden. 'King Arthur' had inherited a financial problem from Grant which was fast resolving itself into a protracted constitutional debate. Tensions accumulated as men argued whether or not to sunder ties with the Presbyterian church in order to further loosen government purse strings and gain access to the Carnegie treasure chest.[1] Elsewhere, Principal William Peterson of McGill University was regularly at odds with the press and public. By his own admission 'a stranger addressing strangers,' the austere Scot felt isolated on 'the outskirts of Empire' and took no pains to hide the fact.[2] Less than tactful, he won scant praise and no little criticism from slighted Montrealers. The vicissitudes encountered by Gordon and Peterson, however, were as nothing compared with the tempests that buffeted James Loudon, president of the University of Toronto. That unhappy man seemed almost to have a monopoly on strife. Bruised and embittered, he was ultimately invited to retire in 1906 after fourteen turbulent years in office. As the news filtered back to Halifax, Falconer undoubtedly took note of the event. For the moment, he probably found the story interesting enough but in all likelihood he viewed it in the same light as developments at Queen's. It was an Ontario matter of little immediate concern to him.[3] He had, after all, no good reason to suspect that his own fate would shortly be interwoven with that of Toronto's beleaguered head.

The winds that swept Loudon from office had been gathering force for a decade and more. In part, he was the hapless victim of circumstance. Aptly described as a 'crazy-quilt,' the institution he sought to administer was at times baffling in its complexity.[4] He was obliged, for example, to balance the claims of several denominational colleges which had warily federated or affiliated with the university after 1887. Methodists at Victoria, Roman Catholics at St Michael's, Presbyterians at Knox, and Anglicans at Wycliffe had cast their lot with Varsity (as the University of Toronto was popularly known) before Loudon assumed the president's chair. In 1904 Trinity College, representing the Church of England, followed suit. These sectarian bodies and the non-denominational University College offered courses in the arts. The university served as an examining body for the whole and also provided instruction in the sciences. Eventually, federation would prove a boon to all concerned. In Loudon's day, however, the structure was not always clearly defined, and there was much jostling among the parties. University College, for example, resented the fact that federation had reduced the range of studies it could pursue. Hitherto, it had boasted a full complement of arts courses. After 1887 it could teach only what Victoria taught and several disciplines were shifted to the university. Many regarded this move as a severe blow.[5] The church colleges guarded their positions jealously. Inevitably, all suggestions concerning the alteration of curricula, salaries, or funding had to be handled with the utmost delicacy.

Professional education was left to the university, but here too a confused system reigned. Engineering and agricultural studies were conducted by provincial schools whose affiliation with Varsity was at best loosely defined.[6] The Faculty of Medicine, although young, was growing; its progress, however, was hampered by the lack of a university hospital. Clinical instruction was carried out at the dilapidated Toronto General Hospital, but only on an ad hoc basis and only at the sufferance of a temperamental board of trustees and a preoccupied resident staff.[7] In consequence, relations among the university, the hospital, and the city's doctors were frequently strained. With these and several other balls in the air at the same time, Loudon had a difficult juggling act to perform. Formidable enough in itself, his task was made next to impossible by a constitution that inhibited him at every turn.

When the Liberal government of Oliver Mowat opened the door to federation in the university, it did so ostensibly to rationalize and co-ordinate higher education in the province. However, the primary motive, one suspects, was that of reducing expenditure by pooling resources. Little was done, in any event, to provide for the effective administration of the new institution; authority was dispersed rather than concentrated. Perhaps this arrangement suited a provincial piper anxious to call the tune. Whatever the case, the university lacked a co-ordinating centre. Understandably, in internal affairs each college was a law unto itself. A senate, often the battleground for warring colleges and faculties, struggled to lay down academic policy. Business matters were conducted by a board of trustees. These arrangements, of course, were neither unusual nor unworkable. Real confusion was to be found in the higher echelons. Here authority was divided among a chancellor, a vice-chancellor, and a president, none of whose powers was precisely delineated. The opportunities for conflict and deadlock were boundless. Loudon thus found himself open to public criticism for events over which he had little effective control. His hands were bound even in the crucial matter of appointments and dismissals. These were the prerogative of the government which not infrequently used a political rather than an academic gauge in reaching its decisions.[8] When an appointment was at stake, department heads often approached Queen's Park directly. It was not unusual for Loudon to be informed only after the fact that a new man had been hired. Similar wire-pulling was normal whenever new courses or departments were proposed. In these cases both the president and the senate could find their wishes thwarted. Loudon, it seemed, was in office but he was definitely not in power.

Government parsimony amplified his frustrations. For Mowat and succeeding Liberal premiers anything like generosity towards the university was politically dangerous. They were increasingly anxious to appease rural and labour voters who regarded Varsity as an abode of the rich.[9] In consequence, the institution was all but starved of support. Its leaders were told to make do with revenue from endowments and tuition. Existing facilities, however, particularly in the sciences, were badly overburdened. Inevitably, therefore, income failed to keep pace with expenses. Accordingly, each year the university was forced to haggle with Queen's Park in an effort to cover the annual deficit. Lacking a secure and sufficient source of supply, the president and his colleagues found long-range planning difficult in the extreme. Furthermore, current financial arrangements only encouraged more political meddling. Worst of all, perhaps, poverty exacerbated internal tensions. Reflecting in retirement on his former plight, Loudon once complained to George

Wrong that 'my office was a thankless one under the old conditions.'[10] This was putting it mildly.

In these circumstances, a considerable measure of statesmanship was required of any man who donned the presidential robes at Toronto. It was of signal importance, therefore, that James Loudon was anything but diplomatic. Indeed, even when a host of unfavourable conditions are weighed in the balance, it must still be said that to some extent he was the architect of his own undoing. Of northern Irish descent, Loudon was born in Toronto in 1841.[11] A mathematician, physicist, and natural philosopher, he held the distinction of being the first native Canadian to be appointed to a chair at University College. In his own words he had to contend 'against a feeling which prevailed in many quarters that the University should continue to draw its professors from the Old Country.'[12] For more than two decades he led 'nativist' forces whose greatest triumph was his own installation as president. Perhaps the long climb upward in what he considered to be a negative environment served to forge a personality with some decidedly sharp edges. In any case, by the time he stood at or near the top of the local pyramid, Loudon was a 'difficult man who carried his own black cloud with him.'[13] Aloof and sensitive to criticism, he found high office an increasingly severe trial. Unbending and tactless, he had no gift for dealing with men and little notion of compromise.[14] On public occasions he rarely shone, since he lacked any oratorical prowess. In time, many came to agree with Joseph Flavelle, that Loudon was inadequate as a university head.[15] For his part, the embattled president became increasingly isolated from colleagues, trustees, and students alike. In the end he came to suspect that all were plotting to undermine his position. As Bliss has observed, his memoirs constitute 'a vitriolic, nearly paranoiac attack on almost everyone else who held office in the university during his presidency.'[16] Like Disraeli, he found that he had scrambled to the top of a greasy pole.

Thus, circumstance and personal deficiency combined to make Loudon's presidency a stormy one. In 1895 there was a noisy student strike. Complaints were made about inefficient teaching.[17] In addition, allegations of favouritism were levelled against the administration, since G.M. Wrong, son-in-law of a former premier, was rapidly promoted, while a popular classics professor was fired.[18] The list of grievances extended to include the muzzling of *Varsity*, the student publication, and the suspension of its editor. Loudon, who for three full days declined to meet Mackenzie King and other student leaders, was branded, perhaps unfairly, as a 'tyrant.' Meanwhile, he and the vice-chancellor, William Mulock, honed an already well-established mutual dislike by bickering over what should be done.[19] Finally, recourse was had to a royal commission which, among other things, passed favourable judgment on Loudon's conduct but left a bitter taste in the mouths of all involved.

Students aside, quarrelsome staff members not infrequently made life miserable for the president. The most celebrated feud pitted the mercurial George Wrong against the eccentric James Mavor. At one level, theirs was a dispute over jurisdiction. At another, it was a dogfight between two men of volatile personality.[20] Wrong, speaking for history, claimed constitutional studies for his department. Mavor wanted them for his own bailiwick, political economy. A compromise solution satisfied neither party and resentments smouldered. Caught between these swordsmen, Loudon had little love for either nor they for him. In his memoirs he berated Wrong as a firebrand 'always going off at half-cock.'[21] But if Wrong was troublesome, Mavor was dangerous. In 1904 he and the president indulged in ill-disguised but equally unsuccessful campaigns to have each other dismissed.[22] Campus politics, it seemed, had caught the flavour of Byzantium in its prime.

Conflict with staff and students, however, did not exhaust the sources of turmoil; the colleges and the trustees also proved difficult. A row with Victoria came to a head in 1900. The college was anxious to purchase some university land in order to construct a women's residence. Typically, Loudon smelled a plot to overshadow University College and drive him from office.[23] When board member B.E. Walker sided with Victoria, Loudon marked him as an enemy.[24] In the future, Walker reciprocated handsomely. College trustee and pork baron Joseph Flavelle was permanently alienated from the president during this affair and on several subsequent occasions sought to have him removed.[25] As confidence in Loudon's administration seeped away, fresh blows had a telling effect. In 1905 J.C. McClennan, erratic president of the Alumni Association, charged him with favouritism in the awarding of scholarships.[26] Another commission of investigation cleared Loudon, but by then the process of erosion had gone too far to be reversed. His string was fast running out.

Meanwhile, a new force was abroad at Queen's Park. After several decades in power Liberals were routed in the provincial election of January 1905. A reputation for corruption and an excessive reliance on rural support combined with numerous other factors to undermine the government of George Ross.[27] His Conservative opponent, J.P. Whitney, had promised to scour the pork barrel and open the provincial purse in the name of better government, social reform, and economic modernization. However justified or unjustified this vilification of Ross may have been, the electors were clearly eager for change, and Whitney emerged from the fray with a solid majority. From the university's point of view, this outcome was significant in that those who favoured change had the ear of the new premier. Flavelle had given him considerable support during the campaign, most noticeably in the columns of the *News* of which he was the proprietor and J.S. Willison the like-minded editor.[28] Perhaps even more influential with Whitney was the chancellor of the university, William Meredith. Prior to assuming the office of chief justice of Ontario, Meredith had been the fiery leader of Whitney's party. Mentor and successor, they got on well together and the older man had little difficulty in convincing his protégé of the need to treat the university generously.[29] When in the spring Loudon warred publicly with McClennan, the Toronto press seized the opportunity to expound on the myriad defects, real or imagined, of his administration and professorial staff. Already persuaded of the need for reform, Whitney moved quickly. In October a royal commission on the University of Toronto was established. A new broom was then vigorously plied.

The commission was a strong one whose members were well disposed towards the university. Flavelle chaired the sessions and brought with him a wealth of business experience as well as an intuitive grasp of the institution's other needs. Meredith was a prominent figure. Intimately acquainted with the university, he could also supply valuable political and legal advice. The venerable Goldwin Smith added intellectual prestige to the body. An international celebrity, he had once been regius professor of modern history at Oxford and had aided in the reform of that university half a century before. The seventy or more meetings of the commission were held at his home, The Grange. Representing the alumni was the Reverend Henry John Cody, an Anglican minister regarded by some as perhaps the most brilliant student of his generation.[30] Another Toronto graduate, the Reverend D. Bruce Macdonald, was principal of St Andrew's College for boys. A.H.U. Colquhoun was currently an employee of Flavelle at the *News* and would later be deputy minister of education. Rounding out the panel was Byron Edmund Walker.[31] Although a leading figure at the Bank of Commerce and soon to be its president, he was no ordinary businessman. A long-time university trustee, Walker was an amateur geologist and a connoisseur of the fine arts. Well travelled and well read, he once confessed that given the choice he would have preferred an academic life to any other.[32] Altogether, the commissioners shared a powerful desire for constructive change but also recognized the delicacy of their task. Given a free hand by Whitney, they conducted a broad-ranging investigation but tactfully refrained from highlighting recent events. Their report, issued in the spring of 1906 and quickly adopted by the government, outlined a plan of reform that was thoughtfully conceived and above all workable.

Where finance was concerned, attention was called to the need for an adequate regular grant from the province. Whitney responded by offering $30,000 per year for the next thirty years to cover the cost of new buildings. Furthermore, his government accepted Walker's proposal that 50 per cent of provincial succession duties be allotted to the university to defray annual operating expenses. With Ontario's population constantly increasing, Toronto's financial security seemed assured. On the constitutional side, the most striking change came with the elimination of direct provincial control. Drawing on British and American experience, a board of governors was established to manage business affairs and pass final judgment on all appointments, promotions, and dismissals. A buffer was thus erected between the university and Queen's Park. The principles of federation were enshrined in a senate through which colleges and faculties set forth academic policy. There were some complaints when University College was placed under the authority of the Board of Governors. Principal Burwash of Victoria and Provost Macklem of Trinity resisted the idea, fearing that the secular college would be favoured over their own institutions.[33] For that matter, classicist Maurice Hutton, principal of University College, objected on the grounds that the college would lose its identity and its capacity to influence the broader lives of its students.[34] While on this particular score their protests were of no avail, Burwash and Macklem had successfully alerted the commissioners to the necessity of treading warily where the denominational bodies were concerned. Smith, for one, sensed the danger and took pains to insist that on other matters 'special caution and strictness' be observed in anything affecting the terms of federation.[35] In the end the church colleges remained internally self-governing and found the Senate and the Arts Faculty Council adequate forums in which to protect their interests.

The old problem of executive confusion was also attacked. Accordingly, the chancellorship was preserved but reduced to largely honorific proportions. The office of vice-chancellor was abolished outright. Henceforth, the president would serve as the hub of the university wheel; his powers were vastly increased to include the exclusive right of recommending appointments, promotions, and dismissals within the university and University College. In addition, he was designated as ex officio chairman of all university councils. On a broader plane, the president's office was viewed as the co-ordinating centre that the sprawling institution had so sorely lacked. One can readily imagine how Loudon must have yearned for the opportunity to begin anew under these circumstances. But such was not to be. Many were convinced that a truly fresh start would involve finding a new president. Never one to pull his punches, Flavelle made this point perfectly clear to Whitney. He advised the premier that 'the capacity to incorporate a new spirit into the University body, the wisdom with which it is done, the encouragement which only good sense and grasp can give are wanting in President Loudon.'[36] Handling the matter as tactfully as possible, Whitney interviewed the unfortunate man privately and suggested that he retire, on full salary, as soon as a replacement was found. Bowing to the inevitable, Loudon agreed to depart peacefully. Predictably, however, he was soon embroiled in a dispute with the governors and resigned abruptly in July 1906. Maurice Hutton was asked to fill the breach on an interim basis. Meanwhile, the hunt for a new president was on in earnest.

In many ways the task proved far more difficult than had the fashioning of a new constitution. From the outset, a search committee chaired by Walker was deluged with unsolicited recommendations. Hutton wrote early, suggesting that it would be wisest to choose a local man. He assured the committee that the senior staff stood solidly behind Ramsay Wright, a biologist and popular dean of the Faculty of Science. 'To appoint him,' Hutton advised, 'would be better and safer than to go afield.'[37] If anything, George Wrong felt even more strongly about the desirability of selecting from within the university family. Among numerous possible candidates, he singled out Walker as the man best suited for the position.[38] The alumni also had their candidate. Speaking for many former graduates, John D. Swanson of Kamloops wrote to expound on the virtues of Cody.[39] Writing privately to his nominee, Swanson confided that he and others were totally 'averse to the appointment of an outsider.'[40] The modest and charming Hutton also received a measure of support, although he appears to have entertained no strong desire to cling to his temporary post.

Writing to Hutton and others who had nominated local men, Walker told them that the committee's only interest was to secure 'the best man available' and that the claims of faculty members would not be overlooked.[41] Publicly open to suggestions, privately the committee members had grave misgivings about drawing on the current staff. At the core of their objections lay a powerful urge to make a completely fresh start. There was a sense of standing on the brink of a new era in the history of a university which, it was hoped, would soon rise to be an institution of national significance. The committee, therefore, was reluctant to perpetuate old rivalries and focused its attention on candidates outside Toronto. Walker later vehemently denied that prominent figures on campus had been given short shrift.[42] However, an earlier letter seeking advice from the president of the University of Wisconsin would seem to indicate that a definite bias was at work. 'There are,' wrote Walker, 'features ... which would make it much more difficult for a member of the Faculty than for a new man to carry out the views of the new Board of Governors.'[43] Goldwin Smith shared this view. Noting the surge of 'nativist' pressure, he toyed with the idea of stridently proclaiming the freedom of the committee to choose as it saw fit. Good judgment, however, militated against this course. Still, he could not help but observe that nativism had paid no dividends under Loudon.[44] He applauded Hutton's conduct as interim president. 'But he looks old,' said Smith, 'and could scarcely be a new start, to say nothing of the jealousies in the Staff which seem to be thought a serious obstacle.'[45]

Preferring to look outside for a president, the committee also entertained a fairly clear notion of the qualities that man should have. Above all else, they agreed, a leader was required. 'It is to be hoped,' Smith wrote to Flavelle, 'that we may find a man of moral force and impressive character as well as administrative power.'[46] The latter was in complete accord and had already confided similar thoughts to fellow board member W.T. White.[47] In replying to Smith, however, Flavelle added a number of other important considerations. The ideal candidate, he explained, ought to display 'sound sense, a knowledge of men, a capacity for organization and a love of learning united in a man young enough to earn distinction by his effort.' Too often, he noted, such positions were filled 'by one who has passed the period when struggle gives pleasure.' In this businessman's mind, therefore, relative youth and solid common sense outweighed the claims of mere academic brilliance. He was not, however, unmindful of the need to secure a man of some intellectual attainment. Indeed, Flavelle sympathized with those who felt that public and political pressure were threatening to tip the balance at Toronto too far in the direction of practical studies. Consequently, he went on to advise Smith that a humanist should be preferred over a scientist.[48] Neither the former regius professor nor Walker, for that matter, required persuasion on this point and the other members of the committee seemed ready to follow their lead.

Establishing priorities was easy enough, but finding a suitable candidate was quite another matter. As the search began, Walker confessed to the governor-general, Lord Grey, that 'so few names occur to us even as possibilities that we really have no idea as to whether we have a reasonable chance of securing an ideal man or not.' He went on to add that 'there will be serious difficulty if we cannot find a Canadian, or a Briton of sufficiently broad and imperial turn of mind to sympathize with Canadian conditions.'[49] Grey suggested George Parkin. Indeed, he launched a one-man campaign to win the post for that champion of imperial federation and first secretary to the Rhodes Trust scholarship scheme.[50] Walker, however, was less than enthusiastic. 'I frankly admit,' he told the King's representative, 'that we hope to get a better man.'[51] When Grey persisted, he was informed that, among other things, Parkin's friendship with a large number of faculty members ruled him out.[52] With no obvious choice looming before them, the committee decided to cast their net broadly in the hope of making a fortunate strike. Accordingly, letters were dispatched to university heads and prominent figures throughout Canada, the United States, and Britain asking them to recommend suitable Canadian or British individuals of their acquaintance. In all, over a hundred inquiries were made and more than eighty detailed replies were received.[53] By December 1906 the list of candidates had swelled to include the names of ninety men of varying degrees of distinction. Most, of course, were easily dismissed. Maddeningly, however, some of those deemed most desirable were simply uninterested. Nova Scotian Jacob Gould Schurman, for example, could not be persuaded to abandon his presidential duties at Cornell.[54] Nor could William Osler, who had enjoyed a brilliant career as a professor of medicine in the United States, be coaxed to leave his more recently adopted home in Great Britain.[55]

The results of these early forays were doubly disappointing because time was rapidly becoming a major consideration. In January the governors made it clear that their patience was wearing thin.[56] An anxious Goldwin Smith warned Walker that 'unless we proceed soon to the election of a President of the University we shall be in danger of losing our power of choice.'[57] It was under mounting pressure, therefore, that the committee drew up a short list towards the end of the month.[58] Michael Sadler, a noted British educational reformer, was the preferred candidate. Negotiations were carried on through Osler, but in mid-March Sadler declined, citing a desire to remain in England and continue his educational investigations.[59] That left three names on the list. Cody's merits were considered sufficiently strong to override most misgivings about a local appointment. A. Ross Hill, Canadian dean of the teachers' college at Missouri University, was also highly rated. In the end, however, the committee decided to approach a man whose name had only recently been brought to their attention. Many were surprised but none was more shocked than Robert Alexander Falconer when he was asked to come to Toronto for an interview.

Not given to fantasy, Falconer had never envisaged himself in Loudon's chair. To be sure, Walter Murray once mused on the possibility, but Falconer had attached little prophetic weight to this flattering comment from a friend.[60] After all, he had neither applied for the post, nor had he any intention of doing so. Indeed, as a cold December deepened into an even more frigid January, his foremost thoughts were of spring and the promised Mediterranean sun. Snow and ice had few charms for a man who had come of age in the tropics. With welcome relief only a few months away, Falconer was battening down for the winter term at Pine Hill when an old friend came to call. J.A. Macdonald of the *Globe* was on a roving commission. Deputed by Toronto's Board of Governors, of which he was a member, to search Canadian universities high and low for a president, he was in Halifax to visit Dalhousie. It was only natural that he should drop in at Pine Hill when time allowed. Macdonald had visited the college in 1905 to speak at the opening session of the new graduate school. More recently, he and Robert had stood shoulder to shoulder at the Presbyterian General Assembly in June when Mackay's proposal had threatened to disrupt the drive toward church union. No doubt their chatter went on far into the evening as they relived old victories and speculated about the future. At some point during his visit Macdonald had a brainstorm. Impressed by the progress made at Pine Hill and fully conscious of his friend's sterling qualities, he recognized in Falconer a solution to Toronto's dilemma.

Thus far Macdonald's university tour had yielded scant results. Now he wrote excitedly to Walker of this fresh and hopeful prospect.[61] The timing was perfection itself. His letter, detailing the merits of a young Canadian of proven administrative capacity and broad humanistic education, arrived just as the committee was straining to produce a credible short list to fend off local critics. If there were a fly in the ointment, it would be the fact that Falconer had taken holy orders and might, on that ground, prove unacceptable to the denominational colleges.[62] Even so, on the strength of Macdonald's recommendation, Falconer was unofficially placed second on the list of four. In all likelihood he was ranked ahead of Cody because he came from outside the university and above Hill because he had no questionable American affiliations. When Sadler declined, partly, some suspected, in response to a nativist outcry against hiring an Englishman, Walker and his associates approached their wits' end. Frustrated and anxious to be done with the matter, they were ready to gamble on a relatively obscure figure, even if he were a cleryyman.

While his name was scarcely a household word, Falconer was not completely unknown in Toronto. Macdonald, of course, spoke highly of him. Furthermore, Knox College had recently offered him a chair. In

1905 he had preached the university sermon. Burwash of Victoria had met him on several occasions during the negotiations on church union, and in this connection, Falconer's well-established ecumenical sympathies stood him in good stead with most of the denominational colleges on campus, as Walker soon discovered.[63] All these factors helped further his cause, as did the testimonials that flowed in at the committee's request. Authorities at Pine Hill described him as an inspiring teacher and an administrator of tact and courtesy. They went on to express their gratitude for having had 'in days of struggle, one so fitted to help them.'[64] Others spoke of Falconer's oratorical gifts and leadership qualities.[65] Of all the recommendations received, however, few probably carried more weight with committee chairman Walker than that of Dougald Macgillivary who represented the Bank of Commerce in Halifax. Writing to his chief, the Haligonian penned a lengthy and penetrating analysis of Falconer. 'He is,' wrote the banker, 'personally a most attractive man, but gives the impression of solidity and sympathy and good sense rather than of brilliancy.' Not for a moment, however, did he doubt the candidate's scholarly prowess. Indeed, said Macgillivary, 'I have heard college men here say that he is a man of quite unusual aptitudes.' Like others, he also remarked on Falconer's capacity for handling men and described him as 'easily the educational leader in the Maritime Provinces.' In this regard, he noted that Falconer was marked to succeed Forrest at Dalhousie and added that he alone offered any hope of leading Nova Scotia's too numerous colleges into a federation. In passing, Macgillivary also commented on Sophie, who, he implied, would be a valuable social asset to any university head. In an effort to round out the general portrait, he isolated 'moral force' as the ultimate source of Falconer's strength. Finally, he summarized the virtues of a man he considered to be ideally suited to Toronto's needs: 'His sincerity, courage, sympathy and broadmindedness are the characteristics of a man who will go on growing. He has an excellent presence, a good manner and is a first rate speaker.'[66] Altogether, it must have seemed to the committee that a veritable deus ex machina had descended to solve their nagging problems. Macgillivary's letter read like a carbon copy of the priorities sketched earlier by Flavelle. And so Falconer was invited to meet the committee.

Years later he could still recall the sensation of 'utter surprise' when this summons arrived.[67] As far as Falconer knew, Sadler had been all but confirmed in the post. He seems to have had no inkling that he was next in line for consideration until almost the last moment. Caught off guard, he scrambled to adjust his schedule. There was at least one saving factor in the situation. His bags were already packed! He and Sophie were due to sail from Boston on Tuesday, 9 April. The committee wanted to meet him in Toronto the Sunday before embarkation. The timing would be tight, but with luck and a good connection in Montreal he could make it. In the end a somewhat breathless Falconer managed the dash to Toronto. At no point, however, did he lose his composure; meeting the committee at Walker's home, he listened calmly to their proposals and in turn was carefully evaluated. Aware of the strife that had riven the University of Toronto for so many years, he made it plain that he had no desire to endure Loudon's unhappy fate. Thus he informed Walker and the others that, should they choose to nominate him, he would accept only if he had the unanimous approval of the governors.[68] Given the university's reputation for factionalism, he must have considered this unlikely. The interview ended, and there was time only to shake hands, grab a few hours of sleep, and catch the train to Boston next morning.

The passage to Liverpool was uneventful, and Falconer had much time to mull over conflicting urges. On the one hand, he was bound by affection and duty to Pine Hill. On the other, he was conscious that so splendid an opportunity came but once in a lifetime, if at all. At least he had the luxury of reflecting quietly on the issue, far from friends, family, and responsibilities. He may even have set the problem aside during a leisurely trip through France and Italy which ended at Naples. There, however, a terse cablegram awaited him. The spartan message, 'Unanimous. Walker. Reply,' came as yet another surprise in an already startling series of events.[69] Originally, it had been agreed that any announcement would be delayed until Falconer's return.[70] Typically, however, word of his nomination had been leaked to the press. Rather than create the impression of indecision and division, the governors met quickly and on 25 April voted to make a firm offer. Once again taken aback, Falconer cabled his intention to cut short his vacation, confer with authorities at Pine Hill, and then make his final decision known.[71] There followed a whirlwind tour of Greece, a brief stay in Rome, and a hastily arranged passage home on the *Winnifredian* out of Liverpool.

His first taste of real celebrity came as he stepped off the ship at Boston to be greeted by reporters from Toronto and Halifax anxious to learn of his decision. Falconer, however, was non committal. Everything, he told them, depended on the results of his forthcoming meetings with the boards at Pine Hill and Toronto.[72] The college trustees were understanding. With J.A. Macdonald in attendance to explain the situation, they reluctantly but generously gave Falconer permission to choose his own course.[73] After meeting the governors in Toronto and assuring himself that their unanimity was genuine, Falconer formally accepted the office of president on 14 June at a salary of $10,000 per year with a free house and moving expenses to boot. A new and challenging adventure had begun.

Rumours of Falconer's nomination and word of his definite appointment sparked considerable comment. Several individuals were quick to convey their private impressions. William Osler speculated that he might one day be 'a great president.'[74] Goldwin Smith, relieved that the search was over, congratulated Walker on his leadership in the matter. He went on to say that 'I saw something of the man when he was here and he struck me as being the right sort, quiet, dignified and strong.'[75] In Kingston many were hopeful that an outsider and fellow Presbyterian would improve the often turbulent relations between Ontario's two principal universities.[76] Thus, one Queen's loyalist wrote to Gordon that the new man 'would do what he could to treat us fairly and might even be rather friendly.'[77] But if some were pleased by the appointment, others had reservations. George Parkin, for example, contacted G.M. Wrong and questioned the wisdom of selecting one who came from 'a smaller position and a narrower social circle' for so demanding an office in the larger arena; this, he submitted, constituted 'a rather serious leap in the dark.'[78]

Wrong was in total agreement. Moreover, he was nursing a full measure of bitter resentment. In a furious exchange of letters with Walker he expressed concern about Falconer's qualifications and flayed the committee for its failure to consider local men. In what might have been a veiled reference to Gordon, he pointed out that not every Maritimer was a G.M. Grant. 'I know,' he wrote, 'of another College which took a "great gun" from Halifax and found he did not rise to the needs of a wider field.' From this general concern he moved to a specific criticism. Although the two had never met, he ventured to state that Falconer lacked the level of 'personal cultivation' necessary in a president. 'I heard him preach once' said Wrong, 'and he struck me as colourless and commonplace.'[79] A few days later Walker was treated to yet another peppery missive in which Wrong denounced the governors' 'open contempt' for their own faculty. 'For the first time in my life,' moaned the professor of history, 'I have felt that I should like to find work elsewhere.' Driving the point home, he observed that if Falconer or Sadler had been employed at Toronto, they would never have been approached.[80] Walker, who could match Wrong tantrum for tantrum, replied in high dudgeon, defending the committee's decision and its methods of selection.[81] Inwardly, however, he must have sagged as the frictions of yesteryear seemed likely to surface anew despite extensive efforts to bury them.

There was another aspect of Falconer's background that troubled some observers. Former Prime Minister Mackenzie Bowell was uncomfortable with the thought that a clergyman would now occupy the president's office. 'As a rule,' he told Walker, 'I have found them in my experience (there are exceptions) narrow in their views and to a great extent impractical as businessmen.'[82] The *Mail and Empire* voiced similar reservations. Noting that Falconer was a very learned man and wishing him well, the editors none the less found it surprising that a layman had not been chosen to lead a secular university.[83] The *News* was more blunt. 'Dr Falconer,' it advised, 'must forget that he has been a preacher and cease to preach.'[84] Springing to the defence of a favourite son, the *Halifax Herald* replied that in Nova Scotia Falconer was viewed not as a cleric but as a 'public man.'[85] Similarly, the *Presbyterian* shrugged off 'whimpers' about appointing a minister, prophesying that 'it will soon be manifest that in Dr Falconer the man is bigger than the clergyman.'[86] Privately, Walker moved to calm fears on this point. To Bowell he wrote that Falconer had accepted ordination only because of his position at Pine Hill. At no point, he continued, had the new president held a pulpit, nor had he any intention of taking one up in the future. Furthermore, he declared that an informal survey of opinion revealed that the Nova Scotian was 'persona grata' as far as the denominational colleges were concerned.[87] He must also have persuaded Whitney on this score, for the latter repeated these assertions in a letter to his brother some weeks later.[88]

Even so, when Falconer arrived to take up his charge he was pointedly advised of sensitivity on the issue. 'It was more than hinted to me,' he records, 'that I should be wise in keeping out of pulpits.'[89] Heeding this advice, he politely but firmly rejected the scores of invitations to preach that accumulated on his new desk.[90] Carefully nurturing an image of sectarian neutrality, he was particularly scrupulous in his dealings with fellow Calvinists. Asked in 1908 to speak at services in Peterborough, he declined on the basis that his position ruled out such activities. Furthermore, he added, 'I should not begin, especially among Presbyterians, for not only would there be no end to the number of requests, but it would not do to appear in their pulpits chiefly.'[91] In short order, Falconer's policy of lying low and his stance on the question of church union dampened fears about his clerical background. In the light of this reserve, therefore, he must have found it ironically amusing when, for the first few months of his administration, Walker of all people persisted in addressing his letters to the 'Reverend R.A. Falconer.'[92]

Despite some qualms about hiring a minister, the press was generous in its initial assessment of the new president. The *News* was taken with the 'optimism and bubbling energy' that Falconer conveyed.[93] He was approvingly described as 'modest' and (inevitably) 'manly.'[94] The *World* embraced him as 'every inch a first-class fellow' with valuable talents in diplomacy.[95] Choosing an economic metaphor, the *Star* cheerfully welcomed this 'Canadian raw material with an imported finish.'[96] In many eyes, indeed, Falconer's nationality more than compensated for the fact that he was in orders. But good-natured regionalism also had its say. Maritimers crowed that they had done it again, as Falconer kept alive the tradition of Dawson and Grant. Wise men, said some Nova Scotians, came from the east. 'Yes,' quipped the Edmonton *Daily Bulletin,* 'and the wiser they are the faster they come.'[97] Not to be outdone, *Saturday Night,* with tongue in cheek, observed that 'every boy in the Maritimes is born with the prospects of a college presidency ahead of him.'[98]

The generally sympathetic reaction of the press undoubtedly buoyed Falconer as he faced the task ahead. There was, however, an element in many editorials which must have intensified the natural pressures he felt. Taking their cue from those who had led the fight for a new constitution, journalists waxed eloquent on the glorious opportunities that lay before the reformed university. Lofty expectations were entertained, and it was made clear that Falconer would be held responsible for fulfilling them. More restrained than most, the *Globe* merely urged him to wrench the university out of its provincialism.[99] Others went further. Toronto, one editor declared, stood on the threshold of great expansion and would shortly become a 'national university of world stature.'[100] The Halifax *Morning Chronicle,* quoting an unidentified member of the Board of Governors, proclaimed that the University of Toronto was destined to be the greatest university in the British empire. It was expected to set the pace for western Canada and attract the brightest students from the dominion at large.[101] The *News* and other papers echoed this heroic theme. Not infrequently, the actual powers of the president were misunderstood and grossly exaggerated. Under the reformed constitution, said the *Halifax Herald,* his authority to effect change would be 'absolute.'[102] Few, of course, went so far as the jubilant but ill-informed *Theologue.* 'The Czar,' it pronounced, 'is autocrat in his dominions, but the autocracy of the Czar is as moonlight to sunlight when compared with the powers of the President of Toronto.'[103] Still, there was a broadly shared assumption that nothing short of patent mismanagement could keep the University of Toronto from an appointment with destiny. The message was not lost on Falconer. Indeed, as he soon revealed, he shared the desire to create a truly national university. Even so, this was a tall order for an institution that only recently had suffered from severe economic privation and bitter internecine strife. With a brilliant future all but taken for granted by the press and governors alike, it must have occurred to Falconer that he was in a very vulnerable position.

June and early July were spent in Toronto as Falconer struggled to gain a sense of his new surroundings. For the moment he lodged with A.H.U. Colquhoun, who patiently explained the intricacies of the constitution and campus politics.[104] There followed a seemingly endless round of introductions to staff members and others of note. In this regard he was particularly relieved to find that Hutton and Wright, both unsuccessful nominees for the presidency, bore him no grudge and were only too willing to be of assistance.[105] Anxious to draw on several perspectives, he sought out Loudon and was surprised to meet 'a quiet, cultivated gentleman, agreeable and not prone to rehearse his past grievances.'[106] At the same time he had his first encounter with George Wrong. The potential for disaster was high. Walker had been informed that the historian had every intention of airing his grievances at the first opportunity.[107] Falconer, no doubt alerted on this score, faced the first test of his much heralded powers of diplomacy. Wrong, after all, was not without influence. As it happened, the two fencers, at first wary, quickly relaxed their guard. Face to face they discovered a mutual affinity. A soul of large spirit, Wrong was willing to concede that he had misjudged Falconer, if not the governors. In the wake of this exchange, he wrote cheerfully to William Lawson Grant that he liked the new president 'very much' and had every reason to hope that Toronto had at last found the right man.[108]

With Wrong comforted, one small problem was solved and Falconer resumed the job of battling the currents in Toronto. Outwardly composed, inwardly he felt very much at sea. To Walter Murray, his 'dear Gualterino,' he confided: 'I am swimming hard and hope that I shall not drown but I am like a fellow who as been pitched in head first.' Drawing out the metaphor, he complained that 'my nose and eyes are full of water and I hardly know where I am.' Somewhat daunted by the very scale of the university, he was also disconcerted by constant reminders of the need to keep his head down amid the rage of faction. Altogether, he confessed that he was looking forward to the September inaugural 'with trepidation.' Loaded down with work and aware that at any moment the slightest miscalculation of local currents could induce calamity, a somewhat lonely Falconer was satisfied 'to live a day at a time.'[109]

Sensing this apprehension, friends in Halifax were determined to give him a rousing formal send-off. A lavish testimonial dinner was arranged. In part, this plan was inspired by a simple desire to toast a man who was genuinely liked and respected, but also the organizers hoped to make a point that would register clearly in Toronto. Dougald Macgillivary, who helped orchestrate the event, explained this deeper purpose to Walker: 'It is intended to give the function a character of as much breadth as possible so that he will go forth a leading and representative Nova Scotian and not merely a Presbyterian cleric.'[110] Thus, on the evening of 15 August at the Halifax School for the Blind, Falconer was hailed by a large and impressive assembly. Among those who paid tribute to him were the lieutenant-governor, the Anglican bishop, the Roman Catholic arch-bishop, civic officials, and the heads of Mount Allison, Acadia, and Dalhousie universities. Premier G.H. Murray set the tone when he declared that Falconer was 'perhaps the best all-round man in Nova Scotia.'[111] In this he was merely proclaiming publicly what he had already relayed privately to Walker.[112] Others dwelt on Falconer's service to the community and his ecumenical spirit. Attention was drawn to the honour paid him in July when he was made a life member of the local Canadian Club. It was a poignant evening, and Falconer was deeply touched. Halifax was dear to him and departure would exact a stiff emotional price. Most difficult to bear was the thought of separation from the companions of his youth. As he lamented to Walter Murray, 'I have never had anything so hard to do as to go leaving Jim and yourself and more recent friends and my old work behind.'[113] It is unclear whether the testimonial dinner had much impact in far-off Toronto. To Falconer, however, it was a sorely needed tonic as he nervously awaited the fast-approaching inauguration.

As it happened, he could have spared himself a great deal of needless anxiety. The crowd that filled Convocation Hall to overflowing on 26 September came to celebrate, not to criticize. A sense of occasion was heightened by the battery of luminaries adorning the platform. Flanked by figures such as Laurier, Whitney and Sandford Fleming, Falconer was no doubt uneasy as the seemingly endless preliminaries dragged on. Preoccupied with his own address, he probably caught only snatches of those delivered prior to his investiture by a stream of delegates from other universities. When the moment finally arrived for him to speak, however, his long-accumulating trepidations were swiftly dispelled. To a man, the audience scrambled to its feet. Thunderous applause reverberated for a minute or more before he had uttered a word.[114] Deeply relieved and stimulated at the same moment, Falconer rose to the top of his form.

As he spoke, it became evident that the new president had a definite flare for public relations. His neatly tailored address was diplomatic but frank in tone. It unfolded as an eloquent plea for understanding between

the university and its many erstwhile critics. After briefly outlining some
general educational values upon which he would expound more fully in
the future, Falconer moved directly to his main theme. The University of
Toronto, he declared, was not a rich man's preserve remote from the
interests and concerns of ordinary men. Instead, he argued, its task was to
seek out and cultivate ability at all levels of society and aid in the
promotion of the general welfare. Pointing to the proliferation of new
departments and faculties, he sought to demonstrate that the University
of Toronto was no fossilized institution wedded to the values of the past.
'The recent expansion of the university,' he alleged, 'shows that it aims at
meeting the requirements of modern life, and is keeping in touch with the
people.' Here he drew attention to developments in the fields of
medicine, applied science, forestry, education and household science in
order to bolster his claim. At no point, however, did Falconer depict
Toronto as a utilitarian institution. 'No true university,' he asserted, 'can
afford to yield to the superficial demand for what is so often erroneously
called the practical.' The Faculty of Arts, in his estimation, would always
remain the core, 'because in it mental discipline and intellectual culture
are found in purer quality.' The humanities in particular were described
as the foundation upon which all professional and specialized education
should be built. But he emphasized that this bias in no way detracted from
the usefulness of the university. Underscoring the point, he chided those
professors who clung to an ivory-tower existence. 'The besetting academical sin,' said Falconer, 'is an intellectual aloofness which occasionally
makes the highly-educated man unable to appreciate the outlook of the
average man; and the aristocracy of intellect is as exclusive as any other
aristocracy.' Such exclusivity, he charged, was foreign to the nature of a
university, which should provide a dispassionate and expert analysis of
society's problems while labouring to define and keep pure the ideals of
the nation. In the latter regard, he contended that Varsity had a particular
duty to help cement the bonds of national unity. Once again, however, he
warned against a narrowing of horizons. Full-blown nativism was ushered
out. But so was a purely colonial mentality. Thus he argued that what was
uniquely Canadian was to be cherished and cultivated with special care,
but not at the expense of broader, more universal currents in western
civilization as a whole. Announcing one of the future themes of his
administration, Falconer called on the university to harmonize a national
with an international perspective. The wholesome fruit of such a blend,
he prophesied, would be a harvest of graduates imbued with the values of
a higher citizenship – people of broad vision, intellectually and morally
capable of providing leadership in a new democracy. In many ways, he

was simply expanding ideas enunciated at his Pine Hill inaugural to suit a larger, secular institution.

Having outlined these glittering prospects, Falconer then raised the issue clearly uppermost in his mind. To him, as to many of his colleagues, it was the point on which all else turned. Addressing politicians and the public at large, he declared that nothing of value could be accomplished unless the university retained its independence. Academic freedom, he asserted, was a priceless possession 'essential to the progress of civilization.' Unconcerned for the moment with philosophical niceties, Falconer did not offer a thoroughgoing definition of the concept. Nothing, for example, was said concerning the participation of professors in public disputes. Similarly, the claims of students were left unmentioned; but the corporate right of a secular university 'to investigate and to teach' without political or sectarian interference was resolutely defended. Speaking bluntly, Falconer emphasized that the appointment of professors 'should be made solely on the ground of attainment, aptness to teach, capacity for research and high professional and personal character.' There were no veiled references here. The president was issuing a straightforward declaration of independence and calling on politicians to honour both the letter and the spirit of promises in the new constitution. Confident of the current premier's blessing, he also understood that leaders came and went and that political moods were quick to change.[115] Relatively little criticism had been levelled against the reforms of 1905, but there were some who regretted the loss of direct government control. Only two days after the inaugural, for example, the Toronto *Star* spoke for those who harboured such feelings. Its editors complained of the inability to bring public opinion to bear on the university and described its administrative scheme as incompatible with the principle of responsible government.[116] This was not the first time, nor would it be the last, that the university's newly won liberty was questioned. Falconer, it seems, was doing all he could to embed the principle of independence in the public mind while the winds of opinion blew fair. It was a case of carpe diem.

His formal début was a resounding success. In emphasizing the broader functions of the university Falconer had struck the right note. Predictably enough, the *News* seconded his plea for independence. The *Mail and Empire* approved of his 'high determination to conduct the university upon modern principles.' Even the *Star* grudgingly conceded that Falconer's vision was a worthy one.[117] With many of the governors, Flavelle felt relieved and vindicated. To Whitney he wrote that 'the courage and capacity of the Government in University affairs deserved the success which President Falconer's address this afternoon assures.'[118]

Falconer's pleasure at his own triumph, however, was not unalloyed. Detecting a small but glaring flaw in the proceedings, he feared that his studious efforts at bridge-building might be undone by an act of simple stupidity. The first six rows in Convocation Hall had been closed to the general public. It had been left to ushers to decide who was to be admitted to these prize seats. Some grumbling inevitably resulted. As far as Falconer could tell, no defensible principle of selection had been employed. Intensely annoyed, he wrote next morning to John Hoskin, chairman of the board, to complain of this flagrant exhibition of the very exclusivity he had been at pains to condemn. 'Toronto University,' he remarked testily, 'has been often charged with social toadyism and if we have any of it this appears to me a good time to extirpate it. We have had a good deal of talk about bringing the University close to the people and one way not to succeed is to deal with the public as they were dealt with yesterday. If there is any institution in Toronto that should not attempt to make class distinction ... it is the University.' He admitted that the matter might appear trifling, but he counselled Hoskin that 'anything affecting the relation of the University to the public is important.'[119] This final comment was no passing observation tossed off and quickly forgotten. On the contrary, it betrayed a habit of mind, acquired at Pine Hill and reinforced by the circumstances of his new appointment, which lingered with Falconer throughout his tenure. The spectre of renewed political interference haunted him, not quite to the point of obsession, but near enough to be always at the edge of his thoughts.

Falconer certainly had no desire to test the public mood while sorting out his new responsibilities. Indeed, he prayed for an extended calm as the university went through a period of adjustment. For himself, he struggled to master the intricacies of his new post. This, as he confessed to Walter Murray, was no mean chore. 'The big machine here,' he told his friend early in 1908, 'is working along, going its own gait while I stand by and watch it go, and doubtless some people fancy that I am an important piece of the gear, but though the watching is very interesting and not a little exhausting I hardly see yet that I am much more than an on-looker.'[120] Keen to reform, he was also conscious of the need to go slowly. If internal harmony were to be promoted, the president could ill afford to move precipitously. Thus, despite strident calls in the press for the removal of 'deadwood,' Falconer reviewed but did not prune the teaching staff. The complaints, he thought, were exaggerated.[121] Within the precincts of the university he consulted broadly, kept his opinions to himself, and assumed a position of strict neutrality. As an admirer later observed, Falconer 'realized that an innocent from abroad had certain advantages.'[122]

Feigning ignorance of local factional alignments he often appointed feuding colleagues to the same committees in the hope of forcing an accommodation. Similarly, he meticulously avoided direct challenges to 'self-assumed authority.' Where change was obviously required, he preferred to work through special investigating bodies rather than proceeding by administrative fiat. The result, said his would-be biographer, was that warring gangs 'had difficulty in determining whether this new comer was totally unsophisticated or as worldly wise at least as any of them .'[123] If controversy were to erupt, Falconer was determined that it would be none of his doing.

Beyond the confines of the university, he acted with similar caution. At this early stage, understandably, time was simply too precious to be frittered away on a potentially ceaseless round of public engagements. Accordingly, Falconer normally cited preoccupation as his reason for ducking external commitments. It was a legitimate but also a convenient excuse for one operating, at least for the moment, on the principle 'the less said the better.' Preaching, obviously, was totally out of the question. But so, it seemed, was affiliation with the plethora of secular groups that sought to employ his voice or his name. Even the Canadian Temperance League petitioned him in vain. Asked for his public endorsement, Falconer replied that he lacked time and in any case was reluctant to identify himself with an outside body until he fully understood the nature of its work.[124] This response must have seemed more than mildly disingenuous to the opponents of drink. It was, however, quite a typical, almost reflex reaction by Falconer during his first two or three years in office. The one major exception came with his enthusiastic support of the Canadian Club. As a founder of the Halifax branch he could hardly refuse invitations to speak from this clearly 'respectable' organization. On these occasions he invariably delivered uncontroversial addresses, extolling the virtues of national unity and the role of universities in promoting it.[125] Playing it softly, Falconer, as he told Murray, was trying 'to keep quiet within the building and to talk as rationally as possible ... outside.'[126] For the better part of a year, this discreet policy kept Varsity out of the headlines, and a valuable breathing space was had. But the hiatus was too good to last.

In the spring of 1908 trouble developed during an attempt to streamline the administration of the Toronto General Hospital. Among other things, it was proposed that clinical services, so vital to the university, be rationalized for the sake of better instruction. With enrolments rising in the Faculty of Medicine it was necessary to squeeze the maximum out of existing facilities. Furthermore, the university authorities entertained a strong desire to keep pace with advances in clinical techniques devised at American schools such as Johns Hopkins. Accordingly, an effort was made to establish two central teaching services under professors of medicine and surgery, respectively. In addition, it was argued that the outside commitments of staff physicians should be severely restricted in the name of greater efficiency. Doctors at the hospital, however, prized their traditional autonomy and succeeded in forcing a dilution of the scheme. In the end, a less centralized system was adopted with three services in medicine and three in surgery. Although a compromise, it none the less represented a considerable improvement over former haphazard arrangements.

Serious complications, however, arose when the appointments were announced. With scant attention to political wisdom, the hospital trustees nominated junior men, mostly associate professors, to these prestigious positions. It was a lamentable gaffe, the more so because four university representatives on the board failed to anticipate the furore it would arouse. Senior professors, backed by former President Loudon, voiced their outrage in the press.[127] Most of the abuse was directed at Flavelle and the other trustees, who had the sole power of appointment, but the university administration was not left unscathed. As he made clear in his first presidential report, Falconer sympathized with the senior men.[128] He could not abide the washing of Varsity's dirty linen in public. To Flavelle he wrote that 'our dignity demands that we should work this thing out ourselves.'[129] At length, a compromise was engineered whereby all future clinical appointments would be approved by a joint committee of the hospital trustees and the university governors.[130] A lacuna in the constitution was thus filled. Still, it had been an embarrassing moment. The only redeeming feature was that the public conflict had been mercifully brief.

If Falconer breathed easily in the wake of this upset, it was not for long. Within the year an even sharper dispute arose whose roots went back to his first days in office and beyond. Barely a month after his installation he was visited by a deputation complaining of a serious breach in the terms of federation.[131] University College, it was alleged, had broken faith with the denominational colleges by poaching on their exclusive preserve: instruction in theological subjects. At issue were courses offered by the Department of Oriental Languages in which, it was charged, the Bible was regularly examined. This procedure, in itself, argued the deputation, was ultra vires according to the University Act. To make matters worse, however, it was said that the sacred text was being interpreted solely in the glare of the higher criticism. Here, one suspects, was the real sticking point. The men confronting Falconer were not known for the liberality of their scriptural views.

Dr Albert Carmen, general superintendent of the Methodist church, was the sworn foe of biblical modernism in all its guises. Doughty champion of the orthodox, he had tackled erring college men before. In 1899 he had hounded Professor George Workman out of Victoria because of the latter's attacks on the concept of verbal inspiration. A persistent harrier, Carmen had pursued when his quarry fled to Wesleyan College. By 1907 Workman resigned in despair. Clearly, this slight, bespectacled, former circuit rider was not to be trifled with. Standing before Falconer, he was supported by William McLaren, the conservative principal of Knox College and N.W. Hoyles of Wycliffe. On this occasion, however, the most determined member of the delegation proved to be the Reverend Elmore Harris. A son of John Harris, the farm equipment manufacturer, he was pastor of Walmer Road Baptist Church, founder of the Toronto Bible College, and a member of McMaster University's senate. He was also, as it happened, a stern and unyielding fundamentalist. In close touch with American conservatives, Harris later helped edit the early volumes of their ringing testament, *The Fundamentals*.[132] For the moment, alarmed by events at University College, he and his associates demanded action.

Falconer listened politely but with little enthusiasm. Initially, he seems to have misread the motives of the deputation. Thus, in an effort to mollify them, he addressed only the legal point. In this regard he suggested an amendment to the University Act to permit the oriental languages department to offer an option in religious knowledge. He could agree that theology was the proper province of the denominational bodies but saw no valid objection to the study of biblical literature and history at University College. On the contrary, he asserted, no arts program worthy of the name could ignore so vast a storehouse of knowledge and experience. The flat refusal of Harris and company to entertain such a suggestion undoubtedly clarified their purpose in his mind. Dropping a conciliatory approach, Falconer made it clear that he was satisfied with things as they were. Furthermore, he refused point blank to raise the matter with the governors so that legalities might be tested. The interview ended on that note. In Falconer's mind, the case was closed. Harris and his friends, however, were far from through.

Over the next several months Harris trundled about gathering evidence for his charges and seeking further support. He went so far as to interview the professor whose lectures were chiefly in question. Dr Thomas Eakin, an Ulsterman by birth, was a graduate of Knox College who had gone on to take a PH D in oriental languages under J.F. McCurdy at the University of Toronto.[133] Ordained in 1897, he was assistant pastor of St Andrew's Presbyterian Church, as well as a lecturer at University College. Face to face, Harris claimed to find him an intractable higher critic, unalterably opposed to a traditional interpretation of the Bible.[134] The meeting, therefore, only strengthened his resolve to see the baneful teaching expunged. In this quest, he was aided by an ally in high places. Samuel Hume Blake, an influential member of the Board of Governors, shared Harris's concerns. Brother of a former premier, Blake was a prominent Toronto lawyer. A co-founder of Wycliffe College, he was a Varsity graduate and had once served as chancellor of the University. Intensely religious, he was a devout Anglican, active in church affairs, and a member of the Layman's Missionary Movement. Like Harris, Blake was an avowed traditionalist deeply suspicious of newer currents in scriptural study. It is unclear whether he had sponsored the delegation to Falconer or had enlisted in the cause later. Whatever the case, by the fall of 1908 he was prepared to raise his voice against the offending courses. Thereafter, the issue could no longer be ignored.

On 30 November Blake wrote to John Hoskin, chairman of the board, outlining the complaints against Eakin and University College.[135] Two weeks later, Hoskin replied that the charges were unfounded. There was, he said, no dogmatic content in the lectures. Furthermore, he added that Semitic studies could scarcely be conducted without reference to the Bible.[136] Not easily turned aside, Blake retorted angrily that the teaching was clearly ultra vires, however well it might be disguised within the oriental languages department. In addition, it was definitely tainted. Textbooks by Samuel Driver and others, he alleged, were heavily biased in favour of the higher criticism. Instructors had encouraged doubts about the virgin birth. Right-minded students, outraged by these excesses, were said to have left the program and complained to him. He even hinted, without identifying his sources, that the federated colleges were deeply disturbed by this infringement on their territory. Hoskin was challenged to answer these allegations.[137] Meanwhile, seeking a broader base of support, Blake forwarded a copy of this letter to Nathaniel Burwash, head of Victoria University. The conflict threatened to escalate beyond manageable proportions.

Much now hinged on the attitude of Burwash. His powerful voice could have shaken the university to its very foundations. In the event, however, Blake had badly misjudged his man. Victoria's chancellor was no narrow dogmatist, nor was he prepared to view the issue solely in terms of his own institution's interests. An architect of federation, Burwash was wedded to the concept and determined to make it work. On scriptural matters, although cautious, he was tolerant of new ideas. In this regard, he had tried to shield Workman from the blasts of Carmen and continued to regret that the professor had lacked the sense to hold his tongue at crucial moments.[138] Thus Burwash placed Blake's irate letter in a larger perspective and urged restraint. He was unmoved by the lawyer's diatribe against the higher criticism. A 'candid search for truth' he replied, need never be feared. He could agree that the teaching in oriental languages was technically ultra vires and added that if it were to be done 'it should not come in by any back door.' This, however, was as much as he would concede to Blake. In fact, he went on to suggest that it would be wise to legalize the teaching of religious knowledge at University College in order to ensure that the Bible was examined closely by students who had no affiliation with the denominational schools. Thus, like Falconer, he suggested that the whole affair could best be settled by an amendment of the University Act.[139]

In the midst of this exchange, even before Burwash had issued a formal reply, Blake resigned as a governor of the university on 28 December. At heart a friend of Varsity, he resisted the temptation to drag the government into the fray. His letter to Whitney cited lack of time as the only reason for his resignation.[140] Meanwhile, he pressed his former colleagues on the board to launch an official investigation. Counting on significant support from the federated colleges, he was shocked when in early January Burwash counselled compromise. In an instant, the best trumps had been stripped from his hand. Bitterly disappointed and livid with rage, he spurned the suggestion of a peaceful settlement. 'No my dear Chancellor,' he thundered, 'I abhor the thought that our Toronto University should aid in the work of shaking men's confidence in the Bible as being the Word of God.'[141] Although stunned, Blake was in no mood to quit. Instead, his hopes now fastened on a committee of inquiry established by the governors on 11 February 1909. For the next few months the investigation would proceed in an atmosphere of mounting tension and growing public interest.

The attack on University College was no isolated incident. Rather, it was part of a general reaction by religious conservatives against what they viewed as a dangerous trend towards scriptural and moral laxity in society at large. A whole way of life seemed threatened, not only by higher critics, but also, one suspects, by immigrants, unionists, and the general pace of change. Challenged, but not subdued, they counter-attacked along a broad front in Canada and the United States. The activities of Blake and company were merely local manifestations of a larger phenomenon. In this regard, Carmen and Harris were particularly busy throughout 1909. The fiery Baptist, when not engaged in stalking Eakin, was testing his mettle against two McMaster professors, I.G. Matthews and George Cross, both of whom, he suspected, were heretics. Life was made sufficiently unpleasant for Cross that he eagerly accepted an attractive offer from Chicago, where his modern views were welcome. Matthews, however, remained and was subjected to increasing pressure until a special committee declared him to be orthodox in May.[142] For his part, Carmen was hot on the trail of yet another modernist at Victoria. This time it was the Reverend George Jackson who felt the sting of his lash. The newly recruited professor had delivered an address on Genesis which at second hand rang heretical in Carmen's sensitive ear. Without pausing to examine the original lecture, the ageing Methodist pilloried Jackson in the press. In the process, he alienated at least two university governors, Joseph Flavelle and Chester Massey, who openly supported his intended victim.[143] Inevitably, his activities did little to aid his case against University College. The Carmen-Jackson dispute raged on and off for a year until both Victoria and the Methodist General Conference came down strongly on the side of the latter. Meanwhile, the conflict served to intensify the already heated atmosphere at the university.

Meeting in the library of Osgoode Hall, the investigating committee interviewed the various parties in the University College case throughout late February and March.[144] Blake had drafted a lengthy pamphlet outlining his charges, and this was used as the initial basis of discussion.[145] At the first session on 23 February the committee, chaired by D. Bruce Macdonald, called on Eakin and his chief, McCurdy, to answer Blake's allegations. Eakin assured his listeners that he approached the Bible strictly as a historical and literary document. When asked if students had ever been shocked by his interpretations, he responded that none had expressed concern. He went on to declare that he shunned theology altogether in the classroom. McCurdy added that this was typical of the department as a whole. Falconer then stepped in to clarify the point. He prodded Eakin to explain that what he did was merely to provide annotations of a non-theological kind as a gloss on the text. Meredith, while accepting their defence, was still uneasy. 'Isn't it our business,' he inquired, 'as a Provincial University, if certain things give offense to avoid teaching them unless it is necessary to do so?' At this point Walker interjected that 'we are entitled to use all proper criticism for the purpose of getting at the truth.' Seizing this opening, Falconer warned that once censorship was applied, there would be little room left for free investigation. 'To be consistent,' he argued, 'I think you would have to go through the whole University and cut out probably fifty per cent of the work, and use the blue pencil freely and say "You must not teach that because it is contrary to somebody's views."' Sensitive though he was to external criticism, Falconer clearly saw that there were other important dimensions to academic freedom beyond the mere avoidance of political interference. Those who have portrayed him as a man willing to sacrifice all for the sake of good public relations have exaggerated their case.[146]

Harris and his friends were due to testify on 22 March. Two weeks before the appointed hour, however, they seriously compromised any hopes they might have had for a sympathetic hearing. Perhaps sensing, not unreasonably, that the committee was already biased against them, they threw caution to the winds and aired their complaints in the press.[147] The *Globe* and even the usually critical *Star* came down strongly on the side of Eakin and University College.[148] The *Evening Telegram,* however, condemned the teaching of religious knowledge at Varsity, and the views of its editors could have had only a negative influence on the university's leaders: 'If the Board of Governors is incapable of acting upon this recognition of truth and duty, the Ontario Legislature ought to intervene and secularize the University of Toronto once and for all.'[149] This prononuncement was like waving a red flag in front of an anxious bull, where men like Walker, Flavelle, Meredith, and Falconer were concerned. For the next few weeks the papers were full of articles examining the merits of various arguments and comparing the dispute with the equally sensational Carmen-Jackson feud. On 12 March Blake intensified his efforts by publishing two angry letters to Bruce Macdonald in the columns of the *Star* in which he implied that the committee was a farce and had prejudged the issue. Desperate and verging on hysteria, he sensed a deep-laid plot. University College, Knox, and even Queen's, he intimated, were partners in a sinister scheme to foster the higher criticism.[150]

While Blake fulminated, Toronto's pulpits echoed the sounds of battle. Lumping the Eakin affair with events at Victoria, the Reverend J.E. Starr of Berkeley Street Methodist Church asked: 'Shall it be Jesus or Jackson?' Dr Winchester of Knox Presbyterian cheered Blake on, noting that Germany, where 'the prisons were full and the churches empty,' was reaping a harvest sown by higher critics. Others, however, took Blake to task for stirring up a 'theological tempest in a teapot.' Castigating the lawyer and his allies, one Congregationalist preacher observed that 'the Roman Catholics have a pope in Italy and we Protestants have any amount of them right here in Toronto.'[151] Methodist pastor Dr Eber Crummy denounced the 'incarnate selfishness' of those who insisted on conformity of scriptural interpretation.[152] And on and on the controversy raged. The very nightmare Falconer had dreaded since coming to Toronto was now hard upon him. He wrote to Walter Murray of the 'hurricane' that had 'knocked our hats off.' Still, he was confident. Legal advisers had assured him that the university was on solid ground. When it came right down to it, he told his friend, he and the governors were 'not going to be run by Sam Blake and Elmore Harris.'[153]

The air was thick with tension on 22 March when Harris and his associates appeared before Macdonald's committee. Speaking for Carmen and the others, the Baptist began by reviewing the history of the case. He then cited the opinions of the *Evening Telegram* concerning the possible need for government mediation. Warming to his theme, Harris damned the higher criticism and all its agents and ended by calling for the abolition of the oriental languages department. Meredith and Flavelle were quick off the mark, responding that the accusations might carry more weight if Harris did not insist on imputing dark motives to everyone. The situation had become very personal indeed. Burwash, preoccupied with the Jackson controversy, refused to be drawn into the argument. Instead, he proclaimed himself happy to trust to the good judgment of the committee and washed his hands of the whole affair. Carmen, for once in a relatively placid mood, said little. McLaren simply urged Macdonald to apply the law. Before leaving the chamber, Harris added that 'I have nothing in heart but the good of young people and the good of the University.' This completed the taking of evidence in the matter. In subsequent sessions one of Harris's key witnesses, a student, reversed his testimony against Eakin, admitting that he had never actually attended class. Another student complainant had earlier been discredited by Hutton, who revealed that he had once been in an insane asylum and had since dropped out to work in a local Jewish mission. A series of slick pamphlets published by Blake were designed to keep up pressure on the committee but appear to have had little effect on its further deliberations.[154] The affair was winding down.

In mid-April Falconer wrote to Zebulon Lash to congratulate him on his preliminary draft concerning the legal question. Lash was a noted attorney and, ironically, a partner of Blake in one of Toronto's most prestigious law firms. In substance, the statement provided the basis of the committee's formal report to the governors in December. The charges against University College were described as ill-founded, but the board was urged to warn instructors against raising theological issues in order to head off any future difficulties. Falconer considered the findings 'admirable' and expressed his confidence in the ability of professors to

draw the proper distinction between theological and literary analysis.[155]
The last few months had been harrowing, and he was glad to put the
whole business to rest. As the dust of battle cleared, however, he may well
have paused to reflect on some positive aspects revealed by the crisis. The
new administrative machinery, after all, had worked rather well in coping
with (or was it 'suppressing'?) a potentially damaging situation. Similarly,
with the exception of Blake, the governors had stood firm under
considerable pressure. It was good to know they could be relied on for
more than garden-party support. Just as heartening was the evidence of
loyalty among the federated colleges. Above all, however, the president
could rejoice that Whitney was as good as his word. The university had
been left alone to sort out its own problems, first with the hospital and
then with Sam Blake. For the time, at least, the ghost of Loudon had been
laid to rest. To Falconer, who had great plans for the University of
Toronto, these developments were very reassuring.

CHAPTER VI

The Organic University

The polar star was not always clearly visible to one engulfed in a morass of administrative detail. Moving abruptly from the intimacy of a small college to the complexity of Canada's largest university, Falconer at times felt like a raw and much harried apprentice. Inundated with committee work, he complained to Walter Murray at Christmas 1907 that he scarcely had time to breathe, let alone reflect. Still, the labour had to be done, and he conceded that 'through it one gets to know thoroughly the working of the machine.' Slowly, he was coming to master the intricacies of his new post as he beavered away at the daily routine. Not content merely to play it by ear, Falconer was also reading broadly on the subject of university administration, carefully sifting the experience of others in search of helpful hints. 'The amount of varied information I have imported during the past few months,' he told Murray, 'exceeds all that I ever acquired before in the like period.' He went on to express the vain hope that 'possibly the large situation will resolve itself into a multitude of small duties to be done faithfully every day, so that the great problems may by degrees solve themselves.' In his heart, however, he recognized that the university required not piecemeal supervision but purposeful leadership at that juncture in its history. Moreover, it was sobering to realize that much of the responsibility for furnishing a galvanizing impulse fell on his shoulders. 'My hope,' he confided to his friend, 'is that I may always be able to do the right thing with courage and not drift into the easiest course.'[1]

In his mind, the effort to infuse the University of Toronto with a coherent sense of purpose was a far more basic, compelling, and difficult chore than fending off a Sam Blake. Strife and penury in the Loudon era had sponsored confusion and drift. Granted, the reforms of 1906 had conferred a new lease on life, but Falconer knew that this golden opportunity could easily be lost unless a clear vision of the university's nature and function were articulated and acted upon. Such was the message he conveyed to an alumni gathering in February 1908. Toronto, he informed his hosts, had for too long lacked a 'cohesive plan.' Without one, he warned, very little real progress would ever be achieved.[2] There was, of course, no dearth of models from which inspiration might be drawn. On the contrary, the western academic world was fairly awash with speculation concerning 'the idea of a university.' Falconer, as it happened, came to power in an age of intense debate which spawned myriad and often conflicting theories of higher education. Americans, in particular, were hurling forth suggestions and devising experiments hand over fist. In the midst of a period of change, therefore, it fell to Falconer to delineate a vision appropriate to the needs and character of what he hoped would be Canada's national university. Typically, in this he drew not on one but on several different streams of thought.

Informed observers recognized that the differences among universities throughout Europe and North America were seldom absolute. A variety of goals and modes of organization was often housed under the same roof, and national boundaries were no guarantee of homogeneity. What differences existed were frequently those of circumstance and nuance rather than of kind. Even so, there were many who felt that certain emphases were sufficiently pronounced to warrant the drawing of a distinction among fundamental ideals. In 1906, for example, the American, Lymon Abbott, isolated three such basic concepts in an attempt to differentiate among English, German, and American universities. The English university, he argued, was dedicated to broad 'culture' and the development of 'gentlemen.' Germany, on the other hand, produced an institution geared to intensive 'scholarship' for its own sake. For its part, he continued, the American university found a raison d'être in preparing the young for 'service' to society.[3] As a description of national experiences this analysis was undoubtedly superficial. Thus, the English 'redbrick' of that day answered the call to practical 'service' as eagerly as the American 'land grant' college or the University of Saskatchewan under Walter Murray.[4] At the same time, Oxford and Cambridge, although continuing to extol the virtues of a liberal education, borrowed heavily from Germany in elevating disinterested research to a place of honour. Still far from utilitarian in outlook, Oxbridge nevertheless was becoming self-consciously 'productive' in the realm of 'pure learning.'[5] Meanwhile, in the birthplace of *wissenschaft* itself, German universities were often forced to accept a compromise between dispassionate scholarship and the demands of the state. All too frequently, ministers of education, who guarded the public purse, insisted on ideological conformity and interfered in order to foster their own notions of what constituted useful knowledge.[6] On the other side of the Atlantic, contemporary America offered a bewildering array of developments. The 'Wisconsin idea,' combining research with intimate involvement in local government planning, captivated many of the mid-western state universities.[7] Johns Hopkins, on the other hand, trumpeted a doctrine of unalloyed scholarship and eschewed a philosophy of simple utility. Yale continued to harbour an older liberal tradition which found its inspiration in 'culture.' In addition, a large number of denominational colleges promoted a less secular version of the cultural ideal.

If Abbott's attempt to stereotype British, German, and American practice left much to be desired, his identification of three broad ideals, at least, stood on firmer theoretical ground. Culture, scholarship, and service had each found its champions among those who sought to define the essence of higher education. The cultural position had nowhere been more clearly or forcefully stated than in John Henry Newman's classic, *The Idea of a University*. In the 1850s that prince of the Roman Catholic church had defined the university as 'a place of *teaching* universal knowledge.'[8] According to Newman, 'the implication was that its object is, on the one hand, intellectual not moral; and, on the other, that it is the diffusion and extension of knowledge rather than the advancement.'[9] Newman's vision has been characterized as an undergraduate ideal, a reflection of the unreformed Oxford in whose life he had played so distinguished a part.[10] The worthy cardinal, in any event, had had little patience with those who would deliver the university into the hands of research scholars and the professions. 'If its object,' he contended, 'were scientific and philosophical discovery, I do not see why a University should have students.'[11] He went on to recommend a division of labour between the university and the independent academy. In part, this suggestion mirrored an assumption that 'to discover and to teach are distinct functions; they are also distinct gifts, and are not commonly found united in the same person.'[12] Thus, while specialized academicians laboured to push back the frontiers of knowledge, university men would offer broad instruction in liberal studies, which Newman took to include not only the humanities but also the theoretical sciences.

A liberal education, he believed, had two basic and closely related purposes. One was to cultivate a 'philosophical habit,' which, being its own end, was 'independent of sequel.' He scorned those who interpreted this process as a vague exercise in 'viewness' in which nothing was learned soundly and intellectual excellence was a thing unknown. On the contrary, declared Newman, the foremost task was always to impress on the student 'the idea of science, method, principle and system.'[13] In truth, he was far less concerned with *what* was studied than with *how* it was taught. Insisting on the oneness of knowledge, he was anxious to promote a breadth of mind and a 'connected view of things.' Hence, the emphasis on system and method. Of the student he wrote: 'Let him once gain this habit of method, of starting from fixed points, of making his ground good as he goes, of distinguishing what he knows from what he does not know, and I conceive he will be gradually initiated into the largest and truest philosophical views, and will feel nothing but impatience and disgust at the random theories and imposing sophistries and dashing paradoxes, which carry away half-formed and superficial intellects.'[14] A mind so fashioned, he asserted, could later grapple easily with any advanced science or profession. The core of this idea proved durable and adaptable. Thus in 1976 Lord Ashby, the celebrated educational theorist, could still proclaim that the mastery of intellectual systems remained the unique function of the university. Newman's shade might have whispered a heartfelt 'Amen' when the master of Clare College went on to state that a liberal education entailed 'a spirit of pursuit, not a choice of subject.'[15]

The second major function of a university, in Newman's estimation, was a natural consequence of the first: to produce 'gentlemen.' He was not primarily concerned with propping up an existing social order, nor was he interested in implanting the 'manners and habits' of a privileged class in his students. These attributes, he pointed out, were, for good or ill, acquired elsewhere. Instead, Newman was anxious to foster the 'force, the steadiness, the comprehensiveness and the versatility of the intellect' that characterized the enlightened individual.[16] Sobriety, candour, reasonableness, and self-control, these were the qualities of the liberally educated man. On one point, however, he was adamant. The university, properly understood, could impart the virtues of civility, but it was not a school of morality or a guardian of faith.[17] Religious and moral instruction were the province of other agencies, principally the church and the home. Distinguishing, rather atypically for his generation, between the Christian and the gentleman, Newman described a university that was resolutely secular in its approach to 'intellectual culture.'

Newman's treatise, while perhaps the most famous, was by no means the only version of the cultural ideal. One highly influential variation on the theme was of older vintage but continued to attract adherents.

Newman's contemporary, E.B. Pusey, canon of Christ Church and professor of Hebrew at Oxford, was one of its most outspoken proponents. Unlike Newman, Pusey was deeply suspicious of the intellect. In consequence, he clung to a traditional position which allotted a moral and religious role to the university. Its purpose, he declared, 'is, with and through the disciplines of the intellect, as far as may be, to discipline and train the whole moral and intelligent being.'[18] The good canon, moreover, was not pleading his case in isolation. 'Mental and moral discipline,' indeed, were the watchwords of paternalistic American colleges before the Civil War and continued to be heard, although in competition with other ideas, long after that event.[19] In Canada, the same notion struck particularly deep roots and a tradition of 'moral concern' remained a potent force at all levels of education well into the twentieth century.[20] In Falconer's day it often surfaced as a call to mould 'character.' Altogether, the concept of a malleable liberal education gave the cultural ideal great strength and resilience whether it assumed an intellectual or a moral form. Many of Falconer's American contemporaries who adhered to the so-called 'general education movement' liked to put their case quite simply. 'There is,' read the calendar of Columbia University, 'a certain minimum of ... [the western] intellectual and spiritual tradition that a man must experience and understand if he is to be called educated.'[21]

There were those, however, who felt that the essence of a university lay not in undergraduate instruction but in professional scholarship and advanced research. Surprisingly, the most uncompromising statements of this position issued not from Germany, but from the United States. After 1865 thousands of Americans flocked to Germany in pursuit of higher education.[22] Inspired by the modern laboratories, the cut and thrust of the graduate seminar, and the professionalism of research, they returned eager to duplicate the model at home. In this movement one returning scholar was prepared to take the lead. Thus, when called to head the newly founded Johns Hopkins University in 1876, Daniel Coit Gilman drew on German precedents in developing the first great American graduate school. The 'Göttingen of Baltimore,' although having an undergraduate section, devoted itself primarily to pure research and the training of advanced scholars in a broad range of specializations. In short order, the experiment inspired widespread emulation as Columbia, Michigan, Yale, Harvard, and a host of others followed suit, at least at the graduate level. By 1900 a flourishing graduate school was taken to be a necessary hallmark of any college seeking university status.[23] But, as many have noted, America borrowed selectively from Germany. The contemplative and idealistic elements in *wissenschaft* had been neglected. German methods were emphasized above German theory. 'The continued lofty evocation by nearly all Germans of an underlying spiritual unity was ignored by research-minded Americans,' many of whom 'identified scientific specialization with the entire purpose of the university.'[24] William Rainey Harper was such a one. Of the recently established University of Chicago he said in the 1890s that 'it is proposed in this institution to make the work of investigation primary, the work of giving instruction secondary.'[25] Professors were promoted on the strength of publication, while the first two years of undergraduate training were hived off and described as 'junior college.' Newman must have clawed his casket's lid in rage.

The most strident expression of the 'scholarly' ideal was penned by Thorstein Veblen. Himself a product of Johns Hopkins, Veblen published his *Higher Learning in America* in 1918, although most of it had been written before the Great War. Alarmed by the encroachments of a burgeoning 'business culture,' he strove 'to preserve the value-free objectivity of the research university.'[26] As he saw it, the university was a self-contained, self-justifying, faculty-centred institution. It was, he wrote, 'a body of mature scholars and scientists, the "faculty" – with whatever plant and other equipment may incidentally serve as appliances for their work.'[27] Pure, disinterested research by highly specialized experts was its sole legitimizing purpose. With Newman he believed that teaching and the advancement of knowledge were incompatible. However, he turned the cardinal's vision on its head in maintaining that the undergraduate college bore 'no peculiarly close relation to the university as a seat of learning.'[28]

Radically opposed in so many ways, Newman and Veblen could at least agree that the university should remain detached from the pragmatic, the vocational, and the ephemeral. The Englishman wished to cultivate 'a wisdom, safe from the excesses and vagaries of individuals, embodied in institutions which have stood the trial and received the sanction of the ages.'[29] The American wanted to liberate investigators from the corrupting influence of 'captains of industry' who would lure them into the lesser realm of applied studies.[30] Each, in his own way, rejected the utilitarian concept of a university devoted to 'service.' Thus, for example, both harboured grave reservations about the growth of professional education. Veblen, in particular, was convinced that such training sullied the university spirit, and he urged its expulsion from the halls of higher learning.[31]

But the call to 'service,' which went beyond merely nurturing the professions, attracted many university leaders. At its crudest, it encouraged a simple catering to the direct and immediate needs of the local economy. Accordingly, the 'A and M' colleges of post-Civil War America specialized in turning out technologically literate agronomists and engineers. In another guise, however, service took the form of an effort to bring university resources to bear on the larger problems spawned by an increasingly complex society. Hence, American 'Progressives,' committed to programs of social reform, called on universities for advice, and many answered. Prominent among these was the University of Wisconsin, under C.R. Van Hise, who turned his institution into a kind of 'teacher-counselor-companion to the people at large.'[32] There and elsewhere the social sciences blossomed as students were 'prepared for life.' Settlement houses flourished. Professional schools expanded and broadened in variety. Extension courses multiplied rapidly as service-conscious universities made useful learning more accessible. Professors were seconded to governments as expert advisers. Civic idealism, it seemed, was running high and not only in America. Scores of Oxonians, their consciences awakened by T.H. Green, served their social apprenticeship in the slums of East London. A few, such as H.H. Asquith, would go on to help fashion the reform legislation of the Edwardian period. Others, like A.L. Smith, who chose an academic life, emerged as leading figures in the extension movement and powerful allies of the Workers' Educational Association.[33] In another sphere, Jowett's Balliol College, reverberating with the master's credo of duty, became a prolific breeder of imperial civil servants.[34]

In far-off Canada as well, the idea of service won support. William Peterson at his 1893 inauguration spoke of the need to make McGill 'a centre of practical usefulness.' Although a humanist by training and proclivity, he recognized the need to fit his university into the context of a commercial city such as Montreal. Under him new departments such as those of social service, commerce, dentistry, and physical education were established. Pragmatic benefactors, headed by businessmen such as Sir William Macdonald and Lord Strathcona, focused their generosity principally on science and medicine. In time Peterson may have regretted his inaugural remarks, since the arts at McGill failed to keep pace with 'practical' studies. Still, it was difficult to argue with success as enrolments and endowments swelled.[35] On the prairies, the philosopher Walter Murray surprised many when, as president, he developed the University of Saskatchewan in imitation of the Wisconsin model. Under his approving eye, great emphasis was placed on extension work among farm boys. Although the arts were not neglected, special attention was lavished on the promotion of agricultural science and the encouragement of professional studies.[36] Less overtly utilitarian but just as heavily charged with the ideal of service was the so-called 'Queen's spirit' inspired by G.M. Grant in the 1890s and carried forward by the likes of D.M. Gordon, Adam Shortt, Salem Bland, and O.D. Skelton in later decades. Shouldering a self-imposed mission to the nation, this relatively small university produced a disproportionately large number of innovative social scientists, fiery social gospellers, and influential civil servants.[37]

In the debate about the nature of a university, some, like Newman and Veblen, were ready to push their conclusions to logical extremes. Others, however, were prepared to see the ideals of culture, scholarship, and service as complementary rather than mutually exclusive principles. Mark Pattison of Lincoln College, Oxford, for example, as early as 1868 set forth a moderate, assimilative position in his *Suggestions on Academical Organization*. He insisted that teaching and research were perfectly compatible and went on to proclaim that Oxford should be regarded as a national institution which served the public interest in preserving and advancing pure learning.[38] This notion, of course, was a long way from the 'Wisconsin idea' of direct service to the state, but it can be described as an early, if tentative, footfall on the road to a reconciliation of the three major concepts of a university. On the whole, the future lay with those who, with varying emphases, promoted such a synthesis. Indeed, there has been in the twentieth century a gradual evolution towards what Clark Kerr in 1963 christened the 'multiversity,' an institution performing several functions at one and the same moment.[39] In the Canadian context this concept was forcefully outlined in 1965 by one of Falconer's successors at Toronto, Claude T. Bissell. A great university, he declared, displayed four basic characteristics. It was a stronghold of learning in 'the pure theoretical subjects,' the fundamental disciplines from which all others derived. It also combined teaching with the advancement of knowledge. Furthermore, it struck a balance between long-range and short-term goals, between a responsibility to disinterested learning and a duty to contemporary society. Finally, the ideal university preserved within itself a 'sense of community,' a wholeness, however diverse and specialized its many branches might become.[40] Had he lived to hear it, Falconer would have applauded much of what Bissell had to say. In his own day, after all, he was, perhaps, the most outspoken and influential Canadian champion of the many-faceted but organically integrated university.

In a revealing letter, Falconer once wrote to congratulate E.W. Beatty, president of the Canadian Pacific Railway, on an address the latter had delivered to McGill undergraduates. 'I am sure,' he told that corporate executive, *that a large element in the value of education of the university is the development in this free atmosphere of the personal powers of the undergraduate, and that if he learns to take a share in the life of the university he is beginning to develop powers that afterwards will be of great value to the community. Always, however, the difficulty is to know where the balance should be. We need men of character in public life. I do not mean only in political life, but men in public life that makes up all the interests of the community. At the same time as Canadians we require highly developed intellect to cope with the rising powers of the world at large. The combination of a developing brain power and a growing character is what we should aim at in all university training.*[41]

Written in 1926, this statement, in fact, could have been drafted at any point during Falconer's tenure. While loosely phrased, it accurately displayed the breadth of his university ideal. Culture, scholarship, and service: each of these concepts appealed to him. Indeed, in a well-rounded university, he thought them inseparable. Consequently, he was ready to sponsor development in several directions, but he did have definite priorities. The University of Toronto, he insisted, had to have a common, life-giving spirit. It required what Bissell would later describe as 'a sense of community.' Thus, while fostering scholarship and service, Falconer accorded special emphasis to his own version of the cultural ideal, which alone, he thought, could supply that much needed unifying factor.

'A university,' he asserted, 'is not a set of public utility schools bundled together by the tie of a common adminstration, nor yet a machine compacted of many parts.' On the contrary, he argued, 'it is an organism with an intellectual, nay a moral spirit, which gives it unity and life.' Like any living thing, he explained, the university had a 'structural integrity.' Energy coursed from an inner core to the remotest tips, encouraging growth and renewal 'by a process of assimilation.' Furthermore, just as, despite superficial changes, 'the individual persists from childhood to old age,' so also the essence of the university remained immutable.[42] Across all faculties, said Falconer, the bonding agent, the 'assimilative' principle, should be an earnest pursuit of the ideal. In following this star, he added, the university would produce graduates of strong moral character who would constitute its greatest gift to society. A man of character, he believed, could be trusted in positions of leadership. He would always take the broad view because he would be 'in permanent possession of moral qualities.'[43] As such, he would be an idealist, one who believed 'that moral forces are finally dominant.'[44] First and foremost a *man*, his gaze would extend beyond mere specialized knowledge. Clearly, in moving to

Toronto, Falconer had not shed his long-standing distrust of the unbridled intellect. Greatly as he valued 'brain power,' he was even more anxious to 'breed men.' Hence, in his inaugural address he cautioned that 'the man must not be lost in the physician, the engineer, the clergyman, the teacher.' As at Pine Hill, so at Toronto, the graduate was counselled to be alien from nothing truly human. Therefore, despite a change of venue, Falconer continued to urge that the intellectual and the moral be cultivated in tandem. Only in this way, he maintained, could character be nurtured while the mind was honed razor sharp. Summing up, he declared that 'it is as creators of intellectual and moral idealism that universities fulfil their supreme function.'[45]

On the surface, these statements might seem little more than a reiteration of the views Falconer had espoused in Halifax. To some extent, this was true. The intellect, after all, was still expected to answer to the spirit. He was not, however, so naïve as to think that he could project unaltered on Varsity an ideal more appropriate to a small sectarian college. In the transition from Presbyterian seminary to provincial university, Falconer made full allowance for the secular nature of his new charge. At Pine Hill he, like Pusey, had employed the terms 'moral' and 'religious' almost interchangeably. At Toronto that practice stopped. Such restraint, of course, was only prudent. Had he sounded a religious note, he would have been pilloried by colleagues, government, and public alike. Nevertheless, while impelled by expediency, he was also prompted by conviction to adjust his approach. The Falconers of Pictou, it will be recalled, were firm believers in the separation of church and state. Similarly, Alex and his sons were ardent supporters of public education. Robert, in particular, had long urged that Nova Scotia's numerous denominational colleges be federated with Dalhousie. Moreover, he vigorously denied that non-sectarian universities were implicitly godless institutions. At his inauguration he made that point clear: 'Did I for a moment imagine that there is any antagonism between the spirit and ideals of a State university and essential Christianity, certainly I should not be addressing you here to-day.' The university, he pointed out, while having no direct religious function, could not fail, in the long run, to promote an atmosphere congenial to the highest religious aspirations.[46] Comfortable in his new office, he experienced no crisis of conscience. In his own mind, he had compromised no principle nor suffered any diminution of purpose in coming to Toronto.

When he spoke as president, Falconer did so primarily as an idealist and only incidentally as a professing Christian. In orientation, therefore, the spirit he touted at Toronto was broadly humane rather than specifically religious. Nowhere was this attitude more evident than in his numerous elaborations on the moral function of a public university. Of these pronouncements, perhaps the most precise is to be found in an article entitled 'Functions of State and Church in Education.' Here he noted that, among other things, the university trained people for specific careers; in addition, it prepared them for their larger role as citizens. These, he admitted, were worthy undertakings. But he emphasized that the duty of the educator went beyond these tasks, because above the specialist, above even the citizen, stood the man. He assumed that 'since good artisans should be good citizens, and if they are to be good citizens they must also be good men, the State should somehow provide an education which ... will create moral character.' Character, he argued, was not to be identified with social or even national 'good form.' Mere conformity with local conventions, he asserted, offered only a flimsy moral base. All too often, it left a man vulnerable in an alien environment. Drawing on Kipling and perhaps on Conrad as well, he noted 'how often where East meets West and "there ain't no ten commandments," the [westerner] finds his inherited decencies stripped from him, his good form a mere rag, and himself naked as a primitive human.' A worthwhile education, he contended, had to bestow something more universal, more enduring. At their best, of course, churches offered a great deal in this area. At their worst, they sometimes dispensed nothing more than Presbyterian, Methodist, or Baptist 'good form.' In either event, he felt that in a world of many creeds and manifold mores there was room for an agency that fostered a 'free and independent morality' based on 'the common virtues of humanity.' There was a need, in short, for the university and the idealism it purveyed.[47]

In this vein Falconer told a Hamilton audience in 1908 that people should 'be ruled by ideas that survive.' Illustrating the point, he drew a distinction between the savage and the civilized man. The difference, he indicated, was not primarily a physical or an organizational one. While admitting the importance of these factors, he nevertheless held that the fundamental divergence was in the realm of ideas. The savage, he explained, was prey to his emotions and normally took a short-range, utilitarian view of things. The civilized man, on the other hand, exhibited self-control and rose above the immediate to be guided by broader considerations. His advantage, said Falconer, was born not of biology but of training. It took a great deal of experience to recognize the permanent good. Only a trained mind, he thought, was capable of sound judgment. In his estimation, therefore, men were to be judged 'by the quality of the ideas they were able to discern.'[48] All these points, he felt, made the cardinal significance of education crystal clear. In this connection, Falconer was fond of inverting a favourite socialist formula in order to drive the point home. He argued that an educational substructure underpinned the economic, social, and political superstructure of a community.[49] Thus, he declared that general ideas, rather than specific information, deserved pride of place at the substructural level if society were to cultivate the arts of civilization. Hence his insistence that the university pursue the ideal.

Falconer, however, never suggested that approved moral maxims be doled out in the lecture hall. Rather, he merely wished to ensure that graduates would develop an ability to choose worthy ideals for themselves and acquire the discipline to live by them.[50] A higher morality would be the natural fruit of idealism. Discipline would result from hard intellectual toil and a growing recognition of the authority of universal truths. He hinted at this philosophy in an early address to undergraduates at Toronto. There was, he told them in 1908, 'an inherent authority' in an orderly universe which, if clearly perceived, kept the thinker free of eccentricity.[51] No more than Newman did Falconer advocate a vague education in 'viewness.' Professors were expected to treat their subjects in an objective and expert manner. But expert teaching, he maintained, involved more than imparting technical detail and a 'soulless professional efficiency.' The best instructor, in his opinion, went beyond the letter of his discipline to embrace and personify its spirit, its underlying principles – in a word, its ideals.[52] In addition to dwelling on particulars, his task was also to highlight the basic precepts of his study and, in broad perspective, place them on the spectrum of knowledge. In this way he would inevitably rear up 'truth-seekers' as well as adroit specialists. Under these circumstances, said Falconer, graduates were more likely to appreciate that 'life is set in a kingdom of law and order' and regulate their thought and conduct accordingly.[53]

This approach, Falconer emphasized, was applicable in all branches of the university. 'The spirit of the truth-seeker,' he proclaimed, 'is one.'[54] Thus, at his inauguration, he argued that it was a fallacy to speak of an antagonism between arts and science. Properly understood, he contended, both led back to the ideal.[55] 'In science,' he observed in 1909, 'a man is shown facts as they are, not as he thinks they are or as he would like them to be'; it was 'a splendid exercise in truth.'[56] 'The true scientific spirit,' he wrote elsewhere, 'is always intellectually eager, always ready to scale the next mountain range over against the valley in which this period of our life's broken history finds its transient abode.'[57] In this sense, he urged that the questing, humble, disinterested ethos of 'pure science' pervade the whole university.[58] In applied studies, such as engineering and forestry, this outlook could be nurtured by reminding students of their reliance on 'pure' disciplines such as physics or chemistry. As for professional education, Falconer had no qualms about enlarging its place within the University of Toronto, so long as those enrolled were first given a solid grounding in general knowledge. The object, he maintained, was to educate 'honorable and efficient specialists who will by their own character set the living standards for the professions.'[59] In these occupations, he believed, 'a mercenary motive is never far off, but it is always corrupting.' He told dental students in 1922 that the only antidote was a good dose of liberal education. Even a dentist had to understand the whole man and 'know the organism on its mechanical, psychological and personal sides.'[60] In general, his advice to students was similar to that offered by the American philosopher, Josiah Royce. Speaking at Harvard, Royce once counselled undergraduates to study the methods and philosophy of their specialization, whatever it happened to be. In this way, he contended, they would be liberated from subservience to routine detail and 'make of [their] technicality a humanity.'[61] With Royce and Newman, Falconer held that a liberal education involved a perspective more than a selection of subject matter.

Even so, he was convinced that certain studies promoted an apprehension of the ideal more effectively than others. In this respect, he believed that the arts, particularly the humanities, had a special role to play. From them, he maintained, there radiated a spirit which should inform the whole university. Thus, in his inaugural address he described the arts as the very core of any institution of higher learning.[62] Again in 1922, he observed that great literature was the best vehicle for liberating the powers of the mind.[63] Similarly, in the last year of his life Falconer wrote that 'it is in the humanities that the spirit of the university has its inmost home', because they concerned 'man as a person, his real self' and the highest things to which he aspired.[64] In practical terms this meant sustaining the arts against the mounting claims of other faculties. In his first presidential report, Falconer noted the pressure on resources that increased enrolment in professional and applied departments was causing. He flatly refused, however, to divert support from the arts into other channels. To do so, he argued, would be to weaken the fabric of the entire institution.[65] Underscoring this point, he wrote to Premier Whitney a few weeks later to urge that, while fees in applied science went up, those in arts should be held down. The tendency at that moment, he explained, was to rush headlong into professional training. But this course of action, he averred, meant 'a loss of breadth and in the long run a crippling of the professional classes in the Province.' His desire was in future to extract a much larger arts requirement from all vocational candidates. To secure this end, he advised that access to the humanities 'should be kept within the reach of as many as possible.'[66]

His bias towards the arts was one specific expression of Falconer's overall devotion to the 'cultural' ideal, but there were others as well. He exhibited a paternalistic alarm at the growing impersonalization of university life. Character, he thought, could not be bred by contact with an anonymous machine. A number of American contemporaries had reached a similar conclusion. Thus, before the war Woodrow Wilson at Princeton and A.L. Lowell at Harvard were striving to reinject a personal note by building or expanding residence halls and establishing a preceptorial system.[67] At Toronto, of course, the federated colleges had long answered this need for some students, a situation in which Falconer rejoiced. Still, as he recognized, there were large numbers who could not share in such intimacy. Accordingly, he was frequently on the prowl for endowments to support new university residences. Perhaps his greatest success was scored late in his tenure with the founding of Whitney Hall.

No single contribution to the corporate life of the student body captured Falconer's imagination quite as fully as the establishment of Hart House. The endowment was all the better, from his vantage point, because it came as an almost wholly unexpected windfall. As he later recalled events, Falconer had gone cap in hand to Chester Massey to ask that he endow an organ for Convocation Hall. He was optimistic that this request would be fulfilled, since the Masseys had long been generous benefactors of the university and had displayed a keen interest in music as well. Compared, for example, with their support of the Faculty of Household Science, an organ costing a mere $20,000 seemed modest. Falconer broached the subject during a friendly chat with the multimillionaire. Meanwhile, in casual conversation, they discussed current efforts by friends to fund new quarters for the YMCA on campus. Massey, as it happened, was well acquainted with the project. Moreover, his son Vincent, a recent graduate, had impressed upon him the need for a building around which student life could centre. One thing led to another until, suddenly, Falconer was aware that Massey was quite prepared to finance just such a scheme. Seizing the moment, he at once replied that he would find money for the organ elsewhere. Meanwhile he sat enraptured as the tycoon unfolded this dazzling new vision. A few weeks later the Massey Foundation submitted a formal offer to finance the scheme and undertook to spend not less than $300,000. Ground was broken in 1911. Delayed by the onset of war, Hart House, so named in honour of Chester's father, was opened in 1919. A magnificent structure of gothic design, even Falconer remained ignorant of the final cost. 'The architects,' he later mused, 'seem to have been given almost *carte blanche* as to expense.' He speculated, however, that in the end well over five times the original offer had been expended. Still, he never for a moment doubted that it was worth every cent. Indeed, for him Hart House became a symbol in stone of the organic university he longed to fashion.[68]

This concern for the personal touch extended to pedagogical matters as well. Wherever possible, for example, Falconer thought that the Oxford tutorial system should be applied in order to combat the alienating effects of swelling enrolments.[69] He was supported and encouraged particularly by humanists, such as George Wrong, who had been reared in the Oxbridge tradition.[70] In another connection, his own experience at Edinburgh had led Falconer to appreciate the value of a core curriculum. He disapproved strongly of the American practice of allowing multiple electives in the early years and also frowned upon the credit system. Preferring a cognate approach to learning, he felt comfortable at Toronto, where a sympathetic faculty helped shape a general course which kept options to a minimum until a student entered his third year. At the undergraduate level his chief enthusiasms were reserved for the traditional honours program. Rejecting sometimes extreme Jacksonian tendencies in American higher education, Falconer was an unabashed élitist, at least in the intellectual sense. The most promising students, he argued, required special attention, if only for the ultimate good of society.[71] Under him there was no talk, as there was, for example, in Chicago, about the equality of students or their standing at graduation.[72] Instead, the University of Toronto sought out and deliberately streamed potential leaders. Yet even here early specialization was discouraged. Towards the end of his career, Falconer was critical of the growing rigidity and narrowness of the honours program, especially in the sciences. As a cure, he casually suggested resorting to the Oxbridge practice of framing comprehensive examinations in the final year.[73] In any case, he remained confident that even the most intense specialization could be combined with a pursuit of the ideal.

Viewed in perspective, Falconer's 'cultural' ideal was a marriage of the positions broadly represented by Newman and Pusey. Along with the latter and scores of earlier Canadian educators, he held that the university had a high moral purpose. However, he interpreted that moral function in predominantly secular terms and thus drew closer to Newman. Similarly, while there was an element of paternalism in his thought, Falconer had no desire to encourage a passive submission to authority.

Should the state, he wrote, 'merely train youth to be blindly obedient to its laws, it [would] dwarf the individual, sterilize his conscience, and prevent him from acquiring the character of a real man.'[74] Anxious to mould their character, Falconer could also be highly critical of Canadian students, who he thought lacked the curiosity, originality, and independence of their British counterparts.[75] Thus, while 'moral concern' constituted an important element in his outlook, so did a desire to stimulate the intellect. Indeed, in this latter regard, he went well beyond Newman in happily grafting aspects of the 'scholarly' ideal onto his conception of the complete university.

At Pine Hill Falconer had taken a keen interest in the promotion of graduate studies. By his own example, he had demonstrated that research and effective teaching could go hand in hand. Not surprisingly, therefore, his enthusiasm for these pursuits only increased when he took command of the University of Toronto. His position was clear from the very outset of his regime. 'The true university,' he said in 1907, 'is a centre for both instruction and research, for the impartation of knowledge already gained, and for the extension of the boundaries of knowledge.'[76] Pointedly, he observed in his first presidential report that Canada had to share in extending those boundaries or remain forever an intellectual backwater.[77] No simple 'nativist,' Falconer valued a free-flowing exchange of thought on the international front. But he had no desire to inhabit a mere colonial outpost, dependent on others for ideas and the men to inculcate them. To be healthy, he contended, the nation had to generate as well as absorb learning. As he explained to a Collingwood audience in 1909, 'we would not be worthy of our race if we were but simply reproductions of Britain.' Equally, Canadians were urged to avoid undue reliance on the United States: 'As a people, we must contribute a unique experience to the history of the world.' Moreover, he added, since thought never stood still, neither could institutions of higher learning. 'Universities,' he declared, 'in particular and in chief are the mediators between the old and the new, they are the transmitters of ideas for which men have fought and struggled, and they not only conserve these ideas in their purity, but adapt them to the new life on which each generation enters.'[78] Predictably, he felt that Varsity bore a special burden as Canada's largest university. Accordingly, he issued a fervent plea for the development of significant research and graduate work in Toronto.[79]

The object of advanced study, he argued, was to transform students into independent investigators. To Falconer, however, this change did not imply a constriction of vision. Instead, he thought that it should inspire the deepening of insight into essential principles. Unlike Veblen he envisaged graduate work as a natural extension of an effort begun in earlier years: it was an intensification of the quest for the ideal. Moreover, he asserted, a lively gaduate program would benefit the entire university. Living models would encourage younger students to excel. The key, as always for Falconer, lay in the approach. Much, inevitably, depended on the quality and outlook of the staff. Somewhat inconsistently, he maintained that, left to himself, the average graduate was tempted to burrow into one narrow corner of a discipline and lose touch with a higher reality. It was the duty of the high-minded teacher to rescue him from this abyss. Shaping his teaching to the character of each individual, the graduate professor was obliged to lead him onto a loftier plain while, at the same time, imparting technical expertise. For this delicate task, special men were needed, experts who combined insight and knowledge. Clear-eyed investigators in their own right, they would induce others to follow; for, as Falconer observed, research was 'essential to the life of a University and almost a necessity for good teaching.'[80] Yet he had no desire to create a group apart. Graduate instructors, he advised, should regularly teach at the undergraduate level. Younger students would profit greatly from their tuition; an awareness and continuity of ideals would be promoted, and there would be no sharp break between the two levels of instruction. For Falconer there were to be no gaps in the seamless fabric of the organic university.[81]

If scholarship found a ready welcome at Falconer's university, so did the concept of service. Many, of course, would have been justifiably shocked had it not, given the president's record at Pine Hill. Admittedly, at his inauguration, Falconer warned against yielding to demands 'for what is so often erroneously called the practical.' This pronouncement, however, was merely to advise that a slavish absorption in the superficial be eschewed. Not for a moment did he counsel that the university function as an ivory tower. Temples of ageless wisdom, universities in his opinion, were also 'useful' contemporary institutions. Indeed, as he said in 1908, they were 'sources from which thought will be translated into action.'[82] Sometimes that translation was direct, as, for example, when a university opened its own settlement house. More often, it assumed a subtler form as idealistic graduates in their many walks of life helped leaven the social loaf. In any case, Falconer was convinced that a university had to be not only in the world, but of it as well. Although he never pronounced systematically on this theme, he appears to have felt that universities had at least four major and often interrelated duties to society. Thus, they were called to nurture leaders, to provide salutory and disinterested criticism, to act as forces for harmony, and, as William Peterson put it, to function as centres of 'practical useful-ness.'

'The educated man,' said Falconer in 1907, 'should be the university's best advertisement in the community.'[83] Care, after all, was taken to mould his character not for his sake alone, but also to endow society with versatile, far-sighted leaders. If a proper balance were struck in his training, the graduate would be an adaptable member of the international community but one equipped 'primarily for service in his own country.' It would be a grievous error, claimed Falconer, to rear students as 'unattached world citizens' indifferent to the enthusiasms and problems of their native land.[84] Idealism was not to be confused with a bloodless stoicism. On the contrary, he thought that 'a thoroughly trained man ... becomes a useful man when his powers of judgment and observation are called into action in social and economic affairs.' Accordingly, even professional students were advised to bring their insight to bear on the troubles that were 'at the base of the body politic.'[85] The privilege of a higher education imposed a commensurate responsibility on an enlight-ened élite. It was a case of noblesse oblige. Speaking to graduates at the University of Alberta in 1913, Falconer rhapsodized somewhat floridly on this theme. His youthful listeners were told of their induction into 'a greater guild of chivalry than the chivalry of the medieval world.' Banners aloft, they were urged to sally forth 'as knights on an intellectual and moral quest.' These latter-day Galahads were enjoined 'to redress wrong' and 'to make this world better, to make it really good, but not for a select circle, not for the few.'[86] Inordinately fond of this image, a few years later Falconer dubbed university men the 'knights of the new democracies.'[87] Expansive flourishes aside, in less exalted moments he was content merely to observe that active citizenship was a cardinal duty of the graduate.[88]

On this score, Falconer emphasized that true leadership was both informed and even-handed. The world, he thought, had bigots, ideolog-ues, and demagogues aplenty. What it lacked in sufficient abundance was 'intelligent sympathy.' Consequently, he insisted that the university, as a seedbed of leaders and an agent of social amelioration, function not as an agitator but as a 'conciliator.' In the heat of the moment, as warring partisans shrieked, its task was 'to show the balance between extremes, to see history's ideals in the present.'[89] Enslaved by no special interest, its duty was to provide perspective, dispassionate criticism and expert advice. At his installation, Falconer declared that the university could not remain voiceless as social problems multiplied. On the other hand, as a state institution it was the property of all the people and had to stand above the rage of faction. In any event, he continued, its response should never be impetuous. Real progress, he asserted, came slowly. It was the hard-won fruit of accurate observation, patient analysis, and deep reflection, activities at which the university excelled. Purveyor of the scientific method, it was equipped to view questions impartially. Furthermore, it was obliged to pass this spirit on to the student. Indeed, said Falconer, the university should 'awaken in him human sympathies and the desire to emancipate his fellows from the ignorance and prejudice which are breeding evil.'[90] As president he himself frequently shouldered this burden. Thus, in 1909, he pointed out to students that Toronto offered an almost inexhaustible store of 'good object lessons' to those interested in diagnosing the nation's ills. He therefore invited them to take to the streets, where problems such as slum housing, immigration, and industrial exploitation could be studied at first hand. He cautioned them, however, not to approach these issues in a partisan spirit, but to think them through coolly.[91]

Obviously, Falconer was anxious to preserve the political neutrality of the university and the intellectuals who comprised it. In part this outlook was conditioned by Varsity's specific connection with the state. In larger measure, however, it was an attitude widely shared by academics of his generation. At Queen's, for example, James Cappon also viewed the university as 'a rational counterpoise to the transient whims of society.' With Falconer, he pictured scholars as a 'mediating class between the Government and the people,' offering advice to both but at one remove from the political arena. His colleague, Adam Shortt, counselled academics to remain aloof from politics lest they compromise their authority as unbiased critics. Closer to home, Maurice Hutton argued that universities could fulfil their highest function only so long as they adopted the pose of disinterested 'mediators' intent on educating enlightened leaders.[92] In time, younger scholars, such as Frank Underhill, would question these assumptions. To some of them, neutrality smacked of complicity in sustaining an unpalatable status quo. But this approach lay in the future. For the moment, Falconer represented the prewar mainstream and became deeply wedded to the conventional vision of the impartial university.

A reputation for impartiality, he thought, was essential if the university were to perform one of its most important services in promoting social harmony and national unity. As a mediator between social groups, Falconer held that the university should labour to deflate the notion that class antagonism was inevitable. Its duty, he imagined, was 'to get that idea out and thereby effect a social revolution of sentiment' based on a higher concept of liberty.[93] As tutor to the nation, the same institution was advised to denounce parochialism and advance a broad viewpoint. An avowed centralist, Falconer saw the university as a means of developing common values and a common culture in Canada. Reflecting calmly, it helped define worthy goals and spare the country 'those experiments which [had proved] to be baneful in older lands.' Graduates streaming to the farthest corners of the nation, ideals in tow, acted as unifying agents. After all, he reasoned, it was ideas and personal links, not institutions or legal enactments, which bound men together.[94]

However, for all his emphasis on lofty detachment, at times Falconer's notion of service could be eminently 'practical.' Recognizing, for example, that the demand for professional education would grow rather than abate, he thought it best that the university accommodate it. The alternative was to leave the dentist or engineer with no opportunity to broaden his vision. Never one to embrace half measures, in 1910 he hinted that the province should concentrate all such training at the University of Toronto.[95] He also responded favourably to pressure for extension courses. The reality, as he saw it, was that newly self-conscious elements were rapidly carving out substantial claims to influence in society. The university could ignore them at its peril or, more construc-tively, could reach out and try to touch them directly. Falconer chose the latter course. Farmers, tradesmen, commercial groups, and others, he believed, could benefit immensely even from brief exposure to higher education. In turn, the university could draw new vigour and a sharper perception of contemporary problems from contact with these elements of society.[96] Taking this aspect of service seriously, in 1910 he toured mid-western American universities in order to study their extension and correspondence schemes. Clearly impressed, he later wrote Earl Grey expressing the hope that similar programs could be financed in Toronto.[97] Moreover, he became convinced that a popular market existed, as a variety of social and philanthropic bodies lobbied his office on this score. Accordingly, early in 1914 Falconer happily announced that a broad range of service courses would be established the following year. These were to include 'practical teaching' in economics, ethics, psychology, and hygiene. In addition, social workers were informed that part-time studies in charity organization, child welfare, recreation, hospital services, and settlement work would be made available.[98] The onset of war inevitably slowed the implementation of these plans, but the impulse behind them did not fade. If anything, in fact, that conflict and the mood of change it engendered intensified Falconer's commitment to social service. In 1908 he had advised Walter Murray not to neglect the example set by Wisconsin as he went about fashioning goals for the University of

Saskatchewan.[99] On more than one occasion Falconer was prepared to heed his own counsel. Indeed, while clearly subordinate to other priorities, 'practical' considerations found a place in his ideal of service.

Taken as a whole, Falconer's concept of the university displayed the same penchant for synthesis that marked the rest of his thought. No philosopher, his phrasing was sometimes careless. The casual reader, therefore, could be forgiven for assuming that Falconer perceived a conflict between an almost limitless number of irreconcilable opposites. After all, references to dualisms such as reason and faith, science and religion, freedom and order, and knowledge and insight abounded in his statements. Nevertheless, garden-variety idealist that he was, Falconer ultimately believed that all these dichotomies were false. Thus, as biblical scholar he sought to unite reason's tools with an insight derived from faith, and as social commentator he linked an earnest desire for reform with a firm respect for authority and a craving for stability. Similarly, as president of the University of Toronto, he encouraged critical inquiry tempered by intellectual and moral discipline. Believing finally in the oneness of all creation and knowledge, he was understandably eager to educate the whole man. Predictably, therefore, he drew eclectically on several sources of inspiration in outlining his goals. The upshot was a broad and flexible vision of the university. For those who listened, there was no mistaking the fact that a change of leadership had taken place. The scientist Loudon, who in any case fought shy of public pronouncements, had generally taken a more pragmatic line.[100] In Falconer, a humanist had come to preach the gospel of idealism. But he did so in an informed and tolerant manner, clearly acknowledging that there were many roads to the ideal. Under him, the researcher, the professional, and the pure, the applied, and the social scientist all could feel at home. To some extent, Falconer's ideal of the university looked back to the moral concerns of nineteenth-century Puseyite educators. In another sense, it prefigured the outlook of later men who championed the more thoroughly secular multiversity. At times his views, by reason of their very breadth, could seem rather amorphous, but in practical terms they were well suited to the needs of a large university that stood on the brink of tremendous expansion. Opportunities for growth could be seized. New developments could be smoothly integrated into the organic whole. And this was as it should be, thought Falconer; for in his mind unity in diversity was vital to the University of Toronto if it were to fulfil its promise as an institution of national significance.

CHAPTER VII

The Larger Context

Ideas flooded his mind faster than Falconer could transcribe them one crisp autumn afternoon in 1913. A unique opportunity seemed at hand and he was eager to grasp it. The centenary of Sir John A. Macdonald's birth had found the Borden government casting about for a fitting tribute. Reflecting on this matter, Falconer outlined a brainstorm for transmission to the prime minister through Joseph Flavelle. It was a long shot, but there was nothing to lose. To be appropriate, said Falconer, a memorial should continue Macdonald's great work by tangibly strengthening the fabric of national unity. There was a need, he argued, to bind eastern and western Canada more closely to each other. Elaborating on this point, he drove to the heart of his message in suggesting that 'if our university can serve to bring and keep them together, we shall perform an immense national service.' Warming to his theme, he further declared that the University of Toronto 'should be the home of true Canadian influence.' In for a penny, in for a pound, Falconer cast fiscal caution to the winds as he speculated on the best way to disburse phantom thousands from Ottawa. Without blinking he proposed the federal endowment at Toronto of a massive Canadian studies program. His imagination, like a schoolboy's at Christmastide, took wing. The luminous sugar plums that danced through his head included new chairs in Canadian history, geography, and natural resources. He dreamt, even more boldly, of a department of sociology devoted to the study of immigration, town planning, social ethics, rural life, and criminology. And all this richness, he exclaimed, could be set in place for the paltry sum of $600,000![1] Sir John A., he thought, would be well pleased.

Not surprisingly, the hoped-for windfall failed to materialize. Borden, after all, was being deluged with requests, and there were many interests to placate.[2] Well acquainted with the ways of the world, Falconer must have expected as much. Still, it was worth a try. Had he succeeded, a giant step would have been taken towards the development of a national university in Toronto. As it happened, he remained confident that there were other ways of achieving his end. His commitment to the idea was too deep to be shaken by Ottawa's predictable rebuff. To some extent he was being prodded by an ambitious board of gvernors; in truth, however, Falconer required little prompting. His appeal to Borden may have been tinged with fancy, but the urge that informed it was the product of long and sober reflection which predated his appointment at Toronto. At Pine Hill, it will be remembered, he had spoken of the crucial significance of moulding 'national character.' This was an intangible yet potent force which he equated with the collective personality and conscience of a people. There was more to nation-building, he believed, than the definition of constitutional niceties and the accumulation of healthy trade balances. Shared ideals born of a mature common culture were, for him, the most abiding source of genuine unity. From them, all else flowed. Thus, he held that 'there is a national character according to which a nation acts and in which sudden changes are not to be expected.'[3]

Pure ideals, he explained, would inspire a strong and healthy loyalty. Where materialism was ushered out, cheap, superficial jingoism and a spirit of parochial self-advantage would also be dismissed.[4] But he warned that salutory growth did not occur spontaneously. Indeed, in 1904 he had cautioned that 'a nation corrupted at the start carries the taint in its blood.' A concerted effort was required to see that a young nation was kept free of polluting influences. In this connection, believing that 'the few create the mind of the many,' Falconer saw intellectuals as the keepers of the national flame.[5] To them would fall the task of purifying Canadian values before those values hardened with age. He had, of course, pursued this duty with vigour at Pine Hill. When he was elevated to the presidency of the University of Toronto, however, his sense of mission intensified. Here was an institution that, if properly guided, could have an immeasurably greater impact on the national conscience. With or without Ottawa's help, he was determined that it should do so. On the broadest plane, this was to be the principal goal of his long administration. Theory and practice meshed in Falconer's quest to build a national university.

With enlarged influence and a broader platform came a mounting sense of urgency. At Pine Hill, Falconer had emphasized the need to overcome domestic difficulties in the struggle to create a wholesome national character. Accordingly, he had harped on the necessity of transcending factors such as geography, class, and immigration. While his concern with these problems did not lessen, in Toronto he became increasingly conscious of an even more disturbing external menace. In the spectacular growth of American universities he perceived a distinct threat to the tender plant of Canadian culture. Their rapid growth, he feared, would seriously retard the development of parallel facilities in Canada, and the country might be reduced to a permanent state of intellectual dependence on its larger neighbour. Canadian universities, he recognized sombrely, lacked the funds and community sympathy to compete for able students and talented professors. He was shocked to find how many Canadians flocked each year to the United States in order to obtain graduate degrees. Furthermore, he was appalled to learn that many of them never returned and thus constituted a dead loss to the nation. As time passed, his annual reports were darkened by frequent references to what a later generation would term a 'brain drain.'[6] On the other hand, he was equally uncomfortable with the notion that those who returned to teach might have imbibed a philosophy of education somewhat alien to his own. Hitherto, Falconer had assumed that patience, time, and devoted labour would suffice to keep the national ethos pure. Now he was not so sure. Time, it seemed, was running out as a wave of materialism rolled in from the south.

Falconer's attitude to the United States was rather ambivalent. He certainly eschewed the crude, almost hysterical anti-Americanism of a W.L. Grant, who in 1910 depicted Canada's neighbour as wallowing in 'horrible depths of degradation.'[7] Travelling widely throughout the United States, he learned to appreciate much of what he found. The man who in younger days was inspired by the Northfield Conferences and later befriended notable Progressives such as the New Yorker, Seth Low, was unlikely to agree with A.J. Glazebrook that America was nothing more than 'an awful morass of mongrel, monotonous, uninspired democracy.'[8] As a university president, he communed with Woodrow Wilson, A.L. Lowell, and others he regarded as kindred spirits, fellow champions of the ideal.[9] On a practical level, he respected American organizational inventiveness and eagerly adapted successful experiments in professional, extension, and graduate studies to Toronto's environment. Above all, he admired the reverence and open-handed support for higher education that he encountered south of the border. On this score, he thought Canadians had much to learn. In imperial councils, Falconer was wont to defend American schools against excessive criticism levelled by British colleagues. At a 1921 conference in Oxford, for example, a number of ill-informed jibes drew from him an irritated response. While conceding that the American university's culture was 'less broad and deep than that of the greatest schools of Europe,' he hastened to point out that it had several compensating factors on its side. One such was 'the unspoiled enthusiasm of the people who show their faith in its future in their financial support, and by sending to it their sons and their daughters in such large numbers for an education which they believe is necessary for the salvation of their democracy.'[10] More broadly, in the 1920s Falconer assumed the role of self-appointed 'lynchpin' speaking and writing at length on the need for greater understanding and amity among Canadians, Britons, and Americans.[11] It is also worth recording that, ever the sun worshipper, in retirement he regarded Palm Beach and its environs as an almost indispensible winter haven. No stranger to America, he laboured long to understand the country and brought to this task a basically sympathetic eye.

On the other hand, while he respected America as a distinguished and powerful member of the English-speaking family, he still considered it very much a 'foreign' country in the moral as well as the strictly political sense. Alert to its finer qualities, he was simultaneously repelled by other traits he deemed less palatable. Ultimately, he rejected the continentalism extolled by figures such as Goldwin Smith, Samuel Moffatt, and J. Bartlet Brebner.[12] Among other things, he was troubled by the evidence of a reactionary tendency in the United States. Americans, he alleged, while embracing material innovation wholeheartedly, were far less hospitable to intellectual change. New ideas, he noted, seemed to grate on intensely conservative nerves. Established groups, said Falconer, although professing democracy, sometimes acted tyrannically in moments of stress. They were, indeed, wont to convert their prejudices into an unyielding standard of patriotism and brand as disloyal all who took issue with them. On balance, he argued, there was 'less freedom of speech in America, east or west, than in Britain,' despite the latter's notorious class disparities.[13] Similarly, the liberal in Falconer found an American penchant for religious fundamentalism exceedingly distasteful. The western states in particular, he lamented, bred 'fanatic movements' which eclipsed even their most rabid Canadian counterparts.[14] To a sober Presbyterian of Falconer's ecumenical ilk, this was a decidedly retrograde phenomenon.

Much of this intellectual, political, and religious conservatism, he thought, was traceable to a common source. Mental isolation, as he saw it, was the father of intolerance.[15] Thus, he disapproved of the inward-looking and narrowly provincial nationalism that seemed to flourish in the United States. An ardent Canadian nationalist, Falconer was also an internationalist, a proponent of empire and, after the war, a spokesman for the League of Nations. At times, of course, he too was guilty of a certain insular smugness. In evaluating America, every now and then he was prone to adopt a morally self-satisfied pose. On one occasion he crowed that whereas Americans were harshly assimilative in their attitude to immigrants, Canadians displayed a more sympathetic approach.[16] This was a strange pronouncement from one well aware of the harrowing plight of orientals in British Columbia. Similarly, it was a less than convincing argument from a man who would later proclaim that 'we want no hyphenated Canadians.'[17] In any event, questions of consistency aside, there were many things which Falconer had no wish to import from America.

At the top of his prohibited list were certain elements in the American approach to higher education. Noting the rapid growth of universities in the United States, Falconer found much to applaud and also much to be feared. On the positive side, he argued, this upsurge had breathed new life into advanced studies on the continent. Vast pools of easily mobilized wealth had ensured success. On the surface, such development was all to the good. At a deeper level, however, he was disturbed by the philosophy that seemed to animate these institutions. Mechanistic values, he thought, had taken hold, where methods of analysis were exalted above all other considerations. In the United States, he alleged, this technical emphasis combined with American habits of parochialism to rivet attention on concerns that all too frequently were purely immediate and material in nature.[18] To him, this was a perversion of the true university spirit, which should be universal as well as national in scope and should develop within the liberal mainstream of western civilization as a whole. The final product, he held, whether fashioned in Europe or America, should be much the same, despite minor regional variations. The crux, therefore, of Falconer's criticism of American universities was that they were too provincial and encouraged both materialism and narrow specialization at the expense of liberal values. There were, of course, notable exceptions, but he was concerned with the whole, rather than with the individual parts.

Falconer also objected to an American taste for uncontrolled mass production and an unhealthy catering to the average student. Both were typical of a materialistic society that preferred quantity to quality. 'Democracy as it exists in America,' he wrote, 'is willing to educate the masses but it is careless of the few who must be carried to a higher proficiency.'[19] Americans, quite simply, were not providing adequate moral or intellectual training for their leaders. Reflecting on the honours system in Canada, he was relieved to note that 'we have not allowed a superficial catchword of democracy to sweep us off our feet, as though in matters of intelligence similar equality exists to that which supposedly is found in the political machinery of our modern state.'[20] He also had harsh words for the credit system, which he thought betokened a quantitative, mechanistic view of education. When the elective principle was taken into account as well, Falconer was not surprised to see a marked variation in the quality of American degrees. Altogether, therefore, he spied much in contemporary American developments that ran counter to his own values. On the whole, he was ready to borrow specific educational forms from the United States, but only when he felt that they could be adapted to the Canadian university spirit. It might be argued that he played a delicate and dangerous game, but Falconer remained confident that right-minded wielders could control the tools.

Materialism, parochialism, social discord, and internal division – these were the windmills against which Falconer was determined to tilt. A glance at the public addresses he delivered during the first few years of his tenure reveals how heavily these matters weighed on his mind. The titles alone suggest the drift of his thought. Thus, in November 1907 he spoke at Ottawa of the need for 'A Broader Outlook in Our National Life.'[21] A few months later he discoursed on 'The Unification of Canada' and 'The Power of Ideas in National Life.'[22] The following year he held forth on 'The Mission of Canada to the Nations.'[23] In 1910 he discussed 'The Individuality of the Canadian People.'[24] Throughout, his central theme was the importance of stimulating and refining an emergent sense of Canadian identity. The fledgling national character, he believed, was essentially British in outlook and he was anxious that it should remain so.[25] The diffusion from the east of 'increasingly approximate ideals and standards in education' was a potent factor in this process but the good work had to be expanded and intensified. In this connection he felt that universities had a special duty to provide leadership. Toronto's role of course would be to stand in the van of this great national effort.[26] It was almost as if he had stolen a leaf from the book of Cecil Rhodes. Thus, as Oxford, thanks to that tycoon's largesse, helped weld an empire together, so Varsity, on a smaller stage, would contribute significantly to a healthier Canadian identity. Indeed, one suspects that, above all other considerations, it was the opportunity to prosecute this mission with enhanced resources that led Falconer to abandon his beloved Pine Hill for Toronto.

It was, however, abundantly clear to him that the Varsity of 1907 was not yet up to so grand a task. Far from displaying the qualities of a national institution, the university drew an overwhelming proportion of its students from the province of Ontario. Indeed, more than half of them were natives of Toronto. This was a trend that Falconer dearly longed to change. But there were other goals to be achieved as well. For example, he drew some comfort from the fact that the undergraduate program commanded considerable respect outside the province, but he lamented that there was little in the way of organization or lofty standards governing graduate work. The professional schools, though hives of activity, were sorely in need of expansion and modernization. All told, he thought that the raw material had promise; the potential existed, but substantial effort and modification would be required before a truly national university could emerge. Not surprisingly, therefore, President Falconer donned a reformer's guise. He did so, however, with full knowledge of the formidable obstacles that lay in his path.

Foremost among them was a tremendous upsurge in enrolment which had been gathering momentum since about 1900. At Pine Hill Falconer had battled drought. In Toronto, he was almost deluged. Between 1897 and 1907 the number of students more than doubled, soaring from 1,353 to 3,545.[27] In 1908 nearly 400 were added to the roll as something of a peak was reached.[28] Thereafter, the tide abated somewhat. Even so, by 1914 the university was home to almost 1,000 more candidates than had greeted Falconer on his arrival seven years before. Thus bloated, the University of Toronto could boast that it was the largest institution of its kind in the empire outside the British Isles. This distinction, as Falconer quickly recognized, was both a blessing and a curse. On the one hand, sheer size gave at least marginal credibility to Varsity's claim to national stature. On the other, the weight of numbers created a series of attendant problems which in combination threatened to undermine the president's goals. It was a bitter irony which did little to sweeten Falconer's cup.

Overcrowding had several baneful side effects. For one thing, it seriously inhibited good teaching. The staff, as Falconer pointed out year after year, was too small to provide the much sought-after personal touch. In his first report to the governors he drew attention to some grim statistics. He noted, for example, that in political science 262 students had only one professor, one associate professor, and two fellows to instruct them. Four men in history catered to 384 candidates. In English the situation was even worse, as four teachers tried to cope with an enrolment of more than 1,000. The same story was repeated across all faculties. Somewhat wistfully, Falconer cited the Blake Report of 1891 in which it had been suggested that no honours course in arts should exceed twelve and no pass course thirty students. Underscoring the point, he alluded to the recommendations of a Carnegie Foundation bulletin of May 1908 in which small classes were described as the only means of maintaining teaching efficiency. Dejectedly, he observed that 'in the case of the University of Toronto the minimum need not at present be considered, since any approach even to the standard of the 1891 report has been less and less possible.'[29] This was a depressing prospect for one accustomed to the intimacy of Pine Hill.

Bad for the student, this situation was also inimical to the welfare of the professor. In an effort to cope with swelling enrolments, classes were subdivided, thus creating smaller, more manageable groups but placing an intolerable burden on the staff. Teachers were condemned to spend long hours delivering tedious duplicate lessons to throngs of pass students. Alarmed, Falconer feared that it would inevitably induce boredom in an exhausted staff. Even worse, he thought it might dry up enthusiasm for other necessary activity.[30] He certainly had no doubt that senior talents which could be more profitably employed elsewhere were being wasted. While he had no desire to impose an unfair load on younger instructors, he was particularly anxious that established men have the freedom to pursue higher interests. 'These professors,' he urged in 1909, 'should not be so overburdened ... that little energy is left for their own reading and investigation, and for the teaching of honour students.'[31] The solution, obviously, was to hire more instructors, and Falconer regularly pressed this point. But he had no wish to adopt the most tempting and least expensive course. The large-scale recruitment of inexperienced junior men would, he thought, only add to a growing imbalance in the university. An enthusiastic supporter of good teaching, Falconer was also an ardent advocate of research. To encourage the advancement of learning, he argued, experienced leadership was required. Thus, he held that the increase in the number of full and associate professors should be proportionate to the rise in the student population.[32] For the moment, however, he was convinced that the chief problem to be attacked was overcrowding.

Nothing brought this need home more sharply than the annual exercise of preparing the budget. Initially, all parties had been satisfied with the financial arrangements of 1906. A 50 per cent share of provincial succession duties seemed likely to provide a secure economic base for the university throughout the foreseeable future. Whitney had consciously gambled that this apparent generosity would not provoke undue political resistance.[33] While some carping took place, it was generally submerged in the euphoria of the moment as a new administration held out the prospect of reform on a broad front. For a time, at least, university finances were removed from the political arena. Unhappily for Falconer, however, such was not to be the case for long. Shortly after he assumed power, succession revenues began to fall short of their projected targets. Complicating the picture, after 1909 the nation experienced its first serious bout of inflation.[34] Thus, costs rose rapidly as burgeoning enrolments ate up restricted revenues. The University of Toronto, it seemed, would have to struggle just to maintain an established level of performance.

The financial skies began to darken as early as the summer of 1908. Meeting in July of that year, the Board of Governors complained of the clumsiness of the new fiscal machinery. 'It is,' they noted, 'impossible to forecast with any degree of accuracy the amount of Succession Duties which will be collected during the next three or four years.'[35] The university was still operating without a deficit, but the margin was small. Concern was expressed as the revenue from statutory grants began to stagnate. Falconer, for one, was sufficiently worried to ask the premier whether additional support could be relied on should the need arise in years ahead. Whitney was sympathetic but cautioned that 'if I can see my way clear to doing anything further it will be with a great deal more hesitation than I had two years ago.' He acknowledged the marked strain that increasing enrolments and a palpable slip in revenues were placing on university resources. Seeking to comfort the president, he speculated that the allotted duties were unlikely to decline much more. 'I think,' he wrote, 'that we should not be easily frightened or discouraged.' Nevertheless, for all his warm moral support, Whitney warned that the public was unlikely to tolerate increases in provincial aid. Pulling no punches, he informed Falconer bluntly that any suggestion of additional grants would be 'a very serious question indeed.'[36]

By 1910 hypothetical fears were translated into a menacingly concrete reality. Expenditures outstripped income. That much was evident even before the formal budget was drawn up. It was a gloomy Falconer who passed the word along to Walter Murray that spring. 'Now is approaching,' he grimaced, 'the horrid season of the estimates – too much for an ordinary man like me to face without shuddering.' In a black mood, he outlined a cruel dilemma. 'They have to be kept down,' he explained, 'and yet we must grow.'[37] Murray empathized and asked to be informed when the final figures were available. Within a month, Falconer replied as he waded through 'the beastliest job of the whole year.' As succession duties fell off, he projected a shortfall of $40,000, which raised the distasteful prospect of negotiations with the cabinet. Depressing as it was, he saw one saving factor: 'The situation,' he told Murray, 'is serious enough, but not so bad as if it were a deficit with an increasing revenue.'[38] Potential critics would be at least partially disarmed. Still, as a wary Falconer knew, he would have to expect some brickbats as the university went begging at Queen's Park. A deft touch and meticulous preparation would be required. But he had lost none of his accustomed optimism. Confronted with this situation he told Murray that 'it is best ... to grow, and to face the indignation of those who tremble at increases.'[39]

If the financial and other obstacles before him were formidable, so was Falconer's determination to surmount them. His plan of campaign, mapped out between 1907 and 1914, involved a two-pronged assault. Internally, he sought to build a case for increased financial assistance, to attack the problem of overcrowding, to modernize professional education, and to upgrade graduate work. Externally, he proposed to combat American influence by playing the imperial card. In this regard, he would try to buy time for Canadian graduate schools by redirecting the flow of advanced students from the United States to Great Britain, where he thought educational values more nearly approximated his own. Throughout, he had the advantage of firm support from the Board of Governors, two of whom, Walker and Flavelle, were rapidly becoming his closest friends in Toronto. With his priorities clearly outlined, he set about the business of building a national university.

Ever alert to the importance of public relations, Falconer lost no time in developing a strong case for the university as it faced an inevitable struggle for financial aid. The problem was carefully studied, and evidence was effectively marshalled. Well briefed, he highlighted the issue in a stark report to the governors for the year 1910–11. In 1901, he noted, registration had stood at 1,624, and the total government outlay had been $233,285. This, he calculated, worked out to an average expenditure of $142 per student. By 1910, he continued, 4,112 candidates were supported by a revenue of $777,809, and inflation had raised the per capita expense to $180. The need for an expanding income, he submitted, was obvious. In virtually the same breath, however, he moved swiftly to allay expected criticism. A plethora of statistics was produced to demonstrate that a spirit of fiscal responsibility reigned at the University of Toronto. Comparing Varsity's performance with that of ten large American schools, Falconer demonstrated that the provincial university was 'endeavouring to do a larger amount of work on a smaller income than [was] undertaken by almost any other similar institution on the Continent.'[40] The following year he drew comparisons with British counterparts and reached the same conclusion.[41] An able president thus armed himself to face the provincial paymaster.

In the eyes of one observer, however, Falconer's argument seemed too clever by half. George Chown, registrar and treasurer of Queen's

University, was positively irate. In a biting letter to B.E. Walker, now chairman of the Board of Governors, he denounced Falconer's reports. They were, he charged, riddled with inaccuracies and fraught with distortions. Having written to the American heads concerned, he had the relevant figures before him, and they did not correspond with Falconer's. In no uncertain terms he condemned the president for consciously manipulating the statistics in order to cast the best possible light on Toronto while indirectly blackening his provincial competitors.[42] At heart, he appears to have suspected Toronto of plotting to steal Queen's share of the provincial pie. An equally incensed Falconer hastened to reply. His comparisons, he stated, were never meant to be more than approximations. In truth, he had said as much in his 1911–12 report. Less forthrightly, perhaps, he denied that he had any intention of criticizing the way others spent their money. Finally, he added that 'I have never made any comparison as to the relative cost of educating a student in Toronto and in Queen's.'[43] In the end, a somewhat embarrassed Chown was forced to admit that he had secured the wrong reports from American Schools. Falconer had drawn on figures for 1910, whereas Chown had requested those for 1911. A self-righteous Falconer crowed triumphantly. 'I hardly understand,' he wrote to the crestfallen registrar, 'why you should say that I shall be interested to know that ... you have received a report from California certifying the figures ... as correct.' Cuttingly he observed, 'I know that they are correct, because I myself received these figures from the University of California.'[44]

This was Falconer at his least attractive. When seriously provoked, he could be singularly ungenerous to an opponent. On this particular occasion, however, his irritation may well have sprung from a sense of guilt as well as from any certitude of literal correctness. Chown's evidence may have been faulty, but his surmise was accurate enough. Privately, Falconer was bent on engrossing as much of the educational budget as he possibly could. He had seen what duplication could lead to in the Maritimes and was anxious to avoid it. Centralization, he imagined, was the only solution to financial distress in higher education. If that meant truncating the development of Queen's and lesser institutions, then, he thought, so be it. These ideas had been confided to Walter Murray as early as 1910: 'Professional and post graduate work have to be more and more developed in Toronto. To establish another university at London would be wrong and Sir James Whitney recognizes this. Of course, Queen's is an established fact, but I am sure that the best results would be got if she were to limit her work to College, early professional work in medicine and what she now has in engineering. The race for large university expansion is terribly exhausting on financial resources.'[45] In October of the same year he met with Flavelle, Meredith, and a few others at Walker's home to discuss the possibility of drawing Queen's and the University of Western Ontario into affiliation with Toronto. The object was to found a truly provincial system with Varsity as the senior partner. Acknowledging the strength of local resistance at the moment, the gathering decided that no action should be taken.[46] Even so, the urge to centralize was never far from Falconer's thoughts. At any rate the race for provincial funding was one he was determined to win.

Meanwhile the pressure to find additional revenue was relentless. In growing desperation Falconer stepped up his efforts to court a reluctant public. Urgent appeals were made to the city fathers. Toronto, it was pointed out, reaped considerable benefits in money and prestige from the local university but rendered not a penny in support. Such indifference, chided Falconer, contrasted unfavourably with the enlightened attitude displayed by the inhabitants of Birmingham, Leeds, and Sheffield. Conscious that their commercial success depended finally on 'trained intelligence,' they happily financed what Torontonians took for granted.[47] But, as Falconer soon discovered, the good burghers of 'Hogtown' were not so easily shamed or cajoled into parting with their brass. This tight-fisted civic apathy remained a source of bitter disappointment to him throughout his days in office.

Nor, as it transpired, did he fare much better with Queen's Park. At first he was optimistic. In June 1913 Falconer and the governors met the full cabinet in order to explain the mounting deficit and to press their claim for a new deal. Writing to the vacationing Walker, the president described the session: 'I told the Government on Tuesday that the ship has been grating on the rocks for two years and if this went on long it would injure the keel.' He was relieved to report that permission to put the budget into effect had been obtained but feared that the university might have to draw on capital to cover its overrun. Nevertheless, he saw hope for the future. The cabinet had understood the problem. Falconer had had 'several conversations' with Whitney, who seemed well disposed to the university's position. He assured Walker that 'they intend next winter to meet the situation somehow ... It is an ill wind that blows nobody good.'[48]

That ill wind, however, gathered hurricane force by the spring of 1914. When final tabulations were made in June, the estimates predicted a deficit of $120,000 for the coming year.[49] Spirits in the university board room sank to a new low. A summons from the premier to attend the next cabinet meeting did little to revive them. Clearly, some members of the government were in a testy mood; for the board's representatives were invited to 'give explanations as to the expected deficit which is to come immediately on the heels of the previous one.'[50] Ready, perhaps, for an argument, no one was prepared for what actually occurred. Falconer, who was abroad at the time, got the bad news in a letter from Walker. The mercurial chairman was furious. The cabinet, he explained, had greeted word of the perfectly predictable deficit 'as if it were a surprise.' Some sparring had ensued and then a telling blow was struck. It was suddenly revealed that the government at the end of the last session had quietly appended an amendment to an omnibus bill which henceforth limited the university's share of succession revenues to $500,000 per year. This meant that the regular annual income from the province was frozen at its already insufficient level. Instead of expanding, statutory support would actually decline as the cost of living rose. The enraged Walker recounted how he had taxed the politicians with the 'extreme folly' of this decision, but to no avail. The minister of education, R.A. Pyne, explained that the needs of Queen's and Western had also to be considered and that, in any event, the universities seemed likely to gobble up an inordinate share of the total educational budget. Appeals to Whitney were pointless. A sick man, he was already fading from the scene, and in any case, he had toyed with a similar idea two years earlier. There was nothing for it. Walker's only hope was that when Falconer returned they two could induce the cabinet to call a royal commission on university finances.[51]

Decades later, Falconer could still recall the 'unpleasant shock' that Walker's letter gave him.[52] It signalled the defeat of one of his most cherished dreams, that of expanding and diversifying the university while steering clear of political entanglements. In future, he would have to bargain with Queen's Park directly over a constantly growing budget. As it happened, the province proved to be remarkably tolerant and generous. While tensions sometimes surfaced, in the end no government ever failed to approve the soaring university estimates. Thus, money continued to be found to sustain growth. Nevertheless, Falconer sensed that a measure of free-wheeling discretion had been sacrificed. For one who deplored this loss of independence, 'the beastliest job of the whole year' became increasingly 'horrid' as time wore on.

While this financial battle was being waged, Falconer launched a simultaneous attack on the problem of overcrowding. He realized, of course, that the tide of new enrolments could not be stemmed altogether – it was a continent-wide phenomenon. Still, he argued that much could be done to slow it down and that some control over the process was vital. Otherwise it would be impossible to promote research and graduate studies. Resources were being squandered on unwieldy first year classes in which a great deal of simple remedial work was done. Moreover, the high failure rate in these courses represented an unacceptable level of waste. This attrition was also testimony to the fact that too many students were being accepted without their having first secured adequate preparation. As a solution Falconer proposed the stiffening of admission and degree standards. Course regulations, therefore, were tightened to prevent the carrying of failures from one year to the next. The university's passing grade was revised. In addition, an effort was made to stream the student population more effectively and thereby reduce the failure rate beyond first year. In the past, too many average students had opted to take the demanding honours program. They were lured by its greater prestige and the opportunity of pursuing special interests more closely. Inevitably, many were unable to meet the exacting requirements. Meanwhile, the honours classes were oversubscribed and suffered as the result of dilution. To combat this problem, Falconer and his colleagues reorganized the pass degree. A new 'general course' was designed. As of old, the first two years involved largely prescribed studies across a range of core disciplines such as language, mathematics, and laboratory science. The new scheme, however, featured a number of electives in the final years which allowed for a modest degree of specialization. These changes, along with the raising of standards, were designed to increase the prestige and attractiveness of the ordinary degree and thereby improve the streaming process. A few years later, the honours program was also recast with a similar view in mind.

These measures and others like them held promise. But Falconer was convinced that a tightening of admission standards was the real key to the question of eliminating waste and shifting the balance of the university. As things stood, in 1907 students were admitted on the basis of a junior matriculation requirement which he felt was insufficiently demanding. Moreover, not all the schools that fed the provincial university applied that criterion with equal vigour.[53] Some candidates came well prepared, while others had not the slightest chance of surviving their first term. To make matters worse, a few were accepted with only partial matriculation. It was this sorry state of affairs, he alleged, that forced the university to channel inordinate energy into the academic upgrading of freshmen. Determined that this waste should end, Falconer, with the support of John Seath, superintendent of education, moved quickly to raise admission requirements. Initially, his goal was to force all candidates to acquire a junior leaving certificate that was a notch above the normal matriculation. This would entail scoring a minimum of 40 per cent on all papers and no less than 60 per cent overall. Through Seath's influence and an endless round of conferences, the co-operation of the schools was obtained. Between 1908 and 1912 the new criteria were gradually phased in and, whether or not it was due to this factor alone, there was a perceptible slowing in the pace of enrolment. In 1913, for example, only fifteen more students were accepted than in 1912.[54] There were other benefits as well. As early as 1910 Falconer reported that a marked improvement in the quality of candidates was noted by all faculties.[55]

These changes were very gratifying, but in the back of his mind Falconer felt that even sterner measures would shortly be required. Numbers might be stabilizing, but he recognized that the phenomenon was merely temporary. Moreover, those huge first-year courses remained to sap the finite energies of the university. As he saw it, the solution was obvious: they had to go. Accordingly, in 1909 he dropped a hint. The time might come, he prophesied, when the entire first year of arts could be usefully transferred to the high schools of the province.[56] For the moment, it remained a mere suggestion. Falconer was testing the wind. In 1911, however, as finances and congestion became more of a problem, he outlined the idea concretely in his presidential report. Noting that the 60 per cent criterion would come into full effect in 1912, he argued that it would be impossible to demand more in the way of grade averages. Then he stated that 'when we are ready for a still higher standard of entrance it must come through abolishing the Junior Matriculation, and creating a new one equivalent to that of the pass work in the first year in Arts.' This senior matriculation, in his view, would do away with the large pass classes in first year which had 'almost outgrown the limits of efficiency.' Professors would have more time for 'advanced instruction culminating in the postgraduate departments.' He envisaged an ordinary degree that could be completed in three years. The honours program would still require four years, but with the last three devoted to more intensive work, standards could be raised. Honours, accordingly, could be made a more efficient preparation for graduate studies.

Falconer also argued that the proposed changes would do much to elevate the reputation of professional education and bring it into line with current practice in the United States. Many of the better American universities, he noted, required either an arts degree or at least two years of college before an applicant was admitted to medical school. Their medical courses usually took four years to complete after these entrance requirements were met – a combined total of six years for the average student once he left high school. In Ontario, he pointed out, the norm was five years. It followed that if senior matriculation were demanded, Varsity's degree in medicine would be made equivalent to that obtainable anywhere on the continent. Such a move, he argued, could only redound to the advantage of Toronto's graduates. The same would be true of applied science and the other professional faculties, should the elementary work of the first year be removed to the high schools.

It was a bold proposal. Aware that eyebrows would be raised, Falconer tried to demonstrate that schools and students would benefit just as much as the university. Teachers, he averred, 'would be stimulated with a new ambition' and find greater outlets for their talents among the older students. More consistency would be brought to the higher levels of the provincial system. Furthermore, the cost of education would be reduced since students would remain at home a year longer and pay lower fees than they currently did for the initial year of arts. This, he added, would be true even for those who had to move to better equipped schools to complete their secondary education. As an added bonus, a year of advanced training would be made more accessible to a broader range of people. Another positive consideration was that the process of streaming could be rendered more efficient and humane. With the present freshman program transferred to the high schools, applicants could be screened at home and thus be spared the humiliation and disappointment of leaving for Toronto, only to return as 'failures.' Furthermore, having attained a higher level of maturity, those admitted would be less prone to take improper advantage of the freedom offered by university life. In passing, Falconer also observed that 'maturity and intellectual earnestness will also tend to restrain the exaggeration of athletics against which all universities have to be on their guard.'

The scheme, he realized, could not be implemented overnight, but he was certain that any barriers could be overcome. Secondary schools, after all, were responding well to the gradual elevation of current standards. There was no reason to suspect that they would fail to meet the new challenge. Offering encouragement, Falconer drew attention to the recent success of similar reforms in Scotland and called on Ontarians to emulate this example. Given time, he felt that most of the province's high schools could make the necessary adjustments without undue dislocation or strain. Rural continuation schools, he admitted, were less well placed to respond. But he emphasized that they had never been intended to prepare for junior matriculation in the first place. In compensation, he called on the province to make special arrangements for rural candidates who would be forced to move to larger centres in order to complete their senior matriculation. Altogether, he looked forward to the inauguration of the plan as early as 1914 or 1915.[57] Having launched this rather weighty trial balloon, Falconer then awaited reaction.

The matter was widely discussed during the next two years. Despite some division of opinion, the university faculties expressed approval of the project.[58] Extensive talks with high school teachers were more successful than Falconer had anticipated. Rural representatives had misgivings about the fate of continuation schools, but a 'large majority' of teachers seemed to favour the plan.[59] Indeed, by February 1912 Falconer told Walter Murray that the scheme was likely to be adopted 'before very long.'[60] All too swiftly, however, his high hopes were dashed. The federated colleges were less than enthusiastic. Worried about a crippling loss of fees, the disruption of the traditional program, and a potential decline of their influence in the federation, they baulked at Falconer's suggestions. More decisively, Queen's voiced its unalloyed opposition, and the rest of the province's universities followed suit. Concerned about a reduction in their revenues, they also resented this implied meddling in their internal affairs. Since Seath had warned Falconer of this probable reaction, he could not have been taken wholly by surprise.[61] None the less, his disappointment was acute. Seeking to counter the blow, in his report for 1913 Falconer noted that other authorities had independently reached conclusions similar to his own. The president of the University of Chicago, he pointed out, had recently declared that the freshman year of arts was an 'anachronism' which should be abolished.[62] For the moment, he accepted a temporary defeat in good spirit, but he was far from giving up. Indeed, he continued to press his case with great regularity throughout the rest of his career.

Meanwhile, Falconer and others chipped away at the problem of reliable testing and uniform standards in piecemeal fashion. In this, Seath was a valuable ally. Past his prime and 'set in his ways,' the superintendent of education thought all educators required constant prodding and supervision.[63] Accordingly, he favoured a high degree of centralization with himself at the controls. Falconer did not share in this low opinion of teachers but for his own reasons was happy to draw on Seath's assistance in streamlining the matriculation process. Moreover, while dead set against senior matriculation, the province's other universities were quite willing to co-operate with Toronto on matters affecting entrance standards. Thus, from time to time some constructive changes were made. Most substantially, a joint matriculation board was eventually established. Representatives of the universities and Toronto's federated colleges met annually to supervise provincial examinations. Normally, Falconer took the chair at these sessions. Standards and content were determined with the help of ministry officials and were ratified by the various senates involved. Joint action of this sort gave the province a more uniform matriculation system and helped improve the quality of freshmen.[64] Yet, although progress was made, Falconer still longed to dispense with the current first-year program. As he told Walter Murray in July 1914, unless senior matriculation were established, little in the way of important graduate work could be accomplished at Toronto.[65] That such work was vital he had no doubt.

In many ways, Falconer viewed the development of graduate studies as the hinge upon which the development of a national university would turn. He recognized, for example, that the proliferation of undergraduate institutions, particularly in the west, meant that Varsity's BA degree was unlikely to attract a growing number of students from outside Ontario. At that level, Toronto, like its fellows, would remain primarily a regional university. A large-scale influx of youthful students was not to be expected. Where graduate work was concerned, however, it was an entirely different story. In fact, there was little domestic competition to stand in the way of Toronto's evolution into a national focal point of advanced studies. Some early efforts notwithstanding, graduate work in Canada was still in its infancy. On paper McGill and Queen's had instituted graduate progams well before the turn of the century. In practice, however, by the time Falconer came to power these arrangements had borne little fruit. Indeed, before 1923 in Montreal these studies had been 'haphazard' and 'ill-co-ordinated,' since conservative elements baulked at drawing up firmer regulations that were criticized as 'new fangled and Germanic.'[66] Queen's, it appeared, engaged in the pursuit more earnestly, but its resources were comparatively slender.[67] Clearly, an opportunity existed in near virgin territory, and Falconer, for a variety of reasons, was anxious to seize it.

Institutional pride and ambition undoubtedly figured in his calculations, but so too did a larger sense of purpose. The national spirit, as he explained in 1908, would be furthered by the development of a thriving graduate school at Toronto. Leading thinkers from all corners of the dominion would be drawn together. They would find a natural home, since an outlet was provided for their energies. Employment opportunities for advanced scholars would save them for the dominion and free Canada from dependence on foreign-trained talent. In addition, something could be done to slow the annual exodus of promising students to the United States.[68] As he pointed out quite frankly elsewhere, the University of Toronto would also reap extensive benefits as it skimmed the cream off the country's student population and thus came to be more representative of the nation as a whole.[69] Happily Falconer's ambitions won warm support among many other Canadian educators. Naturally less concerned with Toronto's aspirations than was Falconer, western university leaders none the less called on both him and Peterson to take the lead in this matter. They too were alarmed by the remorseless southward trek of graduates and their own reliance on external sources of professional recruitment. Operating on thin reserves, they looked to Toronto and McGill to reverse these dark trends. Like Falconer, W.C. Murray and H.M. Tory saw the issue ultimately as a question of national survival.[70] Their encouragement, needless to say, only deepened Falconer's resolve. It was with considerable dismay, therefore, that he viewed the condition of graduate work in his own bailiwick.

Although begun as early as the 1840s, graduate studies were not intensively or systematically pursued at Toronto, even by the time Falconer took command. Regulations governing the MA degree were hazy and loose. Normally, all that was required was a Toronto BA and a thesis. Little more than extended essays, the theses were often less than 5,000 words in length and were of uneven quality.[71] Existing course offerings tended to be slim. In Mavor's department of political science, for example, only one course of systematic instruction for graduates was available.[72] There had been some internal criticism of this state of affairs as far back as the 1880s, and the 'superficial' and 'perfunctory' nature of the MA had continued to irritate a few professors such as Ramsay Wright.[73] Little, however, had been done to improve the situation by 1907. Granted, a board of post-graduate studies for the Faculty of Arts had been established in 1903, but it appears to have had scant success in acting as a centre for the co-ordination of various programs. As one commenter has recently observed, 'some MA students may have got some supervision; it is hard to believe they can have got much.'[74] Doctoral studies, launched in the 1890s, were more carefully defined but attracted few candidates outside the sciences, a fact unlikely to please Falconer. Altogether, Toronto offered few inducements that could lure advanced students or first-class researchers away from the beaten paths to Germany and the United States.

Faced with this situation, Falconer pressed for change. Seeking first to rationalize hitherto scattered efforts, he pinned his hopes on the founding of a faculty of graduate studies. Higher and more uniform standards could thus be applied, while fresh vigour was injected into advanced work. He was confident of support from the Board of Governors. Moreover, strong pressure from some scientists on campus encouraged him to move forward. Accordingly, even as the BA was being reshaped, discussions were also held to consider the future of graduate studies. However, as these 'tedious and repeated' consultations went on, they generated far more heat than Falconer had anticipated. Not everybody, it seems, was persuaded of the desirability of modernization in this area. Indeed, a fierce debate erupted and grew in intensity the longer it lasted. At the level of principle, classical humanists did battle with colleagues of a scientific or 'Germanic' bent of mind. Here the crucial issue was the nature of the thesis. Warring champions hurled salvoes across what they thought to be a yawning chasm. Scientists insisted that theses should make 'additions to knowledge.' Humanists scoffed at such a notion. In the tradition of the Oxford 'Greats' they held that true knowledge was slowly won and involved not the mechanical accumulation of facts, but the mastery of fundamental truths and inherited wisdom. In the arts, or so they alleged, it was naïve to demand original contributions from graduate students. Some feared, too, that undergraduate teaching would be disparaged and suffer should a 'superior' faculty be introduced. It was also said to be unwise to divert badly needed resources from established programs at a moment when enrolments were swelling. Nor was it thought fair that a group of 'super professors' be hived off from the rest and granted relief from undergraduate instruction. In purely practical terms, many pointed to inadequacies in library and laboratory facilities as serious barriers to success. As the conflict of opinion gathered steam, antagonists often descended to personal attacks. Falconer was therefore disturbed to find substantial issues frequently submerged in a welter of biting recrimination.

The president deplored the misunderstandings and misrepresentations which ensued. He was critical, for example, of those proponents of the new faculty who charged their antagonists with blind resistance to change and a desire to bury themselves in comfortable routine. A humanist himself, he understood the fears and the philosophy of those who hesitated. Years later he recalled that 'the underlying misapprehension, or at any rate deprecation, of the ideals of the conservatives was an obstacle in the way of getting a policy, sound in principle, established with the goodwill that would have saved delays.' Yet, while sympathizing with traditionalists to a point, Falconer did not exempt them from criticism. Most obviously, he thought, they failed to appreciate the value of modern scientific methods when applied to their own disciplines. Clearly drawing on his own experience, he noted how new tools of investigation had broadened and deepened understanding of social, economic and religious conditions of the ancient world. Having himself reached an accommodation with newer modes of thought, he urged others to follow. Typically, he sought to close the gap that others perceived between scientific analysis and humanistic insight. On another score, Falconer made it clear from the outset that he had no intention of sacrificing undergraduate teaching or of creating privileged groups within the faculty. Such steps would have been anathema to one who pictured the university as an 'organic' entity. Amid the din of battle, however, his words of comfort went unheeded at times, and the struggle wore on without clear issue until after the advent of the First World War.[75]

To be sure, a few minor improvements were made. Thus, in 1911 Falconer reported that MA requirements had been stiffened slightly to demand at least the equivalent of one full year of work after the BA. But this change, as he tartly observed, was scant progress considering the effort that had been put forth.[76] He had never deluded himself into thinking that a mature and flourishing graduate school could be created quickly. Nevertheless, as he grew ever more conscious of American competition in the field, he chafed at needless delay. Fortunately, however, he believed that a viable temporary solution lay close at hand. Accordingly, while labouring to improve Toronto's offerings, Falconer simultaneously issued an urgent appeal to British graduate schools. If only, he argued, they would open their doors more invitingly to colonial candidates, then Canada might yet buy sufficient time to stand one day on her own two feet.

In Falconer's mind, of course, this was a wholly congenial option. It came naturally to one of his family background and personal experience. Born in one corner of the empire, he had been raised in another and educated in the mother country itself. He had, in short, that grasp of the physical reality of empire that Parkin deemed so essential to a fuller comprehension of its deeper meaning.[77] That meaning would be spelled out in glowing detail as an aroused Falconer later reacted to the Great War. Yet even before that event, his devotion to the imperial cause was made evident. At heart, he ever remained the son of a missionary who had seen in Greater Britain a vehicle for the advancement of Christianity and civilization. In Nova Scotia, Trinidad, and Edinburgh, the empire had been described to him not merely as a manifestation of power but also as a moral force. As he matured, Falconer experienced nothing that shook this fundamental perception. In vain, for example, would one search the entire corpus of his writings for references to contemporary imperial critics such as J.A. Hobson, E.D. Morel, or Mary Kingsley. In Toronto he frequented circles that exuded a familiar and comfortable ethos; Walker, Willison, Flavelle, Hutton, Wrong, and others close to him all were lyrical exponents of the same 'Britannic nationalism' he espoused.[78]

Not surprisingly, therefore, Falconer and several of these fellow travellers were quick to join the Round Table when a local branch was formed. Significantly, this was one of the first outside bodies with which he aligned himself following a period of lying low in the wake of his appointment. The historians George Wrong and Edward Kylie appear to have recruited him. [79] Doubtless they found it an easy chore. Eager to sponsor imperial unity, Falconer could also appreciate the Round Table's tactics. At first disinclined to court the masses directly, its members emphasized a quiet personal approach to those who influenced public opinion. Similarly, elaborate schemes of formal integration were deliberately eschewed, while an informed consensus on broad goals was being stimulated. [80] These ideals, it seems, sat well with Falconer, who as early as 1908 had anticipated just such an endeavour. 'In my judgment,' he had written, 'the future of our Empire depends not upon legislation and external ties but upon intimate knowledge on the part of men in leading positions who become personal links uniting sections of the Empire and who are competent to set forth its ideals either to classes of students or to the more intelligent portions of the community.'[81] In this spirit, he regularly invited notable imperial figures such as Kipling, Milner, and H.H. Johnson to speak at the university.

Accenting personal bonds and moral factors, Falconer was less concerned with the institutional forms of empire. He was not, however, indifferent to or ignorant of the practical problems of imperial unity. Joseph Chamberlain's plea for imperial preference, for example, left him cold. When in 1910 Willison seconded the proposal in the *Times*, Falconer wrote to that newsman and in so doing laid bare much of his own imperial thought. While acknowledging that 'men's sympathies [were] likely to follow their trading friendships,' he nevertheless questioned the wisdom of Chamberlain's scheme. At least two difficulties, he argued, stood in the way. In the first place, it might not be possible to arrange preferences in such a way as to satisfy all sections of the empire. Thus, priceless goodwill could be forfeited for dubious economic benefits. Secondly, Falconer echoed British Liberals of the time and much of later historical analysis in maintaining that Britain had little to gain and much to lose in abandoning free trade. The cheap loaf and a vital but vulnerable network of international trade were at stake. 'I am so staunch an imperialist,' he informed Willison,

that I hesitate to do anything that might make the lot of the poor in England harder. Now she gets wheat from everywhere and without fluctuation. Can she venture to depend upon her colonies, great as their resources are, which with increasing populations of their own, perhaps increasingly reluctant to farm, may take a constantly growing proportion of their own wheat? It's a great venture for England with her great population and small natural resources. I am thankful that I do not have to decide.

Alert to conditions in Britain, Falconer also viewed the issue in a Canadian context. With others of his generation he shared what Carl Berger has so aptly described as a growing 'sense of power.' Ardent imperialism was linked to a fervent Canadian patriotism. Where the senior dominion was concerned, colonial subordination had no place in Falconer's vision of the imperial future. He was at pains, therefore, to congratulate Willison on his effort to allow for local autonomy within a preferential system. In the end, he thought that commentator's scheme unworkable but applauded his sensitivity to Canadian aspirations. For the future, Falconer refused to play the pundit, but he did offer a few suggestions as to how unity might be enhanced. 'Strengthen every tie,' he told Willison. 'Quick lines of steamers, travel, low rates of postage and telegraph, interchange of ideas in public affairs, education, religion,' – all these could exercise a profound influence. As always, he underscored the 'enormously powerful' impact of personal links. In closing, he went so far as to prophesy that an 'Imperial Parliament for Imperial affairs' was not too fanciful a prospect to entertain, so long as Canadians were treated as partners in a global empire.[82]

With thoughts such as these stirring his imagination, Falconer began to attend Round Table meetings in 1911. His decision to do so may also have been prompted by Laurier's drive to initiate reciprocity with the United States, a plan of which he disapproved root and branch. Writing to Walter Murray, he deplored the 'sectional antagonism' that the proposition provoked in Canada.[83] In all likelihood, he was equally alarmed by the prospect of being sucked deeper into the American orbit. A student of empire, Falconer was well aware of the way in which cultural values and trade so often marched hand in hand. When agents of the Liberal government attempted to justify the move, he was unimpressed. He found Laurier's public pronouncements on the matter 'eloquent' but 'too general' and observed that 'the intellectual power at Ottawa is not as great as it should be.'[84] It is unclear whether he took any part in the successful campaign launched by Flavelle, Walker, and others to undermine Laurier's support in Ontario.[85] In any case, he rejoiced when Robert Borden, a fellow Maritimer and solid imperialist, was swept to power. In congratulating the new prime minister on his election, Falconer wrote that all classes in the nation regarded him as 'a leader above reproach from whom they [would] receive efficient and honest government.'[86] Of all those who held sway in Ottawa during his lifetime, it was Borden whom

Falconer most admired. In no small measure this was a result of that leader's approach to imperial affairs. When Borden asked Whitehall to 'call us to your councils,' Falconer heartily seconded the plea. Aboard the steamer *Grampian* en route from England in July 1912, he scribbled excitedly to Murray his impressions on this matter. The request, he enthused, was wholly constructive and likely to be 'of the most permanent advantage.'[87] Murray must have anticipated this reaction. After all, Falconer in his own sphere had been fostering a similar course well before 1912. Rejecting Chamberlainite tariff reform, he had, nevertheless, been preaching the necessity of imperial preference in higher education for quite some time.

As early as 1909 Falconer was urging Willison to bring the University of Toronto and Canadian educational problems generally to the attention of his British readers. The *Times* correspondent obliged and in this modest fashion a campaign was launched which would endure until Falconer retired.[88] Anxious to find a counterweight to American influence, the president sought to forge closer links with British universities whose educational values, he thought, more accurately reflected his own. Oxbridge, he imagined, was the purest font of that moral idealism he held so dear and bred graduates of the finest mettle. 'Few Englishmen,' he later observed, 'are so remorselessly scientific as the Germans, few have the quick intellect of the Frenchman, but in individual genius and in the fine balance of sane intelligence and ethical strength the best Englishman is without peer.'[89] Forging steel of the finest temper, Oxford and Cambridge were also the foremost transmitters of the British heritage that Canadians enjoyed.[90] Falconer's reverence for the great British universities, awakened in youth, ripened with age. It may, however, be suggested that even in maturity he occasionally reverted to a youthful hero-worship. Describing a recent visit to Oxford, in 1925 he intoned sentiments that echoed those roused forty years earlier during his first idyllic sojourn by the Cam. 'We are well known and they take us right into their councils and treat us as familiar friends. But on our part it is a great privilege to be brought up along side their intellectual standards which are first rate. One goes home with an intellectual tonic.'[91] Clearly, first impressions exerted a lasting influence. Thus romance mingled with expediency and conviction. Canada, he thought, was 'still off the highroad of the world's intellectual commerce.'[92] It required a mentor while its own universities matured. Unhesitatingly, therefore, Falconer chose British tutelage as a buffer against what he feared could only be American domination. In practical terms this policy was most obviously mirrored in his attitude to appointments and his sustained effort to gain access for Canadians to British graduate schools.

Canadian universities had, of course, traditionally drawn a high percentage of their faculty members from Great Britain. At Toronto in particular, certain department heads such as George Wrong and James Mavor showed a marked preference for British-trained candidates. The historian, indeed, had very specific notions about recruitment. Thus, of the sixteen appointments approved by Wrong between 1904 and 1920 all but one were graduates of either Toronto or Oxford. The sole exception was W.P.M. Kennedy, who came from Dublin.[93] Mavor cast his net rather more broadly, but once again British recruits were preferred when Canadians were unavailable.[94] In this respect Mavor and Wrong must have found Falconer's leadership congenial, since the policy he adopted was remarkably similar to their own. His influence, moreover, was crucial. He took seriously the provisions of 1906 which vested in the president an exclusive right to recommend to the governors on all appointments. Throughout his regime, Falconer screened all candidates personally and often ventured far afield to interview them. Department heads were always carefully consulted for their views, but the president's word, normally rubber-stamped by the board, was in most cases final. There would be no return to the days when Loudon had awakened to find in the morning papers that such matters had been settled without his knowledge. It was, accordingly, of great significance that Falconer had very sharply defined views on the question of staffing.

Ideally, when on the prowl for new instructors, Falconer preferred to hire Canadians. In particular, he favoured Toronto graduates who had honed their skills abroad and who, he reasoned, would be in tune with the spirit and familiar with the conditions of the university. Furthermore he usually gave priority to native sons who had completed their studies in Britain. Generally speaking, however, even Canadians polished in Germany or the United States were considered before foreign applicants. His principal wishes, however, were not always easily fulfilled. All too often, indeed, Falconer discovered that adequately trained Canadians, wherever groomed, were in lamentably short supply. Many chose to remain abroad. A growing number of domestic universities were also competing for their services. Thus, it was frequently necessary to draw on foreign pools of talent in order to staff an expanding university. In such instances Falconer was prone to exercise his own version of imperial preference. This point was made perfectly clear to Dalhousie's president, Stanley Mackenzie, who in 1912 wrote to ask advice in these matters. 'A strong Canadian,' replied Falconer, 'or a strong Scotchman with an

Oxford training fills our positions splendidly.'[95] In this particular case, Falconer was referring to appointments in history. The statement would hold good as a description of his general policy, especially in the arts, which for him constituted the core of any university. None of the foregoing, however, implies that he was inflexible in matters of recruitment. Ian Drummond has recently described this British bias as a 'qualified tendency' in Falconer.[96] Thus, Europeans and Americans were always to be found on campus, the latter particularly so in the 1920s, when hiring in Britain became more difficult. No ban was imposed. Similarly, no one could count on a position at Toronto as a matter of genetic inheritance, since Falconer insisted that academic qualifications be kept high. Still, given a choice, the president preferred an Oxford or a Cambridge man. In his estimation Canadians or Britons drawn from that milieu not only suited Toronto well but also served a higher purpose. Writing in 1915 to thank a British colleague for aid in finding a new man, Falconer clarified this point. 'I am greatly indebted to you,' he told J.G. Robertson, 'for all the trouble that you have taken in this matter. I console myself, however, in assuming that you are glad to do what is really I think an Imperial service in helping us in this way.'[97] Indeed, on such occasions Falconer was pleased that he could achieve two worthy ends at a single stroke. A good instructor was found and another 'personal link' was added to the imperial chain.

He was aided in his task by a number of talent scouts in the United Kingdom, who were cultivated during the many summers Falconer passed in Britain attending conferences, hunting for professors, or simply vacationing. Over the years he compiled a lengthy list of trusted advisers, men intimately familiar with the British academic scene. Among them, two in particular were relied on for wise counsel. 'If you want an Englishman,' he told Stanley Mackenzie in 1918, 'write A.L. Smith.'[98] Master of Balliol College, Smith was ideally placed at the heart of Oxford and had scores of useful contacts throughout the United Kingdom. Falconer, it seems, was first put in touch with him in 1908 on the recommendation of Milner's secretary, Arthur Steel-Maitland.[99] Thereafter, acquaintance blossomed into friendship as Smith visited Toronto in 1910 and Falconer reciprocated by dropping in at Balliol whenever he was in England. In any case, Smith was always among the first to be consulted when Toronto was in the market for a British recruit. But Michael Sadler was also listened to carefully when such matters were at stake. The vice-chancellor of the University of Leeds, once touted as Loudon's most likely successor at Toronto, enjoyed enormous influence in British educational circles. A noted reformer, he was a leader in the fight to modernize all levels of the educational structure in the face of German competition.[100] As such, he became a noted public figure, who, like Smith, proved to be a storehouse of valuable information. His home, too, became a frequent haven for Falconer during his summer rambles. Other than Smith and Sadler, James Seth at Edinburgh was frequently called on for advice. These three were the men upon whom Falconer most relied to steer good candidates his way. On occasion, however, when a particularly important appointment was involved, he would indulge in a wholesale survey of his many contacts in Britain.

An excellent case study of this process is provided by Falconer's extensive search for an associate professor of political economy in 1909, an appointment judged to be crucial. It was a post, he argued, in which an energetic young man might exercise 'great influence in the Dominion.'[101] Sensing that there was much at stake, Falconer left no stone unturned as he canvassed his British sources. In addition to his usual contacts, he sought help from a large number of other well-placed men.[102] On one point he was adamant. Since no Canadian seemed qualified, he insisted that 'we should prefer an Old Country man to an American.'[103] In clear command of the search, Falconer journeyed to Britain that spring in order to interview potential candidates in person. Despite the active assistance of his many friends, however, the task did not prove easy. By July he was reporting to Mavor that a diligent effort had yet to yield tangible results. Edinburgh and Glasgow had no one available. Cambridge friends suggested C.R. Fay, but he had already made other arrangements. Turning to Smith at Balliol, Falconer received useful suggestions yet left without securing a man. Even Pember Reeves of the London School of Economics regretted to say that no first-class scholars were ready to leave for Canada. Altogether, Falconer was beginning to lose hope and even suggested than an American might do temporarily.[104] As he explained to Walker, the chief difficulty he faced was that salaries in Canadian universities were too low to attract the best candidates.[105] This was a problem that would become more and not less acute as time passed. For the moment, however, persistence finally paid off. A tip from the economist Alfred Marshall at Cambridge led him to the door of G.I.H. Lloyd, who was then an instructor at Sheffield University. After thorough inquiries and an interview lasting several hours, Falconer was both satisfied and relieved when the 'tall, gentlemanly fellow of thirty four' accepted his offer.[106] With his job done by early August, Falconer celebrated by indulging in a trip to the Swiss mountains and a motoring tour of Scotland. Sailing home on the *Virginian*, he returned to Canada tired but well pleased.

The extreme difficulty encountered in the Lloyd episode was exceptional, at least in those prewar days. Economists, it seems, were in great demand at that time, and Toronto was rather less than competitive in a seller's market. The top annual salary for a lecturer was only $1,800, associate professors earned no more than $3,000, while a mere handful of full professors garnered $4,000.[107] Since wages and benefits were generally better in Great Britain and the United States, it was often difficult to attract just the right man. Even so, Falconer's web of connections in the United Kingdom could usually be relied on to produce satisfactory results. In April 1913, for example, a letter was dispatched to Sadler asking him to keep an eye out for 'a man of outstanding character and ability' to fill a spot in Toronto's Faculty of Education. Quick off the mark, Sadler nominated Peter Sandiford of Manchester, whose appointment was confirmed within the month.[108] Altogether his British agents served Falconer well as he laboured to mould a faculty to suit his vision of the university.

Obviously Falconer had great faith in his British advisers. In part, this trust sprang from a shared belief in the essentially moral nature of education. Still the common coin of English educational thought, this concept was regularly propagated even by those who clamoured for more technological instruction in the face of German competition. Thus high priests of the so-called 'national efficiency movement,' such as R.B. Haldane, subscribed to the notion that 'it is not brute force but moral power that commands predominance in the world.'[109] Others, notably Sadler, echoed and re-echoed this thesis.[110] Interestingly, Sadler in 1909 chose to cite Falconer on this point during an address to a British audience.[111] In any event, it was no accident that the two men sat together on the executive of the International Moral Education Conference in 1922.[112]

Beyond this philosophical convergence, however, Falconer and his British friends agreed on another important point. Many of them, as it happened, were also coming to see a direct link between education and the promotion of imperial unity. Indeed, at the very moment when Falconer was calling for closer co-operation, an 'Imperial Studies Movement' was taking shape in Britain. Disillusioned with delays and squabbling in the realm of political, economic, and military integration, some Britons had turned to education as the vehicle for laying a solid foundation for future imperial unity. It was felt that if people were systematically taught to value empire, all else would follow in time. Thus, before the war, organizations such as the Royal Colonial Institute, the Victoria League, and the League of Empire spearheaded a drive to promote imperial sympathy through educational means. History texts were rewritten to accentuate imperial themes. Empire Day celebrations were recommended to school boards throughout Greater Britain. Song sheets, lectures, and a flood of pamphlets were churned out.[113] In all this activity men such as Smith, Sadler, and others of Falconer's acquaintance played vital roles. To them the movement represented a natural extension of the quest for national efficiency. To Falconer it presented a golden opportunity. Indeed, when British enthusiasts raised the question of drawing universities into the service of the empire, they struck a chord long sounded in far-off Toronto.

In July 1910 a welcome letter crossed Falconer's desk. It undoubtedly made a brilliant summer's afternoon all the brighter for him. A congress of the universities of the empire was being organized for 1912 and he was cordially invited to attend.[114] A few weeks later Sir Henry Miers, principal of the University of London and ardent advocate of imperial studies, wrote to fill in the details. No casual assembly, the meeting was being meticulously planned and would include as many universities from throughout the king's dominions as chose to attend. Sensing in it a chance to stimulate valuable co-operation, Falconer plunged headlong into efforts designed to ensure that Canadian views would be articulated unambiguously when the congress convened in London. For that reason, he eagerly approved a suggestion made by H.M. Tory, president of the University of Alberta, that Canadian leaders hold a preliminary conference in order to sort out their priorities.[115] Recognizing, as Tory had, that he and Peterson would have to take the lead, Falconer happily set about contacting his counterparts throughout the country.[116] A rough agenda was requested from congress organizers to facilitate discussion, and that body's secretary, R.D. Roberts, was asked to audit the Canadian meeting. With all in readiness, Falconer and Peterson welcomed seventeen of their colleagues to Montreal in June 1911. This gathering, as it transpired, was the seed from which the Association of Universities and Colleges of Canada would one day grow.[117] For the moment, however, attention was focused on issues likely to arise in London the following year.

In his report to London, Roberts later described the discussions at Montreal as largely 'desultory.' Many present, it seems, had come inadequately prepared, not having thoroughly scrutinized the agenda proposed for 1912. He was struck, however, by the compelling unanimity registered on at least one point: the conference was adamant 'that something should be done without delay to divert the stream of able Canadian students from America and Germany to the United Kingdom.'

Thus the question of improving accessibility to post-graduate facilities in Britain came to the fore. One speaker alleged that 95 per cent of Canadian graduate students were forced to complete their education in either Germany or the United States. The reasons for this state of affairs were obvious in the delegates' minds. Some pointed to a lack of readily available information concerning British programs. Others noted that, compared with American schools, English bodies offered little financial support to colonial candidates for advanced degrees. Finally, many complained that the doctorates offered simply took too long to complete. The conference, 'desultory' on so many other issues, was assertive enough on these points. Above all, its members made it clear to Roberts that nothing was likely to stem the Canadian flood to America until the greater British universities established a PH D degree on terms competitive with those available outside the confines of the empire. The point was not lost on Roberts – he had heard it all before. He was impressed to note, however, that in this even Laval University supported its anglophone fellows.[118]

Pressure for change had been accumulating, especially at Oxford and Cambridge, since the turn of the century. Both universities, to be sure, offered doctorates, but these degrees traditionally required five years of research and were awarded only for 'mature published work.' Accordingly, an Oxbridge D LITT or D SC was won at the cost of long, hard labour and enjoyed tremendous prestige. Nevertheless, very few overseas students took up the challenge. Instead they overwhelmingly preferred to stand for the American or German PH D. Conceived in Germany, the PH D was quickly adopted by graduate schools in the United States, where it soon became the almost obligatory passport to an academic career. Requiring less time and focusing on a thesis not usually meant for publication, this degree had obvious attractions for young scholars anxious to find employment in a world whose tempo was accelerating. By 1900 voices were being raised in a call for British universities to keep pace. The Allied Colonial Universities Conference of 1903 witnessed several such pleas, with Canadian-born Gilbert Parker leading the chorus. In the same year his countryman, H.P. Biggar, wrote bitterly to the *Times* lamenting the lack of adequate facilities for colonial graduates in Britain. Biggar was supported in this plaint by A.H. Young of the University of Toronto. Adding to the din, Charles Eliot of Harvard cautioned that few Americans would take up the newly instituted Rhodes scholarships if all they could hope to obtain was another BA. For the moment this criticism produced no major results, but at least the issue had been raised. In short order, moreover, it would be adopted again by the proponents of national efficiency and the champions of imperial studies.[119] By 1911 men such as Roberts were thoroughly familiar with the arguments for change. Nevertheless the Montreal meeting had usefully underscored the sense of urgency that Canadian leaders brought to the question. Some months later, just to reinforce the impression, Falconer wrote separately to Miers and Roberts reminding them of this concern.[120] When he embarked for England in the *Corsican* the following June, Falconer was certain that Canadian priorities were already well understood in London.

Arriving at his destination, he delighted in the festive mood he found. Delegates from forty-nine of the empire's fifty-three degree-granting universities were treated to a lavish round of pre-congress entertainments. Lambeth Palace opened its gates. Oxford, Cambridge, and their younger counterparts showered honorary degrees on colonial visitors. Inspired rhetoric echoing through academic halls gave vigorous testimony to the abundant good cheer. Catching the spirit, one London daily indulged in a flight of imperial fancy. The congress, it prophesied, was likely to result in a full and formal federation of the empire's universities.[121] Ultimately of course, the conclave managed no such feat. Indeed, R.M. Meredith, reporting to Premier Whitney, observed that the gathering was mired in tedious detail and too little concerned with 'the grand theme of imperial consolidation.'[122] Sober participants, of course, had never seriously anticipated that a federation would be produced. When, from time to time, the idea surfaced, speaker after speaker retreated from the prospect of imperial centralization.[123] This was only to be expected, and Falconer, who dearly prized university autonomy, cannot have been disappointed. Co-operation, not federation, was his goal. Even this goal, however, proved difficult to secure. Indeed, as the sessions went forward, Falconer was unhappy to find the congress 'a rather cut and dried affair.'[124]

It could scarcely have been otherwise, given its format. Mindful of the divisive nature of past imperial conferences, congress organizers made it clear from the outset that, while many issues would be raised, no votes would be taken. Although understandable and perhaps even expedient, this decision itself was sufficient to preclude dynamic action. In addition, an agenda designed to satisfy all interests was too crowded to allow for extensive discussion of individual matters. At times vital questions had to be dealt with in thirty minutes or less, and all too often attention focused on purely technical detail. In any case, when on the last day the question of graduate studies was raised, no concrete action was taken. Peterson introduced the subject and once again forcefully presented the Canadian case. Australian delegates responded by taking up the plea that Britain adapt its programs to meet imperial needs. British representatives, however, quickly dampened colonial enthusiasms. Oxford and Cambridge, in particular, baulked at the prospect of lowering the standards of their advanced degrees. To establish a two-year PH D, they argued, would only encourage unseemly 'degree hunting.'[125] Not for the last time, they heaped scorn on those who would follow Americans down the path of academic 'commercialization.'[126] Unspoken, one suspects, was resentment and fear of outside meddling. In any event, the PH D proposal, along with efforts to effect exchanges and the mutual recognition of degrees, was left up in the air. Thus all attempts to alter existing conditions failed. There remained only one spark to kindle lingering hopes.

It was provided by the only formal resolutions that the congress passed. Clearly dismayed by the indecisive nature of the proceedings, George Parkin took the podium during the closing session and delivered a ringing address. 'I think,' proclaimed that redoubtable imperial champion, 'if we fail to grasp the idea that this is a mighty Empire, that this country is the centre of that Empire, and that the outside Empire is constantly growing and increasing, with thousands of students coming into the Universities to an extent we can scarcely conceive of at the centre – unless we can compare the experience of the past with the great experiments carried on, we will never reach the best organisation and highest influence that the Universities of this country should have.' Blunt words from a bluff-mannered man, they were aimed squarely at reticent English delegates. Going further, Parkin pointed out the obvious dangers of failing to respond constructively to articulated colonial desires. Thus he cited the precedent of Walter Murray, who, in seeking out models for the University of Saskatchewan, canvassed opinion widely in the United States but neither sought nor received assistance from Britons. Such a state of affairs, he chided, was pitiable in any empire worthy of the name. Rising to his theme he argued that London should be transformed into a centre to which all imperial universities would naturally gravitate for leadership and inspiration. To that end, he proposed not only that the congress be established on a regular basis but that a permanent bureau be founded to continue its work between sessions. Serving as a clearing house of information, it might also facilitate at least informal measures of imperial co-operation. Adding, finally, that such steps would redound to the 'enormous benefit' of the empire, Parkin awaited reactions.[127]

They were swift in coming. G. Adam Smith of the University of Aberdeen seconded the motion. He added that a yearbook published by the proposed bureau would end a dependence on the German publication *Minerva*, which was the only regular source of information concerning universities in India. Sadler of the University of Leeds, Tory of Alberta, and Cappon of Queen's threw their weight behind the suggestions. Falconer rose to urge that members of the bureau should not be junior men but people who could speak with authority for their universities. Only in this way, he advised, would that body 'go forward with greater momentum and greater responsibility.' Surprisingly these ideas encountered little or no opposition and were unanimously endorsed. The key to this success, perhaps, lay in the informality of the arrangements. No binding commitments on contentious matters were solicited. Simple, voluntary co-operation alone was requested. And so the Universities Bureau of the British Empire was born. Its headquarters would be in London, but its executive was to be elected by congress on a proportional basis with two of the fourteen seats reserved for Canada. Tory was duly chosen to fill one of these and Falconer the other. It was a position that the latter would retain until ill health forced his resignation shortly before his retirement at Toronto. This result, admittedly, was little enough to show for all the hopes he had entertained before the 1912 meetings. Still, Falconer was a patient man and content to make do with a small opening. Congress, scheduled to meet every five years, was interrupted by the war and did not reconvene until 1921. In the meantime, however, Canadians used the bureau and the platform it afforded to continue lobbying for the PH D and greater access to British graduate schools. The initial congress had been an education, and Falconer was an adept pupil. Eventually he and like-minded associates would be rewarded.

Despite this evident desire to huddle for a time under the protective imperial wing, Falconer envisaged something more than a purely passive role for Varsity within the empire. Colonial subordination was not for him. Instead, while anxious to share in the benefits, he was also eager to shoulder some of the burdens of empire. Indeed, he felt that the University of Toronto could and should play an important part in extending the moral influence of Greater Britain, and he was determined that it should do so as a full and active partner in the imperial cause. As he explained in 1908, 'the more we can do for the Empire as well as for our own provinces and homeland, the larger will be the usefulness of the University.'[128] Forging 'personal links' through recruitment in the mother country was a small if solid contribution in this regard. But he quickly discovered other more grandiose tasks for the University of Toronto to assume. Foremost among these in the years before the war was a sustained effort to broaden Canadian and imperial influence in China by educational means. A lasting interest in the affairs of the Celestial Empire had been born in Falconer as early as his days in Trinidad. Raised on tales of missionary derring-do in the far east, he had also been deeply affected by his father's favourable impression of Chinese immigrants on the island. Informed that they were easily westernized and made excellent converts, he was also told that China itself, once awakened by the clarion call of modernization, would wield tremendous power on the global stage. With so much at stake, cautioned Alex, it was vital that those of British origin help shape the values as well as the commerce of the Middle Kingdom. This was a lesson that Robert never forgot.

An opportunity to translate theory into practice was presented to him early in his administration at Toronto. Former graduates currently active with the YMCA in China wrote home in 1908 requesting Falconer to support their educational efforts. Some of these correspondents were well known to him as former participants in the Northfield conferences.[129] One Toronto old boy, J.H. Wallace, took special care to explain the situation to the new president. The failure of the Boxer Rebellion, he argued, had 'shattered the hope that the Westerner with his civilization could be driven out of the country.' China, he continued, was now a 'learner amongst the nations.' He went on to describe how the United States was making great strides towards capturing the allegiance of reform-minded Chinese, not only through its activities in China but also by opening its own universities to them. Although discouraging large-scale peasant immigration, America placed no barriers in the path of visiting students, many of whom went on to be men of influence at home and encouraged others to look to Uncle Sam for guidance. While applauding such efforts generally, Wallace was concerned that Canada and the empire keep pace, lest by default they find themselves shunted to the sidelines in this crucial portion of the globe. He therefore urged Falconer to make room for Chinese students at Toronto and to induce other Canadian universities to follow his lead. In justifying this proposal, Wallace and others cited arguments that would one day be loudly trumpeted by Canadians alert to the potential of the 'Pacific rim.' The commercial significance of a nation teeming with millions of consumers and 'unlimited natural resources' was obvious to him. But so was the probability that the machinery and supplies for development would be sought in countries where the leaders of a revivified China had been educated. He realized, of course, that there were loftier grounds on which to base his request. As a realist, however, he offered that 'possibly the selfish motive affords the strongest appeal to the average government today.' Thus commercial advantage was emphasized. The vital thing, in any event, said Wallace, was to develop skilled and honest leadership among the people themselves. There were, he admitted, some able and sincere local men, but he lamented that they were submerged in 'the horde of incapable, ignorant and dishonest officials.' Contending that responsible direction would be provided only by Chinese educated in western universities, he asked, 'is it not important that a fair proportion of these future leaders should be trained in British universities and that thus they should look to British institutions for their models and that their friendship should be won for the British Empire?'[130]

Already apprised of the situation, Falconer nodded heartfelt assent to this rhetorical question. In fact, he had written to the British consulate at Shanghai on this score even before Wallace's letter arrived. Officials were asked to keep an eye out for persons who wished to attend a 'British University' but were unable to go to England. Such people, he suggested, would find a thoroughly British environment at Toronto.[131] Moving quickly, he induced the Board of Governors to pass a regulation allowing for the admittance of ten Chinese students to free places every two years.[132] He was gratified by the board's support even though he noted 'a slight antichinese [sic] feeling in some quarters.'[133]

But while clearing the decks in Toronto proved easy enough, Falconer faced a far more serious challenge when he turned to Ottawa. Approaching the Laurier government on the subject, he plucked at an exposed and particularly sensitive nerve. Long hostile to oriental immigration, the Canadian public was in an especially nasty mood at the moment. Racial prejudice, never far from the surface, was throbbing feverishly and nowhere more heatedly than in British Columbia. In 1907 riots had erupted in the streets of Vancouver. Sparked by fears of cheap immigrant labour, they were further stoked by general hysteria concerning a supposed 'yellow peril.' Fearing for their very lives, Japanese and Chinese residents had also suffered severe property damage. Weighing its liberal instincts against political expediency, the federal government opted for an age-old solution. Thus, a royal commission was struck to study the whole issue of oriental immigration. From the start, however, it was clear that the admission of eastern peoples would henceforth be greatly restricted. Conveniently, the Japanese accepted a proposal for voluntary curtailment. When China failed to come similarly to heel, however, not even the patina of liberalism was preserved. Instead, Ottawa slapped a $500 head tax on all Chinese seeking a home in Canada, a move that kept all but the desirably affluent out. British Columbia was thus mollified. Thereafter the Laurier cabinet sought to avoid further entanglement in this thorny issue.[134]

From Falconer's vantage point, needless to say, the head tax was an unmitigated disaster. Stout defender of the British national character that he was, he could understand the desire to prevent a massive influx of oriental peasants. He deplored barriers, however, when they blocked the entrance of students, who in any event would be carefully screened. Such, it seems, were the limits of his own liberal sympathies. In any case, seeking an exemption for bona fide scholars, in 1909 he began the lengthy process of petitioning Ottawa. Appropriately, Laurier was the first to be approached. The prime minister was duly informed of the diplomatic, commercial, and ideological benefits that would flow from such a gesture.[135] Sir Wilfrid, however, was unmoved. He advised Falconer that the issue was simply too hot to handle and that any amendments to current legislation would evoke a storm of protest in British Columbia. Furthermore, and not very convincingly, he argued that any privileges extended to scholars would most likely be abused by others posing as students. In concluding, he added rather curtly that it was unlikely he could help the president in this matter.[136] As one door seemed to close, however, another opened. Sir William Peterson was prepared to add McGill's voice to the call for exemptions. At a special meeting of concerned Montrealers in May, he denounced the head tax on students as 'inexpedient' and likely only to increase American influence in China while Canada's waned.[137] Buoyed up by this timely support, Falconer returned to the fray. This time he directed his appeal to Mackenzie King, minister of labour and one of the architects of the government's immigration policy.[138] A delegate to the recent Opium Conference, King had just returned from China where Wallace and others had attempted to sway him to their views. At first blush their efforts seemed to have had an effect. King's reply to Falconer was cordial and appeared to hold forth the prospect of change. The minister confessed that 'privately' he recognized the wisdom of inviting Chinese students to Canada. He even ventured that it might be possible to lift the head tax on them 'in the not far distant future.' He cautioned, however, that the restriction of general Chinese immigration was 'an absolute necessity' and asked Falconer to treat the contents of the letter as 'confidential for the present.'[139]

On the strength of this optimistic message, the president dispatched a letter to Shanghai informing Wallace that there had been a modification of Ottawa's views on the matter.[140] As the months rolled by, however, and no action was taken, disillusionment set in. Whatever King's 'private' views might have been, he was no more willing to reopen the Chinese issue than was Laurier. Having momentarily soothed Falconer and his associates, he was content to let the matter lie fallow. More substantial questions, such as naval policy and reciprocity, were looming on the political horizon, and Liberals saw no reason to gamble away precious reserves of strength on so marginal a point as the fate of a few Chinese students. When they were defeated in the next general election, Falconer took heart. Even so, it required many more years of persistent lobbying until the Borden government yielded to the combined weight of Canada's university presidents in 1917 and lifted the head tax on students.[141] Meanwhile an alternative line of advance was probed. Barriers in Canada, after all, might be circumvented by working in China itself.

An opportunity to do so came Falconer's way in the spring of 1910. In April of that year A.L. Smith visited Toronto with a clerical scion of the influential Cecil clan in tow. Rector of Hatfield, Hertfordshire, the Reverend Lord William Gascoyne-Cecil and his academic friend were touring North American universities to drum up support for a scheme launched in Britain two years earlier. The intention was to establish in China a university on the Oxbridge model capable of combining 'the highest intellectual efficiency with a system of sound moral training and discipline.'[142] A brochure setting forth the objects of the plan indicates that its proponents had no wish to undermine missionary education in China. They did feel, however, that there was a need for an independent institution that extolled a more liberal spirit than the church schools. They proposed, therefore, a secular university with which interested religious colleges could affiliate. Professors of the central body would offer a full curriculum featuring not only the much sought-after sciences but also the arts. In this way, it was hoped, the higher values of the British peoples would be transmitted, along with their practical skills.[143] As Cecil later explained to George Wrong, 'a materialistic East must be the forerunner of a miserable and materialistic West.' To forestall such a disaster, he continued, a dike had to be raised 'on the boundary of nations which are nearer the danger point.' Oxbridge must be exported to China.[144] Significantly, however, wholesale Anglicization was eschewed; rather, the stated purpose was 'to prepare the way for a real fusion of Chinese and Western thought, which may enable the China of the future to produce a characteristic modern culture of her own.' Like British orientalists in India a century earlier, Cecil and his friends sought to 'naturalize' in China the highest elements of western thought while preserving all that was best in traditional culture.[145] 'The great strength of a scheme like this,' he informed Wrong, 'lies in the fact that it really looks to China to regenerate China.'[146] In the first flush of enthusiasm the details of how this acculteration was to be accomplished were left nebulous. Indeed, the precise points at which British and Chinese culture supposedly intersected were never defined. But even from the outset, one thing was perfectly clear. The task at hand was in scale and expense far too imposing for Oxford and Cambridge to shoulder unaided. Thus Cecil and Smith ventured abroad in search of support for what was coming to be viewed as a necessarily international effort. Aided by their boast that Sadler at Leeds and Miers at London had cast favourable eyes on the project, they found in Falconer a willing recruit.[147]

As chairman of the Canadian committee, Falconer had the assistance of George Wrong, T.A. Russell, and N.W. Rowell. Throughout 1911 they laboured to elicit local support for the projected university, but the scheme was plagued with difficulties from the beginning. Men of wealth and influence paid little heed to their private requests for donations. A mid-year general election monopolized everybody's attention. Consequently, a public appeal was delayed until November. When in that month Falconer published a memorandum outlining the project, he played heavily on the time-honoured Victorian themes of Christianity, commerce, and civilization.[148] The man in the street, however, barely took notice. By January 1912 Falconer had scraped together the $625 that the central committee had designated as Canada's first instalment. In forwarding the cheque, he did not bother to mention that most of the money had come from the pocket of B.E. Walker.[149] Discouraged, but as yet undeterred, he explained this poor showing as the result of public absorption first in the elections and then in the Christmas rush. In truth, it was probably just an ill-timed venture, given the recent furore over Chinese immigration. In any case, he looked forward to 1912 and a renewal of the effort.

Meanwhile, a series of problems arose within the international organization of which his branch was a mere part. Cecil and Smith had been successful in recruiting not only Falconer, but some leading American figures as well. Committees were formed at Columbia, Harvard, and the University of California with general headquarters in New York. Seth Low, a noted Progressive and one-time mayor of New York City, chaired the American group. Seeking to co-ordinate their endeavours, Falconer and Low struck up a lively correspondence and discovered in each other kindred spirits. Broadly interested in the social and political reform of their own societies, both were also deeply committed to developing a better understanding between east and west.[150] On at least one occasion, Falconer visited Low at his Broad Brook Farm estate in Westchester County in order to discuss the university scheme face to face. They agreed that tighter organization and more clearly delineated plans were required if the scheme were to succeed. As a first step they suggested that a president of the university be appointed. The English committee concurred and nominated the Reverend W.E. Soothill, former principal of the Shansi Imperial University. Overseas groups gave their assent, but other points proved more difficult to resolve. In March 1911, for example, Falconer was taken aback by a proposal made by Cecil which seemed to him likely to water down and defeat the whole scheme. The reverend gentleman was urging that, for the time being, individual teachers be sent out by different universities to serve apprenticeships in existing institutions in China. At some unspecified future date, he argued, they could form a nucleus for the new teaching body.[151] Seeing this as a reversal of earlier policy and in any event bound to fail, Falconer rejected the idea out of hand.[152] The suggestion was quickly shelved, but a sharper disagreement was already brewing.

For a variety of reasons, Low and his American colleagues were anxious that the proposed site of the university be changed. The British favoured Hankow, where substantial educational facilities had already been planted by a variety of English missionary bodies. Suddenly, in January 1912 the New York group began touting the advantages of Nanking, where American mission schools had concentrated.[153] To complicate matters even further, Low's associates had begun to question the viability of the whole project. They noted the difficulty of competing for funds with missionary societies. Furthermore, when Lowell of Harvard inquired, he found that American religious colleges in China were less than favourably disposed towards the idea of affiliating with any secular university.[154] With these problems hanging in the air, the Americans felt that useful discussion of a recently drafted constitution was impossible. Everything, they now conveniently maintained, depended on the progress of the British funding drive. One senses that a less than graceful withdrawal was already in progress.

These complications left Cecil's group in a most unenviable position. Ironically, they had counted on American largesse to act as a spur to British generosity. In 1910 they had baulked at trying to raise money in the midst of the clamour that attended hotly contested elections.[155] The following year they found men of substance disinclined to donate because they were uncertain about the long-term effects of Lloyd George's 'soak the rich' budget. Accordingly, in an unfavourable atmosphere it was decided to delay a major public campaign until 1913.[156] Sensible perhaps in a British context, this decision exasperated the Americans. Such apparent stalling only led them to call for a tangible demonstration of good faith. Thus New York refused to move until Cecil's group produced some cash of its own.[157] Moreover, as financial difficulties multiplied, so did complaints about the amateurish quality of Cecil's leadership. Some of this carping was thoroughly justified. Putting the cart before the horse, the naïve peer had assumed that he could delay the formulation of 'the main lines of a definite scheme' until after sufficient capital had been raised. In fairness, however, if Cecil erred in putting forth a hazily conceived plan, Falconer, Low, and others had been willing enough to go along initially and cannot be exempted from criticism. At any rate, by 1912 all the North American committees were complaining of a lack of both co-ordination and communication within the international body.[158]

Predictably, given these circumstances, the United Universities Scheme failed to bear fruit. It wilted under the combined pressures of misman-agement, misunderstanding, and financial dearth. In addition, thinly veiled national jealousies played no small part in its demise. In any case, volatile political conditions in China following the events of 1911 might well have obviated even the best organized efforts to implement such a plan. After 1912 Falconer gave up on the idea and concentrated his attention on efforts to abolish the Canadian head tax on Chinese students. Yet while one endeavour eventually paid dividends and the other failed, both illustrated clearly the context within which he habitually viewed Varsity. An emerging national university, he thought, could only be nurtured at the bosom of empire. He also looked forward, however, to the day when the University of Toronto would play a more mature role as a force for the extension of imperial influence. This was Falconer's version of the 'sense of power.'

Although not immediately aware of it, by 1914 Falconer was standing at the close of the first phase of his career in Toronto. Seven years had been crammed with intense activity. Moreover, they had exacted a toll, if only on his once luxuriant crop of now rapidly vanishing hair. Meanwhile, as though to reciprocate, his erstwhile lean frame was expanding as his locks receded. Confined to a desk, he took less and less physical exercise as the terms rolled by. Small wonder, therefore, that he became progressively more vulnerable to the many plagues that stalk the sedentary. It was a rare cold or flu bug that visited Toronto and did not find him a generous host. In time, one suspects, his general resistance was significantly lowered. For the moment, however, he remained sufficiently robust to delight in even the difficulties of office. Of these, of course, there had been plenty. But there had also been rewards and recognition. Honorary degrees had been conferred upon him by Dalhousie, McMaster, and other institutions. In 1911 he was appointed CMG. Perhaps even more flatteringly, in the same year he was invited to assume the presidency of the University of British Columbia. Touched by this offer, he none the less declined citing as his reason a sense of duty to Varsity and work only just begun.[159] As well, he may have been reluctant to uproot his family. Sophie, besides playing hostess at their draughty residence on St George Street, was enjoying an active role in the local community. President of the Women's Club of Toronto, she was also deeply involved in the affairs of the YWCA. Gilbert and Bobby were thriving. Altogether, the Falconers saw no good reason to leave. Besides, Vancouver was intolerably distant from the Maritimes, to which they returned whenever possible to visit old friends and relations. Renting cottages on Prince Edward Island or in Nova Scotia, the Falconer clan habitually gathered for a few weeks annually to swap stories and to reminisce. Alex was a favourite with the children and regaled them endlessly with stories of his days in exotic Trinidad. He had retired from Prince Street Church in Pictou in 1909 but had lost none of his accustomed energy. Indeed, it was while in Elmsdale, Nova Scotia as a visiting preacher that he suddenly collapsed and died one Sunday in July 1911. Robert was thus bereft of a father who had served as his youthful hero and guide. He was grateful, however, that Alex had not outlived his zest for life and had been allowed to depart this world in harness. Never one to parade his private feelings, Falconer wrote to Murray that 'our memory of him as a good and wise man is a great legacy.'[160] Himself a reserved man, Alex most likely would have appreciated the simple dignity of this epitaph.

Taking the joys and sorrows, the disappointments and the achievements of these years in his stride, Falconer retained his accustomed optimism. Indeed, although not blind to the problems of the hour, he anticipated a future still bright with promise. Speaking in 1913 at the Cleveland convention of the Religious Education Association, he put his hopes into words. He chose progress and the role of science and religion in promoting it as his theme. Reflecting on the nineteenth century, he described that era as a moment of emancipation. The forces of democracy had gathered momentum. A revival of moral enthusiasm had engendered the search for social justice. Above all, however, men had been liberated from their thralldom to antiquated modes of thought. Science of the purest sort shattered superstition and in the process had clarified the essence of religion. 'It has,' he proclaimed, 'removed large portions of what was once thought to be vital, and has sent mankind forth less sicklied over with the pale cast of doubt and has given it the tread of a healthier faith.' Furthermore, he argued, the reconciliation of science and religion had laid the foundation for general progress. Thus civilization, that 'modern City of God,' though still 'somewhat secular' was observably 'more divinely ordered than the older cities.' In simple terms, streets were better illuminated and safer than of old, and despite continued rapacity in the marketplace, society was gradually being 'humanized.' Casting an eye on the international arena, Falconer contended that even there, some temporary disputes notwithstanding, marked improvement had been made. 'The spirit of the twentieth century,' he maintained, 'is cutting away the crudities of a selfish and aggressive patriotism.' Altogether, he looked forward to the revival of a purified common Christianity in a world at peace.[161]

CHAPTER VIII

The Glorious Days
of Our Race
1914–18

With blackout drill in effect, nervous passengers huddled by night in their cabins. The air aboard was stifling as, lights darkened and portholes closed, the *Calgarian* steamed for New York at all possible speed. It was September 1914. Shipboard life had always delighted Falconer. For him it signalled a sweet, if fleeting, release from burdens waiting ashore. This time, however, the cares of the land reached out to trouble him as war's lengthening shadow cast a pall across the North Atlantic. But he at least could keep his mind off larger matters while ministering to the stricken Sophie. Always a reluctant sailor, she was enduring particular torments in the stuffy atmosphere of a ship rigged for emergency. Still, all things considered, they were grateful even for an uncomfortable berth. The *Victorian*, in which they had intended to sail, had been withdrawn from service with the advent of hostilities. Two frustrating weeks of scrambling for alternative accommodation had been passed in a Liverpool rife with confusion and disquieting rumour. So it was a relief just to be moving, and the heat, the crowding, and the anxiety could be borne. In fact, spirits lightened considerably as they neared North American waters and spotted a friendly warship at dawn. Relief, however, was tinged with a sense of loss as they recalled the happier circumstances of the outward voyage.[1]

The problems Falconer had momentarily escaped that spring seemed worrisome enough at the time. Mounting deficits plagued him and he cringed at the thought of going cap in hand to Queen's Park. The university, he confided to Walter Murray, was wallowing in 'the deep waters of financial distress.' He and Walker had tried to impress members of the legislature with the gravity of the situation. On the whole, Falconer was confident that the sombre message had been understood. In any case, he felt sure that the matter could be left in Walker's hands for the next few months. Meanwhile, his thoughts shifted to a brighter prospect. A genuine vacation, the first in years, was close at hand and he was counting the hours. In a reversal of their usual roles, it was Sophie who this time was obliged to travel abroad. A delegate to the international YWCA conference, she was off to Sweden, and Robert had decided to tag along for the ride. With no papers to deliver, no meetings to attend, and no professors to recruit, he was free to chart his own course. His sole concession to official business would be a brief stop at the University of Groningen which was celebrating its three-hundredth anniversary. Apart from that commitment, he gleefully anticipated touring Scandinavia as whim decreed.[2]

The voyage to Europe was everything he could have desired. Never one to haunt the grand salon, Falconer passed the hours curled up in a deck chair devouring carefully selected reading material or locked in earnest conversation. The festivities at Groningen also passed off smoothly. Indeed, he enjoyed reliving his student days in the company of visiting German scholars. Side-trips to universities at Delft and Leyden proved enlightening. In particular and with a touch of envy, he noted how the absence of large junior classes had stimulated graduate studies and research.[3] Finally, his duties done, Falconer left Holland on 2 July and made for the port of Hamburg en route to Sweden. He later recalled that 'at that time there was not even a whisper of war; everything seemed to be going on in a normal way.'[4] Rejoining Sophie in Stockholm, he marvelled at the beauty of the city but was surprised by the temperature which seemed to soar daily. As the YWCA continued its deliberations, he took advantage of opportunities to visit the University of Uppsala and to view a session of the Swedish parliament. When Sophie was at last free, the two moved on to the highlight of their journey, a three-week sojourn in Norway.

Cruising that country's spectacular fiords, Falconer struck up a friendship with a supreme court justice from Berlin. One brilliant afternoon, they joined fellow passengers at the ship's rail to catch a glimpse of the kaiser's yacht steaming lazily in the distance. A few days later six German warships lined the horizon for several hours, only to be gone by daybreak. Whether or not Falconer realized it, those bristling silhouettes were ominous portents of events that would quickly bring his summer idyll to a premature halt.

Everyone, of course, read the warning signs accurately in retrospect, but the rapid descent into war certainly caught Falconer ill prepared.

Originally, he had planned to return to Holland via Copenhagen and then perhaps to spend a few weeks dawdling in England. Suddenly, all was in disarray and the premium was on haste. A new itinerary had to be patched together out of unpromising materials. His greatest fear was of being marooned. With warring legions on the march, Dutch and Belgian ports seemed out of the question. Measuring the odds, he elected passage on a Norwegian steamer out of Bergen. Crammed to the gunwales with human cargo, the tramp vessel offered few amenities as it ploughed through the North Sea. Sophie, more fortunate than most, managed to secure a bed. Robert, however, spent one fitful night stretched out on the floor, and stayed awake the next. There was, in any case, little inducement to relax. The skipper had passed word that the waters they traversed were heavily mined. By whom he did not say, nor is it likely that anyone cared about the national origin of the lurking danger. Breaking free of the explosive threat unscathed, they finally neared the English coast. From out of the gloom, speedy torpedo boats darted in to challenge them time and again. In Newcastle harbour disembarkation was delayed for hours as the alien ship was searched thoroughly while transfixed by a battery of glaring floodlamps. When at last clear of the gangplank, the Falconers hustled to the railway station only to find it choked with soldiers. Normal service was disrupted. Britain was fitting itself out as if for siege. The source of the congestion, as one wild rumour had it, was that 70,000 Russian troops were being shipped south by rail from Scotland. Eventually, jostled and tossed about, the Falconers made their way to Liverpool and with effort arranged passage aboard the *Calgarian*. Thus a longed-for vacation ended in anxious flight as Falconer had his first taste of war.[5]

Upon arriving at home, the weary president communicated immediately with friends who might be concerned for his safety. To Walter Murray he wrote describing the rigours of his journey and speculating on the consequences of the war for the University of Toronto. Disruptions, he noted, had already begun as professors and students flocked to the colours. Enrolment was bound to suffer, but that could not be helped. More alarming was the prospect of severe cuts in government spending on the university. These too were only to be expected, but Falconer feared any precedent that might significantly lower already inadequate grants.[6] For the moment he was content to play by ear an uncertain situation. Meanwhile, where the war itself was concerned, he was confident of the outcome. Writing to Sir Henry Miers in London, he observed that 'the spirit of our people is splendid and we realise that we are one in this matter.'[7] Swept up in the first rush of camaraderie, Falconer emphasized the positive elements in the Ontario mood. But this was early September. A few months later, he might well have been tempted to revise his analysis of the local disposition. All too soon he detected discordant notes in the provincial chorus and himself became the target of sentiments that were far from 'splendid.' Indeed, little did he realize as he wrote to Miers that he was about to face perhaps the most dramatic crisis of his career.

The seeds of controversy had been sown before Falconer's return to Toronto. On Monday, 7 September E.W. Hagarty, principal of Harbord Collegiate, summoned students to a special assembly. By nature blustery and outspoken, the fiery schoolmaster was in a particularly agitated mood. The events of August had roused his martial ardour and he was anxious to stimulate this combative spirit in his youthful listeners. Employing only the broadest strokes, he painted a picture in simple black and white, leaving no room for doubt as to which shade best suited the empire's enemies. Germans and 'Germanism' were roundly denounced as the foes of civilized men everywhere. Sparing none of the Kaiser's minions wherever they might be found, he held forth with passion and self-righteous conviction. Not for a moment did he pause to consider the feelings of at least three boys in his audience who claimed a Teutonic heritage. To Rudolphe, Albert, and Theodore Mueller, however, Hagarty's diatribe came as a crushing personal blow. Not only was their loyalty implicitly impugned, they also faced the threat of ostracism from their adolescent peers. Lashing out, they sought to defend themselves and others of their background only to be rebuffed by Hagarty. One firebrand in the crowd took it upon himself to kick Rudolphe and a scuffle ensued. In the end, the Muellers returned to their Warren Road home acutely embarrassed and threatened with the prospect of expulsion from their school.

As it happened, their father was not the sort of man to take such matters lying down. Paul Wilhelm Mueller had come to Canada twenty-one years earlier. Graduating from Varsity, he had served for a time as pastor of a German Lutheran church in Toronto. After completing further studies, he was appointed to the German department at the university and eventually rose to the rank of associate professor. In 1911 Mueller discovered that his German citizenship had long since lapsed. Consequently, when war broke out, he was not liable for conscription into the Kaiser's legions. Neither fact, however, occasioned regret in the professor, since he had come to consider Canada his adopted country. Even so, he had taken special care to remain silent on the question of the war, fearing that anything he said might be misinterpreted.[8] In August he undoubtedly heaved a sigh of relief as the moderate press urged readers to sympathize with the plight of German-Canadians. The *Globe,* in fact, had denounced the view that this was a war among peoples and instead had insisted that it was only the 'Bismarckian military system' that should be loathed.[9] For a time, then, all had been well and the Muellers had not suffered. And this situation, thought the head of the household, was only just. After all, his sons had been reared as loyal subjects of the crown. Indeed, all three were members of the Harbord Cadet Corps, and Rudolphe, the eldest, had been drilling part-time with the Queen's Own Rifles for almost a year. It came as a shock, therefore, when the boys came trailing in that Monday in September with news of what had transpired at school.

There followed an acrimonious exchange, at first face to face and later in the press. An incensed father tried to arrange transfers to another school, but the stubborn principal refused to sanction them. The Muellers returned to Harbord, but only after Hagarty denounced their conduct and reiterated his own views about the war. Writing to Falconer, the frustrated professor hoped that it would not be necessary to send his family out of the country in order to spare them further embarrassment.[10] Moving to the offensive, Mueller stated his case in the papers. He was, moreover, heartened when six of his colleagues, led by John Squair, issued a public protest on his behalf. The affair was gathering heat. School trustees, sympathetic to Hagarty, rallied to his cause. One submitted that 'I would rather have my boy taught loyalty by Mr Hagarty than to have him listen to Professor Mueller who though for nineteen years a resident of Canada, has not yet been naturalized.' Another argued that the schools were focal points of patriotism but raised doubts about the spirit at the university. 'It is a funny thing,' he contended, 'if universities are to be taught by men from another country.'[11] Gradually, indeed, thanks to the accident of Mueller's employment and the support of some of his colleagues, the focus of criticism was beginning to shift towards the university itself. In the first week of October the Toronto Board of Education met to pass forward resolutions on the matter, and Varsity was dragged into the thick of the conflict. Those resolutions included strong support for Hagarty, condemnation of Squair, and a call for Queen's Park and the Board of Governors to launch an immediate enquiry. A few 'applauding patriots' in attendance even questioned the loyalty of Toronto's professoriate, but suggestions to note this doubt officially were dropped. The resolutions, backed by a petition bearing over 100 signatures, were then forwarded to the premier for action.[12]

The Honourable William H. Hearst, however, wanted nothing to do with the whole affair. Only a few weeks in an unfamiliar office, he had inherited the premier's chair when Whitney died. Faced with all the demands of war, he had little incentive to turn this comparative tempest in a teapot into a major political wrangle. Nor was he keen to interfere in university affairs and thus vitiate the constitution of 1906 which had been of his party's own devising. Accordingly, he stalled. Almost a week passed before he officially raised the subject with Falconer. When he did, it was merely to observe that the issue was one 'for the Board of Governors, not for the Government.'[13] This now familiar formula proved convenient to both parties. Falconer quickly replied that the board saw no reason to take action and Hearst, perhaps relieved, noted that no further discussion was needed.[14] And there the matter might have ended had not other events intervened to give it new life and a more serious twist. The Germano-phobes were not to be so easily turned aside.

In fact, at the very moment that Falconer was exchanging pleasantries with Hearst concerning the Mueller case, an angry letter crossed his desk. Colonel Reuben Wells Leonard, a steel and railway magnate from St Catharines, was positively fuming. Colonel J.S. Campbell had brought to his attention an article published in the *Star* on 14 October which seemed to indicate that at least one Toronto professor harboured dangerously pro-German sentiments. Dr Platon Reich, lecturer in German at Trinity College, had alleged publicly that the press had distorted Germany's role in provoking the war. Britain, he argued, shared part of the blame for allowing relations to deteriorate over the past ten years. Moreover, he continued, it was well known that France had nurtured a spirit of revenge since 1870.[15] These views, of course, would be integrated into convention-al wisdom years later, but in the midst of hostilities Campbell was outraged. 'It would appear,' he told Leonard, 'that the Provincial University is harbouring an agent of "William the Bloodstained."' He therefore urged his friend, as a governor of the university, to recommend that Falconer secure Reich's resignation immediately.[16] Leonard, a graduate of Royal Military College and veteran of the North-west Rebellion, was also a devoted son of empire. Greater Britain, he once contended, was 'the greatest of human achievements' and further offered that 'to serve it rightly is to serve mankind.'[17] In his eyes the 'Hun' who threatened the life of that sacred institution could be viewed only as an enemy of civilization itself. To explain away Germany's patent guilt smacked of treason, and the indignant colonel would have none of it. Accordingly, he endorsed Campbell's call for action: 'This is not the time for such discussions and the liberties of any men who are inclined that way should be curtailed.'[18] Normally a remonstrance from one of the governors could not be circumvented as easily as one from the Board of Education. This time, however, Falconer managed to escape the entangling nets of controversy by calling on solid constitutional precedent. Under the terms of federation he had no jurisdiction over professors at Trinity. Leonard should have known this. Prudently, however, the president sought to soothe him by noting that university faculty members of German origin had been warned to maintain strict silence.[19] Still, in his own mind, Falconer must have cursed Platon Reich, if only for his appalling sense of timing.

Falconer had been fortunate in his efforts to shelter the university from attacks. Very shortly, however, his luck ran out. As October gave way to November various factors combined to inflict increasing pressure on him. There were growing complaints, wholly unfounded as it happened, that the university was shirking its responsibility to encourage enlistment. Falconer moved to counter this slur by pointing out that the University was attempting to form its own officer training corps and that by mid-October over 1,300 of its students had already volunteered for active service.[20] Even so, rumours persisted that certain professors had deliberately scheduled classes to conflict with practice drills. Complicating the picture were allegations that the Toronto campus was becoming a hotbed of party politics. Indeed, concern had been registered about this issue even before the war. In December 1913, for example, there had been heated criticism of a public university which allowed student groups to flaunt party labels. At the time Falconer, although dead set against the practice, had refused to take official action, believing that 'more harm would be done by suppressing it.'[21] Much of the outcry had come from Conservatives, who felt betrayed. Proven benefactors of the university, they bitterly resented overwhelming demonstrations of Liberal support by the students of University College. In the emotional excitement generated by war, resentment evolved into the suspicion that a conspiracy was afoot. By November, in fact, many Conservatives were convinced that the offending student organizations were being secretly funded by the *Star* and other Liberal agents. To make matters worse, some even believed that Falconer, by failing to act, had given clear evidence that he was at the head of this Grit cabal.[22] Nothing, of course, could have been further from the truth. The president saw himself as a servant of the state, above partisanship and loyal to the government of the day.[23] In private he had always loathed party politics in general but, ironically, had personally tended to be drawn to Conservative leaders such as Whitney and Borden. Ever cautious to observe strict neutrality in public, he was understandably angered by rumours to the contrary. But for a time he chose to forgo comment, recognizing that anything he might say would only fuel the flames of speculation. There were, he believed, those who for one reason or another were still dissatisfied with the reformed university and would seize on any opportunity to stir up discontent.[24] It was better to remain silent than to play into their hands by allowing himself to be baited in the public forum. However, when scattered criticism resolved itself into an attack on members of his staff under the evocative banner of anti-Germanism, Falconer dug in his heels.

Feelings against enemy aliens were beginning to run high in Ontario by this juncture. The generous spirit of August was fading rapidly as stories of alleged German atrocities gained general currency. The sensationalist press advertised tales of Belgian babies skewered on German bayonets and of ancient towns laid waste by the 'Hun.' Rifle clubs proliferated, as numerous Ontarians anticipated attacks from German and Austrian expatriots in the United States.[25] Fantasizing about Teutonic Fenians, the public was also receptive to warnings concerning the enemy within. Some papers ridiculed these unfounded nightmares. The editors of the *Star*, for example, criticized indiscriminate propagandists bent on denouncing neighbours who happened to have Germanic names.[26] Pleas for moderation, unfortunately, were lost in the growing din. In particular, an agitation designed to remove all enemy aliens from civic employ quickly gathered strength in Toronto. City fathers yielded to pressure on 13 November as the Board of Control committed itself to dismissing 'all enemies of the King.' The first to 'feel the axe' was a Dr Kohlman, who was forced to resign despite the strong support of Works Commissioner Harris. Meanwhile the Board of Education, more royalist than the king, set in motion an 'alien hunt' of its own. Personnel records were minutely combed in an earnest search for teachers, janitors, and groundskeepers of dubious extraction.[28] In truth, all public institutions were being scanned, as witch hunters probed for agents of the Kaiser. Varsity was no exception. To their unalloyed delight, patriots quickly identified at least three professors who seemed ripe for immediate dismissal.

Mueller was an obvious target, but, in some minds, so were Bonno Tapper and Immanuel Benzinger. All three had been born in Germany. None was as yet a Canadian citizen. Tapper had come to the university in 1913 as a temporary replacement for Professor Toews of the German department, who was then on extended sick leave. A graduate of the University of Chicago, he intended to seek American citizenship in the event that his Canadian post failed to be made permanent. In 1911 the German government had declared him physically unfit for conscription, which was just as well, since Tapper was 'an avowed anti-militarist.'[29] A promising teacher, he was also a popular figure in the junior faculty residence. When Toews proved unable to resume his duties in 1914,

Tapper was quickly invited to stay. Judiciously, he followed Falconer's advice and abstained from commenting on events in Europe. Until the storm broke over his head in November he lived remote from the public eye.

Dr Benzinger, on the other hand, had already attracted at least a small measure of attention. Educated at the University of Berlin, he had lived for more than a decade in Palestine close to the sources of his scholarly interest. It was there that Fred McCurdy had found him while searching for a professor of oriental languages. Benzinger was teaching at a local high school and pursuing his research. This dapper master of many tongues was also running a travel agency on the side. In him McCurdy spied a potential successor to his own headship. Falconer, at first doubtful, finally approved the appointment and eventually came to appreciate the merits of the new man. Thus Benzinger, ironically as it turned out, came to Toronto as a replacement for the once-embattled Eakin, who, with the Blake controversy well behind him, had for other reasons sought alternative employment.[30] In the spring of 1914 Benzinger returned to Germany to collect his family and enjoy a period of study at Leipzig. Clearly intent upon remaining in Toronto, he had secured permission for his son, then a student at Goslar, to enrol at Toronto the following term. The war, however, upset his plans. His son was drafted into the German army and Benzinger himself faced great difficulties in trying to make his way back to Canada. In his absence, the *Globe* speculated that like Professor Stadtler, he too had joined the armed forces of his native land. Falconer, it was suggested, might discover many gaps in his staff when he called the roll.[31] The French, for example, had already conscripted two or three Toronto professors at home on leave. In Benzinger's case, however, this rumour was wholly without substance. At forty-nine and of delicate health, he had never been even a reservist. Consequently, he was technically free to leave Germany at any time. In practice, however, delays were inevitable. Understandably, Germans were not welcome in French or British ports. Thus the former travel consultant was forced to improvise. In September he got word to Falconer through a Swiss colleague that with luck a passage might be arranged out of Rotterdam in October.[32] Meanwhile Falconer wrote to Canadian immigration authorities to smooth his way. In the end, the best accommodation Benzinger could find was a steerage berth. Given these less than satisfactory arrangements, he reluctantly left his wife behind for the moment. By 14 October he was back in Toronto.

On the evening of his arrival a reporter from the *Globe* called at his residence. Rather naïvely, Benzinger agreed to answer a number of questions about German attitudes to the war. He was asked about the German failure to take Paris, the violation of Belgian neutrality and the destruction of Louvain. In each case he described the position adopted by officials of the German government but carefully refrained from offering his own opinions.[33] This fine distinction, however, was lost on the journalist who scurried back to his newsroom thinking he had identified an enemy of the Crown. Fortunately the interview came to the attention of his editor, J.A. Macdonald, before it went to press. Macdonald, a member of the Board of Governors and an old friend of Falconer, communicated immediately with the president and agreed to suppress the article in the interests of the university.[34] The faux pas, however, could not be so easily covered up. Somehow word of the interview was leaked. Thus, on 24 September John Squair wrote to Falconer warning him that Benzinger had issued 'very pro-German statements' to the press. Squair was alarmed that, while the interview had been squelched by 'someone,' the rumour itself could prove very damaging. He therefore urged the president to silence his colleague.[35] Falconer, of course, had already done so, and Benzinger thereafter held his tongue in check. Nevertheless, as Squair had feared, the damage had been done. In particular, the *Telegram* and the *World* began to question Benzinger's loyalty. Soon Tapper and inevitably Mueller were also under close scrutiny. The story circulated that Mueller kept a wireless set secreted in his basement. Benzinger was said to be preventing students from attending military drill. In private Hearst, who was having difficulty keeping some of his backbenchers in line, encouraged Falconer to do something before the situation got entirely out of hand.[36] With pressure intensifying, on the same day that city fathers moved to oust enemy aliens from their payroll, Falconer penned a letter to the press.

In this first public statement Falconer was cautious but firm. After outlining the background of the three men involved, he added that 'they have done nothing that should arouse any suspicion.' Pragmatically, he went on to note that to lose them would be to cripple the work of the university, since replacements were exceedingly difficult to come by in wartime.[37] Moderate in tone, the letter carefully avoided hurling bolts at critics of Toronto. Even so, it provoked a sharp response from several quarters. Most ominously E.B. Osler, benefactor and governor of the university, was livid. Complaining to Falconer, he also wrote to Walker. The chairman of the board was informed that the offending article was having 'a very serious effect.' It was, said Osler, 'being talked about by the most prominent people and talked about very bitterly.' Already 'three or four prominent men' had called on him to protest the retention of the professors. 'President Falconer,' he continued, 'does not seem to realise that one of these men has a son in the German Army and that all of them are openly and avowedly sympathizers with Germany.' 'Personally,' he added, 'I feel so strongly on the point that I am debating upon resigning my position as Trustee of the University.'[38] With Falconer away on business, Walker attempted to soothe the irate Osler but to little effect.[39] Inexorably a crisis developed within the administration itself. A committee of the Senate was struck to confer with Falconer and the board on the question of enemy aliens. An index of the gathering tension was supplied when the governors authorized the hiring of extra watchmen to augment the university guard.

Already-frayed nerves were rubbed positively raw on 2 December. That morning the newspapers published a letter that had originally been privately addressed to Falconer. Spurred by the president's defence of the German professors, Colonel Daniel R. Wilkie, a noted banker, had scribbled his dissent on 16 November. Shocked by Falconer's public statement, Wilkie had rehearsed at length the shortcomings of the university. Its reputation, he alleged, had been 'besmirched by the famous protest of the five professors against British principles being taught in a British school.' Thus the Mueller affair was revived. Furthermore, he continued, the university had been negligent in promoting enlistment. Finally, he condemned Falconer's apology for Benzinger and others of his ilk. Striking a thinly veiled personal blow, Wilkie implied that Falconer was soft on Huns because of his own student experiences in Germany: 'Do not imperil your country, your Province, your university, yourself in an effort in return for many kindnesses to be more than generous to a cruel, ruthless, powerful enemy, a knowledge of whose character can only have been acquired by you through the halls, colleges, the walks and gardens of their universities, and not, as have the sons of many Canadians, on the fields and in the trenches in Belgium and France.' Merely annoying when communicated privately, this insinuation had inflammatory potential when publicly aired. Moreover, it gained immeasurably in evocative force given the circumstances of its publication. Colonel Wilkie had died of an apoplectic seizure a few hours after composing the letter. His bereaved but equally outraged daughter had sent it to the papers. By implication it stood as the last testament of a patriot driven to his grave in a fit of righteous anger. Thus an element of high melodrama was injected into an already feverish situation.[40]

The timing could not have been worse from Falconer's point of view. A special meeting of the governors was due to convene the next day. The Wilkie letter could only further inflame Osler and those who supported him. The news, however, was not all bad. Students, for example, responded to the crisis with an overwhelming vote of confidence in Falconer and the German professors. They had already sent a deputation to his office endorsing his stand. As well, *Varsity* published articles denouncing blatant persecution and calling for 'British fair play' where Benzinger and his colleagues were concerned.[41] More pointedly, two students replied directly to Wilkie's accusation in the columns of the *Star*. Falconer, they declared, was an inspiration to the entire university. Far from inhibiting recruitment. said S.D. Gardiner, the president had consistently drawn the attention of students to their duties in the present war. In particular, he cited Falconer's address of 21 October at Convocation Hall. On that occasion his patriotic words had constituted a virtual 'gauntlet' hurled at the feet of his listeners. What more was required, asked the authors of the article. 'Shall we arm ourselves and with fixed bayonets charge down Yonge Street to show the efficiency of our training?'[42] Under the circumstances Falconer probably found this a tantalizing prospect. In any case he was grateful not only for student support but also for that tendered by Walker as chairman of the governors. The banker had written as soon as he had seen Wilkie's missive to say that he would oppose any effort to dismiss Mueller and the others.[43] Knowing that he could also count on the powerful assistance of Joseph Flavelle and Zebulon Lash, Falconer went to the fateful board meeting determined to resist the Germanophobes.

In an atmosphere crackling with electricity, the board heard submissions on the issue. Falconer took the position that a decision to dismiss the professors would violate the spirit of public policy. He referred to an order-in-council of 15 August 1914 which guaranteed protection to all Germans and Austro-Hungarians who did not engage in espionage or other treasonous activities. Care was taken to demonstrate that Benzinger and the others had committed no such crimes. Thus the president read a statement from Mueller explaining that the wireless set in his house had been used only as a hobby by his son and had, in any event, been dismantled before the war. The circumstances and content of Benzinger's still unpublished press interview were also made clear. Falconer finished by declaring that, since their conduct had been blameless, he refused utterly to recommend the firing of these men.[44] With equal force, however, a senate committee demanded that their contracts be terminated. Finally, when Osler and his allies had also had their say, a motion to dismiss Benzinger, Mueller, and Tapper was tabled.

It was a delicate moment. Far more was at stake than the immediate fate of three men. Walker, for instance, was worried about the long-term implications of the whole affair. He had told Osler earlier that he was 'very honestly trying to think of the position of the University, an institution supposed to be above local prejudices, a few years after the war is over, as having acted in response to clamour in an unusually excited city. I am fearful that at that time we shall regret having acted in a spirit of rather petty retaliation against certain individuals.'[45] Like Falconer, he was anxious not only to avoid perpetrating an obvious injustice, but also to preserve the university's freedom from outside interference.[46] To cave in to popular pressure now would be to create a bad precedent and to encourage similar intrusions later. There also was a specific constitutional point to be considered. No faculty member could be hired or fired without the recommendation of the president. In this case Falconer had flatly refused to accept dismissal. If the board proceeded against the Germans in spite of this veto, the administrative structure of the university would be upset. On the other hand, to do nothing might also prove disastrous. Hearst had kept his distance so far but could not be expected to do so indefinitely in the face of rising public clamour and grumblings within his own party.

There was one other important factor to be considered. At no point had anyone in power even suggested that Falconer himself should step down. Nor had he committed the fatal blunder of formally threatening to resign. Nevertheless he had made it clear unofficially that a vote for dismissal would signal his own departure.[47] Such an event, it was recognized, would only lead to an escalation of the crisis, particularly since he enjoyed considerable support on campus. Four prominent senior professors were ready to go with him. Catching wind of the affair, students promised a massive strike should the president's hand be forced.[48] Popular with students, Falconer had also proved his worth to the administration. His services would not be dispensed with lightly. In the end, it proved unnecessary to do so. No sooner had the motion to fire the professors been tabled than Flavelle and Lash moved to block it. After much heated debate a compromise was suggested and quickly taken up by a majority of the governors. It was decided to grant the Germans a leave of absence at full pay until 30 June 1915. No mention was made of what would happen after that date. Presumably some thought that the war would be over by that time, while others felt that the issue, being temporarily shelved, would simply fade from view. In either case, the public could be assuaged without forcing the president or the professors to resign.

Like most compromises this one left nobody fully satisfied. Benzinger and his colleagues, implicitly condemned, faced the possibility of internment. Osler and two other governors who opposed the settlement felt angry and thwarted. One of them, Dr J.O. Orr, manager of the Canadian National Exhibition, vented his spleen in the press. 'If those German professors had a spark of manhood,' he exclaimed, 'they would not remain on the staff of Toronto University under the existing circumstances.' For him a leave of absence was no solution at all. Capturing perfectly the intolerance of the moment, he poured out a torrent of abuse. 'These three professors,' he stated,

should be either at the detention camp or teaching as usual at the University. They are Germans. We do not have to prove anything against them. It is enough that they are Germans, unnaturalized, and that they have strong German sympathies. The son of one of them is fighting in the German army. The statement that their cases had been investigated and nothing proved against them is untrue. Nothing was charged against them. The precedent set in England by letting Prince Louis of Battenberg go, and also those two Privy Councillors of German descent should be strong enough for us. [49]

Osler, having similar feelings, cited the cases of British universities that had dismissed German professors who were not naturalized subjects of the crown. [50] Frustrated and bitter, he tendered a resignation which the governors refused to accept.

Strong criticism of the board's action bubbled up elsewhere. Public petitions were drafted, one of which reviled the governors for subsidizing 'Munsterbergs to teach our Canadian sons the "benefits" of German Kultur.' [51] An effort was made to stage a grand protest rally at Massey Hall, but it failed to materialize. The Honourable R.F. Preston, minister without portfolio, challenged Falconer's reading of the order-in-council. The government, he said, would not prevent an employer from firing a German, even without cause. [52] Tory backbencher Thomas Hook was even more vocal. 'If we can't get university professors of British blood,' he proclaimed, 'then let us close the universities.' His audience at the North Toronto Conservative Club applauded the suggestion enthusiastically. This 'paid holiday' granted to enemies of the king added 'insult to injury.' At the very least, said Hook, the government should exert firmer control over Varsity as in the happier days before 1906. [53] As other members of the legislature took up the call for drastic action, Hook laboured to channel their resentment into an all-party movement. Rural representatives, always suspicious of the 'rich man's university,' were at the forefront of these legislative protests. [54] Hearst avoided comment as long as possible but was finally cornered on the evening of 15 December. An all-party delegation, backed by several extra-parliamentary groups, laid siege to his office. Significantly, it was noted that the largest number of delegates were from the Conservative side of the house. One member of the throng accused Falconer of trying 'to exercise an autocratic despotism with moneys that came from the public purse.' Board of Education representatives, eager for revenge, raised the Hagarty issue again. All called for a tightening of government control. Thus beleaguered, Hearst moved first to defend himself. No one, he declared, was 'more British' than his government. He did, however, promise 'to look into' the matter and to launch a formal inquiry if necessary. In fact, he was stalling. 'Dismiss them!' shouted a man in the audience. The premier, it was noted, 'smiled but made no comment.'[55]

For his part, Falconer was less than happy with the governors' decision and had voted against the compromise solution. Had he wished to be rigorously consistent, he might have resigned then and there. However, a number of considerations, which he never directly discussed, appear to have induced him to stay. He seems, for one thing, to have thought initially that all was not lost. Indeed, as late as March 1915 he wrote to McCurdy advising him that, while Benzinger probably would not return, it was still possible that Toronto might offer him a position the following spring.[56] Furthermore, he may have felt that out of power he could do little to help the men 'on leave.' As it was, he was still in a position to try to engineer exchange posts for them in the United States. Unfortunately an extensive effort to do so yielded no results.[57] Above all, by remaining in office he could work to ensure that the 'leaves' were not translated into outright dismissals. Beyond these considerations, personal loyalties to Walker and Flavelle, whose motives and problems he appreciated, may have coloured his thinking. Whatever his specific reasons, it is difficult to imagine that he suffered a simple loss of nerve. Indeed, under the circumstances, resignation might have been the easiest course to take. In any case he endured the tide of public criticism while attempting to help the victimized professors as best he could.

As it happened, little could be done to ease their personal predicaments. By the end of December both Tapper and Benzinger had succumbed to unbearable pressure and resigned. The younger man returned to the United States to continue his graduate studies. The orientalist fled first to Princeton and then to a post at Meadville. His trials, if anything, became more acute when word came that his son had been wounded in Poland. He had lain on the battlefield for four days and been robbed five times before he dragged himself to a field hospital. Both father and son were thus scarred by war. It was ironic, therefore, when early in 1915 the German government publicized a notice from Benzinger in which he attested to the satisfactory treatment accorded his compatriots in wartime Ontario.[58] As for Mueller, he fought a rearguard action designed to salvage his situation in Toronto. Rather belatedly he applied for and was granted Canadian citizenship. At the hearing in late December he declared his emphatic hope that Britain would be victorious.[59] Meanwhile, out of his own pocket he paid a substitute lecturer to take his classes. Evidently Mueller was trying to keep a foot in Varsity's door, but it was all to no avail. By June he too had resigned. Fortunately McMaster University, then a private institution, took him in and he went on to flourish in that Baptist haven. Thus, the whole sad affair sputtered to an end.

It was a tragic episode for all connected with the university. Falconer, more fortunate than most, emerged relatively unscathed, having suffered no more than a verbal hammering. Throughout those trying months, he could do little to retaliate directly. As he explained to Flavelle, any public outcry on his part would be interpreted as self-service and might only make the situation worse.[60] Similarly he had no desire to provoke Queen's Park by adding to Hearst's discomfiture.[61] Accordingly, for the most part, he refrained from public comment. Privately, however, some of the innuendo and vituperation to which he was subjected cut him to the quick. Proud son of empire, he may have imagined that an already solid record of imperial service would raise him above suspicion. When, in spite of his reputation, his own loyalty was disputed, Falconer was deeply stung. Writing to Archibald MacMechan at the height of the crisis, his dismay at 'getting abuse as a pro-German' was obvious. Sad and hurt, he reflected, 'How awful war is.'[62] Yet, while war and its side effects might be awful, he never questioned its necessity or the righteousness of Greater Britain's cause. Indeed, as hostilities dragged on he became an ever more vocal, ever more diligent sponsor of the national effort. Hurling himself into patriotic work, he addressed scores of audiences. His pen, moreover, had never been so busy. Much of this activity no doubt flowed from firm conviction. But in some measure, one suspects, he was also striving to redeem himself.

Curiously, for a man who discoursed at great length on the struggle in Europe, Falconer had very little to say about the nature of war itself. On one or two occasions, however, he paused to consider the issue briefly. In December 1914, for example, a Peterborough resident asked whether he thought that the current conflict would lead men to abandon appeals to force altogether. Mulling the question over, Falconer then replied, 'I agree with you that unless as a result of the present war armaments are reduced to the lowest possible stage we shall not have got out of it what we were hoping for. I am not, however, one of those who believe that it would be possible to abolish armies and navies entirely. It seems to me that barbarism will exist in the world for a good while yet.'[63] Disputing the perfectibility of this world, Falconer also rejected the notion that even partial progress was inevitable. On the contrary, improvement was won only through persistent effort in the face of ever-present challenges. Sacrifice, sometimes total, was required from those who would seek moral and material amelioration. Given this viewpoint, Falconer was inclined to doubt the value of pacifism. At times he could be less than generous in describing its practitioners. 'To endure evil patiently,' he wrote in 1915, 'though it is at times heroic, is at times sheer cowardice.'[64] In this regard it is perhaps significant that as late as 1931 he refused to appear on the same platform as Bertrand Russell.[65] Granted, that philosophic peer represented many things that Falconer despised, such as rigorous empiricism and unalloyed atheism. Russell's activities during the war, however, had done even less to endear him to one of Toronto's foremost recruiting sergeants.

Hazy about war in general, Falconer's views were crystal-clear concerning the immediate conflict in Europe. Typically, he interpreted that struggle primarily in moral rather than in political or economic terms. For him it took shape as a titanic clash between the massed legions of materialism and those regiments that marched under idealism's banner. It is a measure of the intensity of this vision that, in this instance, his habitually mediating mind recognized no subtle shades of grey. The contending parties stood arrayed, the one in light, the other in darkness. On this point Falconer never temporized. Indeed, his first major speech on the war, delivered to students in September 1914, was hailed by the press as 'a complete and utterly sweeping condemnation of all things German.'[66] This journalistic assessment distorted Falconer's position somewhat. Even so, the address was merely the first ranging shot of a withering barrage against Germany which he laid down over the next four years. The war, he declared, was 'a clash of two views of life, and one or the other must go.' It was 'a fight to the finish' between 'Prussianism' and all those who boasted civilized values. As such it was necessarily 'the greatest of moral struggles.'[67] This was the simple sermon he preached with clarity and force from 1914 to 1918.

Falconer, of course, was never an all-out Germanophobe. His conduct during the Benzinger affair made that clear. It was not the German people, but the Prussian military caste whom he condemned. The Junkers, in his opinion, worshipping a god of force, had captured the state and corrupted the national character. Slaves to 'organization and things material,' Bismarck's heirs had turned Germany into 'an outlaw waging her campaign of frightfulness like one demented.'[68] In his *The German Tragedy and Its Meaning for Canada,* published only a few months after Benzinger resigned, Falconer described the decline of a once noble patriotism. With near tearful nostalgia, he recalled his student memories and 'the quaintness and charm of the days of Germanic idealism.'[69] He remembered every kindness and all the many sparks of scholarly illumination he had received in Germany as an impressionable youth. Such things, he told Canadians, should never be forgotten. But, he continued, the idealists of that now-changed land had been unable to withstand the advance of Prussianism. Crass materialists, the Junkers spurned Christian principles and took as their guide only the shifting necessities of state.[70] Tearing up treaties and scoffing at international law, they were bent on 'ravaging the sanctities of humanity.'[71] The gospel preached by the likes of General von Bernhardt in his *Germany and the Next War* was dismissed by Falconer as 'an amazing commingling of brutality and claims to culture.' Bethmann-Hollweg's observation that 'it is only steel that counts' was denounced as 'medieval barbarism.'[72] In his own mind Falconer was taking up arms not against the Germany of Beethoven and Harnack, but in defiance of a new creature spawned in the abyss of rank materialism, mechanistic efficiency, and raison d'état.

Vitriolic and strident, Falconer's biting vilification of Germany came as an abrupt volte face on his part. There was nothing in his prewar utterances that foreshadowed such a negative outburst. In fact, right up to the last moment he appears to have assumed there were men of goodwill in all camps ready to compose their differences in a civilized manner. Thus, in 1911 he gladly joined an organization made up of English-speaking people partly educated in Germany who wanted to help ease tensions between the two powers.[73] Like many other people, therefore, he became an outspoken and implacable foe of 'Prussianism' only after the events of August 1914. National and imperial loyalty, of course, impelled him in this direction, but there was a bitterness in his tone which betrayed a sense of personal injury that ran deeper than mere patriotic fervour. A desire to rehabilitate himself in the wake of the German professors fiasco may have been a contributing factor. Yet, at bottom, his reaction was more akin to that of one who felt betrayed and abandoned by an old and trusted friend. Read carefully, his many diatribes frequently reveal an acute sense of loss. 'The Germany we knew and admired,' he once lamented, 'has been trampled down by the rude soldier, the universities are closed, music is silent, and our former German friends are hissing forth anathemas on the perfidious Briton.'[74] Shocked and wounded, Falconer lashed out with all the fury of a lover spurned.

Significantly, however, he never gave up hope that the breach might be healed. At no point did he counsel vengeance as a war aim. Neither did he promote the notion that German civilization was irredeemably corrupt. Rather, he regarded Germany as the victim of a temporary malaise which could be excised. The task at hand, he emphasized, was 'to liberate the German from his present fallen state.'[75] Destroy the Prussian militarists, he argued, and all might yet be well. Moreover there was a valuable lesson for Canadians to learn as they pondered the German fate. Here, he thought, was proof positive of a truth he had long sought to bring home to his compatriots: national character was a fragile and malleable thing. Those who embraced a simple and mindless Germanophobia failed to understand the situation. Any race, he warned, could see its virtues eroded, if once it allowed its moral defences to weaken. Eternal vigilance was the only cure for the corrosive effects of complacency and materialism. Germany had been merely the first to succumb to dangers that threatened all humanity; none was exempt from peril. Canadians, he cautioned, would do well to remember this fact. As always, the crucial thing for Falconer was to 'keep pure the wells of public morals and of religion.'[76]

In this regard he felt that the war, for all its bleakness, had something positive to offer. Like one of Rupert Brooke's 'swimmers into cleanness leaping,' he saw in the dire struggle a potent stimulus to the moral rededication of society. The excesses of propaganda notwithstanding, he sensed a general resurgence of once merely latent idealism. The poet rejoiced at the awakening of 'a world grown old and cold and weary,' and so did Falconer. Canadians, he informed students in October 1914, had entered the war worldly, selfish, and complacent, but they would emerge from it rejuvenated.[77] Already in England, or so he was told, the cleansing experience had served 'to purify the waters of their life which had been growing turbid.'[78] The price, admittedly, was high, but the benefits were great. As increasing numbers of Torontonians began to fall in 1915, he wrote to MacMechan mourning those lost. He remarked that 'it is all very terrible.' But, he added swiftly, 'there is being evoked a spirit of duty and sacrifice that should I think make a better country for our children.'[79] A year later he attempted to explain his views to an American audience. Canadians from all walks of life, he told them, were being drawn together as never before. Close co-operation in a common cause bred an atmosphere of universal sacrifice. From the better mutual understanding born of this shared endeavour he expected to see a common sympathy arise. In this way, he speculated, the war might induce great moral and social changes which otherwise would have been long delayed. If nothing else, he prophesied, 'this generation will at least be sincere.'[80] Altogether he was heartened that Britons had proved themselves equal to the moral challenge of the hour. It was this spirit of sacrifice itself, rather than the prospect of victory or vengeance, which led Falconer to declare these 'the glorious days of our race.'[81]

Lester Pearson, in his autobiography, recalled the vivid emotions of the time. Only seventeen and still a student at Victoria College, he longed for the day when he could enlist. 'I had,' he recorded, 'a normal patriotic instinct – more British, I suppose, at this time than Canadian.'[82] Faithfully reflecting the Toronto mood, Pearson might as well have been describing Falconer's attitude. For the president, one of the most salutory aspects of the war was the way in which it seemed to rekindle Canadians' consciousness of their imperial heritage. In younger people, he alleged, the 'British mind' had become 'almost subconscious.' The average youth rarely questioned himself concerning the origin of his fundamental principles.[83] Now, thankfully, all that had changed. Men, he thought, were coming to realize that the empire of which they were a part was more than an agglomeration of territories, treaties, and trade balances. Rather, in essence, it was a moral entity and, as such, worth dying for. No small portion of Falconer's wartime rhetoric was devoted to driving this message home. In the process he gave expression to his own intensified loyalty and his increasingly precise concept of empire.

In the midst of global struggle, Falconer never hesitated to place the empire in the van of those who stood for moral progress and Christian idealism. Here were the forces of light. From the outset he maintained that 'the heart of the British people is sound and they are impelled by moral purposes which must succeed if one believes in the overruling of Providence.'[84] In keeping with his idealistic persuasions, he described the empire as 'a moral reality.'[85] It was not the physical but the spiritual aspects of imperialism which captivated his imagination. He consistently distinguished between the tangible and intangible attributes of the empire and left no doubts as to the sources of his own inspiration. 'Behind the visible Britain,' he wrote in 1915, 'there is the real spiritual Britain, a corporate life of virtue that speaks through each citizen.'[86] Indeed, the empire was a living organism, greater than the sum of all its parts. Thus, in echoing earlier observers such as Dilke and Froude, he too rejected a mechanistic vision of Greater Britain which would have focused attention on its outward forms. 'The Empire,' he contended, 'is not run by machinery'; instead, it was 'a body politic.'[87] Consequently it mattered little to him in an ultimate sense what forms were employed to make visible this moral entity. After all, he argued, external forms might vary but spiritual realities remained constant. For him the true cement of empire was an inherited national character. 'An imperial conviction,' said Falconer, 'binds Britons everywhere together.'[88] Over centuries of hard-won experience the British character had been forged as an amalgam of ideals, self-criticism, puritanism, and worldly wisdom which had issued in metal of the finest quality. The war, he thought, was merely tempering that steel anew.

Buttressing this vision with appeals to imperial history, Falconer followed conventional lines laid down by the likes of Seeley and Egerton.[89] The empire had not been constructed by conniving politicians and grasping businessmen. Instead, it had evolved as the handiwork of individuals who left England to seek their fortunes without a premeditated design.[90] Initially, therefore, there had been no set creed or ruling idea. Not until well established did Greater Britain come to full consciousness. Falconer identified the Colonial Reformers as the agents of this transformation. Under their aegis, responsible government was made the vital principle of empire. In his opinion this concept, which emphasized freedom and the protection of minorities, was largely responsible for the longevity of the imperial tie.[91] It allowed for the growth of a 'multifarious but integrated Commonwealth' or, as contemporary imperial historians put it, 'university in diversity.'[92] Guided by this idea, the empire had avoided a dangerous emphasis on centralization and officialdom which Falconer said had tainted the German experience. Unlike the Prussian state, Greater Britain had not degenerated into a mere mechanism.

These issues, Falconer contended, were understood instinctively by Canadians of British extraction. For them the war was usefully interpreting afresh 'the inner meaning of the mind of Britain.'[93] More importantly, however, he felt that it was also helping to solve a problem that had troubled him long before 1914. In his eyes decades of large-scale alien immigration had threatened to dilute the British spirit of the new nation. As a result, he alleged, a mature common patriotism had been slow to develop. South of the border, he thought he saw clear evidence of the deleterious effects such ethnic confusion could have. 'The true American,' he said in 1916, 'is drawn as by a magnet towards those who are defending liberty, law, and democracy; the hyphenated American is not stirred by these principles.'[94] Thus the United States, divided within, hesitated to take its part in the noble cause. In this sense, he contended, Canada had been more fortunate. The war, coming none too soon, had acted as a unifying impulse. Indeed, he was confident that Britain's leadership in defence not only of her own interests, but also of 'world-liberty,' had done much to integrate those of alien stock into the mainstream of imperial patriotism. Even the Québécois, he imagined, would be reconciled to an empire that had sided with France in order to uphold 'a common civilization.'[95] Clearly projecting his own feelings on others, Falconer was no doubt guilty of some wishful thinking on this point. In any event, he went so far as to declare that a new imperial allegiance had been born in all sections of the national community. There was here, he said, an opportunity for nation-building not to be wasted. A frank assimilationist, he urged that after the war Canada should restrict the tide of immigration, while making it plain to all who gained entry that they would be expected to embrace British values. 'We shall,' he proclaimed, 'be arrogant towards none, we shall be brothers to those whom we receive, we shall give them the same liberty that we enjoy, it being always understood that our ideals are British-Canadian.' More bluntly, he stated: 'We want no hyphenated Canadians.'[96]

Whether denouncing 'Prussianism' or cheering on his own side, for four long years Falconer strove to clarify the positive and negative aspects of the war in the minds of fellow Canadians. No opportunity to do so was ignored during this period of intense activity. In particular, of course, he laboured to ensure that the university contributed its fair share and more to the national effort. Thus students were constantly summoned to special sessions at which the president and others held forth on the themes of duty and sacrifice. Already a polished speaker, Falconer quickly learned to augment his normally polite style with powerful appeals to emotion. At times he could play on the feelings of an audience with telling effect. His Convocation Hall address of 21 October 1914 was a sterling case in point. Students, who later reminded a critical press of this performance, did not exaggerate his earnestness or his capacity to move men. On that occasion Falconer, arrayed in scarlet-trimmed robes, strode to the podium as the last echoes of 'God Save the King' died away. He spoke with passion of the principles at stake in the war and then announced that the university would shortly be raising its own officer training corps. 'There was,' the *Star* reported, 'a prideful ringing in the president's voice as, facing the solid banks of faces in the big hall today, he said: "We expect the men to come forward now."' Cheer upon cheer greeted the address and 'a sort of glorious pandemonium reigned.'[97] And the men came forward. Indeed, they did so in numbers that must have surprised even Falconer. Within twenty-four hours some 550 of them signed up with the OTC. By December over 1,800 could be seen drilling on the once peaceful lawns.[98] In addition, and perhaps more significantly, with the coming of spring Falconer could report that 1,173 graduates, students, and professors had answered the call to active service.[99] Here, he thought, was an eloquent response to those who charged the university with slackness. Moreover, while he claimed none for himself, at least part of the credit for this lay with Falconer. He had spoken unceasingly that winter, on campus, across Ontario, and even in the western provinces. A few of his addresses were gathered for publication in his *German Tragedy*. In 1915 that volume was adopted for use in schools by the Ontario Ministry of Education.[100] Thus his message was conveyed to an even wider audience.

At this early stage Falconer devoted special attention to the encouragement of Varsity's fledgling OTC unit. Originally authorization had been granted to raise a corps of 1,000 men. So popular did the experiment prove, however, that in short order over 1,500 were enrolled.[101] Young Mike Pearson joined eager classmates who sought to qualify for commissions. They drilled and drilled and drilled again under the guidance of picked professors. After four o'clock, the campus took on the atmosphere of an armed camp all classes having been cancelled to accommodate the manouvres this mortarboard army. Falconer was a frequent visitor as he inspected the troops and observed their earnest strainings. He took great pride in their efforts but quickly realized that the monotony of daily drill would soon take its toll of enthusiasm unless further encouragement were forthcoming. It was, therefore, with consternation that he learned of the cancellation of a general OTC 'concentration camp' planned for the Niagara region that spring. The exercise had been designed to serve as the culmination of the year's activities. Prospective officers were to be tested rigorously in the classroom and in the field. Successful candidates could then expect to receive a commission upon enlistment. The abrupt decision to call the gathering off threatened to drain the OTC program of its incentive. Disappointment was acute, and Falconer feared the collapse of a favoured project. Rather indignantly, he wrote immediately to Borden urging him to reconsider.[102] Powerful supporting fire was provided by Walker. The chairman drew Ottawa's attention to a point which was of great political significance to the university. The work of the OTC, he told Borden, 'has been particularly gratifying to me owing to the fact that certain people in Toronto have always thrown doubt on the public spirit of the University professors.'[103] The prime minister, who had spoken out against the abuse of German-Canadians at the height of the Benzinger affair, appreciated the force of Walker's argument.[104] With Osler and Sam Hughes petitioning him as well, Borden acceded. The camp was held, and Falconer's 'army' went on to flourish.

Pleased by this turn of events, Falconer was also heartened by other developments on campus. In February 1915 many senior medical students responded to government pleas for assistance at the front.

Dozens volunteered to staff casualty clearing stations just behind the lines. Sensing a greater need, the university then offered to raise the men and resources necessary to equip an entire base hospital of over 1,000 beds. It was a generous offer which Ottawa promptly accepted. With amazing speed a funding drive netted the required cash. The alumni alone contributed in excess of $60,000. An able committee of university women secured an ample stock of linen, dressings, and other essential supplies. By spring the unit had sailed for Europe and finally settled down in the Greek town of Salonica. Closer to home, Toronto's physicians and scientists played a crucial role in stamping out an epidemic of cerebrospinal meningitis among troops stationed at the Canadian National Exhibition grounds. Others worked closely with the Red Cross in building up stockpiles of tetanus antitoxin. In the end the university was awarded a contract to produce the substance in its own laboratories. Meanwhile, outside bodies increasingly turned to Varsity for technical assistance in perfecting the engines of destruction. Most notably, munitions manufacturers found the Strength of Materials laboratory ideally equipped to test new shells. For its part, the extension department offered a series of lectures in Toronto and throughout the province designed to sustain public morale. In this effort it co-operated closely with the Speakers' Patriotic League, whose purpose was to stimulate recruitment and victory loans. Falconer of course was prominent among the orators who trumpeted its call.[105]

Those who devoted themselves to fostering enlistment were amply rewarded at first. Volunteers filled the swelling ranks of the first and second contingents of the Canadian Expeditionary Force. The tide of enthusiasm ran high in 1914 and abated only slightly the next year. For its part, the University of Toronto mirrored the contemporary mood. Almost 500 undergraduates had enlisted by the spring of 1915.[106] Impressively, within twelve months that figure rose to over 1,200. When graduates, professors, and others associated with the university were counted, it was revealed that by the close of the 1916 session more than 3,000 men had volunteered.[107] Meanwhile an unaccustomed silence crept through once teeming halls as enrolment dropped precipitously. In 1914 nearly 4,500 students had attended classes. By Christmas 1916 scarcely 1,100 could be found.[108] After the spring campaigns of 1915 casualty reports lengthened appallingly. These losses and the eerie stillness on campus brought the price of war dramatically home to Falconer. 'Laughter,' he later recalled, 'died out in those early years.' A certain boisterousness was conspicuous by its absence. The stadium, for example, was deserted. A few kicked the ball around on the back campus but 'more for exercise than for play.'[109] The whole atmosphere was markedly subdued. At first this seemed to bring some compensations, since students exhibited 'a new spirit of earnestness' in their studies.[110] But as the distractions and strains of war multiplied, this zeal faded.[111] As for Falconer, one imagines him, like Mr Chips, filtering through empty corridors while conjuring up the half-forgotten faces of his departed charges. 'There is,' he wrote to Murray, 'a quietness about the place that makes one realise the change.' Not even the approach of Christmas in 1915 could dispel ever-present apprehensions: 'The overwhelming cloud of war takes the spirit out of the season and one is ever wondering what sad news will come from the front.'[112] A year later this mood had, if anything, deepened. He wrote poignantly to William Peterson, 'there is a great feeling of loneliness about this University.'[113] Persistent coal shortages served to amplify the frosty ambience of a university at war.

Sobered by these realities, Falconer none the less remained ardent in his call for further sacrifice. 1916, however, proved to be an extremely trying year. The gluttonous mud of No Man's Land swallowed up raw volunteers at a furious pace. Alarming gaps formed in the ranks of the Canadian Expeditionary Force. Anxious to plug these holes, recruiters were dismayed to see enlistments slowing to a virtual halt. Growing disillusionment, full employment, and high wages sapped the martial spirits that had flourished in 1914. Farmers, desperate for labour, were more inclined than ever to keep their strapping sons at home. Increasingly, a struggle once identified with the sacred cause of civilization itself was coming to be viewed as a 'European war,' of little direct concern to Canadians.[114] As resolution flagged, men like Falconer lost patience with a recruitment policy that lacked central co-ordination and instead relied on voluntarism and local energies. With others of his ilk he turned, accordingly, to thoughts of compulsion. As rumours spread that Ottawa was considering a program of national registration, if not yet military conscription, Falconer wrote in November to Borden pleading the necessity of just such a step. He claimed to speak for 'a committee of gentlemen in Toronto who [had] long been interested in securing enlistments and in general for promoting public service.' Urging the rationalization of national efforts, he went on to contend that registration would only succeed if it were made compulsory. Otherwise, he noted, those who wished 'to escape scrutiny' would do so and 'we shall be pretty much as we are.' He then proceeded to offer his own services in any scheme that might lead to 'a fairer adjustment in the matter of public service.'[115]

Borden no doubt recognized the merits of Falconer's case, but as prime minister he hesitated to take such definite action. Balancing on a knife's edge, he replied that 'the first duty of the Government is to preserve the seeming unity of this Dominion.' For the moment anything that smacked of compulsion was politically dangerous.[116] Seeking to underline the need for caution, Borden delegated R.B. Bennett to meet with Falconer and his associates that he might explain the situation fully and ensure their silence at this difficult hour. Following the interview, the president acknowledged the delicacy of Borden's position in yet another letter. Even so, he remained convinced that something substantial had to be done. 'It does seem to me,' he told the prime minister, 'that we are in a rather grave condition from whatever point of view one considers the matter.' Accordingly he pledged his support for any measure that might deepen the sense of national service and asked only that Borden provide as strong a lead as he possibly could.[117]

Meanwhile, Falconer was not alone in thinking that relief might soon be forthcoming from an altogether different quarter. Washington, or so it seemed, was rapidly losing patience with Germany. Indeed, Woodrow Wilson had been increasingly critical of the German approach to submarine warfare since the beginning of 1916. At times he had sounded almost bellicose. Countless listeners in London, Paris, and Ottawa took careful note when in the winter and spring the president spoke of the need for a 'preparedness program.' Falconer, of course, was delighted by the prospect of America marching at Britain's side. With allied reserves wearing thin materially and emotionally, assistance from the great republic would come as a tonic and none too soon. In May Washington appeared to compose some of its differences with the Kaiser, but Falconer continued to hope. Visiting Princeton early in December, he was surprised and pleased when the chairman of Wilson's defence committee made a point of coming from the capital to solicit his advice on improving relations between Canada and the United States.[118] Indulging in some wishful thinking, he read more into the gesture than was actually intended. This delusion became clear when Wilson issued a pre-Christmas note to the belligerent powers. To Falconer's chagrin, the president called on the combatants to state their war aims and implied that there was little to choose between the claims of the adversaries. 'The objects,' he proclaimed, 'which the statesmen of the belligerents on both sides have in mind in this war are virtually the same.'[119] Falconer, who knew Wilson to be a man of ideals, found this attitude appalling. In high dudgeon, he wrote to Archie MacMechan declaring that he could not understand the note 'either in its wording or in its time of publication.' He added that he had written to the individual who had sought him out at

Princeton to say that Wilson had done more in one day to estrange Canada than anyone in living memory. 'I am afraid,' he lamented, 'all these hopes are dashed.'[120]

Adding to his frustration were fresh disappointments at home. Borden, still wary of political dissension, had elected not to follow the advice of those who had urged compulsory registration. Instead he called for the observance of a National Service Week to begin 1 January 1917. All males between sixteen and sixty-five were requested to fill out a questionnaire which would provide the government with vital statistics. In addition, respondents were asked to indicate whether or not they would be willing to relocate in the interests of the war effort. The question of military service was not directly raised and registration remained voluntary. This was a compromise and it failed. Relatively few cards were returned to Ottawa, and the scheme virtually collapsed.[121] When an attempt to raise a home defence force met with a similar response, it was clear in many minds that voluntarism had had its day. Of this Falconer was certain. Thus, while Ottawa hesitated, he and the Board of Governors moved. On 11 January he presented a resolution by Caput, Varsity's disciplinary body, calling for 'universal military training' at the university. The board favoured the idea but decided to wait until the Senate had discussed it. Falconer promised to raise the issue with senators as soon as possible. Meanwhile, he stated his intention to issue cards to all students similar to those sent out by the government during National Service Week. But, within the confines of his own jurisdiction at least, there would be no shirking. Indeed, he suggested refusing admission to examinations to all those who refused to fill out the questionnaires.[122] The president was in earnest, and by spring these plans had been approved.[123]

In May Borden returned from a fateful meeting with the imperial war cabinet. Having clung to voluntarism as long as he felt he could, he finally committed himself to imposing conscription, and Falconer applauded. Interviewed by the *Globe*, several notables including Hearst and N.W. Rowell voiced their approval. Falconer, when asked, offered that it was the only fair thing to do: 'It makes it easier now for many a young man to know his duty and he will do it cheerfully.' This surely was a strange conclusion to draw from the evidence afforded by events during recent months. But it was one widely shared by persons in authority at the university. Thus Walker and Cody echoed the president's assessment. Just to drive the message home, Falconer seized the opportunity to deliver yet another rousing address at Convocation Hall. 'Never,' he declared, 'have men been so tested; never proved themselves so splendid.' The going, he allowed, was rough; yet, 'we must believe that a God of righteousness and justice holds the balance and that surely, our inhuman enemies are being found wanting.'[124] Falconer the propagandist, if anything, was becoming less and less tolerant as the war approached a crisis at home and abroad.

That compulsory enlistment would provoke serious opposition was inevitable, Falconer's optimistic words notwithstanding. A tired public in English Canada and a blatantly hostile one in Quebec would have to be mollified. In this situation resorts to shaming were perhaps ill advised. Nevertheless Falconer was present when Presbyterians in the General Assembly of June launched 'an impassioned frontal assault upon the strongholds of slackerdom.' Ironically the gathering had convened in Montreal, many of whose French-speaking citizens were howling betrayal in the face of Ottawa's stated intentions. Undeterred, the Reverend R.B. Taylor, later head of Queen's, exclaimed: 'When I see the kind of gang that comes in from the race-course, I say it is not fair that our willing men should fight for that kind of trash.' Admittedly Falconer did not give vent to this kind of inflammatory rhetoric, but neither did he rise to condemn it. In the end he joined his clerical fellows in strongly endorsing conscription.[125] For himself, he appears to have clung to the myth that basically loyal French Canadians were being misled by a few misguided politicians such as Laurier.

As parliament debated the Military Service Bill that summer, it became apparent that Falconer's rosy prediction of May was in part ill founded. Many English Canadians, of course, looked with favour on conscription, but others did not. Socialists and labour organizations condemned militarism and called for the conscription of wealth as a matter of fairness. Farmers fought for and won some exemptions. The Liberal party, with its large base in Quebec, split over the issue when Laurier refused to sanction the measure. On 24 July, the very day on which parliament passed the necessary legislation, a chastened Falconer wrote to Walter Murray reflecting on the lack of consensus. 'What a muddle we are in politically,' he observed. Liberals who approved of the act, he contended, would have little choice but to support Borden until the end of the war. The alternative, a French-Canadian prime minister, was simply unthinkable at the moment.[126] Others agreed. Indeed, in the face of this parliamentary and national crisis Borden himself began the process of negotiating the construction of a coalition government. Predictably, Laurier demurred. Many of his erstwhile followers, however, decided to cast their lot with the Conservatives. The upshot, after much wrangling, was the formation of the National Government in October. Falconer was overjoyed. 'It is in my judgment,' he informed Borden, 'a piece of high statesmanship, as well as high patriotism and I have admired your infinite patience and sincere purpose as displayed during these months in endeavouring to effect this aim.'[127]

The opportunity to refashion a national consensus was too good to waste. When Borden announced late in October that an election would be held in December to confirm the new coalition, Falconer was with him heart and soul. Although he felt bound by his office to remain publicly neutral, in private he was quick to tender advice to Borden on the best means of ensuring electoral victory. Writing to the prime minister as 'a strong supporter and admirer,' he passed on some rumours he had overheard in the lobby of the Chateau Laurier Hotel. Although disillusioned with Laurier, many Liberals, it seemed, were resentful of Conservative efforts to monopolize all the reins of power in the new government. The danger lay in playing into the hands of Liberal party organizers, who wanted to attract former comrades back into the fold. 'This,' said Falconer, 'would be a great calamity.' But it was a distinct possibility, as 'mutual friends' in Halifax had recently warned him. He therefore counselled Borden to make 'some public utterance' on the matter before it was too late.[128] The prime minister thanked him for his note and passed it on to a number of colleagues.[129] In the end Borden moved to calm the fears of waverers and the National Government carried the day.

This involvement, of course, is not to suggest that Falconer played a major role in shaping the outcome of the election. Borden had already realized the necessity of assuaging his Liberal allies.[130] The episode, however, does illustrate Falconer's commitment to a man and a government he thought indispensible to the war effort. Despite many public professions of neutrality, he was coming to be closely identified with Borden. Moreover, some people thought that the federal Conservatives returned this admiration in full measure. In June, for example, Falconer was knighted, along with his friend Flavelle, in recognition of his 'splendid work in patriotic endeavours.' The honour was unquestionably merited. Commentators remarked on his revival of the university, his role in promoting the empire, his recruiting activities, and his efforts to help forge better relations with the United States.[131] Falconer was deeply moved. Almost immediately he wrote to Walker, his 'friend and guide,' to thank him for opening new doors to him in 1907.[132] Gracious and humble in his acceptance, he must nevertheless have experienced a sense of inward triumph in the light of the long-remembered German professors affair. Quite properly, there was not the slightest hint of dissent when the knighthood was announced. But in some quarters there was anticipation that it was only a prelude to even greater honours. Thus, as negotiations proceeded that summer towards the formation of a coalition, rumours began to circulate that Falconer was to be invited into the new government as a respected outsider with no formal party affiliations.

Somehow the story took wing that, as talks between federal politicians bogged down, Falconer was mentioned as a compromise candidate for the leadership of the dominion.[133] In 1967 F.C.A. Jeanneret repeated the tale in a biographical sketch of his late friend and leader.[134] Apparently he based his assertion on information obtained from Falconer's younger son Bobby.[135] Thus the latter recalled a noisy interview heard through a closed door at the Falconer home during which Borden himself supposedly tried to persuade a reluctant university president to accept the prime ministership of the country.[136] There is, however, no other evidence to indicate that such a proposal was ever made. Both the Falconer and the Borden papers are silent on the matter. Moreover, in August 1917 Falconer dismissed the story as groundless rumour-mongering in a letter to Walter Murray, his closest friend and confidant.

I heard the rumour which appeared in the Toronto 'Star' but have, of course, regarded it as an irresponsible suggestion. I cannot believe that there is anything more in it, and I sincerely hope that this is the case. To enter political life would be the last thing I should think of. It has no attractions, but the reverse, and I do not believe that I have the qualifications and especially the strength of character necessary. My present job is hard enough, but I should hate to think of giving it up for a cabinet position: in fact I don't see how I could at present. That I hope is the end of the matter.[137]

This statement, of course, may not have been 'the end of the matter.' Borden might have interviewed Falconer at a later date. A cabinet post could have been offered. Still, in the absence of direct evidence, the story is perhaps best regarded as apocryphal – an intriguing but unlikely possibility. Nevertheless, the fact that it was aired and believed by some is testimony to Falconer's growing prominence as a national figure.

Whatever the case, in the wake of December's election Sir Robert Falconer redoubled his patriotic efforts. In his own way, for example, he tried to soothe the feelings of Quebeckers. Thus representatives of the Bonne Entente movement were encouraged to visit the University of Toronto, where they were received with studied displays of warmth and respect. Furthermore, the French ambassador to Washington was invited to accept an honorary degree and to address convocation. Perfectly frank about his motives, Falconer told the Honourable J.J. Jusserand that his intention was to demonstrate Toronto's high regard for France in order to impress Quebec.[138] The ambassador, detained by weightier responsibilities, was unable to attend but the degree was awarded in absentia. It is doubtful, however, that this symbolic gesture had much impact. Quebec's grievances, after all, were home-grown and had little to do with the treatment accorded to France.

More fruitfully Falconer took a lead in promoting the work of the War Lectures Bureau. In this effort he joined forces with noted personages such as J.W. Dafoe, N.W. Rowell, J.S. Willison, and Vincent Massey. The bureau's goal was to buttress sagging spirits as the war dragged on into its fourth trying year. A store of easily distributed five-minute lectures was amassed. The content was deliberately simple and stridently patriotic. Partisan politicking was discouraged. As a guideline to volunteer lecturers, Falconer helped circulate a sample entitled 'The Crucial Hour.' Scarcely a work of rhetorical excellence, it drummed away noisily on emotive themes. Promising victory, it declared that Canadians were still 'cubs of the old Mother Lion.'[139] In a hundred only slightly modified forms this message was churned out over and over again. Under Falconer's signature letters advertising the bureau were sent to theatre managers all over the nation. Nor was the clergy neglected. To countless reverend gentlemen Falconer wrote explaining that 'one of the many objects of the Bureau [was] to use every pulpit in Canada as a medium of appropriately chosen propaganda.'[140] It is unclear how many of his clerical brothers answered this call. One may assume, however, that many did, since the clergy as a whole had been solidly behind the war throughout its troubled course.

Despite being heavily engaged already, in 1918 Falconer happily took on yet another wartime responsibility when he agreed to chair the board of the newly founded Khaki University of Canada.[141] The project held an obvious appeal for him. It was designed to provide basic courses for those troops abroad who wished to commence or continue their university education. Dynamic leadership in the field came from Henry Marshall Tory. Indefatigable, Tory and his assistants laboured ceaselessly to establish study camps and libraries not only in England but also just behind the lines in France. Reputable lecturers were recruited from the ranks of those Canadian professors who, like George Wrong, were anxious to serve but either by reason of age or infirmity were unfit for military duties. Classes opened in the summer of 1917 and quickly proved popular. By July of the following year over 10,000 men had attended at least one lecture. Given this success, the YMCA, which had originally sponsored the scheme, sought help from the universities and the government of the dominion. It was here that Falconer, with other academic presidents, played a key role. Together they secured recognition from their respective senates of the programs of study. Additionally, they granted leave to professors willing to take part in the project. Finally, they added their not inconsiderable weight to the pleas for official government sanction. Falconer had the crucial task of acting as liaison among the overseas body, the universities, and the government. Efforts to woo Ottawa were furthered by the interest in copying the experiment displayed by the British, New Zealand, and Australian armies. At last, on 19 September 1918 Borden's cabinet granted official status to the Khaki University as a unit within the Canadian forces. Tory was given the rank of colonel and set up headquarters at his 'Beaver Hut' in London.

For the most part the day-to-day load of administration fell on Tory, and his task was far from light. Particular difficulty was encountered in sustaining work near the front lines. Transport and materials were always in short supply. On one occasion books destined for France had to be shipped in cast-off champagne crates. When some were pilfered en route, the Colonel chuckled: 'Imagine the surprise of the thieves when they found two cases of Hall and Knight's Algebras!'[142] Some problems, however, were not so humorously dismissed. The gradual transition from civilian to military control placed a strain on some personal relationships within the emerging KUC. Thus, as negotiations with Ottawa went ahead in the spring of 1918, some early organizers began to grumble at the prospect of falling under Tory's leadership. Prominent among the disgruntled was Falconer's old Edinburgh classmate and successor at Pine Hill, Clarence Mackinnon. Active in the work of informally educating troops in England since 1917, he suspected that Tory was about to claim sole credit as the originator of the scheme. The latter, not to be outdone, argued that the early efforts of Mackinnon and others had been largely haphazard. To Falconer as Canadian chairman he wrote, contending: 'I, therefore, felt justified ... in assuming that the idea of systematized educational work for the Army on broad lines in relation to home problems was my real contribution and an original contribution.'[143] The situation became even more difficult when Tory had a falling-out with his second-in-command, Edmund Oliver. Sensing that valuable work was in jeopardy as old friends quarrelled, Falconer resolved to play the peacemaker. He had been considering a visit to England for some time. There were a couple of teaching positions to be filled, and he felt called to visit students who had enlisted. When Tory invited him to come, ostensibly to lecture but also, one suspects, to act as a mediator, Falconer booked passage for July.[144] The governors granted him leave and the KUC covered his expenses.

Arriving in England, Falconer went immediately to Oxford in order to see A.L. Smith. The two men discussed potential candidates for the vacant posts in Latin and medicine at Toronto and exchanged the latest academic news. Although he failed to find any suitable new professors, Falconer left Balliol refreshed and ready for what turned out to be an exhausting round of activities. A little wire-pulling won him permission to visit contingents in France. Eager to see as many former students as he could, at times he was within hailing distance of the front lines.[145] Then it was back to England and an extended tour of the Canadian camps, where he lectured for the KUC. Meanwhile he endeavoured to restore harmony among Tory, Mackinnon, and Oliver. As it transpired, he had lost none of his flair for dealing with men. Ruffled feathers were smoothed all round, and nothing more was heard of that spring's dissensions. By November, indeed, Walter Murray could inform him that the trio seemed fully reconciled and now constituted 'a very hilarious and happy party.'[146] At peace with itself, the Khaki University was just shifting into high gear when the armistice was signed.

Busy as he was, speaking, writing, and organizing for the war effort, a seemingly tireless Falconer nevertheless also found time to fulfil older continuing commitments. His involvement in the Round Table, for example, intensified during the early years of the conflict, which of course was only natural. Anticipating as he did that the war would nourish a new imperial allegiance, he was understandably anxious to speed the process along. Writing to Murray in January 1916, he felt the moment opportune to 'consider what steps may be taken to bring about some closer union in the way of government between the various Dominions and the Motherland.' He was unsure about the precise details of such a plan but was convinced that this was 'the crucial period for strengthening all the English and British influences throughout the Empire.' This, he told his friend, had been the theme of recent meetings of the Round Table, and, while he baulked at some of the rumours of full political integration which were circulating among its members, he none the less applauded the general drive towards unity. His own preference was to iron out disagreements and establish a consensus at a general Canadian conference before the organization committed itself to any course of action. He therefore urged Murray to suggest prominent men who might be willing to contribute to such a conclave.[147]

This letter, in fact, was part of a campaign initiated by Toronto Round Tablers who were seeking to broaden their base of support throughout the country. Many were alarmed by the suggestion of Lionel Curtis that the movement should go public the following spring.[148] From the outset the plan had always been to proceed slowly and to concentrate on quietly influencing men of prominence. Now 'The Prophet,' as Curtis was dubbed, seemed likely to spoil everything by precipitous action. In response, the Toronto group sought to tighten its organization and to extend its influence in order to better withstand inevitable criticism from anti-imperialists. Accordingly a 'genuine Canadian "Moot"' was formed in imitation of the London model.[149] Among others its executive included J.S. Willison, B.E. Walker, Vincent Massey, R.W. Leonard, and Falconer. Day-to-day administration was assumed by the organizing secretary, A.J. Glazebrook. Much of this activity had been prompted by the appearance of Curtis's *The Problem of the Commonwealth*. Even the most ardent Canadian imperialists took sharp exception to the latter portions of the book in which a comprehensive unification of the empire was urged. Plans to publish the book, indeed, precipitated what Edward Kylie christened 'the great Canadian revolt.' Willison, Walker, Glazebrook, and others were eager to dissociate themselves and the local membership from Curtis's views.[150] Falconer, in similar fashion, found the 'Prophet's' approach too strident, too 'cut and dried' and simply impractical.[151] While favouring the development of a common imperial policy for defence and foreign affairs, Falconer wished to maintain a far greater measure of dominion autonomy than Curtis envisaged, particularly where fiscal matters were concerned.[152] Above all, he objected to the rigid nature of the plans outlined in *The Problem*. A Burkean in this sense, Falconer always recoiled from overly detailed blueprints for social or political action. They smacked of the 'officialdom' he disliked in Germany. Curtis, he argued, ignored the complexity of Canadian aspirations. To be sure, the war had occasioned a growth of imperial loyalty, but it had also encouraged a new sense of national self-confidence which would seek an outlet in partnership rather than in submersion within the empire. Furthermore, he felt certain that the uncompromising tone adopted by Curtis would only play into the hands of critics such as Dafoe. Altogether, as he told Glazebrook, Curtis had overlooked 'certain very serious effects that are most obvious to those who have had time to feel the pulse of the country as a whole.'[153] In fairness, Falconer sometimes misread or deluded himself about public opinion, just as Curtis had. On this occasion, however, he undoubtedly had a point.

When, in spite of Canadian objections, Curtis insisted on broadcasting his prophecy, Falconer and his colleagues scrambled to minimize the damage. The upshot was a carefully worded memorandum setting forth the general goals of the dominion moot. A desire to strengthen the imperial tie was noted, but care was taken to avoid any hint of colonial subordination. 'Effective organization,' ran clause two, 'must not involve any sacrifice of responsible government in domestic affairs or the surrender of control over fiscal policy by any portion of the Empire.' Some commitments to imperial foreign policy and defence were described as necessary, but it was said that such details could be settled only at a full conference of all the parties concerned.[154] Deliberately vague, the memorandum left many difficult questions unanswered. For the moment the object was merely to restore unity within the Canadian Round Table and head off criticism from without. In the end, however, all these efforts were to no avail. Neither Curtis nor Falconer had been correct in his assessment of the imperial significance of the war. Canadians grew not less but more enamoured of autonomy, and even the best laid plans for closer union went astray. Moreover, the demands of total war left less and less emotional energy for other things as the struggle dragged on. Glazebrook, for one, came slowly to understand this point. In 1917, as he explained to Milner, the battle over conscription simply overshadowed all other issues and little could be done to arouse or sustain public interest in the memorandum.[155] Dynamic younger men who might have aided the cause were away in France or absorbed in more pressing work. As well, the allegations by Dafoe and others that the Round Table was a sinister cabal plotting to rob Canada of its independence cut deeply. By the spring of 1918 Glazebrook was in despair. Understaffed and unpopular, the organization, he lamented, could do nothing at the moment and might even have to change its name after the war. His one hope was that men would come to their senses and make Milner 'dictator for the war.'[156] After 1917 Falconer said little about the Round Table and appears to have gradually drifted out of its orbit. No doubt he too was disappointed with its collapse. Even so, he never lapsed into the right-wing fantasies entertained by Glazebrook. After all, and again along with Burke, his real faith was in those bonds of empire which although 'light as air' were 'strong as links of iron.' These ties, he thought, endured beyond all temporary political arrangements.[157]

As the fortunes of the Round Table sagged, so did those of another of Falconer's established interests. Indeed, despite promising beginnings, church union had fallen on hard times even before the war. In 1910 both Methodists and Congregationalists had given the recently drafted 'Basis' overwhelming support. It was otherwise, however, within Presbyterian ranks. A plebiscite in 1912 revealed that almost a third of those who voted stood opposed to union. The principal citadels of resistance, much to Falconer's dismay, were in the conservative eastern provinces, where the need for co-operation was less pressingly felt. The west, where thin resources were dispersed over boundless tracts, rallied impressively behind the ecumenical thrust, as did a majority of central Canadians. However, church leaders, faithful to their democratic traditions, hesitated to move without an expression of near unanimity. Accordingly the 'Basis,' already a moderate document, was slightly revised in order to appease its critics. Allowing time for tempers to cool, the General Assembly then waited until 1915 before testing opinion again. The opposition, however, had only gained strength in the interval. More active than their rivals, opponents of union had used the breathing space to sow further doubts among the faithful. The result was a vote in which nearly 40 per cent of Presbyterians expressed their disapproval of amalgamation. Desperate to head off a fatal crisis, some members of the union committee moved that all public discussion of the issue be suspended for the rest of the year, but the motion was defeated.[158] Altogether, as Falconer sighed, things looked 'very blue for Union.'[159]

If anything, skies grew even darker the following year. Sensing pressure from anxious would-be partners, Falconer and others on the Presbyterian union committee advised the General Assembly to commit itself firmly to the cause but to leave the date for merger open.[160] Accepting this counsel, the Winnipeg assembly signified its intention to consummate union at some point after the war. But the 'antis' would not be stilled. Indeed, the Winnipeg decision evoked a storm of protest from dissenters which led to the formation of the Presbyterian Church Association at a large rally in October. Dedicated to resisting union, the association's members had already delivered a series of blows at union and its proponents that summer. Anticipating as much, Falconer, now convener of the union committee, moved early to parry such attacks. Hitherto the champions of union had been slow to grasp the importance of propaganda, and the field had been left clear for their opponents. But the university president turned recruiting sergeant had clearly learned some lessons during the war. No sooner had the Winnipeg assembly ended than he wrote to members of his committee urging that pro-unionists begin to manufacture publicity in a systematic way. As he informed Murray: 'a strong propaganda is about to be undertaken by the *antis* and ... we must forestall it.'[161]

At the urging of Falconer and others a publicity committee was finally established in July. By September it had ceased to rely on notices in newspapers and instead was publishing pamphlets on its own. Intended for wide distribution, these flyers were levelled at the case put by Ephraim Scott and other dissenting publicists. Thus a series of 400-word statements were churned out, each designed to allay specific fears raised by the 'antis.'[162] Meanwhile the committee issued a general 'Message to Sessions' setting forth a defence of the assembly's actions. As convener, Falconer added a note of his own in which he gave full vent to his ecumenical convictions. Above all he tried to assure fellow Presbyterians that union would signal not the obliteration of their church but a fulfilment of it. [163] The text of the message was conciliatory and moderate, but even so, Scott refused to publish it in the *Presbyterian Record*. Such censorship, of course, was a blatantly partisan misuse of an official church organ, and Falconer was duly outraged. Inflamed, he despatched a scathing letter to the stubborn editor but received no reply.[164] Evidently the gulf of bitterness between the contending parties was widening as it deepened.

Flickering hopes, however, were kept alight by events on the prairies. Careless of formalities, impatient with delays, and urged by necessity, westerners were spontaneously organizing local union churches of their own. Affiliating in a spirit of tolerance and mutual sympathy, joint congregations flourished, especially in Saskatchewan.[165] Thus, by example added pressure was exerted on parent bodies in the east to follow suit, and Falconer was glad. By December he was urging Presbyterians to support and expand the prairie experiments. Indeed, he warned them that more was at stake here than purely ecclesiastical matters. Good in itself, he also viewed religious amalgamation as a necessary contribution to national unity. In his mind it followed that easterners could not long allow the aspirations of the west to go unrecognized. An accord among churchmen in the older provinces, he reasoned, would go a long way towards heading off potential western alienation.[166] Others, as it happened, shared his view, and early in 1917 steps were taken to co-ordinate more fully these local unifications.[167]

Meanwhile all eyes turned to Montreal, where the General Assembly was convened in mid-June. A score of items graced a crowded agenda, but no one doubted that the crucial debates would focus on the question of union. There was a brief moment of unanimity as the conclave voiced its unreserved support for universal military service. However, when Falconer rose immediately thereafter to table the report of the union committee, the tension could be felt throughout the hall. He was quick to remind his listeners that the Winnipeg assembly had committed the church to a definite course of action. In broad outline, he contended, it could no longer be considered debatable. This being the case, his committee had operated on the assumption that they had no mandate to consider alternatives. He went on to draw attention to the fact that Scott had refused to publish the 'Message to Sessions' but passed no further comment on this. He did, however, refer to the campaign of the

Presbyterian Church Association and criticized it for failing to recognize the authority of the Winnipeg gathering. At this point protests from dissenters, who sought to justify their stance, were hooted down. When the tumult subsided, Falconer warned that Methodists and Congregationalists would regard any attempt to backtrack as an unpardonable breach of faith. 'Presbyterians,' he declared, 'are not fickle people; when they have come to a decision after long and careful consideration they abide by their decision and keep faith.' Speaking for the union committee, he therefore advised that the resolutions passed at Winnipeg be regarded as beyond discussion. Falconer, however, was careful to leave the door to compromise at least slightly ajar: the great issue might have been decided, but details were still negotiable. Accordingly he proposed that, while the assembly sat, the union committee should receive submissions from those who entertained reservations. By a slim majority of nineteen votes his report and suggestion were approved.[168]

The enlarged committee worked feverishly over the weekend but succeeded only in producing two radically opposed recommendations. The majority, for whom Falconer spoke, upheld the policy of proceeding towards union within two years of the conclusion of the war. Minority representatives called instead for yet another plebiscite to be held on that date. On one point, however, an understanding was reached. Continued public wrangling was deemed not only disruptive but also unseemly so long as the country was at war. By mutual agreement, therefore, Thurlow Fraser of the Presbyterian Church Association rose immediately to second a plea for the suspension of debate. These proposals apparently came as something of a surprise to regular delegates, and the hall went 'stone silent.' Then 'a great wave of applause passed over the house.' A standing vote proved unanimous, and the whole gathering spontaneously sang the Doxology. As a gesture of reconciliation Falconer urged that his reference to Scott be deleted from the record of proceedings. The *Globe* prophesied, inaccurately as it happened, the imminent dissolution of the Presbyterian Church Association. 'Thus,' it reported, 'the Church Union controversy passed by an act of devotion into history.'[169] In truth, of course, nothing like this had occurred. But for the moment the issue was shelved, and the truce generally held good until 1921.

Had he no other responsibilities, Falconer's efforts to promote church union, imperial unity, and a score of patriotic schemes would still have left him very busy indeed. But he remained the president of a major university, and the task of running it continued to provide the focus for the bulk of his considerable energies. Falconer took great pride in the response of the university to the call for sacrifice, but the war also brought its disappointments. From the outset he was resigned to the fact that the exigencies of total war would force Toronto 'to mark time.'[70] Even so, it was galling to have to abandon important initiatives launched in peacetime. Obviously a permanent solution to the problem of inadequate funding was out of the question so long as government resources were necessarily being channelled elsewhere. Similarly there was little hope of forcing sweeping changes in the provincial matriculation system while Ontarians were obsessed with more demanding priorities. Nor could the old case for reform be put with much vigour as enrolment not only declined but plummeted. Thus, yielding to circumstance, Falconer was willing to let these issues remain dormant until peace returned. There was, however, one vital matter which he absolutely refused to shelve. The war, he insisted, had increased rather than diminished the urgency of stimulating graduate work within Canada and the empire. On this question there could be no compromise.

In his presidential report for 1913–14 Falconer reserved his final paragraphs for a blunt and forceful presentation of his case. The great danger as he saw it was that Canadian universities would spend the war in a state of suspended animation while American schools moved dramatically forward. Nowhere, he contended, was the peril greater than in the field of graduate studies. He predicted, rightly as it transpired, that fewer and fewer Americans would venture abroad in search of advanced education while the war lasted. Instead they would place new demands on their own universities, whose leaders were bound to answer with rapid expansion. This development, said Falconer, would inevitably have one ominous side-effect. Canadian students, cut off from Europe, would be tempted to flock to the United States in ever greater numbers. From sad experience he went on to point out that all too many who went south to study failed to return. He therefore argued that, wartime difficulties notwithstanding, Canada had to be prepared to expand its own graduate facilities or forfeit its self-respect: 'Such advanced work is costly, but without it we shall have the chagrin of watching our neighbours shoot past us, and we shall have to be content with obtaining from them such trained teachers as they can spare us.'[71]

Falconer's concern with American competition in the graduate field was perfectly genuine, as his many prewar declarations attest. During the early months of the war, however, other considerations impelled him to call for the improvement of advanced work at Toronto. As the German professors affair raged, attempts were made to stir up disaffection among the alumni. In part this took the form of growing complaints about the failure to develop a first-class graduate program. The administration, it was alleged, was letting the university down. Falconer, understandably, was furious. On the surface, as he conceded in a letter to MacMechan, the complaint was reasonable. However, he deeply resented the implication that he had been laggard in his efforts. The real problems, he argued, were a lack of money and division within the staff. He looked forward to peace and the return of prosperity to solve the financial difficulties. Time and the infusion of new blood, he thought, would break down the factional strife that still bedevilled the question. Thus, while angered by innuendo, he remained cautiously optimistic about the future of graduate studies. As he told MacMechan: 'If our old troubles had all been buried deep enough, we should hear less of the struggle between graduate and undergraduate, but unfortunately the personal element still remains, though with the advent of younger men the friction is distinctly lessening.' Still, the accusations of slackness stung, and he was quick to retort that, for all its limitations, Toronto was even then 'doing a good deal of really excellent work of graduate standard, though often it is not recognised.' Soberly he added that 'it is not an easy task to do the right and expedient thing at all times and you know how much even in university circles is determined not as you would expect by reason but by personal predilections.'[172] Feeling himself a victim of 'personal predilections' at the moment, Falconer redoubled his already strong commitment to bolstering graduate work.

Accordingly he ensured that discussion of the subject was not blotted out as the university laboured to cope with the war. By 1916 tangible progress was made. A new board of post-graduate studies was constituted and important changes in the regulations were approved. Courses were more carefully defined. Attendance was made obligatory unless special dispensation were granted. In addition, particular efforts were made to draw students from other provinces. To this end an old rule requiring candidates to have completed a Toronto BA degree was abolished.[173] Similarly, Falconer took personal charge of a drive to elicit graduate fellowships in support of those who came from outside Ontario. For the moment he confined his appeal to wealthy governors of the university who might be expected to sympathize with his goals. To Flavelle he wrote of the need 'to show the West that we mean business and will do our best for them.'[174] Osler, Leonard, and Sir John Eaton received similar letters. In the end, three of them donated a total of $2,000 in the form of four annual fellowships. Eaton agreed to help after the war. It was a modest beginning but one on which Falconer thought he could build. More importantly, he believed, it was a clear signal that Varsity intended to serve the nation as well as the province in the field of graduate studies.

Intentions, however, were one thing, but the immediate escalation of the American threat was quite another. Therefore, while Toronto revamped its own program, Falconer restated his plea for closer national and imperial co-operation in graduate studies. In this vein he took the lead in calling for a conference of Canadian university presidents in 1915. 'The increased necessity of postgraduate work in the Dominion by reason of the war may soon become urgent,' he informed his colleagues.[175] On the eve of the gathering he went further in explaining his purposes to R.A. Pyne, Ontario's minister of education. The war, he contended, offered a priceless opportunity to bind the country together. Too many on the prairies, he argued, knew little of the east and were prone to look to the United States for their values. However, he continued, a co-ordinated system of higher education could do much to repair this, particularly if future western leaders were induced to spend a few years of graduate study in the older provinces. The trick, he advised, was to strike while the patriotic iron was still hot in a nation drawn together by war.[176]

These thoughts were in the forefront of his mind as the meeting convened in Toronto that June. Taking the chair, Falconer dwelt forcefully on such themes in his keynote address. Others took up the cry, and a consensus emerged on the need to foster graduate work in the larger eastern universities.[177] Lamentably, however, it was also generally recognized that some major obstacles would be hard to overcome. For example, the conference stumbled on the question of establishing mutually acceptable matriculation standards; regional variations reflected differing local realities that could not be wished away. Similarly, it was obvious to all that adequate funding would be difficult, if not impossible, to obtain during the war. Yet the will to stave off a perceived American challenge was strong. Moreover, the merits of meeting annually to discuss shared problems were obvious. Accordingly it was decided to establish the conference on a regular footing. When, in 1916, the members met again in Montreal, they formulated a constitution for the new organization and elected Falconer its first president. With few interruptions meetings were henceforth held each year as the National Conference of Canadian Universities took shape. The 1916 session was also notable for its efforts to solicit British assistance in the graduate field. Members resolved that 'in order to strengthen the unity of the Empire, the Universities of Great Britain should be urged to modify and increase their graduate facilities to meet the needs especially of students from the

Universities of this Dominion.'[178] A committee of four under Falconer's leadership was directed to communicate this resolution to university heads in the mother country. In due course a strong appeal was issued over Falconer's signature. Striking an imperial note, as well as emphasizing the American threat, the letter reiterated many things said before the war.[179] The message was not new, but the circumstances and reception were different. Indeed, Falconer's missive was well timed and had a considerable impact on deliberations in Britain.

Pressure to accommodate foreign students by the adoption of the PH D degree had been mounting in Britain even before 1914. A desire to emulate the more economically proficient Germans had contributed to this. So had appeals from the empire. Some people also questioned the political wisdom of allowing Germany to educate the majority of Americans who sought higher degrees outside the United States. Little, nevertheless, had actually been done, since conservative British educators resisted 'Germanic' innovations and the supposed diluting of their cherished Oxbridge doctorates. The war, however, gave fresh impetus to the drive towards establishing the PH D. Imperial overtures carried more weight as Britain's reliance on her overseas possessions was underlined. Similarly, and especially before 1917, there was much talk of trying to undercut German influence in the United States by drawing more American students to Britain. That a market existed could not be doubted. In 1916 the American Association of University Professors wrote to British vice-chancellors urging them to recognize foreign BAS and to make graduate work more accessible. Given the general desire to court American favour at this juncture, the request was difficult to ignore. Sadler at Leeds and H.A.L. Fisher at Sheffield stepped up their campaign for the adoption of a 'foreigners' doctorate,' obtainable after one or two years of residence at a British university. Their arguments were compelling, but many of their colleagues still baulked at caving in to the 'commercial' motives of Americans. Falconer's blatantly patriotic appeal, however, was seen as quite different and met with a far more positive response. It undoubtedly allowed many to approve a course of action that, although patently necessary, could henceforth be undertaken as a grand, and therefore palatable, imperial gesture. The note, moreover, arrived only a few weeks before conferences intended to address the issue were scheduled to open. Coupled with American requests, pressure from the Universities Bureau of the British Empire, and the lobbying of Sadler's friends, Falconer's letter helped persuade some of the reluctant. On 12 May 1917 the Northern Universities Conference expressed joint support for the introduction of the PH D. A week later the United Kingdom

Universities Conference followed suit. It recommended a special program for foreign candidates consisting of not less than two full years of
research and advanced study. Older doctorates, of course, would be
retained. Unfortunately, however, the resolution was not binding on all
members of the conference. Individual senates would still have to
approve the measure.[180]

Oxford, the most imperially minded of British universities, moved
quickly to implement the scheme. But other institutions, notably Cambridge, London, and Glasgow, dragged their feet. Falconer found this
hesitancy irritating in the extreme. 'What some of these English Universities do not realise,' he told Walter Murray, 'is that the United States ... is
going to be an increasingly strong source of attraction for our men, and
that if we are to be able to divert the stream they must do everything in
their power to help us.'[181] Partial measures were not enough. From
England H.M. Tory wrote to explain that old divisions had resurfaced
after the Universities Conference had adjourned. He was particularly
disappointed in the quarrelling he had encountered. Part of the discord,
he speculated, was the result of generally poor organization. 'The lack of
co-ordination and cohesion and almost of good will between the Universities over here,' he told Falconer, 'at once strikes one as so peculiar and
makes one feel what real progress we have made to date in our Canadian
Conference.' He did, nevertheless, advise that there was reason to hope.
At Cambridge he had discussed the PH D question with representatives of
the senate. 'I am afraid,' he joked, 'their self-complacency was slightly
disturbed by the breezy manner in which a wild Westerner presented the
scheme for recognition of the work done in Canada.' Even so, he was
happy to report that the vice-chancellor seemed very well disposed
toward the idea.[182] In the event Tory's optimism eventually proved well
founded. By 1918 over half the British universities had adopted the PH D.
Cambridge, not wishing to be left behind, gave its approval a few months
after the armistice. London, the last hold-out, yielded in May 1919.
Needless to say, Falconer was pleased by this turn of events. He did,
however, point out that there was one more problem to be overcome. In
the absence of a generous program of fellowships, Canadians of average
means would still find it difficult to pursue the British option. None the
less he could rejoice that an important battle in this continuing struggle
had been won. Meanwhile the war in Europe mercifully drew to an end.

When the guns at last fell silent, Falconer was as relieved as the
next man. Unlike many Christian idealists of his generation, however,
he survived the war with his basic confidence in modern society still
intact. Others, such as Archibald MacMechan and Maurice Hutton, felt

increasingly estranged from a world seemingly gone mad, first with violence, and then with peacetime materialism. Falconer, on the other hand, although chastened, retained his accustomed optimism. To be sure, like his friends he sensed that his most cherished values, indeed his whole world view, would be subjected to mounting criticism. Thus he too mourned the decline of religious practice and the rise of a frank hedonism which followed the war. Significantly, however, he never gave into despair or retreated into a dignified but sombre isolation. In part this may have reflected no more than a difference in personality, but it is likely that Falconer's experience of the war differed markedly from that of a man such as Hutton. Both had greeted its outbreak as an opportunity to burn away moral complacency and build a better world on a foundation of clarified ideals.[183] The classicist, however, gradually adopted the stance of a disillusioned spectator as events took an unforetold and harrowing course. It was otherwise with Falconer. Indeed, for him the war could not have begun in worse fashion. Accused of disloyalty during the German professors affair, he was beleaguered from the outset. In many ways, therefore, the blackest days of the conflict for him came early. There followed an unbroken period of intense activity during which he not only rehabilitated his reputation and won a knighthood but also had the sense of being in the thick of things and of contributing ultimately to victory. Thus, far from feeling like an irrelevant fossil, Falconer experienced an increase of influence as his personal stock rose. He never imagined, of course, that he could stem the rising tide of materialism single-handedly. The historian in him, however, was convinced that time and effort would repair much of the moral damage wrought by war. Society, as he saw it in broad perspective, had momentarily plunged into one of those valleys that dotted the landscape of human history. But the peaks would be scaled again, and progress, never automatic, would continue to be made, however slowly, however painfully. Such was his faith in men and providence. Determined to help accelerate the process of recovery as much as possible, he looked forward with zest to a period of reconstruction. It was no casual whim that led Sir Robert in 1917 to choose as his knightly motto the word 'Service.'[184] Indeed, for him, as for J.S. Willison, N.W. Rowell, and other activists among the British-Canadian élite, the war had served to sharpen what John English has described as an 'ideology of service.'[185] Born in Falconer as early as his Pine Hill days, this urge to address the problems of Canadian society, largely without reference to party, had been powerfully confirmed.

CHAPTER IX

Service, Tact, and Diplomacy

Where stability had been longed for, dislocation reigned. Where plenty had been prophesied, unemployment flourished. Inflation gnawed at wages; doubt wrestled with conviction; harmony dissolved in strife. To Falconer, as to many others, the first fruits of victory tasted far from sweet. He never doubted, of course, that had Germany won the war 'a chilling ice-age of materialism would have crept over the earth.'[1] Not for a moment did he imagine that the four years of costly struggle had been wholly in vain. Still, the reward for sacrifice fell lamentably short of once-bright expectations. 'It is wrongs unanswered,' he recognized, 'that breed unhappiness.'[2] War, for example, had seemingly increased rather than diminished the dominance of master over man. Thus he sympathized with disgruntled workmen who took to Winnipeg's streets in frustration: 'Sore disappointment rankles in the hearts of many who have fought for freedom only to find themselves fastened into an industrial system in which they have little or no recognition of the dignity of their function and receive a small return from the proceeds of their toil.'[3] Similarly, he could understand why some men rejected established values and were seduced by the siren song of Bolshevism. The times, after all, were sadly out of joint. Want on one hand and lavish display on the other quite naturally bred extremism in the dispossessed.[4] All this he comprehended, but he refused to concede that the cure lay in class warfare or in the application of force by any group. Instead, as of old, he recommended the forging of a grand consensus based on higher concepts of liberty and social justice. Enduring ideals, he advised, could yet be adapted to new conditions.

As the postwar era dawned, Falconer issued a clarion call for the reconstruction of society. His *Idealism in National Character,* published in 1920, was expressly designed to highlight the intellectual and moral qualities he deemed essential for this renewal. In its pages he once again displayed the 'progressive-conservatism' that had long marked his social thought. If anything was new, it was Falconer's increased emphasis on the need for evolutionary rather than revolutionary change. Clearly, he was deeply alarmed by the prospect of social disintegration. Unrestrained capitalism still left him cold, but so did radical calls for its violent overthrow. Nor did he warm to utopian visions, whether generated by the left or the right. Rather, he thought that wisdom dictated the gradual reform of an always imperfect world. Some measure of social justice, he argued, would be had only when man acknowledged the primacy of three interrelated ideals: law, righteousness, and liberty. By law Falconer understood not particular legislative enactments, but 'the permanent moral relationship which holds mankind together.' A determination to live in accordance with law, for him, constituted righteousness. Liberty, therefore, he defined as the condition enjoyed by men who had the opportunity to live a righteous life. It was, however, 'a gift which [could] only be realized in a regulated universe and an ordered society.' Thus, he slammed the door on those who fostered class hatred, anarchy, or tyranny.[5] Such notions, of course, had been familiar since at least the age of Burke. Yet, whatever their vintage, Falconer saw scores of new applications as Canada struggled to cope with peace. In large measure they served as guideposts for much of his action in the troubled years ahead.

Of the various exponents of radical change, Falconer feared communists far less than he did social gospellers. Marxism he regarded as an alien plant, too exotic to strike deep roots in Canadian soil. Even in hard times, he argued, the average person had 'too large a stake in the country' to contemplate an end to private ownership. The 'red peril,' he therefore prophesied, would wither with the first breath of prosperity.[6] The social gospel, however, was different. Posing as evolved Christianity, it had a home-grown flavour and a potentially greater appeal. Before the war Falconer had denounced it as a perversion of scripture, but his tone had been measured and his arguments primarily academic. When, however, late wartime militants called on the godly to impel the state towards socialism, his criticism became at once more biting and more loudly voiced. Fearing would-be theocrats, he undoubtedly overestimated their influence. At any rate, the social gospel became an obsession that haunted him long after it had ceased to be a significant force. Scant weeks before his death in the early 1940s, he was still belabouring its long-vanquished exponents.[7]

His scholarly and religious objections to the social gospel remained unchanged. In his 'Moral Standards in Primitive Christianity' and 'The Book of Acts Once More,' published in 1919 and 1922, respectively, Falconer reiterated his contention that Christ had neither prescribed nor foretold a social revolution.[8] Elsewhere, however, he began to add political criticisms to these academic reservations. With increasing stridency, he warned that both experience and common sense militated against church interference in the affairs of the state. In part, the voluntarist in Falconer was offended by collectivist pleas issuing from labour churches and the like. Beyond this, one suspects, he was also anxious to dispel the notion, current among reluctant Presbyterians, that church union would lead to the creation of a 'religio-political machine.' Moreover, as the decade wore on, he was disturbed by events south of the border that seemed to confirm some of his worst fears. Falconer believed that when churchmen meddled directly in affairs of state, they also opened the door to publicly endorsed intolerance. The Scopes trial of 1925 and the mental habits that induced it served only to strengthen this conviction. In 1922, when the Kentucky legislature came within one vote of prohibiting the teaching of evolutionary theory, Falconer was outraged. Writing immediately to Willison, he expounded on 'the danger of tyranny from majorities.' 'Politically,' he snarled, 'it is all too evident, but also at present on this continent there is a recrudescence of obscurantism in religion which is endangering intellectual freedom.' The rantings of William Jennings Bryan he described as 'incredible.' 'It is sad,' he continued, 'that an influential contemporary has gone the way of the backslider, for he will pull others down the slippery places.' Indeed, said Falconer, 'the danger is not all over; and there are only too many indications that it is hovering in the offing here.'[9] Perhaps recalling Sam Blake, the president of a state-supported university winced whenever fundamentalists challenged freedom of inquiry. The Butler Law and subsequent 'Monkey Trial' in Tennessee did little to allay his misgivings. In his mind even moderate political activists who paraded under the banner of religion represented a threat to the liberty of conscience. It was probably unfair to identify social gospellers, such as Salem Bland, with the likes of Bryan. The former, after all, shared Falconer's ecumenical sympathies and his distaste for rigid dogma. In times of stress, however, reality and perception are all too frequently at odds, and so it may have been with Falconer. Whatever the case, the social gospel was a path he refused to follow in pursuit of reconstruction.

Within the compass of his own jurisdiction he preferred to urge the merits of the politically neutral but socially active university as an agent of reform. Along with culture and scholarship, service had always formed part of his vision of the ideal home of higher learning. Indeed, he had ever held that, to be truly useful, universities had to adjust to the needs of each generation. Thus, as the 1920s presented new challenges, Falconer was more than prepared to help Varsity meet them. Without sacrificing either culture or scholarship, he laboured to amplify his own ideal of service. Such, he argued, was the university's clear duty. It was also the simplest political wisdom in an era when established institutions, and the University of Toronto not least among them, were subjected to increasing pressure as society whirled in a state of flux.

In 1921 Falconer informed an Oxford audience that universities everywhere were living 'in a new state of affairs.' He continued, 'Old orders are being dispossessed and have to range themselves alongside new classes, such as artisans or farmers, who see that power is ultimately based on knowledge.'[10] Demanding access to and sensitivity from the university, these rising groups required attention. Frequently, he observed, their needs would have to be met in novel ways. Among other things, therefore, summer sessions and extension services would inevitably grow in volume and importance. Similarly, while traditional faculties would continue to give the university its character and cohesion, changing economic and social realities would have to be reflected in the development of a multitude of attached departments.[11] He went on to add that none of these changes need alter the essence of the university. 'In short courses for young farmers,' he argued, 'there is nothing alien to its spirit, provided they are taught by those who can create an inquiring mind.'[12] The task, as he saw it, was to bring the university closer to all the people that it might better serve them and, in so doing, demonstrate its continuing relevance. A year later he told Toronto students that the university stood as a stabilizing force in any society. Both 'conservative and progressive,' it relayed inherited wisdom which each new generation of forever young students subjected to purifying criticism in the light of contemporary concerns.[13] Thus, forms and emphases varied with the exigencies of the moment, but the ageless spirit of impartial inquiry remained, informed by the past and responsive to the present.[14]

It was not difficult to identify the first order of business to which the postwar university could usefully turn its hand. The returned soldier would have to be reintegrated with a changing community. Falconer, of course, had little power to affect the fate of demobilized farmers or workmen in the mass, but aspiring undergraduates in the armed forces were another matter. The success of the Khaki University encouraged him and others to believe that a significant number of troops would seek to further their education once they had been mustered out. As early as February 1918 he approached the Board of Governors with a request to remit the fees of a former student who had returned from France. It was a trial balloon. The governors, although sympathetic, feared to set a costly precedent and therefore rejected the plea. Ottawa, they told the president, should assume the expense of educating returned men.[15] In principle, Falconer agreed, especially when he considered the generous loan and scholarship schemes being planned in Britain and Australia. Surely, he believed, Canada would do no less for her own faithful servants.

Meanwhile, in May Canadian university leaders exchanged views on how best to alter their regulations so as to accommodate this special type of student. Among other things, it was suggested that some academic credit be awarded for military service and that prepatory courses be set in place.[16] In November Bruce Taylor, Gordon's successor at Queen's, urged that all men holding matriculation certificates be demobilized early in order that they miss as little of the university term as possible.[17] A few weeks later he wrote to Falconer urgently underlining the need for government assistance for the returned soldier-student. 'His old civilian clothes are moth eaten or worn by his brothers,' said Taylor, 'and he has to face an expensive training without any immediate possibility of earning money.' Anxious to help these men, Queen's was prepared to absorb the cost for a year, but could do little when the expected flood came later. Accordingly, an apprehensive Taylor turned to Ottawa for financial support and urged Toronto to join in the appeal.[18]

Unknown to Taylor, Falconer had already begun quietly to test the wind on Parliament Hill.[19] The task, however, was less than easy. A veritable forest of special committees, each designed to oversee some aspect of demobilization, was springing up in the capital. All too frequently bureaucrats jostled one another in jurisdictional disputes or described inconvenient requests as somebody else's affair. To Falconer it was painfully obvious that only a concerted assault by the universities of Canada would suffice to break up the log-jam of red tape. Taylor's letter, therefore, came as a timely prod in this direction. Meanwhile, encouragement was forthcoming from another source. In December the Great War Veterans Association, impatient with delays, petitioned the federal government to move swiftly towards clarifying its policies concerning returned men. Among other things, the GWVA asked that generous grants be offered to those who wished to enrol in the universities.[20] As pressure mounted the Repatriation Committee decided to call the various interested parties to a conference in Ottawa. University leaders, veterans' groups, and the Dominion Trade and Labour Council were invited to send representatives. Falconer expected a sympathetic hearing, since Vincent Massey, long a friend of Varsity, was a prominent member of the government committee. The January meeting was cordial. J.A. Calder, minister of immigration and colonization, received submissions as chairman of the Repatriation Committee and seemed genuinely anxious to help. Massey too was encouraging. In the end, however, it was made clear that nothing could be done without the approval of a cabinet which was seriously divided on the issue. Thus, Falconer and the others left Ottawa having presented their views but without having secured a definite commitment.

This first brush with Ottawa's demobilizers demonstrated the need for more systematic and determined lobbying. Over the next few months Falconer worked to forge an alliance among university leaders, veterans, and labour groups interested in the issue. Tom Moore of the Labour Council and W.D. Tait of the GWVA were sounded out and proved amenable. There was even talk of holding a general conference under federal auspices to settle the whole matter of soldier education. Meanwhile Falconer helped to draft a resolution, approved by all these groups, which called on Ottawa to cover the expenses of returned students for one year and to reimburse the universities for the special prepatory courses involved.[21] Members of parliament, particularly those associated with the demobilization committees, were deluged with letters and petitions. For himself, Falconer wore out a seat on the Ottawa train as he interviewed key politicians in person. Most notably he and others laboured hard to break down the resistance of Sir James Lougheed, powerful head of the Department of Soldiers' Civil Re-Establishment.[22] Without that prairie cabinet member's approval, little could be done.

By March it appeared that all this effort had been in vain. The Repatriation Committee, in the person of Vincent Massey, informed Walter Murray, then president of the Universities Conference, that the proposals aired in January had been rejected. Murray was almost crushed by the news. Dejectedly he wrote to Falconer that 'these conferences are very pleasant things to attend, but very disappointing.'[23] Momentarily stunned, Falconer quickly recovered and set off on another round of intense lobbying. Polite but pointed letters were fired off to Lougheed and Calder as once more the rationale for aid was set forth.[24] In addition, copies of the letters were sent to university heads throughout the country, who were implored to write Ottawa in support. Moore and Tait added their voices to that of Toronto's president. Once again, therefore, the cabinet table was littered with petitions. Finally, harried ministers agreed to reconsider the question. Calder, indeed, sounded an optimistic note. 'I am in hopes,' he told Falconer, 'that some arrangement will be made whereby the necessary Federal assistance may be granted for this work.'[25]

It was a stunning blow, therefore, when two weeks later the same minister took refuge behind a banal, if well-tried, gambit in rejecting these pleas yet again. Education, he informed Falconer, was deemed to be a provincial concern in which Ottawa could not interfere. Going further, he gave notice that the federal government refused to call or participate in any general conference devoted to the matter.[26] Bruce Taylor, for one, had no doubts about where to lay the blame for this boycott. He had already written to Falconer describing Lougheed as the chief 'stumbling block.' Said Taylor, 'When our recommendations came before him, he simply waved them all aside with some remark that since the Universities had asked so much, they would not get anything.' Even a supportive telegram from Lord Milner had failed to make a dent in Lougheed's stubborn resolve.[27] Taylor thought he knew why: in his unpublished memoirs the principal bluntly observed that 'Sir James, a product of the early west, took us for a group of theorists, making far too much of so intangible a thing as education. He was playing politics. He would help a soldier established on a farm in the north-west, because one soldier-farmer was one vote for the Government; a student trying to recover his languages or mathematics was, from the electoral point of view, of no importance at all.'[28]

In a sense Taylor was correct. Political considerations did lie at the root of Ottawa's reluctance to assist the returned student, but this reticence was not confined to Lougheed, as the principal of Queen's seemed to suggest, as other events soon made clear. Fed up with trying to hack their way through the bureaucratic undergrowth, in May delegates to the annual Universities Conference decided to go straight to the top. A lengthy resolution was drafted and forwarded directly to Borden by Falconer.[29] The two men later met to discuss the matter privately. The prime minister then mulled the question over for a month, but not without being subjected to further entreaties, chiefly from N.W. Rowell, who strongly seconded the universities' stand.[30] By mid-July, however, Borden could stall no longer. He advised Falconer that federal monies would not be made available, because to do so would open an already strained Treasury to a host of far less reasonable demands. 'We all foresee,' he wrote, 'a tremendous outcry and disturbance of public opinion if we should make general provision for assistance to Students at Universities and should fail to make the like provision for vocational training for assistance in embarking upon business enterprises, etc.' Resources, he alleged, were severely limited. 'If,' he added, 'assistance of this character is granted I do not know at what point we could stop.'[31] Somewhat later Borden explained to H.P. Whidden of Brandon College that student aid was perceived as a class issue and was therefore potentially explosive.[32] And that, for all purposes, was that. For a year or so Falconer attempted to reopen the matter, but Ottawa turned a deaf ear. Provincial governments were no more helpful. Thus, the universities and the soldier-student were left to fend for themselves.

In the final analysis most Canadian universities managed to accommodate a share of the demobilized through privately or institutionally sponsored loan programs. At Toronto it was decided to employ part of the War Memorial Fund for this purpose. Thus, of the substantial sums donated by alumni to commemorate the university's fallen, part went to the construction of Soldiers' Tower and the rest helped finance the education of returned men. By 1922 over 400 former soldiers had been granted interest-free loans which totalled in excess of $120,000.[33] This represented a heavy investment on the part of a university that was badly in need of revenue. Yet, however stiff the price, Falconer considered the money well spent. The 1,200 erstwhile soldiers who eventually enrolled at Toronto displayed a maturity and an earnestness that deeply impressed the president. Moreover, notwithstanding some forecasts to the contrary, they did remarkably well as a group in examinations.[34] Altogether, in spite of his failure to win governmental support, Falconer's initial attempt at fostering reconstruction met with at least limited success. Still, one wonders how many more soldiers might have had the benefit of a university education had nervous politicians not trembled on the brink of obligation.

Apart from stimulating his interest in the fate of returned soldiers, the war and its aftermath also deepened Falconer's commitment to older forms of service. The University Settlement, for example, continued to benefit from his active support. Located at the corner of Adelaide and Peter streets, the house stood as an outpost of academically sponsored concern in the heart of one of Toronto's manufacturing districts. Its small resident staff was augmented by a corps of student volunteers who distributed aid to the needy and in addition ran a variety of social and educational clubs. A summer camp enabled hundreds of urban children to taste the pleasures of the countryside. A baby clinic saw to the needs of the very young, while a circulating library helped entertain and inform the more mature. During the great influenza epidemic, the settlement house functioned as an emergency 'flu depot' responsible for the care of over a hundred families. Parties were held on special occasions, and the president was regularly on hand to distribute parcels at Christmas.[35] More substantially, Falconer helped keep the operation afloat by personally soliciting cash from his wealthier acquaintances.

In the same spirit he strongly encouraged the university's emerging Department of Social Service. The first of its kind in Canada, it had grown out of a handful of part-time courses launched just before the war. Not surprisingly, the demand for at least partially trained field workers sharpened in the 1920s. As attendance rose, R.M. McIver was charged with overseeing the expanding program. When in 1920 he decided to devote the whole of his energy to political economy, James Alfred Dale was imported from McGill to serve as the department's first full-time director. Although designated a 'department,' social service did not lead directly to a regular degree. Instead, a two-year curriculum culminated in a diploma. The vast majority of candidates were part-timers.[36] Even so, graduates from the department were in demand as social problems and agencies designed to cope with them multiplied. By 1929, however, E.J. Urwick, who succeeded Dale, was complaining of the deficiencies of a less than fully professionalized department. He argued that there was a need to bring the training into closer line with rapid changes in field conditions and to integrate fully the theoretical and practical aspects of the program.[37] Efforts were therefore made to upgrade course offerings and to co-ordinate them with the requirements of major social agencies. To an extent these modifications seem to have been successful. Urwick, at any rate, was later satisfied that, with Falconer's help, progress had been made. In 1932 he told the president that 'the continued life and the present vigour of the Department are due to your care and your unfailing support; and this knowledge is shared by the whole body of Alumni and by the still greater body of social workers in the community.'[38] This generous note undoubtedly pleased the service-conscious Falconer. Even more heartening was the substantial development of graduate studies after the war.

From his first days in office Falconer had worked patiently to improve and expand advanced studies at the University of Toronto. Acutely aware of the scholarly benefits of such work, he had also stressed the service that a strong graduate school could render to the community. Most vitally it would stand as a bulwark against American intellectual domination and as a focal point of national unity. Furthermore, he contended, intensified research by professors and students was bound to produce some results that would have practical application beyond the groves of academe.

James Playfair McMurrich shared this vision and brought with him a determination to see it realized when he was appointed chairman of the Board of Graduate Studies in 1919. The dynamic professor of anatomy made his position clear in accepting the post. To Falconer he wrote: 'It is understood that my endeavour will be to make the Department of Graduate Studies what it seems to me it ought to be, at least the equal in rank to any of the other departments of the University.'[39] Assisted ably by the philosopher George Brett, R.M. McIver, and others, McMurrich and the president co-operated over the next few years in tightening requirements and defining programs. The upshot, in 1923, was the establishment of the School of Graduate Studies with its own council and a dean. In one sense, of course, this was an innovation on paper only. The Board of Graduate Studies had been in existence for years and had brought greater standardization and co-operation in advanced work throughout the university. But symbols are important, and the creation of a distinct school was intended to dramatize 'a fuller recognition' of and 'a new impulse' to this crucial field of endeavour.[40]

The gesture was crowned with success. In 1921 there were 163 students proceeding towards graduate degrees at Toronto. Of these the vast majority were products of Varsity itself.[41] By 1932, however, 675 persons were enrolled in graduate courses.[42] This healthy leap in absolute numbers was gratifying, but even more so was the changing composition of the graduate population. All along Falconer had insisted that mere size was not his primary goal. Instead, his object had also been to attract graduates of other institutions. Only in this way, he argued, would Toronto fulfil its mission as a national university. Accordingly, he took great pride in the fact that of the 675 graduate students on campus during the last year of his presidency, 307 had taken their first degrees at sixty different universities.[43] These figures, furthermore, were in line with a long-term and welcome trend. In 1924 74 per cent of Toronto's graduate students held local BAs but in 1930 that percentage dropped to 61.[44] Many of those from outside Ontario had come from the prairies, lured by the increasing respectability of Toronto's program and by the opportunity to remain in a Canadian environment. A lucky few were attracted by the special fellowships, whose number had grown to ten by 1929, thanks in large measure to Falconer's personal efforts.

Inevitably there were still problems to overcome. In 1930, for example, McMurrich informed Falconer that the University of Toronto was failing to provide adequate support for its own graduates. Only two fellowships were available to those who had taken their first degrees at Toronto. The University of Chicago, by contrast, offered 115 scholarships to its graduates.[45] There were also serious questions about the quality of the candidates entering Toronto's graduate school: At one point fully three-fifths of them failed to attain a second-class standing in examinations.[46] Clearly, some fine-tuning was required. Nevertheless, by the close of Falconer's administration the foundations of a mature graduate program had been solidly laid. Understandably, therefore, the president was rather miffed when in 1927 Dean Laing of Chicago described Toronto as having the best BA but the worst MA on the continent.[47] As one historian has recently commented, this might have been true in 1917 but it was patently false in 1927.[48] Falconer merely observed that the good dean had been sadly misinformed.[49]

Meanwhile the University of Toronto was gaining prestige as a centre of research. The successful liquefaction of helium was accounted a major development. As well, the seminal work of scholars such as Harold Innis added lustre to Toronto's reputation. But nothing in the 1920s advertised the university to the world more dramatically than the discovery of insulin. Heated quarrels among Banting and his associates, although worrisome, paled beside news of their findings, which seemed to many little short of miraculous. There were initial embarrassments as jury-rigged efforts to provide adequate supplies of the precious substance faltered. Soon, however, a world-wide licensing network was established. Thus the suffering of thousands was allayed and substantial royalties helped support further research at the university. Insulin was a godsend, not least of all to Falconer. By 1923, with Banting and Macleod hailed as Nobel laureates, he had indisputable evidence that the University of Toronto was, indeed, a 'useful' institution.[50]

Anxious to advertise Varsity's growing service to society, Falconer lavished considerable attention on extension work and publicity in the 1920s. In the past the university had been criticized as a rich man's haven, aloof from the mundane but pressing problems of everyday life. To a degree this public image had some basis in reality. Few of society' s less privileged members could afford the luxury of a university education. Few, indeed, had traditionally felt the need for one. Moreover, rural elements tended to be suspicious of an institution that appeared to be overwhelmingly urban in its outlook and yet gobbled up significant portions of the public purse. To make matters worse, the university had hitherto paid little systematic attention to long-term public relations. It would respond to crises but tended to neglect opinion on the shop floor and concession lines when not immediately challenged. By the war's end, however, the need to take a more active role in moulding public perceptions was obvious, a need made plain by urban unrest and the advent of a farmer government in Ontario. Thus, as Falconer understood, it was not enough for the university to provide service to a changing society. It had to be seen to do so. However justified or unjustified old allegations may have been, Toronto could ill afford a reputation for ivory-tower isolation and class indifference in the turbulent 1920s. In short, urgent necessity sharpened sincere commitment and impelled Falconer to reach out to a broader constituency.

Before the war extension work had been rather casually undertaken. There were summer sessions, correspondence courses, and numerous occasional lectures, but no long-range planning or careful supervision. In 1918, however, the formation of the Workers Educational Association brought the first major stimulus to the development of a more systematic approach. Inspired by and modelled after successful British experiments, the WEA offered short, specially adapted university courses to interested labouring men. In part, its purpose was simply educative. In addition, however, middle-class founders assumed that 'the root of social harmony lies in like-mindedness.' There was an immense danger to any country, said one of its champions, 'in the existence of two languages, the language of the cultivated and the language of the street, neither of which is really comprehensible to the other.'[51] To men who shared this view the WEA recommended itself as an agent of assimilation capable of wedding the 'better sort' of working man to established values. Some, such as A.J. Glazebrook, even believed that this vehicle could be employed to win the workers' hearts for the empire.[52] Many, of course, also looked upon the movement as a form of public service to workers anxious to improve the quality of their lives. Falconer, who was well acquainted with Albert Mansbridge and other British architects of the WEA, shared most of these motives and helped both launch and sustain the Canadian effort.[53] By 1920 classes were being held regularly in Toronto and Hamilton. With only 160 people enrolled, the experiment had yet to prove itself, but organizers assured Falconer that a much larger market existed. In order to tap it, they told him, more money and better management were required.[54]

Meanwhile, as the university moved to accommodate the WEA, other interest groups quickly demanded similar attention. In 1919 a Bankers' Educational Association came into being and approached Falconer with a request that Varsity devise special programs to meet its needs. Significantly, the bankers offered to defray all the costs involved.[55] Here, thought Falconer, was a golden opportunity to solve several problems at one stroke. Handsome fees could be extracted from the 265 applicants put forward by the association.[56] This money, in turn, would help offset losses incurred in subsidizing the WEA, whose members paid only a token subscription. The bankers' classes would also be a boon to hard-pressed junior professors who craved extra income. Vincent W. Bladen, for example, had been reared at Oxford under the wing of A.L. Smith, who exuded the spirit of Toynbee Hall. Like many of his young colleagues, therefore, Bladen laboured for the WEA at least partly out of a sense of public duty; but he was equally happy to teach bankers at double the fee.[57] Altogether Falconer wasted little time in approving this particular scheme which offered all the benefits of public service and 10 per cent!

Besides workmen and bankers, farmers also engaged the attention of the university. Wisdom, indeed, dictated that they should, since the provincial elections of 1919 had catapulted the United Farmers of Ontario into power at Queen's Park. From the outset of E.C. Drury's administration, it was apparent that rural opinion was not entirely well disposed towards the provincial university. Early financial negotiations between Varsity and the new government were conducted in an atmosphere of increasing tension. Under these circumstances proponents of higher education would have to bring their message more forcefully to the concession lines. This, at any rate, was the way things seemed to Professor E.F. Burton as he contemplated the future of Toronto's extension work. Writing to Falconer in the spring of 1920, he noted the growth of farmers' clubs and suggested that they constituted a field that the university might sow with benefit to all concerned. 'From conversation with some members in close touch with headquarters,' Burton was led to believe that these clubs would 'welcome such work on the part of the University.' Furthermore, he saw in this action an opportunity to win the support of Queen's Park for the expansion of extension services generally. 'If the demand came from farmers themselves,' he advised Falconer, 'a very considerable movement towards the adult University would be very sympathetically considered by the government of the province.'[58] Accordingly, when in November the UFO asked the university to offer rural classes in economics, public health, literature, and architecture, the president quickly offered support to the project.[59]

By 1920, therefore, the University of Toronto boasted a growing array of extension programs in rural and urban districts. It was felt, however, that better planning and supervision would soon be required for the sake of efficiency and in order to extract the maximum advantage from these efforts. A committee, chaired by Burton, reviewed current activities and made inquiries concerning the extent of public demand. American organizational models were also scanned for helpful hints, and a general report was tabled in the spring. It was found that in addition to WEA and bankers' classes, a hundred or more single lectures had been offered extramurally, 'the subjects being pretty well scattered over all departments.' Staff members expressed a willingness to participate in serious educational projects but displayed a growing reluctance to go out 'merely as entertainers of heterogeneous audiences.' Occasional lectures to church groups, Sunday schools, and high school commencements were seen as time-consuming and unprofitable. Taking the hint, Burton's committee sounded out the Social Service Council of Ontario and found its leaders anxious to co-operate, and farmers' groups were also approached. Altogether, a considerable demand was said to exist for systematic adult education. The committee, therefore, offered Falconer several recommendations, most of which involved calls for the better funding of a more centrally co-ordinated effort. In particular, it was emphasized that a director should be appointed, one who could give his full time to a clearly defined extension service.[60]

Two American models captured the attention of Toronto's planners. The Wisconsin plan featured an extension division that operated almost independently of the regular departments of the university, having its own faculty, leadership, and buildings. On the positive side, this system allowed for intensive and extensive work in the field. It did, however, have one great drawback: it involved considerable duplication and therefore heavy expense. Financially more attractive, the Michigan plan worked through established departments and faculty. Admittedly, it did not produce as lavish and varied a program as that evolved by Wisconsin. Nevertheless, a central office did channel the efforts of various departments quite effectively.[61] Given a bottomless purse, Falconer might have preferred the Wisconsin approach. In an hour of financial dearth, however, it was the Michigan scheme that was generally followed in Toronto.

Much, of course, depended on finding the right man to pull together Toronto's scattered extension services. In appointing W.J. Dunlop to the directorship, Falconer chose wisely and well. Combining a knowledge of academe with no small measure of wily entrepreneurship, Dunlop proved his value from the outset. He understood perfectly the dual nature of the task he was assigned as director of extension and publicity. It fell to him to co-ordinate and expand extramural teaching as cheaply and efficiently as possible. At the same time, he was told to seize every opportunity to improve the university's public image. Purists of an older vintage might have found the latter chore repulsive, but Dunlop relished it. When Falconer asked for a report on publicity early in 1921, the director was primed and ready. 'It is impossible,' he told the president, 'to distinguish between extension work and publicity.' They fed one another: 'Our extension courses bring the University the best of publicity, and the publicity work results in requests for more extension work.' As a case in point, Dunlop noted the special courses for the UFO. They received wide coverage in the newspapers and 'did a great deal to propagate the idea that the University is a democratic institution, anxious to serve all the people.' Publicity of this sort was invaluable, he argued, especially in rural areas. Eager to stir up more, he was sending weekly releases to the papers in which Varsity's public services were described in glowing detail. His motives here went beyond promoting extension courses. 'In all of this newspaper work,' he told Falconer, 'I have been trying to "sell" higher education, that is to get the people to realise the importance of the University's work and to see that it is worth all the financial support for which it asks.'[62]

Typical of Dunlop's salesmanship was a circular to the press entitled 'The Provincial University's Service.' Issued under his hand, it had, in fact, been edited and amended by Falconer. A few words were devoted to the university's 'chief task,' the training of undergraduates. Graduate studies were also briefly highlighted. In both areas it was the element of practical service that was underscored. Thus, care was taken to illustrate that Toronto's graduates had for seventy-five years and more provided educational and religious leadership, healed the sick, prevented disease, upheld justice in the courts and pioneered in science. This said, however, the main burden of the piece fell heavily on extramural teaching. 'The Provincial University's service,' it was proclaimed, 'is not confined to those who are able to attend its regular courses.' On the contrary, through its extension program, Varsity was said to meet the educational needs of all aspiring students, whatever their station in life. The University of Toronto, indeed, was touted as 'the servant of the people.'[63] As its pitchman, Dunlop rarely missed a trick. He was confident that, if all went according to plan, 'a very large development of extension and publicity work [could] safely be predicted.'[64]

This prognostication proved correct. As early as 1923 Dunlop was able to report that well over 2,000 people were enrolled in extension classes. Particularly gratifying was the substantial increase in the number of those participating in the WEA. Almost 1,000 working men were taking part. Furthermore, the program as a whole was paying its own way. Thus, when the fees from teachers, bankers, farmers, and the like were calculated, they offset the losses incurred in subsidizing the WEA and summer sessions.[65] Success of this sort encouraged further expansion. In 1927, therefore, evening classes were launched as far afield as Windsor and Fort William, where American universities had previously made extramural forays.[66] The University of Western Ontario murmured in protest at these jurisdictional incursions by Toronto. In reply, however, Dunlop argued that the provincial university was obliged to answer any calls for assistance within the boundaries of Ontario.[67] Given the aggressive nature of Toronto's extension drive, this response was rather disingenuous. Indeed, few stones were being left unturned as Dunlop and Falconer sought out opportunities to 'sell' the university. No technique, however novel, was disregarded if it promised to yield dividends in the form of better public relations. Film-makers were therefore commissioned to develop promotional movies.[68] The directors of the Canadian National Exhibition were petitioned to make space available for the university.[69] One, of course, hesitates to suggest that Falconer served as a judge in the *Star*'s 'Loveliest Child Competition' out of a lust for publicity, but a series of radio lectures in 1932 was at least partly undertaken as a form of advertising.[70] The impact of all this activity on the public mind is impossible to determine with any accuracy. The health of Toronto's extension department, however, seems to indicate that it was not wholly without effect. By mid-decade an average of 2,500 students were enrolled in all courses combined. Albert Mansbridge, therefore, did not exaggerate when in 1929 he described Toronto as a 'power' in Canadian adult education.[71]

This virtually obsessive concern with public relations is best understood as the reaction of a university whose leaders felt increasingly vulnerable to external pressures. The shifting composition, balance, and priorities of postwar society were sufficient to generate new demands on Varsity, but an acute sensitivity to public criticism was the particular fruit of deepening financial distress and a correspondingly greater dependence on political goodwill. In 1914 the Whitney government had placed an upper limit on statutory grants to the university. Plummeting enrolments during the war had temporarily muted the impact of this decision. The full after-shock, however, registered devastatingly in the 1920s. Continuing waves of inflation and a massive influx of students combined to gobble up a static and already insufficient regular income. Prices, which had roughly doubled between 1907 and 1915, doubled again by 1920. In the same year enrolments, which in 1918 had totalled only 2,800, jumped to over 5,200.[72] Thus, regular burdens grew, while a commitment to expanded 'service' imposed more. The inevitable result took the form of prodigious deficits. Budgetary plans for 1919 had predicted a shortfall of $250,000. Next year the all too accurate forecast was for a 100 per cent increase. Understandably worried by these developments, Falconer and his boardroom colleagues were even more depressed by the outcome of their calculations in the spring of 1920. Having pruned and pared, they were nevertheless confronted with a staggering projected deficit of $880,000 for the coming year.[73] For the first time since 1906 requests for supplementary aid were greater than statutory grants. The governors acknowledged a financial crisis and the president trembled as he considered its implications for a university supposedly insulated from political meddling.

His fears on this score, accumulating since 1914, grew in proportion to the deficit. Alarm bells sounded when, in its last months in office, the Hearst government began to complain of Varsity's seemingly insatiable appetite for cash. After some grumbling, Queen's Park had approved the university's estimates for 1920, but the premier had added in a personal note that a thoroughgoing review of financial arrangements would soon be in order: 'It, of course, will be impossible for the Province having regard to its present sources of revenue to continue making increased yearly grants to the University.'[74] Although ominously phrased, this pronouncement cannot have been wholly unexpected. Nor, one suspects, was Falconer unduly disturbed by the prospect of renegotiating financial arrangements with the Tories. After all, both he and Walker had called for a new permanent settlement in 1914. Furthermore, the Conservatives were a known quantity with a tradition of supporting the provincial university, momentary disagreements notwithstanding. But in October 1919, as Hearst went down to defeat and a new era of populist government was ushered in, there was fear that the rules of the political game were about to change. New to power and still struggling to organize itself internally, the cabinet of E.C. Drury must have seemed a wild card to Falconer and his associates. Loudly proclaiming the virtues of retrenchment and a new broom, the farmer government also represented a constituency that had displayed little love of Varsity in the past. The United Farmers of Ontario, moreover, had put their hand to the provincial plough just as the university's fiscal problems were becoming acute. It was a coincidence that did little to reassure Falconer.

Difficult to play under the best of circumstances, the president's hand was further weakened by the fact that no small proportion of his estimates in 1920 took the form of a request for an across-the-board salary increase of 25 per cent for faculty and staff. Critics, accustomed to thinking of the professoriate as a leisured class, complained that a similar raise had been approved in 1919. To a rural audience, Walker's public pleas on behalf of a professional group that was having difficulty affording domestic servants must have seemed less than heart-wrenching.[75] To George Wrong, however, who had once taken such things for granted only to see his standard of living eroded by inflation, this was a serious matter. Writing to A.L. Smith at Oxford, the historian lamented that he and his wife found themselves alone in a big house, bereft of housemaids and cook. Seeing little hope in the immediate future, he was determined to soldier on as best he could. 'I do not know,' he wrote, 'whether our old civilization is to be bowled over ... I could make my own bed and black my own boots quite well, but I am doubtful about cooking my own dinner! Anyone, however, who can learn to run an automobile can learn to cook a dinner.'[76]

While older, established men bemoaned the flight of their butlers, younger professors tried to cope with more pressing difficulties. As Falconer pointed out time and again, there had been no general upgrading of salaries between 1907 and 1919. Meanwhile prices had soared. Seeking public support, in the summer of 1920 he used the columns of the *Telegram* to describe the conditions of faculty distress. He recalled an interview with one professor, who had informed him that 'I cannot go on any longer.' Unable to sleep because of the strain of taking on additional work to cover necessary expenses, the man was near exhaustion and anxious to procure alternative employment. Resignations by the young and the gifted, warned Falconer, were looming. The university, the province, and the nation could not afford to lose them. To those who argued that such men were overpaid and underemployed, Falconer retorted that 'when you think of the years they have spent in preparatory work, and the efforts put forth to make ends meet, it is pitiful and unfair.'[77]

In taking their case to the newspapers, Falconer and Walker were trying to prod a reluctant government. Pledged to economize and yet facing massive outlays for hydro-electric development and other schemes, Drury and his fledgling cabinet were torn on the question of university spending. Annual grants to Toronto, Queen's, and Western were already outstripping all other educational spending combined. On the concession lines such matters were often viewed as class issues, likely to stimulate unrest. The premier considered himself a friend of higher education. The minister responsible, R.H. Grant, was ready to compromise with Falconer. But the provincial treasurer, Peter Smith, was opposed to granting Falconer's request. Cabinet members were divided between the poles represented by Grant and Smith. The result was an impasse which left the estimates sitting on the table throughout a tense spring and summer.[78]

By late July the situation was becoming desperate. With a new term fast approaching, the university required approval of its operatlng expenses. Convinced that the only way to break up the log-jam at Queen's Park was to appeal directly to Drury, Falconer twice sought an interview but was ducked on each occasion. Turning to Walker, he asked the banker to try his luck in the hope that the premier would 'see the serious condition of affairs if approached personally.'[79] Urged in the same direction by fellow board member T.A. Russell, Walker managed to pin Drury down, and a meeting was set for 2 September. Meanwhile Falconer drafted a lengthy memorandum concerning the estimates for the benefit of Smith.[80] At the appointed hour Walker and Russell were initially dismayed to find that, instead of the promised full cabinet, only Drury and Grant attended the meeting. Conspicuous by his absence was Smith. The premier claimed to be ignorant of his whereabouts; the treasurer later stated that he had not been informed of the gathering. In all likelihood, Drury had left him out so as to avoid a noisy confrontation. In any case, both Walker and Russell came to regard the absence as a stroke of good fortune. 'I feel,' the former told Falconer, 'that we should probably not have succeeded if the Treasurer had been present.' As it stood, the going was heavy enough. 'We certainly had a hard battle,' recalled Russell. Drury tried to dodge a commitment by suggesting that he would relay university opinion to the cabinet for discussion. Not to be brushed off so easily, Russell and Walker pressed their case for an hour and a half. Finally they induced the two politicians to recommend approval of the budgetary requests.

The able Russell appears to have made a favourable impression on Drury. Following the formal interview, the premier drew him aside and expressed 'great nervousness about what he was doing.' He went on to suggest that further conferences be held 'with a view to putting himself in the best possible shape to meet the house.' Quite by accident, Russell ran into Smith at the Canadian National Exhibition grounds later in the day. In a testy mood, the treasurer bluntly warned his listener that he would certainly 'queer' anything that had been done if it did not meet with his approval. Somewhat taken aback, Russell tried to soothe him but broke off the conversation, convinced that Smith was not strong enough to oppose both Drury and Grant. All told, like Walker, he considered the matter settled and advised Falconer to relax in his Huntsville retreat.[81] Unfortunately, they had misread the situation.

Smith's faction in cabinet was more powerful than the university representatives imagined. Indeed, the politicians continued to wrangle over the estimates, and in the end a compromise was struck. On 14 September Grant informed Falconer that his budget would indeed be approved. There were, however, two significant catches. In the first place, the government agreed to grant the desired salary increases, but only as a temporary measure and only to teachers. There would be no general raise covering administrative and maintenance workers. Furthermore, the supplements were to be awarded on the basis of merit alone, and in no case were they to exceed $500. Secondly, Grant announced that a royal commission would be established 'to report upon the whole question of Provincial aid to the universities in order that a definite and comprehensive basis may be arrived at.' Falconer was then told to revise his estimates to accommodate the new salary policy.[82]

The Board of Governors, taken aback, called for a conference with the full cabinet. Meanwhile Falconer issued another memorandum on the budget. It was not possible, he argued, to draft another set of estimates with the opening of term so close at hand. Moreover, he continued, even if they could do so, the conditions laid down by Queen's Park were unacceptable. Mechanics, technicians, and administrative staff would be justifiably outraged if their claims to a raise were neglected. Already, he noted, the International Association of Machinists had asked for an increase of more than 25 per cent. In these circumstances, he alleged, to reward professors and omit others would destroy morale at the university. As for the professoriate, Falconer maintained that $500 would be insufficient to retain the services of many valued men. Numerous specific instances of looming or already tendered resignations were cited. Nor, he added, would the vacancies be easy to fill, given the attractive force of higher pay scales in Britain and the United States. Appealing to provincial pride, he pointed out that Toronto was falling behind even McGill in this respect. Searching for a way out, he offered a temporary solution to the problem, suggesting that half of the proposed raise be designated as a bonus for that financial year. A more comprehensive settlement could be deferred until after the royal commission had reported.[83] When the government accepted this expedient a few days later, the decks were cleared and attention shifted to the approaching hearings.

The next few weeks were anxious ones for Falconer. As he told Willison, rumours abounded concerning the potential composition of the commission.[84] Government intentions were far from clear. However, when the letters patent were finally issued in October, the president heaved a sigh of at least partial relief and also gained a new respect for Drury. From the list of men appointed, it became immediately clear that the premier had decided to treat the matter in a statesmanlike and non-partisan manner.[85] Instead of the half-expected clutch of suspicious farmers, noted businessmen and allies of higher education were named.

Of the six, Russell, Willison, and Cody were long-time friends of Falconer. The only full-time farmer was J. Alex Wallace, a cattleman from Simcoe. Yet even he was known to be well disposed towards the universities and later served as one of Varsity's governors. With Cody in the chair, a fair hearing was assured. It remained only to draft a solid case. Hopes began to revive that a workable financial arrangement might yet be devised.

The commissioners visited the universities in question, pored over their books, and took evidence from a wide range of interested groups. Falconer submitted a seventy-one-page brief in which little new was said. From Queen's O.D. Skelton wrote to urge that the province return to the old system of funding higher education out of a proportion of succession duties. Adopting an avian metaphor, he argued that this 'would yield the maximum of feathers with the minimum of squawking.' The Royal Canadian Institute called for government generosity to overcome research deficiencies and 'deplorable' salaries. Indeed, all went smoothly for the universities until the United Farmers of Ontario injected a disquieting note. Their delegate, George Waldron, issued a fervent plea for 'greater frugality and extensive decentralization.' The University of Toronto, he alleged, catered to an overwhelmingly urban and 'foreign' population. Unrepresentative of the province as a whole, it also gave undue emphasis to professional training and too little to 'culture education.' It provided an expensive medical program, whose graduates normally disdained service in the countryside. Waldron criticized extension work on the concession lines as 'feeble and trivial.' In the end, he called for the creation of small, rurally based affiliated colleges, which could bring literary studies to the people, while Toronto specialized in scientific education. The thought that Queen's and Western should strive to duplicate programs offered at Toronto was dismissed as absurd. Above all he counselled that the university be returned to direct political control and that its budgets be subjected yearly to close scrutiny. Somewhat later the UFO spokesman J.J. Morrison echoed this entreaty.

Predictably, the commissioners almost completely ignored the pleas of Waldron and Morrison. In the event, this snub was probably a political error. Some effort to mollify agrarian opinion, if only in token fashion, might have softened hard feelings that surfaced later. For the moment, however, Falconer rejoiced in an official report that offered him everything for which he could reasonably have hoped. Most importantly, it was recommended that funding be returned to the basis outlined in 1906. Furthermore, a grant of $1.5 million for much needed construction was advised. On the administrative and political fronts, the idea of abolishing the Board of Governors and returning to direct legislative control was quashed. In addition, it was suggested that first-year work be transferred to the high schools, should the numbers seeking entrance to university continue to rise. This idea, of course, was dear to Falconer but was unlikely to be implemented in light of the well-established resistance from Queen's and Toronto's affiliated colleges. A number of lesser provisions rounded out the report. Altogether it seemed too good to be true.[86]

In fact, it was. Such lavish long-term financial commitments to higher education as recommended by the commission were simply unsaleable in political terms, and Drury knew it. For a time the government quietly ignored the report and then finally shelved it. By mid-April it was clear that no action would be taken. Instead, Grant informed the governors that their original estimates would be approved along with a disbursement of $500,000 to launch a new anatomy building. Thus, the controversial 'bonuses' were saved, but it was a hollow victory in Falconer's eyes. Flavelle was certain that Drury's hesitancy stemmed from the fact that he had already borrowed $34 million on the money markets to help finance hydro and was preparing to ask for more. According to Flavelle, this move had led to raised eyebrows in financial circles. 'Under the present uncertain outlook it is natural that the Premier should be disturbed.' Indeed, he continued, 'I think it would be unfortunate if he were not disturbed.' Understanding, if not necessarily condoning, Drury's position, Flavelle also appreciated Falconer's plight. On the whole, however, he was confident that Varsity's needs would continue to be met on an annual basis.[87] But the president yearned for more. Craving the independence and stability tantalizingly symbolized by the report, he lobbied for its adoption. As late as October 1922 he endeavoured to enlist alumni in a campaign to force its implementation.[88] The die, however, had been cast.

Thus, spring, a relief to so many others, remained a gloomy and burdensome season for Falconer as each year he pored over his budgets. Contrary to expectations, enrolment did not stabilize, but surged upward as the 1920s rolled on. By 1928 it had climbed to 6,000, only to top 8,000 three years later.[89] In nightmarish lock-step, deficits followed suit, reaching $1.5 million in 1931.[90] Small wonder then that, as Falconer confided to a friend, 'worries and cares' about finance continued to plague him.[91] Flavelle's estimate of the situation ultimately proved correct. Governments regularly covered these mounting shortfalls, despite some carping from time to time. Even so, Falconer remained painfully conscious of the potential for serious confrontation and of the political as well as the economic implications of this situation.

Fortunately, there had been more of smoke than fire in this first brush with the farmer government. Mostly extra-parliamentary sparks had never truly been fanned into flame, despite some menacing talk of increased political control over the university. Still, a wary Falconer had been put on guard, and subsequent events only amplified his anxiety. In July 1921, for example, Alex Wallace was appointed to fill a vacancy on the Board of Governors. Given his able performance on the recent royal commission, the choice was natural enough. In fact Falconer, then vacationing in Britain, was glad to have him as a colleague,[92] as was Walker. But the chairman did have some misgivings about the method of appointment. The cabinet, as it happened, had made the decision without even the semblance of prior consultation with the board. Although Queen's Park had acted within the strict provisions of the University Act, Walker found this move somewhat high-handed and irritating.[93] When the procedure was repeated some months later, he grew even more annoyed. On 18 January 1922 Walker read in the morning papers that William Good, UFO member for Brant, had been installed as a governor to fill the place of the late Dr Hoskin. Scribbling angrily to Falconer, he grumbled, 'I do not know anything about Mr Good and it does seem rather hard to bear, so far as a mere matter of courtesy is concerned.'[94] The president could at least console him that Good was a worthy candidate, a graduate of Toronto, and deeply interested in university affairs. Moreover he thought that it might be helpful to have as a governor one who enjoyed excellent connections within the ruling party. Yet, like Walker, he found the method of appointment distasteful. The UFO, it appeared. was rather careless of niceties in dealing with the provincial university. This attitude, perhaps, betokened a style from which more serious consequences could flow. Speculation aside, however, Falconer was prepared to make the best of the situation. 'While we dislike the manner of the appointment,' he told Walker, 'it may work out alright.'[95] And, indeed, it did. Good maintained a low profile on the board during a brief tenure which ended shortly after Drury fell from power. In any case, minor irritants aside, a far more serious storm was brewing. By January 1922 the newspapers were echoing a gathering controversy in which Varsity's administration was characterized as autocratic, dictatorial, and badly in need of reform.

The origins of the tempest were to be found in a reorganization of the Faculty of Medicine launched just after the war. Changes wrought before 1914 had, in part, been inspired by examples south of the border and in far off Edinburgh, where efforts had been made to systematize the education of would-be physicians. Particularly admired was the innovative work of William Osler, one-time head of medicine at Johns Hopkins University. That Canadian had been given charge of a unique experiment in 1893 in which an endowed hospital was fully integrated with the university. Members of the teaching staff were expected to forgo extensive private practice in order to concentrate on their pedagogical duties. In addition, classroom, laboratory, and clinical instruction were closely articulated in a carefully structured educational scheme. So fruitful was this approach that one Toronto admirer later hailed it as 'the beginning of a new era in medical education among English speaking peoples.'[96] In time Baltimore's lead was followed by most of the prominent universities of the United States.

In 1908 Toronto had taken some tentative steps in the same direction. However, a veritable torrent of protest from doctors had crippled designs for a more thoroughgoing reorganization. To be sure, some limits were placed on the external commitments of physicians associated with the university. Furthermore, three 'services' were established in the departments of medicine and surgery to help co-ordinate instruction.[97] Thus, a start was made, but several key figures were less than satisfied with these compromises. Alexander McPhedran, for example, had pressed for the adoption of Osler's system in the 1890s and did so again in 1908. Frustrated by half measures, the influential occupant of the chair of medicine continued to urge reform.[98] Joseph Flavelle, as it happened, shared McPhedran's views. Ever an exponent of efficiency, the pork baron disliked a dilution of leadership among three heads in each department.[99] His bridge partner and colleague, President Falconer, was of the same mind. From his vantage point the necessity of keeping pace with American advances was patent. In this respect, a cue might well have been taken from the experience of Queen's. Like Falconer, the head of that institution, R. Bruce Taylor, recognized that North America was fast becoming 'one country' for the purposes of medical education.[100] It was a matter of some concern, therefore, when Queen's American Medical Association rating slipped from 'A' to 'B' just before the war. This drop effectively barred Kingston's graduates from practising in the United States and, perhaps more significantly, made it difficult to tap external sources of grants. A lack of efficiency in clinical services at the local hospital had led to this lower rating. It was a blow to its prestige from which Queen's did not recover until 1919, when a newly constructed general hospital was brought into closer affiliation with the faculty of medicine.[101]

Toronto had escaped a similar fate, but Falconer was in no mood to take chances. In March 1918 he tabled a tentative plan for medical reorganization; it included a call for the establishment of a full-time professorship in medicine, a post designed to consolidate leadership in that department.[102] The precise genesis of this scheme is unclear. At the time Falconer was quietly conferring with Sir John Craig Eaton, from whom he hoped to secure a major new endowment. In any case, whether the idea emanated from the president or from the tycoon, it was swiftly translated into a plan of action backed by a donation of $500,000 from Eaton. Writing to Flavelle in November, Falconer urged the speedy adoption of the design. He speculated that the time was right, with so many senior men still in the armed forces and others ripe for retirement. Under these conditions, a changing of the guard coupled with the introduction of new organizational principles might be accomplished with less friction than would normally be expected.[103] In the event, Duncan Graham, a relatively young lecturer in bacteriology, was catapulted into the new position and given considerable power to direct the combined services in medicine. Two years later the department of surgery was similarly reorganized under Clarence L. Starr with the substantial financial assistance of the Rockefeller Foundation.

For some this was an administrative dream come true. For others, however, it was cause for growing disillusionment and bitter complaint. As part of the general reorganization, some old positions were eliminated and the men let go. In addition, honoraria formerly paid to city physicians who doubled as part-time clinical instructors were abolished. At the time of their inception these changes had met with relatively little criticism, chiefly, perhaps, because the men consulted were heads of services unlikely to be aversely affected by their results. When the full implications of the reorganization became apparent, however, once-muted protest began to swell. Prominent among the early dissenters was Dr F.W. Marlow, associate professor of gynaecology. Having resisted change from the outset, he wrote personally to Falconer in November 1921 to voice strident objections after hearing that his honorarium had been discontinued. He took it as discourteous that so fundamental a change in his status was made known only in a general circular, rather than in a personal letter. Noting the slight, he moved on to more basic considerations. Thus Marlow bitingly denounced the adoption of 'Germanic' and 'American' models which cramped individuality and encouraged a mechanical, uninspired uniformity. Urging Falconer to return to the 'old established methods of the British School,' he also bemoaned the loss of independence entailed in relying on external 'gifts' which came with strings attached. Finally, he decried as hypocritical a system under which a supposedly 'full time' head competed with his unpaid clinicians for private business. Speaking as a recent president of the Ontario Medical Association, Marlow advised Falconer that the university had few 'boosters' and all too many 'knockers' among the general public. 'One is forced to believe,' he concluded, 'that there is something radically wrong with the institution somewhere.'[104]

Verbally more restrained, but equally disenchanted, was Dr Kennedy C. McIlwraith, associate professor of obstetrics. He objected strongly to the implications of the rhetoric that had accompanied reorganization. It was made to seem, he alleged, 'that new men and a new system [had] effected a great change for the better,' while the contributions of older loyal servants had been denigrated or ignored. When Falconer apologized for any unintended slur, McIlwraith was temporarily assuaged. Later, however, he added his voice to those who railed against the lack of consultation and the exercise of 'autocratic' and 'despotic' power by an administration that curried American favour in its search for 'alien funds.'[105]

These internal complaints were troublesome, to be sure, but they soon gained added significance when dissenters took their case to both the press and Queen's Park. By January 1922 newspapers and journals were carrying stories of the squabble at Varsity. In particular, the *Canadian Practitioner* denounced the innovations in medicine and the means employed in carrying them through.[106] At first Falconer was tempted to remain silent and let the ill wind blow itself out. As criticism gathered force, however, he responded in the *Globe*. Charges of autocracy were dismissed as unjustified. He denied that personal considerations had entered into the firing of excess staff. Furthermore, the Rockefeller grant was described as a largely unconditional gift which had merely allowed the university to implement schemes already locally conceived. As for the emotive suggestion that 'German' methods were being introduced, Falconer simply retorted that 'Germany has nothing to do with it.' Indeed, he noted that the same system was being adopted in Britain at that very moment.[107] Having stated his case, the president expected the furore to peter out shortly. Walter Murray advised him not to worry about the self-interested mutterings of a few 'sore heads.'[108] A like-minded Falconer replied that 'We have had a great fuss as you have noticed in the papers made by certain members of the Faculty of Medicine, but I think that the gist of it is that they were dissatisfied men who took this way of expressing their dissatisfaction. Such we must expect from time to time.'[109]

The problem, however, could not be brushed aside so easily. In some minds there was more at stake than the personal interests of a few disappointed doctors. The Great War Veterans Association, for example, saw in all this discord the betrayal of a sacred national obligation. Several of the dismissed men were returned soldiers who had staffed military hospitals overseas. Snatching up the cudgels in their defence J.R. Nicholson of the GWVA wrote angrily to Drury, advising him that 'no further monies be paid to the University until this matter has been investigated by a Representative Commission.'[110] J.F. March, dominion secretary of the Grand Army of United Veterans, also heeded the call to arms. He drew Drury's attention to charges of discrimination against veterans which had been levelled by Colonel Thomas Gibson, lawyer to the Alumni Association. In high dudgeon he too issued a plea for a full-scale investigation.[111] Meanwhile former officers in the legislature began to raise questions in the house. These were quickly united with the by then standard criticisms from rural interests, who complained of the urban isolation of a university that churned out scientific specialists but supposedly neglected the nurturing of badly needed general practitioners. The premier, as it happened, also had misgivings about the growing emphasis on impersonal specialization. His romantic idealization of the intuitive 'GP' may have inclined him to give a sympathetic hearing to critics of Toronto's new system, some of whom, like McIlwraith and Marlow, were deeply suspicious of a trend towards 'scientism.'[112]

Amid the growing clamour few blasts could match that issued in May by *Saturday Night*. Vitriolic and broad-ranging, it testified stridently to the intensity and diversity of the passions on which the medical controversy fed. Autocratic habits of mind were said to be the natural fruit of a defective constitution. A 'cloistral' attitude of an administration insulated from public criticism had insured that 'follies and ineptitudes' had gone unchecked. The Board of Governors was reviled as a latter-day 'star chamber' within which a 'small and irresponsible clique' wielded great influence. Meanwhile, it was alleged, the Senate had been emasculated and the alumni lacked an effective voice. The inequities spawned during the medical reorganization were described as typical of a larger pattern of the abuse of power. Even more telling, the author continued, was the evidence of fiscal irresponsibility as revealed in soaring deficits. 'Can it be,' he asked, 'that the Board of Governors felt that it could take greater liberties with a Farmer administration ...?' If so, he crowed, Varsity's leaders had made a final, costly error in judgment, for it was rumored that Drury was considering a public investigation into the whole matter of university government.[113]

Falconer had caught wind of this rumour too. Yet, far from being intimidated, he almost welcomed the prospect of a show-down with the recalcitrant physicians. Incensed, he assured Walter Murray that the public would quickly sour on 'a miserable quarrel of disappointed doctors.' Moreover, he confided: 'the Prime Minister knows our side, the Minister of Education is with us and I fancy that the worst that may be done will be to have a committee of the House to investigate.' Flavelle, he noted, had his 'dander up,' and in a recent address on the issue had 'called a spade a spade.' The board had requested a hearing before the legislature. If the affair were pressed further, he was confident that 'the attackers [would] get more than they bargained for.'[114] Girded and even eager for the fray, Falconer waited to see if battle would be joined.

Even so, when the first ranging shots were actually discharged, Falconer and his colleagues were taken by surprise. Having misgauged the temper of the legislature, they had expected that any public inquiry would be confined to a confrontation with McIlwraith and his friends over the limited facts of the medical dispute. When, in the first week of June the government suddenly announced that a select committee would investigate the whole structure of Varsity's constitution, they were caught off guard. The affair was widening menacingly. To make matters worse, no one at the university had been consulted on or even advised of this decision in advance. Meanwhile, efforts to secure an audience with the cabinet had failed. For some this treatment was all too reminiscent of the discourtesy that had attended the appointments of Wallace and Good. Moreover, it seemed in this instance to imply a thinly veiled hostility on the government's part. Flavelle, for one, was both worried and angry. To the senior civil servant A.H.U. Colquhoun he wrote, asking who was responsible for the turn of events and what motives lay behind it. 'Surely,' he added, 'this declaration ... is an ungenerous way of communicating the Government's views to the Board.'[115] Colquhoun replied that repeated efforts on his part had failed to uncover the source of the decision, although he was 'reasonably sure' that the idea had originated on the government side of the house.[116] Whatever the case, the terms of the inquiry and its method of publication sent tremors through the university board room.[117]

In what to Falconer must have seemed tortuous detail, from 25 October to late January the select committee probed into university affairs. Often heated, the sessions furnished ample dramatics for the local press. Charges and counter-charges concerning medical developments were aired. Particularly damaging to the board's case was the revelation that restructuring at the hospital had taken place without the official consent of the lieutenant-governor. Granted, this step was only a formality. A request, or so it was alleged, had been forwarded through channels but somehow had been delayed or gone astray. Furthermore, an interesting twist was added to old complaints when McIlwraith contended that Falconer was at the head of a Scottish cabal that monopolized key appointments in medicine.[118] In a masterly passage of innuendo, another aggrieved doctor, G.W. Ross, offered a variation on this conspiratorial theme. 'In a word,' he told the committee, 'there has existed and one wonders whether there does not still exist what might fairly be termed an "obscure influence," an elusive something that has exhibited a certain liveliness from time to time in various ways.'[119]

With the door thus nudged open, others happily barged through to address the question of general administrative and constitutional reform. Speaking for the alumni federation, Colonel Thomas Gibson led the charge. Describing the university machine as 'autocratic in the extreme,' he called for the reservation of several board seats for graduates elected by the alumni. Going further, he urged that the 'unwieldy' Senate be reduced in size and given greater power. He went on to criticize not Falconer personally but a constitution that loaded too many responsibilities on one man, particularly in the realm of faculty appointments. A champion of democracy, Gibson argued that 'qualified men should pass upon the capabilities of men for posts of wide distinction and recommendations should go on to the Senate and lastly to the Board of Governors.'[120] In a roundabout way this was to suggest that the alumni should be given decisive weight in the management of the university, since they already had substantial representation in the Senate. When these proposals were resubmitted a month later by Angus MacMurchy, president of the Alumni Federation, Drury's opinion as chairman of the committee was sought. Asked whether the Board of Governors should be composed chiefly of Toronto men, the premier said he thought not. 'Toronto,' he proclaimed. 'has quite the village point of view.' Indeed, he went on, 'its mind is isolated.'[121] Significantly, however, he did not criticize the basic thrust of MacMurchy's suggestion.

But others did. Arguing that a more far-reaching change was required, the Toronto District Labour Council offered a class analysis of the situation. In a submission addressed to Drury, John Young wrote from the Labour Temple to declare that 'taxation without representation [was] undemocratic.' In the past, he observed, the Board of Governors had been the almost exclusive preserve of business and professional men. The time had come to provide for labour representation as well so as 'to bring the University and the masses into closer sympathetic touch.' Perhaps then, he speculated, 'lower fees for lower classes' would be instituted to render the University truly egalitarian. Referring to specifically medical issues, Young complained of 'class prejudice' in the treatment of different groups of patients. He also condemned an excessively lengthy course of study which made it all but impossible for the less well-to-do to acquire a medical education.[122]

University representatives, of course, did their best to deflect this and other bolts hurled their way. Lengthy memoranda were conjured up to justify recent actions and to defend the established constitution. College heads expressed continuing satisfaction with the working of federation. McPhedran praised the new arrangement in medicine, as did Dr George F. Young, despite the fact that it had meant a demotion for him.[123] The *Globe* as well offered a timely boost in pointing out a supposed anomaly in the whole situation. Drury, it noted, was lending an ear to those who called for popular representation at the university, while incongruously denying municipal authorities any say in hydro developments.[124] For his part Falconer attended every sitting of the committee in order to parry opponents' arguments as they arose. In the end, however, he and his colleagues could have spared themselves the trouble. Of the committee members only G. Howard Ferguson seemed at all sympathetic, and even he signed a final report whose recommendations must have delighted all but the most implacable 'knockers.'

The committee stopped short of recommending the abolition of the Board of Governors and a return to direct control by the legislature – but only just. Meanwhile the pleas of Gibson and MacMurchy were translated into a call for fully one-third of the board to be elected by the Alumni Association. Furthermore, labour representation was to be given serious consideration once the WEA had established itself securely on a province-wide basis. As for the president, his discretionary powers in the realm of appointments, promotions, and dismissals were to be whittled down considerably. Thus it was declared that henceforth he be guided in these matters by faculty committees, whose views 'should not be ignored except for very weighty reasons.' In addition, Falconer and his associates were to be bridled when it came to accepting external grants. Such gifts, it was suggested, ought to be approved by the Senate in the first instance. There were, it should be noted, some recommendations which undoubtedly pleased Falconer; for example, more generous support for extension work and scientific research was urged. However, on the crucial matter of general funding there was to be no change. Current methods, it was stated bluntly, furnished a 'satisfactory check upon University expenditures,' which should not be removed. In effect, therefore, the cabinet was unwilling to relinquish its whip hand in what amounted to a system of dual control in university affairs.

Not forgetting the dispute that helped give it birth, the committee commented at length on medical matters. It decried a tendency towards specialization and called for the increased voting power of clinical instructors in the faculty's councils. The reorganization was described as 'illegal and unauthorised,' since it had overturned a previous statute without legislative approval. Consequently its architects faced the agonizing prospect of having to seek political authorization in an altogether unfavourable climate of opinion. The chances of securing this from the present regime seemed bleaker still when the dismissal of certain doctors was described as tactless, legally questionable, and abrupt. Finally, the Eaton and Rockefeller gifts were said to have bound, if not explicitly then at least implicitly, the university to conditions that were 'highly undesirable.' In sum the report roundly criticized all those concerned with the restructuring of medicine since 1919.[125]

There was one gleam of hope for Falconer during that otherwise gloomy spring. Even as the report was being tabled, a bitterly contested provincial election campaign was heating up. With Drury himself standing at the bar of public opinion, the Board of Governors prayed for a Conservative victory. On 25 June their entreaties were answered. A 'broadened out' but diluted and disillusioned UFO crumbled in the face of Tory attacks on its northern, hydro, and liquor policies. In a humiliating upset, Drury lost his own riding. Had Falconer been a devotee of Bacchus he most certainly would have cracked open a bottle of vintage champagne. There was no guarantee, of course, that Ferguson would dump the committee's report. But the farmers, at least, were gone, and a measure of revenge was no less sweet for being indirectly inflicted by the electorate. Meanwhile, for the next few months Varsity's leaders held their collective breath as their new political masters settled into Queen's Park. In September, however, relief pervaded the boardroom when Walker reported that private talks with Ferguson had 'laid the basis for good relations in the future.'[126] The Tory chieftain, after all, was an old boy of University College who had displayed a benign attitude towards his alma mater in the past. For reasons that are not entirely clear, he had signed the Special Committee's report. Thus, there had been some anxious moments until Walker was informed that the new administration had no intention of implementing it.

In this drawn-out fashion an episode that Walker had characterized as an exercise in 'despicable politics' sputtered to a close.[127] As far as Flavelle could see, it was 'an unhappy experience, with no compensating advantages.'[128] Continuing tirades concerning the peremptory and discourteous behaviour of the Drury regime were, perhaps, understandable. In fairness, however, it should be noted that Falconer and the board had helped bring this treatment on themselves. After all, some measure of courtesy and acumen had been wanting on their side too. For one thing, they had neglected to secure legislative approval for major alterations in a faculty whose constitution was defined by provincial statutes. Furthermore, there can be little doubt that in 1919 they tried to obviate opposition by taking advantage of the absence of several potential dissenters. Again, the decision to dismiss some returned medical veterans was, at a minimum, less than politically astute. When frustrated critics took their case elsewhere, Falconer and the others seriously misgauged the nature and extent of the public furore which arose. Consequently a stiff price was very nearly exacted for these errors in judgment. That an escape was found was purely a matter of luck. One wonders, therefore, how much self-recrimination and disillusionment were implied when, shortly after the dust had settled, Falconer wrote to a British colleague that 'the Headship of a University calls for the exercise of as much tact and diplomacy as a self-respecting man can be expected to exercise.'[129] One thing, at least, is certain. Falconer's innate fears of political intervention had been greatly intensified by his encounters with the farmer government.

CHAPTER X

Skylarking on the
Ragged Edge of Folly

The political demise of the United Farmers of Ontario came none too soon for the embattled Falconer. But the passing of one crisis did not signal a new era of olympian calm in university circles. Granted, the provocative issue of constitutional reform was allowed to slip quietly from view. Yet others soon arose to render Falconer's last decade in office at times less than easy. Indeed, in the 1920s and early 1930s he would find himself at the centre of numerous conflicts, great and small, which turned on the emotive question of academic freedom. Few aspects of his long career have attracted more comment from subsequent observers, whose assessments have ranged from lavish praise to biting criticism. Thus, one aspiring biographer maintains that Falconer is best understood as an ardent champion of academic liberty.[1] Antithetically, another scholar has described Sir Robert as so 'mildewed with discretion' that he readily abandoned beleaguered professors who ran afoul of the press, the public, or the politicians of that intolerant age.[2]

In part, no doubt, this variance reflects the different vantage points of different assessors. Perspectives aside, however, interpretation has also been influenced by the tendency to focus on celebrated incidents rather than on long-term practice. Recognizing the bias implicit in the case study approach, Hofstadter and Metzger rejected it in chronicling the history of academic freedom in the United States. As they observed: 'To write only about the outstanding violations of freedom would be to treat the story of academic freedom as though it were nothing but the story of academic suppression.'[3] Hence, we are advised to view individual episodes as parts of a general context. In the complicated case of Robert Falconer, this caveat is well worth heeding.

In February 1922, before a packed house at Convocation Hall, Falconer delivered a long and carefully researched address on the theme of academic freedom. His clearest statement on the subject, it had been prompted by a variety of circumstances. The continuing joust with Queen's Park undoubtedly weighed heavily on his mind. Again, he may have been anxious to chide disgruntled university physicians who had gone to the press and the premier with their complaints. Beyond these considerations, however, he had a far more pressing, if little publicized, reason for speaking out. An irritating and potentially dangerous storm was brewing in his own boardroom. A notably generous but moodily cantankerous governor was thirsting for the blood of one of Falconer's supposedly 'radical' professors. The besieged president, assailed from without, could scarcely afford an untimely assault from within his own ranks. Choosing expediency, he might simply have dumped the alleged revolutionary and curried some much needed favour among the defenders of traditional values. Significantly, however, Falconer elected to follow a different course.

To describe Colonel Reuben Wells Leonard as a conservative would be to understate his devotion to the established order of society. Thriving in the rough and tumble of frontier capitalism, he had amassed millions through investments in railways, mining, and other enterprises. A noted philanthropist, he was also on the governing boards of several educational institutions such as Queen's, Varsity, and Wycliffe College. Sincerely interested in higher education, Leonard was generally open-handed. But his largesse was rarely dispensed unconditionally. Shortly before the war, for example, he offered to provide new residence buildings for male students at Queen's. He insisted, however, that Royal Military College officers be placed in charge and that military discipline be imposed along with compulsory drill in order to help mould a new generation of responsible leaders for Canadian society. When Daniel Gordon refused to relinquish direct university control over these students, the tycoon withdrew his offer.[4] Clearly he had pronounced views about the values to be extolled by universities. Indeed, he seems to have considered their ivy-covered walls as sturdy bulwarks against moral and social change. The aftermath of war only reinforced this outlook; even halting and well-diluted efforts at social reconstruction roused his ire. Thus, when asked by Falconer in 1920 to endow a small scholarship, the doughty Colonel replied: 'I am rather fearful that the regrettable tendencies of the day towards class legislation and the confiscation of the savings of the industrious and thrifty to give to the shiftless and lazy will tend to dry up many sources of funds for such good works as your Post-Graduate Fellowship.'[5] In this agitated state of mind Leonard found the reformist views of political economist Robert MacIver distinctly unpalatable.

Born in the Outer Hebrides, the lean, bespectacled MacIver had been educated at Edinburgh and Oxford. In 1916 he left a post at the University of Aberdeen to take up an associate professorship in Toronto. Falconer had approved the appointment enthusiastically. After all, the new man had much to recommend him. The son of a Presbyterian minister, MacIver had attended all the best schools and was warmly praised by several of Falconer's most trusted British contacts.[6] The president, no doubt, felt that he was recruiting yet another well-rounded man of conscience who would diligently pursue the ideal. And in this he was perfectly correct. The only problem was that MacIver's conception of the ideal was somewhat at odds with that entertained by more conservative Torontonians, particularly where social and economic matters were concerned. He did, however, find a congenial home in the department of political eonomy within which, as one of its members later recalled, a 'moderate radicalism' had taken hold by the end of the war. Like his colleagues C.R. Fay and Gilbert Jackson, MacIver, while no Marxist, was sharply critical of unrestrained capitalism and urged that the period of reconstruction be used to fashion a new society founded on co-operative principles.[7] No armchair theorist, he was instrumental in helping develop the department of social service at the University of Toronto and was unstinting in his service to the WEA. Nor did he shrink from publicizing his views to a wider audience. Thus, his call for a new social order was trumpeted in the press with regularity. In a city where fear of radicalism ran high, especially after events in Winnipeg, it was only a matter of time before MacIver was singled out as suspiciously unorthodox.

By January 1921 Colonel Leonard, for one, had had enough of those who encouraged the shiftless to milk the thrifty. In a letter to Walker he denounced MacIver as a dangerous radical whose utterances fuelled unhealthy public discord. The fiery missive was passed to Falconer, who wrote immediately to the fulminating millionaire. The professor, he assured Leonard, was no extremist. Indeed, having read his books, the president was certain that MacIver was actually a 'steadying influence' on the moderate trade union men who were attracted to the WEA. Significantly, however, he added that even if this were not true, it would be folly for the governors to restrain or dismiss him. 'The genius of the British people,' said Falconer, 'always has been advanced through discussion, and the most treasured privilege of the University is freedom of thought.'

Clearly he had no intention of bridling MacIver, despite Leonard's financial importance to Varsity. Calling on his own experience, Falconer added: 'You may think that I am optimistic, but I have gone through so much discussion in theology, science and economics that, although I suppose my tendencies would be regarded as very cautious and old-fashioned, even I believe that in the long run in our environment unrestrained discussion results in good and in the stability of the people.'[8]

Despite Walker's full support for the president's position, Leonard was far from mollified. He continued to insist that MacIver represented a grave threat to the social fabric. Expanding the bounds of intolerance, he wrote Falconer to say that 'nearly all our labour and socialistic troubles are fomented by self-appointed leaders from Wales, Cornwall, Scotland and the North of England.' Continuing in this vein he averred that 'we have very few native-born agitators in Canada, and I do not think we should educate them.' Twisting the sense of Falconer's words, Leonard went on to scoff at the idea of unfettered freedom to teach. Only half-jokingly he suggested that 'If we are to encourage in the University the teaching of one line of extreme, unusual or dangerous doctrine, why not encourage others, such as anti-vaccination etc., or now that Mrs. Besant has played out in India we might bring her over here, or Lenine [sic] when Russia should get tired of him.' More seriously he asked whether MacIver had been hired in spite of or because of his views. In any case, Leonard was 'very jealous that criticism ... against Professors in the University should never be warranted.'[9]

Meanwhile Falconer had taken care to alert MacIver concerning this attack. In private conversation he asked the professor to outline the core of his views so that Leonard's thrusts might be more deftly parried. He did not, however, in any way reprimand MacIver or even imply that a 'defence' was required. On this basis, the instructor was happy to oblige, and a statement was drafted for Falconer's personal use. In it the political economist argued that 'all that should be required from the outside of a teacher of economics is that he should not advocate or support any proposals which strike at constitutional ways and means.' Making it clear that he had always rejected violent solutions, MacIver further noted that his views had been solicited regularly by the Montreal *Star* and its Toronto namesake, neither of which could be accused of sponsoring incendiary radicalism. Nor, it seems, did the federal government find cause for alarm in his pronouncements. Indeed, Ottawa had approached him twice in 1920 with the offer of a civil service post. In addition MacIver alleged that his opinions on industrial peace were in line with those of younger economists throughout the western world and did not really go beyond the 'enlightened capitalism' favoured by men such as Lord Leverhulme. As he saw it, proposals for a minimum wage and a modicum of worker representation in industrial boardrooms were commonsensical antidotes for unrest in the workplace. Moreover, said the minister's son, these measures and others like them would fulfil, rather than corrupt, the spirit of simple Christianity. Even so, he admitted that economics was a less than exact science in which there was always 'a legitimate difference of opinion.' In short, while confident that he was on the right track, MacIver was no dogmatic pleader.[10]

Falconer was reassured by MacIver's statement, but Leonard, who never saw the letter, kept up desultory sniping for the rest of the year. In December, however, he renewed his frontal assault after a careful reading of MacIver's *Labour in a Changing World*. Even Falconer found the opening of that work 'rather startling,' while taking no objection to its overall drift.[11] But the volcanic Leonard was moved to full-scale eruption. Venting his outrage on Falconer, he rumbled that if such views were to be aired at Toronto, then the governors had best do the honest thing and appoint MacIver to a 'Chair of Political Anarchy and Social Chaos.'[12] His patience wearing a trifle thin by this time, the president responded in a three-page letter which contained a veiled rebuke to the tenacious colonel: 'Personally, not being an economist, I am unable to form more than a superficial opinion as to the validity of these principles.' In case the subtle hint was lost on Leonard, he brought his attention to recent Marxist attacks on MacIver's thought, implying, of course, that the professor could hope for no better character reference.[13] The businessman, however, remained adamant. Taking his case to Walker, he lamented that 'it is a great pity that the seething brain waves of these academic thinkers could not be tempered with some practical knowledge of human nature.' Hammering away at MacIver's 'dangerous' teachings, he questioned the amount of latitude that Falconer allowed to 'Marxians and other cranks and lunatics.'[14] Leonard, it seemed, could not be persuaded to alter his assessment of MacIver. Accepting this lamentable fact, Falconer therefore changed his own strategy. Indeed, he drew up plans for a pre-emptive strike which would make it awkward for Leonard to press his case any further.[15]

The artful blow was delivered on 14 February 1922. Taking the podium at Convocation Hall, Falconer discoursed broadly on the concept of academic freedom. With studied moderation of tone he called for a balancing of individual liberties and collective interests. Scanning recent history, he illustrated the danger of emphasizing one side of the equation at the expense of the other. German experience, he claimed, demonstrated the pitfalls of direct state supervision. Impressive theoretical constructs of *Lernfreiheit* and *Lehrfreiheit* had not sufficed in the long run to ward off the corrosive effects of political management. Eventually ultra-nationalist orthodoxies had taken hold in the universities, and dissenters had been persecuted. Thus, knowledge had been advanced, but freedom and the ideal had languished. By contrast, English universities had experienced the ill effects of excessive individualism prior to the late-Victorian period. A tradition of jealous independence had flourished, but freedom and security were often abused by the indolent. Truly innovative thinkers all too frequently worked outside the university. As a result, Falconer observed, England had suffered 'by insisting too strongly upon the power of isolated genius.' Indeed, for want of better organization and co-operation, many a good idea had been left dormant, while others had been fully elaborated only by foreigners.

Where the United States was concerned, Falconer acknowledged the difficulty of generalization. Conditions varied widely throughout the great republic. As a rule, however, he observed, older foundations in longer-settled regions were relatively free from outside interference. But, he alleged, it was otherwise with younger institutions serving less well educated constituencies. Indeed, he was alarmed to note several 'crude and harsh exhibitions of partisanship' during the last decade. Citing examples in Oklahoma, Montana, Iowa, and Kentucky, he illustrated how numerous presidents had been dismissed without warning for treading on political or religious toes. Nor had professors been exempt: he referred specifically to one case in which trustees had fired instructors for dancing and smoking in public. Generally speaking, he contended, such unrestrained meddling was at its worst in private colleges whose benefactors and alumni sometimes went to reactionary extremes.

But history, argued Falconer, provided more than litanies of abuse. It also offered clues to the proper understanding of academic freedom. Seen in perspective, it was but an element in the growth of toleration and political liberty. Calling on Milton, Locke and others, he sought to show that appeals for political and intellectual emancipation had traditionally gone hand in hand. He noted, however, that these twinned concepts were far from static. Instead, while retaining a common thrust, they had been constantly adjusted and refined in the light of changing experience. Of particular moment was one such modification undertaken in the nineteenth century. Inspired by John Stuart Mill, mid-Victorians had embraced an atomistic vision of society, a view mirrored in the isolation of England's unreformed universities. By 1870, however, fears of national decline had coupled with a quickened social conscience to produce a new concept of liberty. Thus, thinkers such as Caird and Green envisaged 'a closer and more organic relation between the individual and society.' They had, in seeking balance, defined the 'higher' notion of liberty that Falconer himself later extolled. It thus became 'a man's right to make the best of himself, and to make the best of himself was to take a share as a responsible citizen in the life of the State to which he belonged.' And here, thought Falconer, was the vital clue. Freedom and social responsibility were not polar opposites, but two sides of the same coin.

Nowhere, he maintained, was this proposition more valid than in the case of the university. As an institution its highest social obligation was to search for and impart truth. But it could fulfil that function only when it was free to investigate the full range of human thought. There could be no prescribed or proscribed ideas for the devotees of higher learning. 'Universities,' said Falconer, 'are not pontifical colleges for the propaganda of authoritative doctrines.' Indeed, 'orthodoxy' was a word that had no place in such institutions. 'What university,' he asked, 'would adopt Marxian economics as its standard, or protection, or free trade, or Kantian philosophy, or republican, or monarchical government?' Rather, its duty was to discuss them all without fear of external censure. The university, he continued, was a meeting place of old and new in which conflicting ideas were constantly engaged in a battle for attention. It was, therefore, only natural that to the timid or conservative outsider the college might seem a hotbed of unrest; an ever-present threat to the stability of society. In reality, however, as Falconer assured his audience, rash libertinism was rare. 'The genuine university man,' he argued, 'is too earnest in his search for truth to think that it is to be furthered by flippancy.'

Here, the great restraining factor was the nature of truth itself. Manifold rather than singular, always partially shrouded rather than fully revealed, it was the exclusive possession of no man or group. Moreover, it was always apprehended through a subjective veil. The competent scholar, said Falconer, understood this and so, he implied, should the extramural critic. Thinking, no doubt, of both Leonard and MacIver, he observed that 'the theories of society so thickly strewn over the pages of our magazines are only semi-scientific, and the reception they get in the reviews depends chiefly upon the cast of mind of the reviewer.' His message to the state and society was that, properly understood, their own interests were best served when the autonomy of the university was respected. It was a question of tolerance and confidence, which in turn were the earmarks of a mature community.

He proceeded to aver that 'we can measure the rank and stability of a university by the security given to a professor to pursue and expound his investigations without being compelled to justify himself to those who differ from him.' But, seeking to instil 'tolerance and confidence' in his listeners, Falconer was careful to emphasize that academic freedom was never absolute. Appearances to the contrary, he argued, there were numerous checks and balances within a self-regulating university community. Some were self-imposed by the individual, the result of scholarly humility in the face of partially illuminated truth. Others arose dialectically in a competitive world of ideas. Thus the unfounded, the slipshod, and the fanatical were quickly exposed and humbled. In this regard, one of the most potent restraints was supplied by the student population. Unlike many American contemporaries, Falconer had no fear that unwary neophytes would be seduced into error by manipulative special pleaders.[16] The student, he argued, was no empty vessel but a keen evaluator who, being regularly exposed to rival ideas, soon learned to discriminate among them. Building on this idea, Falconer went on to contend that students had a positive right to be introduced to all shades of opinion; for only then could they learn to think for themselves. And if, from time to time, they received unpleasant shocks, they would still profit from having to probe more deeply into the foundations of their own beliefs. At this point one suspects that the president was waxing autobiographical. In any case, he had underscored the fact that, even without extramural constraints, the professor's freedom did not amount to licence.

Having touched on conditions internal to the university, Falconer then raised the sensitive question of professorial forays into the public forum. Reiterating the organic theme, he advised the teacher to remember that he was 'independent but not isolated.' 'Secure he is and free from many of the cares of others, but only in order that in matters of the intellect he may become the servant of the nation.' Like most scholars of his generation, Falconer pictured the academic as a detached critic who forfeited his moral authority and betrayed his lofty function when he adopted a partisan stance in political matters. He would never have taken this view to the extreme, as did Maurice Hutton, who advised that professors should be 'in the world but not of it.'[17] Instead, his views were closer to those of Adam Shortt. The political scientist, while cautioning against party entanglements, had seen a positive role for professors as impartial social critics and expert advisers.[18] Falconer, in this vein, compared academics to judges who served the people as a whole rather than particular parties. Their moral obligations to the nation required that they rise above the momentary rage of faction. But so, he counselled, did simple expediency. The professor, he noted, was a member of the university community whose welfare depended on public goodwill. When he spoke in public people were prone to assume, however unjustifiably, that he did so in the name of his colleagues. It was, moreover, a sad fact of life that 'the thoughtless or ill disposed portion of the public will find only too good grounds for an attack upon the whole university in the political utterances of the indiscreet or thoughtless professor.' This, of course, Falconer regarded as a formula for disaster. Inevitably, therefore, for both theoretical and practical reasons, he argued that professors should take no active share in party politics or 'burning political questions.'

In closing Falconer had some advice for university governors. Above all, he asked them to be broad-minded in their selection and treatment of professors. The temptation to hire only 'safe' exponents of accepted views was, he admitted, always strong. But in the long term it was also utter folly. 'A university whose professors were chosen by popular vote,' he cautioned, 'would soon lose its freedom and its prestige would disappear.' As for disciplining the unorthodox, the president pleaded for tolerance. To challenge a professor's competence, he maintained, required a technical expertise that few governors possessed. To argue that there was no place in the university for a particular type of thought was even more unwise. 'The history of universities,' Falconer contended, 'makes it clear that it is safer to tolerate an erratic or even provocative teacher than to have the University, which is a most sensitive human organism, suffer from shock due to the inhibition of normal functioning in one of its parts.' Besides, he continued, a prophet might well appear and, like most of that breed, find the times out of joint: 'Lest he be a true prophet, it is well to be very tolerant.' Calling for goodwill all round, he ended his address with the words of Jeremy Taylor: 'I can see no reason why this pious endeavour to find out truth shall not be of more force to unite us in the bonds of charity, than the misery it shall be to disunite us.'[19]

While there was little of novel theoretical import in the speech, it was, nevertheless, the fullest statement on academic freedom offered by a Canadian university head in Falconer's time. Far from idiosyncratic, the views outlined were widely shared and not only, one suspects, by administrators and politicians. Indeed, later whiggish assumptions aside, it remains to be demonstrated that the majority of contemporary Canadian academics found them unreasonable or repressive. To be sure, some undoubtedly chafed at restrictions on public expression, and their ranks would soon grow. But it surely deserves mention that Falconer's address bore a striking resemblance to the report on academic freedom issued in 1915 by the American Association of University Professors. Like Toronto's president, that body had argued that scholarly liberty was never absolute. The Americans spoke of 'neutrality and competence' as conditioning factors. Falconer implied as much in describing the restraining effects of open dialogue within the university. On another point he proved more liberal than the signatories of the report. The AAUP had condemned 'oracular teaching' because it presumed students to be immature and gullible. Falconer denied this assessment and was willing to grant a fair measure of toleration to the occasional classroom proselytizer. Where governing boards were concerned, the American professors had taken a firmer rhetorical line. Regents and the like were described as trustees for posterity rather than as proprietors. And it was to posterity, rather than to regents, politicians, and popular moods, that academics were said to be finally answerable. However, having gone this far in theory, the authors of the report almost immediately drew back in the face of harsh political realities. Thus, they advocated discretion on the part of professors who were tempted to voice unpopular opinions outside the sanctuary of the university.[20] Reduced to its essence, Falconer's message was much the same; academic freedom was internal to the university.

Altogether, the *Globe* probably erred in covering the address under the caption, 'Professors in Politics Are Read Stern Lesson by Sir Robert Falconer'.[21] The president's intent and his words were more balanced than this headline would imply. Walker, indeed, thought that he understood Falconer's purpose quite clearly. Commenting on the printed version, he quipped: 'I hope our dear friend Colonel Leonard will take it to heart.'[22] The belligerent tycoon, as it transpired, was not entirely won over, but he did allow that the case had been presented 'in a very unbiassed and convincing way'. The chief inference he drew was that extreme caution needed to be exercised in recruiting professors, who, being unworldly, were often too easily gulled by professional agitators. A dent, in fact, appears to have been made in Leonard's once unshakable position, since MacIver was demoted from the status of cunning revolutionary to that of naïve dupe.[23] As for the professor himself, despite Leonard's objections, within the year he was promoted to head of his department on Falconer's strong recommendation.[24] MacIver, however, had been disillusioned by the whole affair and in 1927 accepted a post at Columbia University. His ties with Falconer, however, remained warm, although he declined an offer from the president to return as principal of University College. Significantly, perhaps, it was MacIver who in the troubled 1950s headed Columbia's academic freedom project, among the finest fruit of which was the landmark historical study by Hofstadter and Metzger.

Falconer may have stumbled during the medical crisis, but his management of the MacIver affair was certainly adroit. A valued professor was shielded and a volatile critic subdued without public furore or political repercussion. The end of the episode afforded momentary relief, but the president was under no illusions about the need for continued watchfulness. After all, with G. Howard Ferguson in the provincial saddle, a certain wariness was well advised. The new premier regarded himself as a champion of higher education. He was also on good terms with Flavelle, Russell, and other governors of the university. When Walker was elevated to the chancellorship in 1923, Ferguson appointed his old friend Harry Cody as chairman of the board. Thus, a new intimacy coloured Varsity's relations with Queen's Park. Moreover, the premier, anxious to defuse explosive educational issues, did his best to keep university matters off the floor of the House. There would be no more of Drury's special committees. Yet, for all that his was a boardroom style, Ferguson left no doubt as to where final authority lay. Acting as his own education minister, he once quipped, only half-jokingly, that 'I am the boss of the Toronto University'. In firm control of a stable majority, the Tory leader was a force to be reckoned with on those not infrequent occasions when he exercised personal influence in university affairs.[25]

That Ferguson would not be a passive overlord was soon apparent. In 1924, for example, there were numerous enquiries from his office concerning individual students. Disappointed parents had asked him to induce Falconer to relax various regulations as they applied to their less than successful offspring. One aggrieved MPP thought it arbitrary and unjust that his son was barred from readmission for the want of a few marks; in fact, the benighted lad had failed all his regular and supplemental examinations.[26] On another occasion, Ferguson passed on similar complaints from the leader of the opposition. Proceeding carefully, Falconer investigated all these questions personally and replied to each at great length.[27] Invariably he supported the senate and appeal boards in their decisions but always phrased his answers in diplomatic tones. Strident proclamations of university independence, he realized, were more likely to alienate than to impress Ferguson. For his part, the premier was usually content to let Falconer have his way. He was, one suspects, simply going through the motions at times in order to mollify colleagues and constitutents. As he told the president: 'My regret is that matters of this kind get to the public in a way that gives a wrong impression of the situation and prejudices the position of the University in the public mind.'[28] To Falconer, however, these intrusions upon academic discipline were both irritating and ominously revealing.[29]

More worrisome by far, however, was Ferguson's tendency to harass members of the faculty. The premier, suspicious of foreigners and despising radicals, imagined the true university to be a school of patriotism and sound opinion. Less than tolerant of dissent, he would one day advocate the summary deportation of foreign-born communists. Sensitive to popular moods, he was also ready to act as the guardian of public morality. Furthermore, he had no qualms about impinging on any supposed academic or literary immunities, as his Public Libraries Act of 1926 would soon attest.[30] Falconer, however, had become acquainted with this aspect of the premier's character much earlier. In June 1924 an agitated Ferguson had written to complain about seditious reading matter at the university. 'An outstanding businessman,' he informed the president, had found a particularly offensive booklet in the vulnerable hands of a nineteen-year-old female student. Outraged, that sterling entrepreneur had impounded the loathsome document on the spot and dispatched it to Ferguson for swift action. So hateful was the work in the eyes of the premier that he could not even bring himself to inscribe its title in his letter to Falconer. It was, in fact, *The Communist Manifesto*. 'As you are doubtless aware,' he chided the president, 'this is one of the prohibited publications for the Dominion.' He demanded to know, therefore, why 'a professor' had been allowed to sneak over to Chicago in order to import numerous copies for distribution to his students. In a passage rife with chilling ambiguity, Ferguson stormed: 'I think you will agree that not only should these be exterminated, but if it is true that members of the staff either encourage or condone this kind of doctrine, they should be summarily dismissed.' Calling for an immediate investigation, Ferguson thundered: 'the matter is too serious to be ignored.'[31]

Falconer, however, was not about to be stampeded into a witch-hunt. Indeed, he might have been mildly amused to find that the professor in question was none other than Gilbert Jackson of political economy, a well-known and vocal anti-Marxist. After interviewing Jackson and consulting with MacIver, he informed Ferguson that *The Communist Manifesto* was in fact employed as a teaching instrument and had been for some time. But, he hastened to add, no clandestine operations had been involved in its procurement. Thus, Falconer undoubtedly took no small measure of wry satisfaction in noting that the work had been removed from the national prohibited list shortly after the war. Having caught the premier out in an embarrassing faux pas, he then seized the moral initiative and subtly put the case for academic freedom. Jackson, he told Ferguson, ranged over the whole history of economic theory in his third-year course. Such, he implied, was his obvious duty. As socialism was a major brand of economic thought, it could not and should not be avoided. *The Communist Manifesto* was analysed like any other document, without fear or favour. Jackson, he assured the premier, set forth Marx's theories dispassionately in the classroom. Playing a good trump card, Falconer then related how three former radicals had publicly renounced Marxism after attending his lectures. Closing out a strong hand, he drew attention to recent complaints from 'radical labour people' about Varsity's approach to their ideology. Finally, he invited Ferguson to discuss the matter further if there were any questions lingering in his mind.[32] There is no evidence that the offer was taken up.

Outmanoeuvred in this instance, the Tory chieftain was back in 1925 to denounce yet another political economist, C.R. Fay, as a suspected fellow traveller.[33] Three years later Fay's colleagues E.J. Urwick and H.A. Innis drew Ferguson's angry fire when they criticized conditions in the mining camps of northern Ontario. In no uncertain terms, he told the professors to tend to their books and keep their noses out of public affairs.[34] In October 1928 it was the turn of newly recruited historian Frank Underhill to taste the premier's lash. Word, it seemed, had reached Queen's Park that Underhill's loyalty was suspect. In what was described as a 'course of lectures' on the origins of the First World War, he was said to have left the impression 'that the British were as much if not more to blame for the war than the Germans.' Such apostasy was not to be countenanced. 'I should feel compelled,' Ferguson informed Cody, 'if I thought it was true, to take steps that might be thought drastic.' Given the documentation and literature freely available, the premier thought it 'quite uncalled for that any member of the staff should be exploiting his own views to the students as to the cause of the war.'[35] Clearly, Falconer's incantations about the freedom to teach had made little impression on the patriotic Ferguson.

The accusations took Underhill by surprise. As he told Falconer, he was not giving a 'course' on the war, nor had he even lectured on the subject. As best he could recall, he had mentioned it only once in a brief reference to nineteenth-century Anglo-German imperial rivalries. He had, on that occasion, simply observed that this overseas competition had more to do with the roots of the war than did any disputes over Belgian neutrality. In saying so, Underhill felt that he was merely voicing what, after all, was 'a commonplace among informed persons.' Hence his shock at being tarred with disloyalty.[36] Falconer, who had helped to recruit Underhill just a year earlier, seemed equally taken aback by the charge. For Ferguson's benefit, therefore, he recounted the enviable war record of the new man. Resigning the safety of his position at Saskatchewan, in 1915 Underhill had enlisted as a private in the Princess Patricia's Light Infantry. Later commissioned a lieutenant, he saw considerable action until he was wounded in the grand offensive of 1918. 'He thus demonstrated,' said Falconer, 'the quality that is within him when the great call was made.' As to the specific charge, Underhill's response was relayed to Ferguson along with the president's conviction that the accusations were groundless. It is interesting that Falconer did not add his usual hints about the freedom of professors within the university. Perhaps, after much experience, he felt they would be lost on Ferguson. He did, however, note that he had urged Underhill 'to be careful in his casual remarks.'[37] Was this a sop to the premier or did Falconer have an inkling that the professor could prove rebellious? It is difficult to tell. At any rate, if Underhill took offence at the suggestion, he gave no indication at the time. For his part, Ferguson accepted the president's explanation and described the incident as closed. Typically, however, he added that 'It indicates ... how careful those occupying teaching positions should be in discussing this subject.'[38]

A few months later, responding to an article by Underhill in the *Canadian Forum*, Ferguson told Cody that he might be tempted to 'tick off a number of salaries' of university men who meddled in politics.[39] Fortunately, it never came to that. Seen in retrospect, there was more bark than bite in Ferguson's tirades. At times, of course, he disarmed himself by acting precipitously on ill-substantiated rumour. Thus, he had little choice except to back down in the case of Jackson and his first assault on Underhill. On other occasions he seemed content with bluster and vague threats. In these instances, his desire after 1926 to restructure freshman programs across the province may have provided a restraining factor. As formidable opposition to these measures grew, especially in Kingston and Toronto's affiliated colleges, he may have been reluctant to alienate Falconer, his only major ally on this issue, by blatant displays of heavy-handed interference. Whatever the case, he took no formal disciplinary action against individual professors. Still, as his biographer suggests, Ferguson's intimidating style may well have dampened faculty enthusiasm for public involvement.[40] After all, no one could be certain that he would be content merely to bark forever. Indeed, it was probably fortunate for all concerned that he resigned the premiership in favour of a diplomatic plum just before a veritable maelstrom enveloped the university.

If expressions of popular paranoia were taken literally, one could only assume that in 1929 Toronto was ringed round by the massed legions of Bolshevism. The onset of the depression and attendant fears of social disintegration helped sponsor this feeling. So too did xenophobia in a city experiencing the rapid dilution of its British matrix. Alarm among the traditionally Christian at an advancing culture of secularism only accentuated general anxiety. Hogtown, or so it seemed, was in dire peril. Lending at least superficial plausibility to this perception, the Communist party of Canada had stepped up its propaganda efforts in recent months, anticipating, perhaps, that Canadian capitalism was staggering towards its inevitable doom. The stage, in short, was set for confrontation. Guardians of the public citadel rallied vigorously to stem an anticipated red tide. In the van stood Chief of Police Brigadier Denis Draper and the Toronto Police Commission, as redoubtable an anti-communist phalanx as ever Toronto had produced. Plunging headlong into battle, they ordered constables to disperse seditious gatherings lest the pollution spread. Warming to the task, Toronto's finest plied their truncheons with effect in the heat of August. It was in the course of one of these sweaty melées that T.J. Meek, professor of oriental languages at University College, stumbled momentarily into public view.

While walking abroad for his own purposes, the unfortunate Meek was suddenly swept up by a disorganized throng surging along College Street. The mass was being impelled by baton-swinging police who had broken up a socialist rally and were now in hot pursuit. The professor, when ordered by an officer to 'step lively,' retorted that he was unable to do so given the tremendous crowd about him. Impatient with resistance, the constable is said to have shoved the academic, in addition to favouring him with a phrase that the papers demurely declined to print. Unaccustomed to rough handling, verbal or otherwise, Meek nevertheless stood his ground and demanded the policeman's number. When he paused to write this down, his wrists were reportedly seized and further discouraging words uttered. When the dust settled the outraged Meek took his complaints to an informal interview with Brigadier Draper but left without so much as an apology. Proceeding with a formal complaint, he had to wait until November to be told that the Police Commission would not take disciplinary action, despite the corroborating testimony of several witnesses.[41] 'The University,' writes one historian, 'had not interfered in the Meek affair, and there is no written record of the feelings of the august Board of Governors nor of the ever-proper President, Sir Robert Falconer.'[42] Long on innuendo but short on logic, the implication of this statement is clear. Spineless administrators had thrown a valiant professor to the wolves. In response, however, one might ask on what basis they might have intervened. It would, for example, be difficult to describe this as a case of academic freedom violated; the fact that Meek was a professor was quite beside the point. Rather, it was a question of common assault involving a private citizen and a particular policeman. After the Police Commission's verdict was announced, an angry Meek condemned official efforts to suppress free speech. Predictably, the pro-Draper *Globe* and *Telegram* pounced on him for offering aid and comfort to the agents of Moscow. Shortly thereafter Meek faded from the public eye. 'It is not known,' interjects another historian, 'whether added to this was a suggestion from the University authorities that he keep his opinions to himself.'[43] Again, one questions the use of innuendo in lieu of evidence. Altogether, if Meek deserves a place in the pantheon of academic freedom, it is surely among the lesser gods of that temple.

Systematic efforts to smother communist agitation continued unabated throughout 1930. However, during this period, it should be stressed, not a peep of protest issued from any section of the university community, apart, that is, from a polite Hart House debate at the tag end of the Meek affair. 'In principle,' writes Michiel Horn, 'communists were probably believed by many professors to have a right to preach ... without hindrance.'[44] While this statement is undoubtedly true, there was also *probably* some who agreed with the more conservative professor, D.J. Gibb Wishart. In his opinion communists were 'like snakes, like wild beasts that must be destroyed and it is not a question of free speech with them.'[45] In truth, the academic community was *probably* divided on the question, with many of its members remaining indifferent. Just where the heaviest support lay we shall never know, because opinion on the matter was never directly tested. In any event, even those who felt communists to be victimized failed to speak. It was only in January 1931, almost two years after the sustained police crack-down had begun, that some professors sallied forth in defence of free speech. It is doubtful, however, that they did so because they were finally moved by the continuing suppression of Lenin's heirs. Instead, the timing suggests that it was the extension of repression to more 'respectable' elements of society that sparked their protest.

Swept forward by the momentum of their anti-subversive drive, authorities had steadily expanded the range and the tools of police control. By January 1931, however, some Torontonians felt they had gone beyond what was strictly necessary to check the reds. Thus, efforts to fingerprint the city's taxi drivers met with considerable opposition. The ostensible purpose was to prevent Chicago-style racketeering in the industry. The *Globe* claimed that a majority of legitimate cabbies favoured the move.[46] Even so, pressure from the *Star* and others concerned at the growth of police power induced authorities to rescind the measure. Although rebuffed in this venture, the Police Commission could still count on extensive popular support in its campaign against visible agitators. Thus, when it denied the Fellowship of Reconciliation a licence to hold a meeting, it was confident of public approval.

In reality, of course, the FOR was anything but a hotbed of violent revolution. It had been founded in Britain in 1914 with the object of solving social, racial, and other problems through open discussion. A latecomer, the Toronto branch had not been chartered until May 1930. Its membership, however, was patently 'respectable.' Ecumenical to a fault, the fellowship included Baptist, Quaker, United Church, and Jewish leaders within its ranks. A lawyer, a labour leader, the editor of the *Canadian Forum* and a couple of Varsity professors also took prominent roles.[47] In normal times such men banded together in the name of peace were unlikely to strike fear into the hearts of the multitude. But the times, alas, were far from normal. Two years of unrelenting depression and numerous revolutionary scares had prepared many to see communists under every overturned rock, the scepticism of a few notwithstanding. Such was the fate of the FOR.

Anxious to clear the air and make way for fruitful discussion, the fellowship challenged Draper and Police Commissioner Emerson Coatsworth to a debate on the issue of free speech. The brigadier, however, declined, describing the FOR as a front for the communists. Furthermore, a permit for the proposed 11 January meeting was denied, making it difficult for the fellowship to secure a hall. Spokesmen for the group, therefore, threatened to institute legal proceedings against the authorities. Rival newspapers, scrambling to boost circulation, took up the story with relish. The *Star,* as was its wont, assailed the police. The *Globe,* as it had for many months, backed Draper's boys in blue to the hilt. The latter questioned the motives of the FOR, noting that some if its members had disavowed Marxist ties, but at least one, who remained unnamed, was said to have written a magazine article 'some time ago' which 'showed pro-Soviet sympathies.'[48] Letters to various editors poured into Toronto's papers in response. One irate citizen argued that if sniping against the police were allowed to continue, the city would soon decline to the level of Chicago, 'where peaceful citizens never know but that machine-gun bullets will be pumped into them.'[49] Meanwhile, less than subtle sidebars in the *Globe* detailed the supposed infiltration of otherwise conservative American trade unions by subversive agents.[50] Caught in a whirlwind of others' devising, the Fellowship of Reconciliation was sucked into the eye of a storm whose ferocity can scarcely be overstated.

It was at this moment that some professors stepped into the fray. Sixty-eight signatures were appended to an open letter drafted on 15 January by Frank Underhill and Eric Havelock.[51] 'The attitude,' it read,

which the Toronto Police Commission has assumed towards public discussion of political and social problems, makes it clear that the right of free speech and free assembly is in danger of suppression in this city. This right has for generations been considered one of the proudest heritages of the British peoples, and to restrict or nullify it in an arbitrary manner, as has been the tendency in Toronto for the last two years, is short-sighted, inexpedient and intolerable.

It is the plain duty of the citizen to protest publicly against any such curtailment of his rights, and, in so doing, we wish to affirm our belief in the free public expression of opinions, however unpopular or erroneous.[52]

As it appeared in the newspapers, the letter gave no indication of the affiliation of its signatories. Since, however, some of them were among Varsity's most prominent senior men, few could have doubted that the connection would be swiftly made.[53]

In assessing their motives, Horn comments: 'Having spoken out in defence of traditional British liberties, thereby presumably adopting fairly safe ground, many of the sixty-eight may have been surprised to find that they had done something controversial.'[54] This argument, however, seems open to question. It implies a degree of political naïveté which would be unusual even in the most cloistered academic. The flames of intolerance had been raging brightly for two years. The letter of protest itself is witness to the fact that the heat had penetrated Varsity's walls. Furthermore, just days before, the FOR had raised the banner of free speech only to be branded communist. Altogether, only the insensate would have failed to recognize that they were stoking an already well-laid fire. The sixty-eight, however, numbered among themselves many who were far from naïve. Indeed, E.J. Urwick, Gilbert Jackson, and Frank Underhill each had personal reason to know just how hot the public arena could get for the professor errant. True, they may not have fully anticipated the level of controversy that their missive would inspire, but it is hard to believe that they expected nothing more than polite criticism to materialize. After all, it was against intolerance writ large that they were tilting. In like manner, as Horn documents so well, professors of that day were well aware of university policy concerning academic interventions in heated public disputes.[55] In challenging the Police Commission the sixty-eight were, at the very least, taking an unusual step.

Press reaction was immediate and predictable. The *Star* applauded the professors and opened its columns to those who inclined in the same direction. The *Globe*, however, led the march of the outraged. Describing the letter as a 'ridiculous document,' it went on to denounce free speech as a 'red herring.' The pun was no doubt intentional. Every gun in the arsenal of prejudice was touched off. The sixty-eight, it proclaimed, were pandering to communists and furthering 'foreign propaganda' whose purpose was 'to supplant Christianity with atheism.' A dash of anti-intellectualism was added for good measure. The police, so the editorial ran, were coping with real threats, not with mere 'theories from textbooks.' In sum, the *Globe* advised that 'the tender-hearted bosh about the Bolsheviki ought to be stamped out once and for all.'[56] On the following day this 'challenge to law and order on behalf of communistic "free speech"' was tied to threats of murder and arson directed at Coatsworth over the telephone by a man who spoke in an 'educated voice.'[57] This incident led to further denunciations of the 'theorizing pusseyfooters' and their 'idealism run amok.'[58] Increasingly, charges of veiled atheism were hurled at university men. In this regard, it probably did the image of the sixty-eight little good when E. Haldiman-Julius, hailed as the 'high priest' of American atheism, offered to journey to Toronto to stand at their side in company with Clarence Darrow, the scourge of southern fundamentalists.[59] Articles of rebuttal by Gilbert Jackson and W.S. Wallace, the university librarian, were, for many, only further examples of professorial folly. For a month or more, and despite friendly words from the *Star,* demands for the censure of the sixty-eight reverberated deafeningly.

To Falconer, of course, the situation was a veritable nightmare. For him personally, moreover, it could not have occurred at a worse moment. As it happened, he was a very sick man; long years of toil had finally exacted a heavy price. On 5 June 1930 doctors had broken the sobering news.[60] A nagging sensation of weakness, which Falconer had long shrugged off as inconsequential, was diagnosed as symptomatic of a severe heart disorder. Ordered to bed for seven weeks, he had passed a troubled summer at his beloved Huntsville retreat. In late August he was permitted a few turns around his verandah, but Sophie was still handling his correspondence.[61] Soldiering on, he returned to work in the fall, but at reduced hours and, as he confessed to a fellow sufferer, still 'pretty well crocked up.'[62] How long he might be able to remain as president was a matter of conjecture. By the new year his attention was focused on February and the promise of an extended leave in Trinidad. 'I hope,' he confided to a British friend, 'that the sun and warm weather will drive out any lingering trouble that may still lurk within me.'[63] Thus preoccupied and weakened, Falconer was ill-placed to take a leading role when the clouds suddenly burst over the university.

The issue could not be ignored. No sooner had the controversial letter been aired than reporters were hammering at Falconer's door and those of the governors. Cody told journalists that the professors had acted on their own and in no way represented the university as a whole. After this disclaimer, however, he quickly added: 'It is a free country and they have a right to give expression to their own opinions.' Asked if the board would take action, its chairman replied: 'I don't know just how it would come under the purview of anybody.'[64] Initially, at least, the good canon seemed to hint at an extension of the bounds of academic freedom. Although the evidence is slight, this attitude may have reflected his own discomfort at being harassed a year earlier when he publicly endorsed the government-controlled sale of liquor.[65] For his part, Falconer uttered a few words in defence of free speech, denied seeing the letter before it was published, and said no more.[66] In private, however, he was more forthcoming. When Professor Wishart wrote furiously to urge that the sixty-eight be disciplined or even discharged, the president rejected his proposal. 'I, myself,' he wrote, 'am like you thoroughly British, and I am of the strong opinion that the safety of the community, just as the safety of science, in the long run depends on free speech.' Alluding to the evolution controversy in the United States, which had long obsessed him, Falconer continued, 'our danger on this side is getting more of the American spirit ... and I, myself, believe that it is far better to give a good deal of rein than to curb too much.' He granted that the gentlemen in question had probably acted inexpediently, but he made it clear that mass firings were not being considered.[67] There were, of course, very practical reasons for ruling this course out: sixty-eight men were not easy to replace. Even more, one senses in his words to an angry alumnus a concern for the broader moral repercussions that such action would have. No doubt his mind ran back to the German professors affair when he had intoned similar misgivings. 'I am afraid,' he told R.H. Lloyd, 'that if the Governors were to adopt the method you propose and offhand dismiss the professors bag and baggage on account of the letter that they sent to the public they would find that the University would have been so injured that it would be long in recovering from the blow.'[68]

Not all university authorities, however, were in so tolerant a state of mind. The chancellor, Sir William Mulock, was fuming. More significantly, the influential Sir Joseph Flavelle was thoroughly disenchanted with the sixty-eight. While not applauding Draper's excesses, he understood why the police chief had been tempted by stern measures. Acutely, he analysed the mechanisms of conflict within an excitable Toronto. 'Men of small calibre,' he told George Wrong, eagerly exploited any conditions that could serve their own immediate ends. Newspapers, in particular, always stood ready to trumpet 'any cry that might bring grist to their mill.'

Irresponsibility and self-interest notoriously abounded. Accordingly he had little sympathy for academics who had plunged willingly into this 'mess.' Indeed, grumbled Flavelle, they 'should not be surprised if someone hit them over the head.' At a stroke, he complained, they had put the financial well-being of the university in jeopardy. In his view the professors were little more than 'a group of innocents ... led into the trap by designing agitators.'[69] Fortunately, the newly installed premier, George Henry, showed no inclination to meddle in the affair. Ferguson, one suspects, would have played a more dynamic role. In any case, Varsity's deeply troubled leadership was left alone to cope with the matter, and for this, if nothing else, they were surely grateful.

The upshot was a long debate on 22 January, the details of which were never recorded. In the end Falconer was instructed to convey the misgivings of the board to representatives of the sixty-eight in a private interview, which he duly did on 3 February. Six unnamed professors and Alfred Tennyson DeLury, soon to be acting president, were invited. Falconer informed the group that the governors had decided to make no public statement on the merits of the case. Nor, he went on, would there be any resolution of censure. But Cody's offhanded hints notwithstanding, it was also made clear that no fundamental revisions of university thinking on academic freedom were being contemplated. Thus, Falconer explained the inexpediency of professors engaging in public controversy. He tried again to demonstrate the wisdom of curtailing external involvements in order to protect institutional autonomy and the freedom to research and teach. Typically, he dwelt on the sad experience of several American state universities which had been victimized in partisan political disputes. Proceeding diplomatically, he felt that his message was taken to heart. As he told the governors, 'these gentlemen responded to my presentation of the case, and undertook to use their influence with the members of their staff to refrain from further discussions on this or political matters.'[70] From his point of view this was the end of the matter and he swiftly decamped for two months of much-needed rest in the Caribbean sunshine. A week later the board issued a brief statement dissociating the university from the protest of the sixty-eight. Unfortunately, this move came after a speech at the Royal York Hotel in which Mulock vented his ire on the communists. Like the professors, the chancellor spoke for himself, but again, like theirs his words were interpreted as an expression of his colleagues' views. Thus, an impression flourished to the effect that the governors had read the riot act to the sixty-eight.[71] In reality, of course, they had done no such thing.

Falconer's sojourn in the Caribbean was a balm to his spirit as well as his weakened frame. From Port of Spain he wrote to Archie MacMechan of the refreshing joys entailed in retracing his youthful steps. 'Life,' he mused, 'has been telescoped for me during the past three weeks.' The island, however, was 'more beautiful than ever' and he delighted to observe several 'great improvements.' There was particular pleasure in introducing Sophie to boyhood friends, most of them now sedate grandparents. He was relishing the idea of a fortnight in Barbados before sailing for Boston in the last days of March.[72] Indeed, one suspects, time at that point could not pass too slowly to suit him. Disturbing news out of Toronto, moreover, made the prospect of return less than enticing. The recent atmosphere of discord had simply refused to evaporate. The furore sparked by the sixty-eight had scarcely begun to subside when students provided new ammunition to critics of the university. With exquisitely bad timing, on 24 February *Varsity* featured an article in which it was alleged that 'practical atheism' had many adherents within the professoriate and student body. Seeking not to condemn but merely to comment, the youthful journalists nevertheless precipitated yet another public outcry.

Allegations of their unchristian proclivities had coloured many of the press attacks on the sixty-eight. Suspicions planted in January flowered in the wake of *Varsity*'s editorial. Sensing, as Flavelle would have it, ample grist for its mill, the *Globe* pontificated: '*Varsity* is right or it is wrong. If right, the University of Toronto needs purging with unrestrained ruthlessness, or closing up altogether, if wrong, much more than a penalizing of the directors of the undergraduate publication is necessary ...'[73] Not to be outdone, the *Telegram* speculated that the offending article was a 'firecracker that might well tear the university to pieces ... Until the university has been purged of the mongers of atheism, it has ceased to be a worthy recipient of State funds.'[74] Opposition MPP Harry Nixon had come to the same conclusion. In the House he argued that 'not one dollar be voted in sessional estimates to the support and maintenance of the University' until a full public inquiry was held. Meanwhile, he seized the opportunity to lambaste Henry for reserving the educational portfolio for himself instead of delegating it to one who could devote the whole of his energies to that ministry.[75] The premier refrained from public comment but blocked Nixon's initiative in the legislature.

To the great relief of the Board of Governors, the Student Administrative Council moved independently to discipline *Varsity*'s staff. The journal was suspended for the rest of the year by the SAC and its editor, A.E.F. Allan, was fired. Caput, the university's disciplinary body, confirmed the resolution and the governors happily nodded approval.[76] But limited action of this sort was not enough to satisfy crusading journalists and their scandalized readers. The hard core of atheism, after all, had still to be excised. Thus the papers howled on. Rising to the bait, on 27 February angry students and some professors gathered on the lawns of Hart House ceremoniously to commit copies of the *Globe* and the *Telegram* to the flames. In righteous indignation those journals replied with calls for a religious census of the university.[77] Thus fuelled, the controversy rolled on through March.

Towards the end of that month Nixon again raised the question of withholding university grants. Once more Henry countered by expressing his confidence in the governors' ability to manage the situation. Meanwhile he wrote privately to DeLury. Quoting only the second and third paragraphs of the letter, Horn sees it as a subtle warning from the premier that he might not refrain from intervention should similar incidents be allowed to crop up again.[78] Read in full, however, the tone of the communication seems rather less ominous than this interpretation would suggest. 'Replying to your favour of the 19th instant,' wrote Henry,

regarding the question in the House concerning the University and the editorial in 'Varsity,' let me say that I feel quite sure that the staff of the University and the other governing bodies are quite capable of dealing with the situation that has been raised.

Unfortunately, from time to time there arises some discussion as to some of the teaching that is carried on in the University. I have a daughter taking an Arts Course and she sometimes brings home ideas to her Mother who gets very much concerned about it at times. I sometimes feel there are discussions in the classes with the youths that are being trained that would be better confined to more mature minds.

I am looking forward to getting more closely in touch with the affairs of the University and hope that Sir Robert Falconer will shortly be back and improved in health that he may undertake his position as President, and that things will right themselves and that the confidence of the public will not be disturbed by similar incidents in the future.

I want to thank you for the confidence the University authorities are placing in me. I have received many personal expressions of thanks since the incident occurred in the House.[79]

While a vague threat may have been implied here, it was at most a veiled and distant one. Indeed, in the context of the moment, Henry's actions spoke far more eloquently than his words. Having allowed the university a free hand with the sixty-eight, he was now prepared to let the governors deal with the *Varsity* affair. Moreover, his letter came hard on the heels of one from the attorney-general of Ontario in which that minister expressed his personal good wishes. With Nixon blocked effectively in the House, he confessed himself 'glad indeed that nothing further was done.'[80] All things considered, therefore, it is unlikely that DeLury and his colleagues were unduly disturbed by the premier's note.

Popular opinion, however, still required adequate soothing. This task was left to Falconer who, after almost a quarter-century of service, had come to symbolize for many not only Varsity but Canadian higher education itself. Drawing heavily on his accumulated prestige, on 7 April Sir Robert faced a hushed audience at Convocation Hall. His message, aptly framed, was brief, personal, and pointed. 'On behalf not only of the University of Toronto,' he declared, 'but of all the universities of Canada, I wish to say ... that in this Province there is no cause for alarm as to what issues from this university. I have for many years known the University of Toronto, known it in all its aspects and efforts and achievements, and I say emphatically to you that this is a healthy place, morally, physically, spiritually and industrially.' Men, he admitted, often spoke rashly; the young, in particular, were prone to be incautious. But, he told his audience, on the whole there was a 'constructiveness' about what was thought, said, and taught at the university. The students were worthy representatives of 'the finest stock on this continent.' There was, in short, nothing to fear: 'That,' he concluded, 'is my testimony and my message to you tonight.'[81]

The only argument here was one from authority. Falconer had offered nothing more than his personal assurances. Somewhat surprisingly, they seemed to be enough. Even the habitually hostile Globe described the speech as 'extremely gratifying.' Remarking on Falconer's intimate knowledge of the place, it was willing to concede that Varsity had probably been in error about the extent of atheism at the university. 'At any rate,' said the newspaper, 'now that President Falconer has spoken with certainty, the public will hope that there will be no apparent excuse for repeating the charge in the future.'[82] Had the venerable president performed a miracle single-handedly? Probably not. He had struck, to be sure, a noble chord. But angry critics had turned deaf ears before. Again, he may have won some sympathy when, shortly after the speech, he announced that he would retire the following June. A stricken man, after all, has certain moral advantages. In the end, however, the controversy was probably subsiding on its own. For weeks the papers had milked the issue until it neared dessication. Queen's Park had repeatedly signalled its disinclination to act. As well, student journalists had paid the price of their presumed folly. Little, in short, was left to be said. Doubts might have lingered, but excitement was rapidly draining away.

As the crisis ebbed, Falconer looked forward to a relatively quiet final year in office. Of academic freedom he had probably heard enough. The time for rest was at hand. Unfortunately for the president, however, the ever-active pen of Frank Underhill was still at work. Unchastened and maybe even spurred by recent events, that most political of professors was in the news again by June. In the columns of a British weekly he bitingly condemned R.B. Bennett's handling of imperial relations. The *Mail and Empire* immediately took him to task for meddling in political matters. Falconer must have suffered a particularly nauseating attack of déja vu. Writing to Underhill, he cautioned him about engaging in political journalism, noting that 'it endangers the autonomy of the University.'[83] When fully two months elapsed without a response, the president must have imagined that his strictures had been at last taken to heart. In fact, however, the letter only caught up with Underhill, who was out of town all summer, much later. Meanwhile he had received encouragement from a most unlikely quarter. In a spectacular tour de force of wholesale inconsistency, the *Globe* leaped to his defence. Fired, one suspects, more by political bias and a desire to outdo the 'Tory morning organ' than by any new-found respect for academic freedom, it applauded Underhill's critique of Bennett and championed his right to speak. 'The *Globe*,' its editors declared, 'does not always agree with the views of university professors but can see no reason why an attempt should be made to keep academic thought within the bounds of party exigency.'[84] Somewhat later the *London Advertiser* rallied to Underhill's side, condemning those 'busybodies' who would, in forever hectoring them, reduce professors to the level of civil servants.[85]

Thus fortified, Underhill replied to Falconer's letter on 24 September. Noting favourable comments in the press, he observed that 'I don't think that you realize how much common sense and liberalism there is still left in Ontario even after the long Ferguson regime.' Given the occurrences of that winter and spring, Falconer must have winced at this statement. More deftly, Underhill went on to recite the lengthy list of professors at home and abroad who had regularly contributed to political discussion in the press. At one time or another, for example, his own Toronto colleagues, George Wrong, Chester Martin, George Glazebrook, and W.P.M. Kennedy, had aired their views in the pages of the *Globe*, the *Manitoba Free Press*, the *Round Table*, and other such forums. Overseas, the respected G.D.H. Cole was a frequent contributor to the *New Statesman* as was the brilliant Australian historian, W.K. Hancock. 'In the light of all these cases,' said Underhill, 'I fail to see what is so particularly reprehensible in my own conduct.' Cogently he continued: 'If professors at Toronto must keep their mouths shut in order to preserve the autonomy of the University then that autonomy is already lost. A freedom that cannot be exercised without danger of disastrous consequences is not a real freedom at all. In the midst of all the intolerance which is rampant in the world at present a University plays a sorry part if it does not raise up its voice for freedom of speech.'[86]

However compelling its logic might have been, Underhill's letter left the president cold. To him, after all, the central question had never been one of principle so much as it was one of expediency. Logic, he seems to have felt, was at best a flimsy armour against political interest and public prejudice, once aroused. Thus he wrote: 'Your letter leaves me still of the same opinion as to the inexpediency of professors in the University of Toronto taking part in political journalism, by which I mean discussing current politics in such a way as to bring party criticism upon the writer.' It was pointless, he continued, to draw analogies with practice in Britain or America. They simply did not apply in Toronto. Although not saying so here, Falconer had always thought the United States far less and Great Britain vastly more hospitable to academic freedom than his own constituency. Dealing, therefore, with Hogtown realities rather than with theory, he favoured caution. Indeed, in seeking to counter Underhill he willingly conceded one of the latter's points. Sometimes professors had to keep their mouths shut precisely because university autonomy was not yet fully secure. 'Not infrequently,' he reminded the historian, 'I have had to defend the professors in their right to teach their subjects with complete freedom.' And teaching, he emphasized, was their primary duty, one that secondary concerns should not be allowed to undermine. He told Underhill, 'Your references to the press carry little weight with me'; the *Globe*, as he pointed out, showed 'no manner of consistency,' and he urged his reader to remember that newspaper's vitriolic campaign against the sixty-eight.[87]

Having stated their respective cases, both parties then quit the field unmoved from their original positions. Underhill continued to pursue his journalistic avocation, especially in the *Canadian Forum*. For his part, Falconer reiterated his views that fall, this time for the benefit of students. Clearly recalling the *Varsity* affair, he informed them that 'now, more than ever, skylarking on the ragged edge of folly irritates onlookers.'[88] Following this speech came welcome words of sympathy from Carleton Stanley, now president of Dalhousie. 'I began to realise last winter', wrote Stanley, 'what a difficult time the university administrator has with the yelping, yowling pack of average minds whose first instinct is to hunt down anything original or critical or independent.' These banal harriers, he continued, 'were not bad people in their way, and yet, if unresisted, as much the enemy of Truth and Decency as any base self-seeker.'[89] Both Underhill and Falconer could have whispered 'Amen.' They differed only, if substantially, on what might constitute the wisest form of 'resistance' to the baying of the ill-informed.

Much to the president's relief, his direct dealings with Underhill were over. Whether by chance or by design, the historian was out of the limelight during the last six months of Falconer's tenure. Even so, and much to his chagrin, the latter was not quite finished with troublesome professors. Indeed, mere weeks before his own retirement was to come into effect, Falconer felt compelled to require the resignation of one of his staff. Ironically the strongest disciplinary measure he ever meted out was directed at one, not in the traditionally sensitive departments of history or political science, but in the normally inconspicuous field of forestry. Initiative in the matter was supplied by the dynamic dean of that faculty, C.D. Howe, who in May 1932 forcefully demanded the dismissal of Associate Professor W.N. Millar. In a lengthy memorandum Howe catalogued complaints against Millar which stretched back over several years. The professor, it was alleged, was an abrasive fellow, almost wholly devoid of tact or common courtesy. Over time, said Howe, he had managed to alienate not only his colleagues, but more damagingly, most of the public and private forestry agents upon whom the faculty depended for access to field training. 'Several of our alumni,' said the dean, 'holding responsible administrative positions and upon whom we would need to depend for co-operation, have told me quite positively that there was no point in attempting to give the students more extensive practical experience so long as Professor Millar remained on staff.' There was more involved here, he continued, than a simple personality conflict: 'To me the most significant point in the whole matter ... is that whenever there is a forestry discussion it is always assumed that Professor Millar will take a violently hostile attitude.' Moreover, all too often his criticism was 'irresponsible or exaggerated or unsubstantiated.' The dean, in fact, thought the professor an unscientific crank. But the principal charge levelled against Millar was that he was failing to carry out his duties as a teacher. His chief task, as Howe explained, was to introduce students to the fundamentals of silviculture, the scientific study and management of forest resources. The prevailing view was that this job was best accomplished through an intensive examination of the entire forest as a biological unit. Millar, however, was said to object both to the general approach and to the amount of time given to the subject. Furthermore, said Howe, he regularly indulged in scathing classroom denunciations of the school, his colleagues, and the policies of all levels of government. To make matters worse, while delighting in 'tearing things down,' he rarely offered constructive suggestions. Altogether, he was said to have disclosed 'a type of mind unfitted to carry on the work of a professorship in a university.'[90]

Uncharacteristically, Falconer seems to have made little effort to investigate the case personally. Perhaps, with his mandate very near its close, he felt constrained to act on Howe's pointed advice. Of course, he could have delayed until his term expired. But that would have left his friend and successor, Harry Cody, with a dismal first task to perform. In any event, he transmitted Howe's memorandum to the governors along with his own recommendation that it be implemented. Thus Falconer and Millar departed Varsity, albeit under radically different circumstances. For both of them, however, a difficult passage had come to an end.

Taken as a whole, Falconer's approach to academic freedom was governed far more by practical concerns than by considerations of theory. From the very hour of his appointment one thing above all had been impressed on him. His greatest challenge and foremost duty, he understood, was to avoid a repetition of the Loudon years, when appointments, dismissals, policies, and programs had been subject to blatant political manipulation. The problem, of course, was a familiar one to university heads throughout North America. On the whole they elected caution and chose to interpret academic freedom as something internal to the autonomous university. Accordingly, it was easy for critics, such as Thorstein Veblen, to burlesque these men as 'Captains of Erudition,' timid public relations men ready to bow to external pressure at every turn.[91] Veblen, however, did not have to contend with politicians and benefactors who often mirrored in sharp detail the prejudices of a very nervous age. From Falconer's vantage point, the continuing threat of public intervention was more than a vague spectre. Indeed, to him the need for tact was obvious. The memory of Loudon, the battle with Sam Blake, the tragedy of the German professors, and the many tempests of the 1920s affected him deeply. They seemed parts of a recurring pattern of life in Toronto which made the university's independence appear tenuous at best. Escalating financial pressures added to this sense of vulnerability. Clashes with the United Farmers of Ontario only deepened already entrenched fears. Falconer's anxieties, in short, were genuine and to his mind well founded, rather than bogies conveniently conjured up in order to mask ulterior administrative designs. Thus, with almost monotonous regularity, he urged professors to be prudent in dealing with a temperamental public.

While consistent in his definition of policy, Falconer was less so in his actual practice. Chiding professors who indulged in political journalism, he none the less frequently engaged in it himself. In self-defence he might have replied that his office, by its very nature, sometimes required no less. This would be an effective retort had he limited himself to matters that impinged directly on the university or on higher education in general. In fact, however, he often addressed himself to issues that bore little immediate relation to his expertise or duties as president. One thinks, for example, of his support for conscription and his impassioned pleas for social reform while at Pine Hill. Whenever he had perceived the greater good of Canadian society to be at stake, Falconer had rarely practised self-censorship. He may have felt that his position of leadership conferred a special licence or a special obligation to speak. Whatever the case, it is difficult to reconcile his personal practice with his public admonitions to professors.

It is vital to recognize, however, that Falconer's staff was also given latitude to wander the gap between theory and practice. On this score Underhill was perfectly correct. Despite formal injunctions to the contrary, journalistic forays by Toronto's professors were far from rare. Although they would one day demand far more, in fact Varsity's academics enjoyed considerable leeway in the area of public expression. In 1979, for example, Barker Fairley recalled the 1920s as 'happy days,' when, under no particular pressure to conform, he felt free to help launch first the *Rebel* and then the *Canadian Forum*.[92] Why then, it must be asked, were some who ran afoul of extramural critics defended by Falconer, while others were disciplined? What, for instance, would account for the difference in his treatment of MacIver and Underhill, whose cases seem so similar? Did the president play favourites? There can be no denying that considerations of a personal nature sometimes coloured his decisions. MacIver, although harbouring unorthodox views, was a mild-mannered individual who eschewed rigid dogmatism. In other words, he fit Falconer's image of the scholar as a disinterested and constructive critic. Underhill did not. His grating, often sarcastically self-righteous style could not but rub the president the wrong way.

In fairness to Falconer, however, there were factors beyond personality that led him to handle the two men differently. For one thing, Underhill must have seemed incorrigible, a habitual transgressor who cared little for the problems with which others had to cope. Indeed, between 1928 and 1932 not a year passed without his becoming embroiled in one public row or another. MacIver, to be sure, had continued to address topical issues long after his brush with Leonard. But he did so without arousing serious controversy. And therein lay the crucial and wholly pragmatic difference. Much, it seems, was permitted so long as it could be defended as responsible, non-partisan comment. C.D. Howe made this point plain in his condemnation of Millar. 'There would be, I am sure,' he advised the president, 'no objection to Professor Millar's public criticism of our forestry problems if only they [sic] were dignified, dispassionate and constructive.'[93] Similarly, it will be recalled that in chastising Underhill in 1931, Falconer had warned him against inexpedient exercises in political journalism, 'by which I mean discussing current politics *in such a way* as to bring party criticism upon the writer.'[94] Tone, timing, and posture, he was saying, mattered even more than substance when it came to drawing the line between acceptable and unacceptable public statements by the staff. That line admittedly was a fine one, and too much depended on the will of him who defined it. Falconer, however, generally tried to be liberal and in practice urged prudence rather than silence on his professors. Unfortunately, the acid tests of prudence were supplied by circumstance rather than by stated policy. As a result, academics gambled on public reaction when they took to the press or the platform.

When professors miscalculated or ignored the consequences of their pronouncements, Falconer's was a delicate task. In administering such cases was he, as has been alleged, 'mildewed with discretion'? Underhill probably thought so. Yet it is doubtful that MacIver did. Likewise Thomas Eakin, sheltered from the wrath of Blake, had good reason to be grateful for Falconer's protection. For that matter, few had suffered more than Immanuel Benzinger. As their later correspondence clearly attests, however, that unfortunate victim of intolerance bore no animus towards the president, who, virtually alone, had tried to defend him. A character reference can even be had from at least one of the celebrated sixty-eight. Although a moderate left-winger and then married to 'a communist of sorts,' Barker Fairley got on well with Falconer, who always remained his 'ideal president.' As university leaders go, mused the professor in his nineties, there had 'never been as good a one since' at Toronto.[95] Of course one testimonial issued decades after the events in question cannot a reputation make. But neither should it be ignored. After all, perspective can sometimes clarify as easily as cloud one's vision.

By no stretch of the most sympathetic imagination can Falconer's era be described as a golden age of academic freedom. Yet neither was it a period of stagnation or utter darkness. Plainly, professors were inhibited in the full exercise of what a future age would define as their civil right to address matters of public import. Some, who went beyond what was conventionally deemed acceptable, were rebuked. For the most part, however, the 'punishments' meted out were remarkably mild. Thus the sixty-eight were disowned but not censured, and even Underhill was let off with little more than a measured dressing-down. Millar, of course, was dismissed, but this action seems to have been occasioned primarily by his refusal to adhere to the curriculum and by his disruption of the work of his department. Moreover, for all those who were disciplined, several more were shielded, even in the face of considerable pressure. From the standpoint of individual freedom, in other words, Falconer's was an uneven record. From an institutional perspective, however, his was a considerable achievement. If he sometimes hindered free expression, it was in order to guarantee university autonomy. In retrospect, it might be suggested that he fought and largely won a battle that had to be prosecuted before any significant extensions of academic freedom were conceivable. In a curious sense, although both surely would have grimaced at the notion, Falconer helped make a Frank Underhill possible.

CHAPTER XI

Beyond the Office Walls

Despite the nearly insatiable demands of office, Falconer's involvement in the larger world never waned. Indeed, a variety of extramural causes engaged his attention in the 1920s, not the least of which was the unsettling matter of church union. The truce he had helped negotiate with anti-unionists in 1917 was respected throughout the remainder of the war. But, while animosities among Presbyterians were temporarily restrained, they by no means vanished. As the period of grace neared its agreed end late in 1920, Falconer and others braced themselves for a resumption of strife. It was clear that the 'antis' would not go down without a fight. Seeking to forestall a permanent rift, S.W. Dyde, principal of Queen's Theological College, advised Falconer, the convenor of the Union Committee, to arrange an informal conference between extremists on both sides before too much heat accumulated.[1] Sir Robert, wary of facilitating confrontation, rejected the suggestion. It was better, he told Dyde, to air the matter in the open, 'sniff the wind,' and then prepare for the next General Assembly.[2]

The 'wind,' it soon became apparent, carried more than a whiff of acrimony. The assembly of 1921 confirmed the decision to proceed with union 'as expeditiously as possible.' To those of Falconer's persuasion this meant 'forthwith.' To the leaders of the Presbyterian Church Association, however, the formula implied an indefinite delay, and warnings were issued to the effect that any attempt to employ coercion would lead to their secession.[3] The potential for conflict was obvious. For a time, a desperate search for compromise served to mute hostilities, but the dam burst once and for all during the Port Arthur Assembly of 1923.

Scrambling to find a way out of the growing impasse, the Reverend D.R. Drummond of Hamilton suggested that federation, rather than organic union, be tried. The antis were enthusiastic but the majority unionists voted the resolution down. To adopt it, they argued, would be a breach of faith with Methodists and Congegationalists, who had been promised full amalgamation on numerous occasions. When, shortly thereafter, unionists decided to seek legislative approval from the provinces and the federal government, the die was cast and the long-feared split became all but final.

In the spring of 1924 private members' bills won assent on the prairies and in the Maritimes. Following their progress closely, Falconer was particularly heartened by the show of support in the west. Ontario was a different matter. As a well-orchestrated and vehement opposition gathered force, Sir Robert advised Walter Murray that 'there will be a warm fight here.'[4] This proved to be an understatement. No sooner was a bill formulated than Ferguson was inundated with demands that it be blocked.[5] One dissenting Presbyterian observed that 'no legislature can force a man into a church in which he does not believe.'[6] Another, who smelled conspiracy, warned that the premier would pay a heavy political price if he allowed the matter to go forward. 'If,' said A.W. Paton of Lindsay, 'Dr Gandier, Rowell, and the few *invisible* war profiteers (adepts at organization et.) who are the prime movers in Church Union, succeed ... it will certainly create disruption and result disastrously not alone to the Presbyterian Church but, to your Government as well.'[7] Subjected to similar pressure by proponents of union, Ferguson avoided making public commitments.

Meanwhile, in committee, opponents succeeded in so diluting the bill with amendments that by mid-April it was withdrawn. Its sponsors decided to try their luck in Ottawa before tackling Queen's Park again. Christian brotherhood was at a low ebb. Fratricidal Presbyterians were locked in earnest combat. Methodists were berating Anglicans, who had helped to stall the legislative process. Reports from Nova Scotia told of the bitterness dividing old comrades. 'It has been a testing time,' Falconer told Murray, 'and we must try not to lose our old friendships.' He was proud to hear that his brother Jim and his old classmate Clarence Mackinnon had carried the torch of union valiantly at home. As for the opposition's tactics in Toronto, he described the campaign launched by Thomas Eakin and others as 'scandalous.' 'They will pick up any stick to beat the enemy,' he observed. For a moment he probably regretted that he had not fed Eakin to the sharks in 1908. He could understand the urge to indulge in pulpit rhetoric, but, he wrote, 'I am a Calvinist and I try to keep calm and quiet.'[8]

Clearly, much hinged on the outcome of proceedings in Ottawa. The Private Bills Committee of the house held hearings on the matter from 30 April to 9 May. Falconer was the first witness to be called. That evening he wrote excitedly to Walter Murray describing the scene: 'I opened the ball this morning with a speech of an hour and a quarter succeeded by a grilling of three quarters of an hour.' The stage, he recalled, had been dramatically set. The room was full to overflowing as over 700 people sought admission.[9] Always at home in front of a large audience, one suspects that Sir Robert rather enjoyed his moment in the limelight. Asked about the situation in the west, Falconer assured the committee that the many spontaneous local mergers were interpreted there as definite commitments to organic union. When probed further on the possible effects that a failure to pass the needed legislation might have on the prairies, he responded that chaos would likely ensue. He went on to assure his questioners that, contrary to opposition arguments, the bill in no way altered the 'Basis' agreed to in 1908. Furthermore, he rejected the call for yet another Presbyterian plebiscite, noting that the antis had said time and time again that they regarded the whole business as unacceptable in principle. To Falconer this stance implied that 'the side of the majority did not count' in their eyes. Accordingly, he viewed the proposal for yet another vote as an obvious effort to stall. The next witness, a Mr Mason, was asked to answer the claim that the General Assembly lacked the constitutional power to dissolve the church. Adroitly, he countered that the Presbyterian church itself was the outcome of the union of four separate bodies in 1875. If the assemblies of those groups had not the power to dissolve themselves, said Mason, then there never was and never could be a Presbyterian church in Canada.[10]

Altogether, Falconer felt that these opening blows had been well struck. The antis, however, were sure to put up stiff resistance. Moreover, they could count on the support of many Catholic MPs from Quebec who feared the emergence of a united Protestant church. Thus, he anticipated that the struggle would be keen and that the outcome was 'by no means assured.' Even so, he was confident that unionists would eventually carry the day. 'A few indications,' he informed Murray, 'lead me to think that the Government will not want the burden of killing the bill.' In the first place such a move would 'work into the hands of the Conservatives in Toronto,' a development unlikely to please Mackenzie King. Secondly, English-speaking champions of the bill could count on some assistance from Quebec. 'There is a good deal of doubt about the Frenchmen,' he admitted, 'but tomorrow Geoffrion may fix them.' Above all, King, he was certain, realized the furore that would be unleashed if he moved to stifle the legislation.[11] In the end, after much squabbling, the bill was passed and royal assent was given in July.

Having secured the moral advantage of dominion approval, in the spring of 1925 unionists reintroduced a bill at Queen's Park. Once again Ferguson found himself the target of a barrage issuing from both sides. 'For God's sake and your own reputation,' wrote one concerned dissenter, 'block the efforts of the invisible heads of the proposed new church to purloin church property ... They have no more moral or legal right to Presbyterian property than Cabinet Ministers, who leave a government, have to their portfolios or office furniture.'[12] As this letter indicates, the antis had almost given up on the prospects of preventing union and were now concentrating instead on the question of how the assets of the Presbyterian church were to be divided after the split. In selecting this tack they played their cards wisely. Unionists had long feared a legal contest in the light of a Scottish court's decision in the Overtoun case, according to which secessionists forfeited all rights to the property of their former church. Unwilling to test this precedent, unionists eventually struck a deal with their opponents. The bill was passed, but claims to the property of non-concurring congregations were relinquished. Saddest of all for Falconer and his brother-in-law, Alfred Gandier, was the loss of Knox College with its splendid library.

There followed a last fierce round of electioneering as Presbyterian congregations across the nation opted in or out of the new church. The west, predictably, responded positively to the call for final union, but Falconer was depressed when western Ontario and his boyhood home, Pictou County, rejected invitations to join. The dreams implanted in him by Harnack of a grand Christian confluence had fallen short of Falconer's once-bright hopes. When the United Church at last took formal shape in 1925 it left one-third to one-half of Canadian Presbyterians behind. Great tribulation had complicated its birth. Falconer's chief consolation throughout was that the new church was likely to prove all the stronger for having passed through the fire.[13]

This ecumenical streak in Falconer's thought extended beyond purely religious matters. Indeed, throughout the 1920s an ever-increasing proportion of his extracurricular energies came to focus on the very secular realm of international affairs. As he surveyed the global scene, it seemed to him that the major lesson arising from the First World War had yet to be fully understood. Enduring peace, he felt, could be built only on the foundation of a more co-operative and closely integrated world order. Yet, looking about, he found that narrow nationalism still held sway. He was particularly disturbed by its North American variant, a myopic isolationism born, he thought, of an almost wilful ignorance. 'This Continent,' he lamented in 1923, 'is woefully defective of knowledge of what it owes to the world at large.'[14] Correcting that defect became something of a personal mission for Falconer. In setting out to combat exclusivity and mutual suspicion he called, predictably, on those of British blood to take the lead in promoting a new spirit of harmony. Theirs, he imagined, would be the crucial initiative as they provided models of co-operation through the League of Nations, the empire, and a projected Anglo-American entente. Writing, speaking, and travelling widely, he brought this message to Canadians, Britons, and Americans throughout a troubled decade.

Even as the war was reaching a fevered pitch in 1917, Falconer had paused to contemplate the requirements of a lasting peace. Chief among these, he speculated, would be 'the promise and potency of a supreme court of the civilized world.'[15] Anarchic individualism among the nations had proved disastrous. Increasingly, therefore, he was attracted by the idea of a league of nations, a collective arbiter that could mediate conflicting interests. His enthusiasm for the scheme rose when, during a 1918 visit to Britain, he encountered others of the same persuasion. On his return journey in the *Adriatic,* he enjoyed long talks with league proponent Lord Charnwood. Their relationship quickly mellowed into 'real friendship.'[16] If nothing else, Falconer thought that such a league would put an end to the secrecy that had marred prewar diplomacy. Whole populations had been left in the dark and had thereby been encouraged to embrace either indifference to foreign affairs or an explosive xenophobia. It is unclear whether he was in any way influenced by the writings of E.D. Morel or others who condemned veiled diplomacy. Whatever the case, he shared many of their misgivings. Accordingly, a few days after armistice, Sir Robert dashed off some advice for policy-makers in Ottawa in a letter to N.W. Rowell: 'I am rather sorry,' he told that privy councillor, 'that the whole question of terms of peace has not been discussed more in public in Canada for I am sure it would have had a very fine educative effect upon our people.' While recognizing that the government was under foreign pressure, he thought that frankness was nevertheless in order. 'I am,' he continued, 'a little afraid of the effect on the public mind of having terms of peace declared and drawn up without the people having been told beforehand as to the main principles that will be laid down.'[17]

As those 'principles' were slowly revealed, Falconer became even more apprehensive about the future. The vindictive tenor of the treaty seemed to him more likely to aggravate national jealousies than to obviate them. Increasingly, therefore, he turned to the idea of an international council of revision as an antidote. The face of Europe had been transformed but its heart had not changed. Ancient hatreds and suspicions fed new animosities. The Balkans and central Europe alone, he warned, held ample tinder for a new conflagration. Furthermore, he believed that gruesome atrocities, such as those inflicted on Armenia, would multiply so long as others refused to interfere lest they be criticized as meddlers. 'In the next generation,' he told an audience in 1919, 'the rights of nations must be closely defined so that no one nation can contravene the universal human conscience simply because it has the power to do so.' A league of nations, he maintained, would have at least two fundamental purposes. It would help to rectify the errors of the peace settlement and would act as a warden of international law. The alternative was a return to the balance of power, which, he swiftly noted, had already caused 'a collapse of the world amid cries of woe.' Surely, he observed, 'we have had enough of that.'[18]

By this time friends of the league in Britain were urging Falconer and others to organize local support for the cause. In October 1919 Percy Hurd, MP, wrote Sir Robert to tell him of the good work done at Westminster by the league's parliamentary committee. In passing he asked Falconer to speculate on the chances of forming a similar all-party group in the Canadian House of Commons.[19] The president, in responding, was dubious about the possibilities. Indeed, he was 'much disappointed' by the attitude of Liberals who seemed bent on avoiding any foreign commitments. However, he assured Hurd that he and other university leaders stood ready to promote any concrete suggestions as to how the 'League spirit' might be promulgated.[20] Fortunately, he did not have long to wait. Newton Rowell, in fact, was even then in touch with Lord Robert Cecil and other British organizers of the League of Nations Union.[21] The idea was to develop a private Canadian group based on the British model. Working feverishly throughout 1920 and 1921, Rowell enlisted several prominent Canadians in the project. Particularly enthusiastic were members of the old Round Table clubs. Many of them, as much internationalists as imperialists, viewed the scheme as a natural extension of their old work. Thus, W.L. Grant argued that 'the peace of the world depends – so far as human eyes can see – on the League of Nations being made a living reality, on the British Empire taking its proper place in it, and on the prevalence in it of the British spirit.'[22] He had almost taken the words out of Falconer's mouth. In minds such as theirs, the emerging commonwealth would serve its highest purpose if it provided an example of how a multi-racial, multi-national world order could be made to function. The unification of South Africa, co-operation among the new dominions, and dyarchy in India all seemed tangible evidence that these hopes were not in vain. Although ultimately chimerical, these prospects seemed bright enough in 1920, and Falconer, for one, embraced them wholeheartedly. Thus, with Round Tablers Vincent Massey and A.J. Glazebrook, he was listed by Rowell as one of the league's keenest supporters in Toronto.[23]

It should not be imagined, however, that Canadian imperialists gravitated towards the league as a unified body. Colonel Leonard, for example, declined to join the general committee. 'The League,' he told Sir Robert Borden, 'appears to me to have been conceived and drawn up by idealists who do not realize the radical differences in mental and moral make-up of the different races, which differences are I believe, inherent and irradicable [sic].' In addition, Leonard thought that the league and concurrent proposals for a separate Canadian embassy in Washington were indicative of trends likely to disrupt the empire. Finally, he felt that in signing the covenant Canada had assumed obligations that she was 'utterly incapable of carrying out.'[24] While recognizing the sufficiency of these objections, the uncharitable observer might add that with R.M. MacIver on its executive, the league must have seemed doubly suspect to the doughty colonel. In any case, this little episode suggests that one can speak a little too freely perhaps of 'Canadian imperialism' as though it were a monolithic school of thought. Granted, the colonel shared with Falconer, Grant, and others a 'sense of power,' but the goals of power and the vehicles of its expression were not matters of universal agreement. Thus, differences arose which were more than merely tactical in nature. They involved disputes over ends, as well as means. In the postwar era, imperialists fell into at least two camps. There were those like Leonard who, to borrow from Northrop Frye, adopted a 'garrison mentality' towards empire. For them Greater Britain was akin to an Anglo-Saxon fortress, a bulwark against a fundamentally alien and hostile outer world. To those of Falconer's stripe, however, empire was not an end in itself but merely one stage in the general evolution of global integration. Its fulfilment would come only with its absorption in a diversified but harmonious whole.

By the spring of 1921 league recruitment had proceeded far enough to allow formal organizational steps to be taken. Sir Robert Borden, Arthur Meighen, and other prominent political figures gave credibility to the proposed body. Among academic leaders A.W. Currie of McGill, H.M. Tory of Alberta, and Falconer were named to a central committee. Finally, on 31 May the League of Nations Society in Canada was founded at a gala hosted by the governor-general at the Chateau Laurier. Within the year branches popped up in Hamilton, Ottawa, Montreal, Halifax, and Saint John. Falconer chaired the highly active Toronto group. In so many respects an heir of the Round Table, the new society adapted many of the former's tactics to its own purposes. Better publicized and less secretive than the older body, the league's champions nevertheless concentrated on the same stratum of society. Thus, the group poured its chief energies into converting the moulders of public opinion. Members of the provincial and federal legislatures were strenuously lobbied. Executive officers of major national organizations were approached, as were professors and teachers. Monthly bulletins were fired off to all who in any way might induce others to follow.[25] All told, it was a busy time for Falconer and all concerned.

Initial success on the home front was gratifying. In full measure, however, Falconer shared the dismay arising from American failure to ratify the covenant. Wilson, he thought, had made an 'awful mess' of the entire matter.[26] While acknowledging that president's finer attributes, he could only lament that 'Mr Wilson was such a solitary figure and found such difficulty in working with men.' Harsher criticism, however, fell on Senator Lodge, who had done 'very serious injury to the world' out of 'personal antagonism' to the president.[27] Falconer realized, of course, that isolationism was not universally espoused in America. Moreover, he did not consider recent events irreversible. Even so, he remained quietly sceptical of movements south of the border that, in his eyes, posed as pale alternatives to action through the league. Publicly, for example, he praised American efforts at the Washington Conference in the columns of the New York *Herald*.[28] In private, however, he had his doubts. 'In this Disarmament Conference,' he told a Halifax friend, 'it seems to me that the United States is endeavouring to retrieve her error in not joining the League of Nations which her conduct pretty nearly rendered null and void.' Arguing that Americans, rather than Canadians, needed to be awakened to their international obligations, Falconer contended that the latter should concentrate on the league and not be seduced by half measures.[29]

On this point he never wavered. A well-known figure in the United States, in the 1920s he was asked to join several American peace groups. Invariably he declined. Thus, when Minneapolis organizers of the World Peace Union asked for his endorsement, Falconer, while sympathetic, wired that he was unwilling to do anything that might divert attention from the League.[30] Not even a plea from that venerable journal, the *Christian Century*, could sway him. In 1926 its editor, Charles Clayton

Morrison, invited him to write an article seconding a legislative resolution outlawing war. Appealing to Sir Robert's pride, he said: 'your prestige on both sides of the line in international thinking would invest any utterance from you with particular significance.'[31] Although flattered, Falconer politely refused. 'I am aware,' he told Morrison, 'of the desires of a very large number of my best American friends that the United States should also soon become a member of the League, but they tell me that politically this is now hopeless.' In these circumstances, he felt compelled to refrain from expressing 'any opinion as to an effort ... to secure what I think would be better secured through the League of Nations.'[32] A recent trip to Geneva had convinced Falconer that the league, although weakened by America's absence, was still a viable organization and the best vehicle for promoting international harmony.[33] Accordingly, he avoided entanglements in American-based schemes.

However, while urging Canadians to adhere to the 'League spirit,' Falconer never imagined that this was the only way in which they might foster healthy international relations. Thus his devotion to the cause of imperial unity remained as bright as ever. Indeed, he felt no need to choose between these two enthusiasms but tended, instead, to regard them as perfectly compatible. To him the empire was a microcosm of what the league might ultimately become. Therefore he continued to work for the consolidation of both. On one occasion, at least, this took the form of a call for formal action in the imperial sphere, something he had largely avoided in the past. In 1920 he speculated on the possibility of uniting Canada and the West Indies. His thoughts were set forth in a letter to Sir Charles Prestwood Lucas, a former Colonial Office official and currently a leading figure with the Royal Colonial Institute. The islands, he warned Lucas, were in danger of falling into the American orbit as seductive trade links multiplied. Were they to veer even closer to the United States, 'a grievous loss to the British Empire' might result. Was not the time ripe to sponsor their political union with Canada?[34] An experienced hand, Lucas immediately poured cold water on the scheme. Any hint of annexation, he advised, would only provoke unrest in the West Indies.[35] Accepting this reality, a more sober Falconer comforted himself with the thought that islanders would shun absorption by the United States, given that nation's treatment of its own black population.[36] It never occurred to him that they might also spurn Canada for precisely the same reason. After all, the condition of blacks in Nova Scotia was far from idyllic. In any case, he quickly set this whim aside in favour of more promising plans to encourage imperial solidarity.

As of old, he placed his greatest faith in informal links, especially educational ones. Thus, he remained an ardent champion of the Universities Bureau of the British Empire. His commitment was no doubt strengthened when, in 1919, the bureau's secretary mused that the body might one day expand into a 'League of Universities,' capable of furthering the good work begun at Geneva.[37] That was for the future. For the moment, however, the bureau was not without its problems. Chronically short of money, it was also experiencing internal difficulties. In August 1920 Professor J.W. Cunliffe returned to the University of Alberta after a visit to bureau headquarters in London. In a biting letter to H.M. Tory, Alberta's president, he vented serious misgivings about the health of the metropolitan organization. The bureau, he said, 'strikes me as being altogether too bureaucratic in character.' It had the foetid air of a government office rather than the 'active personal feeling' that such a body should exude. For this lack he blamed its secretary, Alex Hill, a man he thought lacked the verve and tact necessary for his post. 'My impression,' he advised Tory, 'is that the spirit as well as the machinery of the present administration is hopeless.'[38] Tory had already confided similar thoughts to Falconer, as had imperial historian A.P. Newton during a recent visit to Toronto.

Sir Robert, however, opposed plans to fire Hill. Personally, he had always enjoyed cordial relations with the central office. Furthermore, he sympathized with a man who had very little scope for initiative within an organization whose only mandate was to arrange meetings and facilitate the exchange of information among autonomous universities round the globe. Clearly, he felt that if the bureau were to lead to greater things, then some of the momentum would have to be supplied by the universities themselves.[39] In a sense, of course, this dilemma was shared by all who sought co-operation within the rapidly changing commonwealth. It was a question of trying to co-ordinate, very late in the day, elements that had long been allowed to mature in relative isolation from each other. The task, however, seemed far from hopeless at the time, and Falconer thought it wrong to load the blame for occasional set-backs on the shoulders of a mere intermediary.

His own response to this challenge was to intensify his personal efforts. Accordingly, recognizing that educational conclaves tended to lapse into considerations of tedious pedagogical detail, he did his best to see that the Congress of the Universities of the Empire of 1921 was occasionally reminded of higher things. The stage, at least, was well tailored to his purpose. Lavish entertainments preceded and followed the formal sessions throughout early July. Delegates were fussed over by service organizations such as the Royal Colonial Institute and the League of the

Empire. Visiting dignitaries were showered with honorary degrees. Falconer himself was so saluted by Oxford and Dublin. The atmosphere, in brief, fairly crackled with imperial bonhomie. Eager to take advantage of the mood, Falconer seized his first opportunity, which came following a speech of welcome by A.J. Balfour at the Savoy Hotel. Responding on behalf of all overseas delegates, Sir Robert intoned a favourite theme. With German universities temporarily out of fashion, the time had come, he argued, to make Britain the educational home of students throughout the empire. He declared, 'I hope that one outcome of the Congress ... will be the creation of a new psychological atmosphere, which will cause the thoughts of the Dominions and of India to turn naturally to the British Universities, and the scholars and scientists of the Homeland to expect that students will come to them from every quarter of the Common-wealth.'[40] In truth, he expected little immediate action. Instead, he was settting out an agenda for the 1920s. The battle over the PH D had been won. Now he wanted to encourage a habit of mind that would lead to its full utilization.

The Universities Bureau and the congresses were means to that end. Throughout the decade Toronto's grant to the bureau was higher than that given by any other participating university.[41] But there were other educational means that could be used to develop imperial consciousness, and Falconer was prepared to try them. Part of his motivation was still supplied by his desire to counter-balance American influence in Canadian higher education. As he told A.B. Macallum in 1920, 'the American Universities are growing rapidly and there will be an exodus to the United States of many of our best young men and women.'[42] Granted, Toronto was making great strides in graduate studies, but there would always be many who wished to travel abroad for their education. In this case he was determined that they should look first to Great Britain. There was, however, at least one major obstacle to their doing so: adequate financial incentives had not accompanied the birth of the British PH D. By the late 1920s patterns of student migration had altered little. Thus, in 1927 Canada and Newfoundland together sent 156 candidates for all degrees to British schools, whereas Australia alone was represented by almost 200.[43] On the other hand, Falconer noted two years later that over 600 Canadians held academic posts in the United States, and this figure did not include the numerous professional people and graduate students who resided there.[44] While many at the time saw this exodus as a contribution to Canadian-American friendship, Falconer regarded it as a 'serious loss' to the dominion.[45]

By 1929 Sir Robert felt that time was running out. Accordingly, in

November he drafted a lengthy memorandum detailing the advantages of transforming London into a centre of graduate work for the whole empire. Illustrating Canadian need, he drew attention to the flood of students southward. Casting an eye on international developments, he noted French efforts to refurbish the Sorbonne as a place attractive to foreign candidates. London, he continued, therefore had to act decisively if it were to emerge as a major educational force on the world stage. Fully co-ordinated, the magnificent resources of the metropolis and those of nearby Oxford and Cambridge represented facilities 'unsurpassed in the world.' Moreover, a large market existed and required only to be stimulated. 'Those who speak the English language,' he wrote passionately, 'if their hereditary or spiritual derivation is British, must in the nature of the case desire that Britain, and especially London, shall not fail to give the lead to their intellectual interests.' The financial burden, he alleged, need not be extreme. It was, instead, largely a question of making better use of existing materials. Funds for scholarships and hostels could be raised privately amid the ranks of the well-to-do. He concluded that the opportunity was there, but it had to be grasped quickly.[46] Understanding the clubbish nature of imperial circles, Falconer sent a draft of this appeal to the governor-general, Lord Willingdon, and then let matters take their course. As expected, Willingdon passed the document on to friends in Britain. Certain of these, to Falconer's initial delight, seized on it with a good deal more than polite interest.

Although eloquent, there was nothing particularly novel in Sir Robert's memorandum. There had been dreams of making London an educational seminary of empire since before the war. Indeed, groups such as the Royal Colonial Institute had adopted the notion as one of their raisons d'être and an 'imperial studies movement' had retained at least a shadowy existence into the later 1920s.[47] Talk, therefore, had been plentiful, but relatively little had actually been achieved. Interest, however, was reviving even as Falconer took up his pen. Metropolitan planners were projecting renewed schemes, some of which meshed nicely with Falconer's. For instance, plans were afoot to confer broader management powers on the University of London over a variety of hitherto independent bodies. As a start, it absorbed the London Day Training College for Teachers. The idea was to duplicate the success of Columbia's Faculty of Education and turn the new department into 'a great educational laboratory for the Empire.'[48] At the same time it was announced that a new teaching hospital would be built and made attractive to overseas medical students. The latter development drew particularly high praise from Falconer.[49] Under these circumstances, his memorandum was assured a warm welcome among its intended readers.

British enthusiasts, however, tended to focus on one particular suggestion in Falconer's general statement. Among many other items, he had underscored the desirability of constructing hostels, so that overseas students could enjoy at least a taste of college life. An influential committee in London had come to the same conclusion and was in the process of raising money. The group included H.A.L. Fisher, Leopold Amery, Max Aitken, Sir William Beveridge, and others, who quickly saw to it that attention was drawn to the supportive words in Falconer's circular.[50] In return they asked Sir Robert to enlist Canadian aid for the 'London House' project. A site in Bloomsbury had already been purchased, but extensive construction would require considerable fresh capital.[51] In October 1930, however, Falconer gloomily reported that little could be expected from Canada, since the depression was drying up pools of ready cash.[52] Nevertheless he was able to provide some crucial assistance through his contacts in New York. Thus, F.P. Keppel of the Carnegie Corporation was persuaded by Sir Robert to channel some of that foundation's money into the scheme.[53] London House was duly opened in 1932, and Falconer was no doubt pleased. Still, he must have regretted that more was not done to fulfil his principal recommendation that travelling scholarships be significantly increased. At any rate, although some of his efforts had paid dividends over the years, by the time of his retirement his dream of an empire knit together by legions of London-trained graduates was still a long way from realization. Lack of co-ordination at the centre had been a constant problem. The depression had added further difficulties. But above all, dominion and colonial universities, like their parent states, had generally preferred to nurture independent as opposed to pooled resources. To a degree, Falconer had run against the grain.

Throughout much of his imperial thought and action, Falconer's continued ambivalence towards the United States was plainly evident. Nevertheless, even as he strove to bolster imperial unity, he also laboured hard to foster a spirit of Anglo-American concord. Such an entente, he thought, was a necessary precondition of general stability and well-being. Americans might shun global commitments, but he continued to hope that they could be induced to play a more constructive role closer to home. Moreover, Canadians, he thought, had unique qualifications and a compelling moral obligation to serve as intermediaries between the two great branches of the British family. Above all, they could interpret the one for the other and so heighten awareness of their mutual interests and traditions. Falconer, of course, was neither the first nor the last among his countrymen to entertain such a vision, but he was one of the most vocal and persistent promoters of the idea in the 1920s. Although he recognized that a university president could have little influence on high diplomacy, this thought scarcely bothered him, since he felt that the real work of persuasion had to be done at the level of popular perception. Accordingly, he defined his personal task as an educative one in the broadest sense.

That it would not be an easy one was readily apparent. Canadians, he realized, would have to overcome home-grown prejudices before they could function effectively as honest brokers. In particular, they would have to forgo a penchant for blanket criticism of the United States, a deeply ingrained habit which threatened to become a blind reflex. At times Falconer was provoked to anger when he found this cast of mind on his own doorstep. In 1920, for example, Toronto organizers had cancelled a planned address by Jane Addams, an American expert on social service. Miss Addams, it seemed, had alienated some Canadians by calling for a negotiated peace at the height of the war. Hard feelings on this score were soon linked to complaints that the University of Toronto was importing far too many guest speakers from the south. Sir Robert reacted to these barbs sharply. In the first place, he was outraged, but not entirely surprised, by community efforts to muffle free expression; but he also deplored the unconstructive anti-Americanism revealed by this episode. 'Surely' he wrote to the editor of *Varsity*,

they (Americans) are to be welcomed as enabling us to get a better understanding of one another. The well-being of the world depends upon the increase of good-will between the British Empire and the United States. At present the enemies of this entente cordiale *are seeking to produce a reaction and none are more delighted than pro-Germans and Sinn Feiners at sectional differences which they hope will serve to cause estrangement between the British and American peoples.*[54]

While fully aware of America's shortcomings, Falconer none the less sought to prevent such a falling-out. Thus, he tried to break down some of the stereotypes that fed prejudice and suspicion within the English-speaking world.

Ever the inveterate traveller, it was a rare year when Falconer did not address several convocations and service groups across North America. Almost as regular were his appearances in Britain. Increasingly, wherever he went he raised the issue of Anglo-American comity. The second Congress of the Universities of the Empire, for example, gave him a splendid opportunity. Invited to address the gathering, he surprised some by dwelling, not on a Canadian theme, but on the achievements of the

United States in the field of higher education. Well aware of a British tendency to trivialize American contributions in that sphere, he was anxious to paint a clearer picture for his audience. On other occasions he voiced misgivings about certain features of American university practice. At the congress, however, he sounded a highly positive note. Thus, he lauded American reverence for higher education. 'Has democracy,' he asked rhetorically, 'ever shown itself to better advantage than in the readiness with which States, such as Michigan, Illinois, Wisconsin and California make grants ... for the maintenance of their Universities?' While admitting that the cultural sea on which these schools floated was not as broad and deep as that in Europe, he bade his listeners remember that few interpreters of the classics had proved as adept as Basil Gildersleeve of Johns Hopkins or Paul Shorey of Chicago. As for the sciences, Falconer described American scholars and their facilities as a match for the best in the world. Comparing the American university with the Renaissance academy, he declared that it too was 'expressing in its national form the ancient and perpetual ideals of humanism and science.'[55] This ringing tribute came from a man whose knowledge of the subject could not be denied. In a sense it was Falconer's British debut as an interpreter of America.

An even better chance to disseminate his message soon cropped up. In 1923 he was invited to take up the Sir George Watson chair of American history, literature, and institutions for 1925. Offered a generous fee and travelling expenses to Britain, he was asked to discourse on a topic of his own choosing. Previous incumbents had included two Britons, Lord Bryce and A.F. Pollard and two Americans, Presidents Arthur Hadley of Yale and Nicholas Butler of Columbia. In approaching Falconer, organizers were seeking to balance perspectives by appointing a Canadian. Their only stipulation was that he address himself to some aspect of Canadian-American relations.[56] Sir Robert eagerly accepted this spacious platform. 'I am sure,' he replied, 'this is a recognition on the part of your Committee that Canada may be influential in increasing understanding and good-will between Britain and the United States.' He therefore proposed that his lectures take 'Canada as an Interpreter' as their central theme.[57]

Sailing from Halifax on 30 March 1925, he and Sophie went first to the French Riviera for a fortnight of sun and relaxation. Then they were off to Britain and a hectic round of activity. The strain proved to be considerable. Rather than settling in one place, Falconer delivered each of the six Watson lectures at a different university. Such a program, of course, guaranteed maximum exposure, but it also meant that he was constantly on the move, criss-crossing the United Kingdom from London, Cambridge, and Oxford, to Bristol, Glasgow, and Edinburgh. The basic itinerary was not too taxing, but the numerous side trips to address service groups left him barely a moment to himself. Gradually, both he and Sophie were worn down. Eventually the two fell victim to particularly nasty spring colds that confined Lady Falconer to an Edinburgh bed for the better part of a week. Under these circumstances, as Sir Robert moaned to Walter Murray, it was difficult 'being constantly on one's mettle.' Nevertheless, although 'greatly under the weather,' he managed to honour all his appointments, despite at times being 'fearful of not being able to pull through.'[58]

The lectures that a sneezing Falconer delivered amounted to an extended exercise in comparative history. At the time of their conception he had told British contacts that he wanted to offer something different from what he had hitherto seen in print. Aware of his own limitations, however, he had added that he 'could hardly venture to undertake to make any real contribution to the understanding of American and Canadian history as such.'[59] In the sense that he did little or no primary research, this was certainly true. But he did try to cast information gleaned from published sources in a new light. Indeed, in adopting a North American-wide framework for the study of his subject, he anticipated many of the themes that professional historians, such as J.B. Brebner and J.T. Shotwell, would later examine more systematically.[60] This is not to suggest that Falconer fathered the continentalist school of North American history. Rather, it is merely to note that Sir Robert, who was well acquainted with Shotwell and Brebner, shared in the internationalist spirit that led naturally to this perspective. His Watson lectures, in other words, were an early manifestation of a growing general phenomenon.

Tracing his theme, Falconer first drew attention to the formative influence of American events on the rise of Canadian nationalism and Canadian institutions.[61] Next he discoursed at length on the trading links between the two peoples. Here he argued that the spectacular economic success of the United States, in conferring wealth and recognition on the republic, had taken the edge off America's territorial ambition and thereby greatly eased its relations with Canada.[62] Rejecting an exploitive interpretation, Falconer maintained that 'the interdependence of Canada and the United States economically makes for the permanence of good will.'[63] There was, however, more to North American amity than crude self-interest; thus he emphasized the bonds of culture and blood that linked the two northern peoples, which cross-fertilization had done much to encourage. Loyalists were merely the first of a long line of Americans to settle in Canada. Similarly, thousands of Canadians had moved south and were particularly welcome because they helped augment the British streak in the American population.[64] All told, said Falconer, Canadians and Americans were inextricably bound together by historical ties which spanned the full range of experience.

Not for a moment, however, did he suggest that they were or would become indistinguishable. Indeed, he had harsh words for Goldwin Smith and others who prophesied full continental integration.[65] Canadians, although 'Americans,' remained a distinct people. The large francophone element guaranteed this uniqueness, as did long-term membership in the British empire. On the whole, he contended, Canadians were less provincial than Americans, less fearful of new ideas, and less prone to religious extremism.[66] Drawing out this litany of contrasts, Falconer also identified major differences between Canadian and American educational philosophies.[67] In like fashion, he could not agree with those, such as Roy P. Baker, who held that 'the literature of the United States was the literature of Canada.'[68] A large number of Canadian intellectuals, said Falconer, were British-trained and continued to look across the Atlantic for their inspiration. As well, he observed that Canadian prose, poetry, and painting were beginning to draw more heavily on local scenery and history. America, he admitted, had a profound impact on Canadian popular culture, but he asserted that 'in general it may be affirmed that the United States has not been a primary source of influence on Canada in respect of literature and the fine arts.'[69] While this was perhaps an overstatement, the Group of Seven, had they been asked, might well have agreed.

Noting significant differences, Falconer nevertheless returned again and again to the argument that 'Americans of Anglo-Saxon origin and English-speaking Canadians are more alike than any other separate peoples.'[70] Thus, as he turned from the past to consider the present and future, he declared that Canada's role would be to serve as an interpreter between the United States and the empire. Through contact with the dominion, Britons would gain insight into American manners, conventions, and habits of mind. For their part, Americans, in understanding Canada, could be led to see that the commonwealth was not the empire of 1776, but an altogether more liberal entity. In the end, he speculated, 'the British and American peoples will be united effectively only through mutual understanding, not diplomacy.'[71] Working to encourage this happy consummation, Canada would fulfil a lofty historical purpose. The dominion, he concluded, 'in her history, her character and her position holds a unique privilege, and, if she takes advantage of it, the world of the future will judge that she will have played a part given to few nations in the progress of humanity.'[72] Such, in his eyes, were some of the further implications of 'the sense of power.'

Falconer considered that spring well spent, despite his near exhaustion. 'A good reception everywhere' had helped spur him on.[73] Sensing what he thought was the mood of the hour, he felt that Britons, as never before, were eager to solidify overseas friendships. The war, subsequent economic hardships, and escalating labour unrest had gone a long way, he asserted, towards deflating insular smugness. Describing the atmosphere to Willison, Falconer held that only isolated 'die-hards' still clung to a 'colonial' vision of the empire. It would, he admitted, take some time to dispel British ignorance of conditions abroad. But the new mood offered hope.[74] Indeed, Sir Robert was certain that in a changing Britain the Canadian interpreter would find a growing and attentive audience.

Across the Atlantic his words reached Americans, when the Watson lectures were published under the title *The United States as a Neighbour*. Widely reviewed, the book was generally considered a positive contribution to Canadian-American relations.[75] The *New York Times* praised Falconer's 'skill and discernment' and declared that the section on Canada's role as an interpreter was 'full of political good sense and good feeling.'[76] C.D. Allin, in the *American Political Science Review,* accurately described the work as 'essentially popular in nature' but quickly added that the author had proved himself 'a keen critic and observer of our national psychology and *kultur.*' Allin thought Sir Robert 'sympathetic,' 'fairminded,' and 'discriminating,' especially in his analysis of the 'weakness and intolerance of American democracy.' However, as for the suggestion that Canada could serve as a North Atlantic linchpin, the reviewer had reservations. 'It is somewhat doubtful,' he wrote, 'if many of the Canadian public have yet risen to this high statesmanlike concept, if one can judge from the utterances of many of the politicians and papers during the recent electoral contest.'[77] Harvey M. Watts, who assessed the book for the *Forum and Century,* later wrote directly to Falconer to voice similar congratulations and misgivings. The tone, he said, had come as 'a balm' to one who had endured 'the unparalleled brutality of British criticism' while visiting Canada during the election. He recalled, moreover, hearing a speech by the touring Anglican bishop of London who had described Americans as 'the enemy.' Outraged, Watts had decamped for Philadelphia and advised his sister to sell off her 250 acres of prime Ontario land. 'After long editorial experience,' he told Falconer, 'I have come to the conclusion that the case is hopeless; that even your good offices will not change the Empire Loyalists and that they certainly have been a curse on Canada.' Still, like virtually all other reviewers, he applauded Sir Robert's sterling effort to heal the old breach: 'You have tried in naught to extenuate Canadian hostility, nor to set down aught in malice in stating our position.'[78] In reply Falconer acknowledged that hasty generalizations were often heard, but he disputed the notion that Canadians were the sole offenders. In any case, he maintained that 'it remains with us if good relations shall continue and we in the educated classes have more in common than any other peoples, and should not be too much disturbed by ordinary newspaper talk or by what thoughtless people say.'[79]

Even before the lectures were formally published, invitations from American groups began to flood Falconer's office. In September 1925 he declined offers from the New York State Bar Association and the George Washington Sulgrave Institution. Pleading fatigue, he was also being cautious on a point of decorum. 'I suppose,' he told his would-be hosts, 'that neither Dr Butler nor Dr Hadley received any such recognition on their return, and it would I am afraid not be becoming for me to do so.'[80] By 1926, however, he was ready to resume his personal mission. An ideal opportunity presented itself in December. The English-Speaking Union, headquartered in New York, sought his services at a gala dinner. Catching wind of this invitation, the American Association of Insurance Presidents asked him to address their luncheon on the same day. Hustling off to a wintry New York City, Falconer regaled the insurance men with some brief observations on the chief characteristics of North American civilization.[81] His most pointed and ringing phrases, however, were carefully saved for that evening's gathering at the Biltmore Hotel. Hailed as the author of *The United States as a Neighbour,* Sir Robert delivered a message that was the mirror image of his Watson lectures. Thus, he sought to introduce his listeners to a clearer vision of the mind of imperial Britain. After underlining recent pronouncements which made it plain that the dominions enjoyed 'the status of equal nationhood' within a flexible commonwealth, he dwelt on the common ideals and shared trust that united those of British heritage everywhere. All branches of that global family, he observed, spoke a simple and direct language which revealed the 'forthrightness of character from which the words issue.' Britain and the United States, he argued, shouldered a general trust for their various colonial peoples. As such, he contended, they should be singers of a common 'song,' one compacted of 'freedom, humanity and reverence for the divine.' He exclaimed, 'these are the notes that we wish to join in sending throughout the world.'[82]

He emphasized, however, that racial intolerance and the use of force had no place in the pursuit of that mission. Instead, he argued that differences among peoples would remain and should be cherished: 'It takes all the nations of the earth to make up a complete humanity.'[83] He merely held that in purifying their own 'song' and in cultivating the arts of friendship, English-speakers could lead the world by example. In essence, this was the core of the message that he repeated throughout the 1920s. Canadians therefore were told that, although they were a 'distinct type,' they belonged 'essentially to this continent' and were in the broadest sense 'Americans.'[84] Above all, he continued to deride isolationism as folly in a world grown so interdependent that a shock in any one region quickly registered around the globe.[85] Altogether, he went beyond many later continentalist historians in embracing an enlarged vision of North America's role in the world.

Meanwhile, as he became an ever more prominent figure, honours were heaped upon him both as an internationalist and as an educator. The Watson chair afforded early recognition, as did a string of honorary British degrees. Americans were no less generous in their accolades. On one occasion the University of Michigan asked him to stand in as orator of the day for the president of the United States.[86] In 1926 Union College of Schenectady made him its honorary chancellor to mark his contributions to international amity.[87] An LL D degree from Harvard was, in part, similarly inspired. Even higher praise came in 1929, when Falconer was appointed to the joint commission that monitored relations between the United States and Paraguay under a treaty signed in 1914. Its members included the presidents of the two nations, two of their personal nominees, and a commissioner at large named by both sides. Sir Robert was invited to fill the latter post for 1930. Assured by the American chargé d' affaires that no taxing duties would be entailed, Falconer happily accepted this 'high honour.'[88]

Of all the honours bestowed on him, however, none moved him as deeply as the one that issued from his alma mater. On 3 April 1929, while he and Sophie were vacationing in Atlantic City, he received letters offering him the principalship of the University of Edinburgh. Caught off guard and genuinely surprised, he felt the powerful tug of mixed loyalties and wrote immediately to Flavelle for advice. The offer, he recorded, was 'unanimous and cordial.' A handsome salary and a house added to the attraction. The lord provost and others spoke 'appreciatively' of Sir Robert and thought his vast knowledge of the North American scene an incomparable asset. Stunned and exalted in the same moment, Falconer confessed to Flavelle: 'In my wildest dreams as an undergraduate during my six years in the old grey city I never romanced with such an idea.' Now, all at once, he was being offered 'the greatest academic honour that could be paid to me.' The temptation to accept, fired by rekindled allegiance, was almost overwhelming. And yet, as he pondered the issue more carefully, he admitted that both he and Sophie were inclined to stay in Toronto. 'Canada,' he told Sir Joseph, 'is my own country and will I hope be the country of our sons.' Furthermore, at sixty-two, he felt that any influence he might have would be greater at home than that which he would enjoy in Scotland. He recognized, however, that the governors at Toronto might be happy to have him take up the post: it would be a feather in their cap and would make way for a new and younger man as president. Flavelle was asked to comment.[89] Meanwhile Falconer pounded the boardwalk as he more deeply searched his own heart.

His mind must have flown back to 1907, when another cable had disrupted a vacation and opened up a brilliant new vista. The parallels were striking in all but one important detail. Falconer was no longer a vigorous forty. After much painful indecision, therefore, he wrote to Sir Alfred Ewing, Edinburgh's current head, to decline the handsome offer. The call of the blood, he conceded, was compelling. So was the chance to recharge his 'flagging energies' in a new environment. Furthermore, he believed that in Edinburgh he would live 'in an atmosphere of more bracing academic freedom than here.' But some 'hard facts' outweighed all these pleasant considerations. Thus Sir Robert was forced to admit that his 'elasticity' was not what it had been. Indeed, he confessed that he was looking forward to retirement in the not distant future. Above all, he was concerned about security in his old age. A generous pension guaranteed by the Carnegie Foundation and the governors was too much to cast aside so late in life. Having virtually no private means, he felt that within eight or nine years of going to Edinburgh he would find himself out to pasture and 'in very difficult circumstances.' Accordingly, he had decided to stay in Toronto.[90] Nevertheless, he would long remember the invitation as 'a fine imperial gesture' and 'the greatest honour of my life.'[91]

As luck would have it, this decision worked to the benefit of all parties concerned. Edinburgh appointed the vigorous Sir Thomas Holland in Falconer's stead, while, within a year of refusing the offer, Sir Robert was felled by a serious heart attack. At first he entertained hopes of a rapid and full recovery. In September 1930 the doctors assured him that a return to health was merely 'a matter of time.' By then, recuperating at Huntsville, he was able to walk 'short distances in the open on level ground' and had even taken part in celebrations attending the marriage of his eldest son, Gilbert.[92] In his heart, however, he knew that time was catching up with him. Writing to Stanley Mackenzie in December, he congratulated the latter on his retirement and reflected on the fading generation of which they were a part. Their whole group, he observed, was leaving harness. Mackenzie had resigned at Dalhousie, Tory had left Alberta for a government post, Bruce Taylor had departed Queen's, and Murray was thinking of giving up his position at Saskatchewan. 'In some sense,' said Sir Robert, 'we have made an epoch of our own, and I doubt whether our successors will have as much real intimacy as we have enjoyed.' Probably, he ventured, the country would be better for a change. Wistfully he concluded, 'has not our epoch, almost without our being aware of it, been drawing to a close?'[93]

The various crises of 1931 did little to ease his physical torments. Having no desire to linger on as a 'delicate man,' in June he announced his intention to resign. The governors and the premier had already advised him that there was no need for him to worry about the financial future.[94] As good as their word, in the end Falconer had a yearly pension of $10,000 from all sources combined.[95] No sooner was his resignation tabled than testimonials poured in. The governors remarked that 'the success of the new form of University government depended to a very large extent upon the new President.' Since 1907, they continued, Sir Robert had been more than equal to the task. Fairness, unselfishness, patience and loyalty were noted as his trademarks.[96] The chancellor of Syracuse University, a Varsity old boy, wrote: 'We have been proud of your scholarship, your dignity and your genuine manliness as President of our Alma Mater.'[97] Rush Rhees, President of the University of Rochester, observed to F.C.A Jeanneret that 'we consider your man Falconer the outstanding university president in America.'[98] And so it went. For his part, Sir Robert was conscious primarily of the tremendous weight that seemed suddenly to fall from his shoulders. To one professor he confided: 'While I shall regret to leave my colleagues, it will be a relief to lay down my duties.'[99]

A rousing farewell dinner at the Royal York Hotel on 16 December attracted over 500 guests. During a speech in which he surveyed the previous twenty-five years, 'the vast and learned audience hung on every word Sir Robert spoke.' Typically, he urged younger scholars to pursue 'without haste but without rest ... those entrancing but illusive visions of pure learning.'[100] There were other dinners and other speeches. Unfortunately, there were also further medical problems as first Robert, then Sophie, underwent surgery for the removal of tonsils and a gall bladder, respectively. Adding to the drain on his slim reserves, in March Falconer was bedridden with influenza. Under these circumstances his words of the previous November to Archie MacMechan acquired added force: 'I have had a happy life, a very happy life, though by no means an easy one.'[101] Understandably, as his rewarding but often turbulent career drew to a close, Falconer finally embraced retirement as a sweet release from care. The prospect, after all, held no horrors for a man whose vision of life had always extended far beyond his office walls.

CHAPTER XII

Emeritus

Unlike many an old war horse put out to honourable pasture, the now president emeritus had no itch to return to harness. He had followed the drum long enough. On the other hand, he had never been the sort to loll about in a state of gracious inactivity. Given free rein, liberated from the thousand and one demands of administrative routine, he viewed retirement as an opportunity rather than a curse. Of course less than perfect health imposed some annoying restrictions, but he had no intention of frittering away the precious hours left to him. Taking first things first, he and Sophie spent a few months settling into their new home at 81 Glengowan Road. Then it was down to work. For years a frustrated Falconer had watched as a growing body of biblical literature accumulated while he, distracted, had tended to the needs of the University of Toronto. Indeed, it had been one of his few regrets that of necessity he had lost intimate contact with the field of scholarship that had so fired his imagination in youth. Now, with time to spare, he plunged joyfully again into that deepening pool; not with abandon, but with a clear sense of purpose.

His purpose, however, was not defined by issues at the very cutting edge of contemporary religious thought. These had been raised by Karl Barth and the prophets of what would soon be called 'neo-orthodoxy.' That Swiss thinker, far more concerned with meaning than with attribution, urged men to take a theological approach to the Bible. Inspiring followers and opponents alike to ask primarily spiritual questions, Barth had helped set the main agenda in a troubled age. Although awake to the importance of such matters, Falconer was not theologically oriented. A biblical critic, his skills and interests were historical and philological in nature. Thus, while at the heart of affairs in the 1890s, by the 1930s he was neither equipped nor inclined to enter into the central debates of the era. Even so, he was no fossilized dilettante. Indeed, in choosing to investigate the origin, purpose, and character of the pastoral Epistles, he was tackling a difficult and demanding task which had long engaged the attention of serious scholars and would do so again.[1]

The pastorals, so named because of their obvious concern for orthodoxy and decorum, comprise three supposedly Pauline epistles: First Timothy, Second Timothy, and Titus. The mystery surrounding them involved problems that offered Falconer full scope for the exercise of his particular talents. Given in Paul's name, the letters, nevertheless, differ in language and in thought from acknowledged Pauline writings. Moreover, they suggest a chronology at odds with accepted descriptions of Paul's movements as registered in Acts. The fundamental questions, then, concerned authorship, reliability, and interpretation. The challenge, in short, was strikingly similar to that which Falconer had faced in dealing with Second Peter and may have provided the initial spark of attraction for him. He began wading through the sources while still at Pine Hill, only to be sidetracked by the call to Toronto. In 1932, scanning now yellowed notes, he was dissatisfied with the tentative analysis he had launched so long ago and decided to start afresh. Accordingly, for four years he immersed himself in the documents and secondary literature, intent on producing a full-scale commentary of his own.

The result of this foray was the publication in 1937 of *The Pastoral Epistles*, Falconer's magnum opus as a biblical scholar.[2] The work included a new translation rendered by the author who glossed his text with elaborate notes designed to clarify troublesome passages. In an introduction running to some seventy-two tightly written pages, Falconer analysed the style, language, structure, and purpose of the epistles. While indulging in the minutia of word-counting, he also rose to a higher plane. Thus, for example, he drew attention to the concept of *eusebeia*, which he alleged was a unifying factor in the letters.[3] Denoting 'piety' or 'godliness,' *eusebeia*, he argued, accurately reflected the changing religious atmosphere of the late apostolic age. It implied, he said, 'a reverent, worshipful attitude of heart' which the author or authors tried to inculcate.[4] This attitude, he maintained, betokened the more settled piety of an era in which 'the earlier rapture of mystical faith, as it is seen in the great Epistles of Paul, is passing into eclipse.'[5] The pastorals, therefore, had been written rather late in the day and included a good deal of non-Pauline material. Unlike many, however, Falconer was not convinced that they were the work of an obscure pseudonymist who had merely stirred a few Pauline 'fragments' into a questionable stew of his own concoction.[6] On the contrary, as Sir Robert noted in his preface: 'They appear to me to give glimpses of the life of the Apostle Paul and of the Pauline tradition which are afforded nowhere else.' Dissecting each letter in great detail, he argued that Paul had written part of one himself and that sections of the rest had either been dictated by the Apostle, or were the records of his conversations with disciples.[7] Later, all three were edited by a single person 'who gave them much of the unity in language and outlook which they possess.'[8] They assumed final form, he contended, shortly after the Gospel of Luke and the Acts of the Apostles appeared and bore some striking resemblances to these major works in terms of language and ideas.[9] Altogether, therefore, while stating his case in cautious terms, Falconer maintained that the pastorals offered important clues to an understanding of the later Paul and the early church.

Contemporary reaction to the book was generally positive, despite the fact that few reviewers accepted his argument concerning authorship. The problem of the pastorals, said the *Times Literary Supplement,* was almost as intractable as the mystery of Edwin Drood. Noting recent contributions from P.N. Harrison, F.J. Badcock, and others, the reviewer declared that 'the final word has not yet been spoken ... The same must be said of Sir Robert Falconer's interesting thesis.' Questioning Falconer's dating and his tendency to compartmentalize small sections of the epistles, he quipped: 'Not all of the conclusions reached ... could be substantiated in a court of law.' Even so, he felt that enough of a case had been made to cast doubt on the tendency of modern scholars to assign a very late date to the letters. Furthermore, he applauded Falconer for recognizing that the pastorals did not record the existence of a completed church hierarchy. Finally, he said of the book that 'as a piece of painstaking and original research it deserves high praise.'[10]

In a more detailed critique, E.F. Scott, himself a noted proponent of the 'fragments' theory, also rejected Falconer's solution to the authorship question. Quickly and generously, however, he added that the issue was a relatively minor one. Indeed, he chided others who dwelt on that puzzle while ignoring the larger value of the Epistles as a record of Christian history at one of its most critical moments. 'It is the merit of the present book,' he proclaimed, 'that it concentrates on the really vital questions.' Referring to Falconer's analysis of *eusebeia*, Scott commented: 'For the sake of this discussion alone the book will be indispensable to all future students.' The section on genealogies he described as 'a little masterpiece of philological and historical research.' Sir Robert, he continued, demonstrated 'the patience and honesty of the true scholar.' As evidence he noted how Falconer went 'out of his way repeatedly to supply the evidence on which we might build some other theory than his own.'[11] An experienced hand, Sir Robert was probably satisfied with these evaluations. Had he lived, however, he would no doubt have been delighted when, in 1982, C.F.D. Moule cited his work approvingly, while arguing that Luke had composed the pastorals at the living Paul's personal request.[12]

As he laboured to produce this treatise, Falconer's health slowly deteriorated. In 1934 a mild case of diabetes was added to his other ailments. Still, his heart seemed to have stabilized for the time being, and, all things considered, he was 'feeling well enough.'[13] At times, however, he reflected on the inexorable march of time and lapsed into wistful musing about 'a better world to come.' Confiding such thoughts to Walter Murray, he wrote:

Why should we not imagine that future in terms of the best things we have known here, our greatest joys and purest hopes? Memory means much, but the present so soon becomes the past that we at our age are apt to live too much in that memory. And I find it so elusive and so unsatisfactory, so full of that which one did very badly. Really, I never had the courage to do what it was in me to do. So I look to the future with much hope: there will be a new chance, and we shall take with us the best that is in us. That at least is what I believe. How short is the step between belief and knowledge ...[14]

Yet, while occasionally speculating on his eternal reward, Falconer still felt very much a part of the life he saw around him. Thus, in 1935 he accepted the presidency of the Canadian Institute for International Affairs.[15] In like manner, he regularly attended sessions of the Royal Society, and his activities on behalf of the League of Nations Society scarcely diminished. Speaking engagements continued to lure him far afield. 1936 was an especially hectic year: touring the prairies to deliver convocation addresses and promote the league, he visited Winnipeg, Regina, Saskatoon, Calgary, and Edmonton. A week in the company of Walter Murray was a tonic. By the time he and Sophie reached Edmonton, however, Falconer was nearing the end of his tether. 'Their commencement,' he recalled, 'went off well and though it was a hot afternoon and the gown was heavy, I got through 25 minutes without too much fatigue.'[16] Surprisingly he rallied when, after crossing the mountains, they descended on Vancouver. A side trip to Victoria proved positively bracing. The colouring of the city, he observed, was 'gorgeous.' 'It must be,' he wrote, 'an ideal place for the *Emeriti*, if they have some friends here and not too much surplus energy.'[17] Although sorely tempted to sink his lot with these geriatric lotus-eaters, Falconer had time only to pause before being whisked off to Vancouver and yet another league luncheon. Arriving home late in May he splurged, taking two full days of rest. Then he was on to Ottawa for a general meeting of the league's Canadian friends.[18] Meanwhile he was recruited to serve on a special committee studying adult education. Given this demanding round, it is a wonder that he found time to write *The Pastoral Epistles* at all.

In the long term, of course, the pace was just too much for him. His heart rebelled in December 1936. Ten weeks of absolute rest saved Falconer from total enfeeblement, but he was forced to recognize that his strength was much less than he had imagined. Following this confinement he was permitted 'to go out for a drive nearly every day and walk quietly round the garden.' The doctor told him that he had made a remarkable recovery, but Sir Robert admitted to Murray that he would have to 'guard against fatigue and excitement' in the future. 'The public appearances,' he lamented, 'will henceforth be merely memories.'[19] Fortunately Sophie was well able to care for him. Following the removal of a long-troublesome gall bladder, she felt rejuvenated. Accompanying Robert on his many travels, she had also nurtured her own interests including a leading role in the Canadian Girl Guides. Indeed, Falconer must have sometimes envied her reborn vigour. Although regaining some lost ground, he did not expect, henceforth, to be able 'to do more than meet people and listen.'[20] For a man of his mental energy and moral enthusiasm, this prospect must have been chilling.

His solution, of course, was to ignore infirmity as much as possible and to press on with the business of living. After all, periods of enforced relaxation were not wholly unpalatable when passed in the proper surroundings. Thus it was that in 1937 Falconer took the first of what would become habitual winter treks to Florida. Drawn by the sun and the companionship of the Murrays, he came to glory in 'the ripples of the Gulf Stream.' With Sophie at the wheel, he enjoyed the long drives and the chance to visit universities along the way. Decked out in a Palm Beach suit and the inevitable straw hat, he was becoming quite man of leisure. Lake Worth, Daytona Beach, and similar Florida locales became familiar haunts. By 1939 he was part of the little migrant colony of retired Canadians who, on leaving for home, regularly pledged to meet again next year. In the off-season, when the humid summers of southern Ontario drove sensible persons to distraction, Sir Robert could be found by the shores of Lake Vernon, his Huntsville retreat. It was an altogether pleasant round and Falconer enjoyed it to the full. But occasionally he resurfaced as a public man. Old habits died hard.

April 1938 found him in Houston, Texas, a guest of the Rice Institute. The thermometer readings alternately soared and plummeted, and as the air hung stiflingly still one moment only to be whipped into icy gales the next, Falconer delivered the inaugural version of the Rockwell lectures.[21] Given over three evenings, his presentation took the form of autobiography. In the published version, *Religion on My Life's Road,* Sir Robert candidly discussed the many factors that had shaped his own religious outlook. He clearly enjoyed this structured reminiscing about his father, Trinidad, and his happy student years. As he moved closer to the present, however, his focus grew less personal and his tone more sombre. The Florida sun had not blinded him to ominous developments in contemporary Europe. Shaken by what he saw, Falconer had begun to question moral progress more than was his wont. 'Savage passions,' he warned, 'slumber so lightly, awaiting only appeals to self-interest or suspicion to be aroused.' Nor, lamentably, was there any lack of those who would play upon these feelings. Europe, indeed, was 'yielding to the impulses of a barbaric mind,' spurred on by dictators whose only genius was 'an untutored naturalism.' As always, Falconer depicted such events primarily in moral terms. 'Superficially,' he argued, 'the contest may seem to be one between Naziism [sic], Fascism, or materialistic Communism on the one side and Democracy on the other. But it reaches down far further: the savage, primitive nature of man is in deadly wrestle with the cultural accomplishment of his higher spirit.'

Sniffing powder on the wind, he flinched at the prospect of yet another, seemingly inevitable war. The last great conflict, he noted, had been fought in the name of freedom, and yet, he continued, there was probably less freedom in 1938 than in 1913. War, he therefore observed, must often seem worse than the disease that spawned it. Still, he asked: 'might we not now be in a still worse case if we had refused the issue?' Evidently Falconer was emotionally girding himself as well as his audience to face another cataclysm. Typically, however, he refused to end on a sour note. 'I do not,' he said, 'yield to despair in regard either to myself or to my fellow mortals.' Hope remained so long as some clung to the ideal: 'I find my assurance in the steadfast truths of the moral firmament, which are mere outliers of light in the nearer reaches of an infinite spiritual universe.' His was still a message of comfort as he looked to the long run of human history. For the short term, however, Falconer was less optimistic.[22]

Next year, when Europe finally plunged over the brink of war, Sir

Robert was acutely depressed. Once again, he had no doubt that Britain and France were in the right. 'Without their resistance,' he told Walter Murray, 'Hitlerism like a cancer would have eaten into the life of our Western World.' But he prayed that hostilities would not last long enough to erode the spiritual inhibitions that alone held man's darker nature in check. The experience of the drawn-out First World War had to be avoided. Fortunately it seemed to him that the allies were far better prepared than they had been in 1914. So he hoped for the best. There was personal relief, at least, in the fact that his two sons, while volunteering, had both been rejected by the armed forces. Gilbert, now a prominent physician, was told to train more doctors. The eager Bobby, an engineer, was considered essential by Ontario Hydro, whose leaders, unlike the army, cared not a whit about his flat feet. Mercifully, therefore, Falconer did not have to live with the spectre of personal tragedy as the legions clashed in Europe.[23] For himself, Sir Robert had decided to forgo the pleasures of Palm Beach that winter. 'During war-time,' he told Murray, 'one wants to be with one's own people.'[24]

Hitler's lightning conquest of Denmark, Holland, and Belgium and the ensuing collapse of France dashed Falconer's dreams of a short and decisive war. Canada, it now seemed obvious, was in for a long haul again. With the Vichy regime blessed by the pope, he was worried that opinion in French Canada might turn against the national effort. Indeed, to him the whole situation called for far more dynamic leadership than Ottawa seemed able to supply. The government, he thought, was acting efficiently, but he saw little 'idealism or personality at the head of it.' As he put it, there was some comfort in the fact that 'our academic isolationists are quiet for the time.' Quite accurately he prophesied: 'they will have to find new arguments for the future.' If nothing else, he hoped that the war would lead Canada to a clearer understanding of its international obligations.[25]

Throughout these dark hours Falconer himself was far from idle. An honorary vice-president of the Red Cross Society, he was deeply involved in the affairs of the Toronto branch. In 1942 with others he petitioned Ottawa to increase public aid to the society. Maddeningly, however, the group sensed only 'a great lack of co-operation' in its dealings with Mackenzie King. Indeed, rumour had it that the cabinet was about to curtail its grant. Furthermore, it was feared that Ottawa would force all such bodies to campaign independently for donations, rather than spearheading a united drive. Efforts to secure an audience with the ever-elusive King proved fruitless. Meanwhile the Red Cross faced insolvency by February. Worried, but not panicked, Falconer felt that the cabinet was merely biding its time until the society moderated its demands. For the moment he and his colleagues struggled to keep the work going.[26]

As 1943 dawned with no end to hostilities in sight, Falconer's concerns about the moral effects of a prolonged war grew sharper. In particular he was alarmed by trends in the United States, which seemed to put the future of the humanities in jeopardy. Asked by military authorities whether a liberal education was of value to the war effort, American college leaders shocked Falconer by responding in the negative. At a meeting of the American Association of Universities and Colleges, President Emeritus W.A. Neilson had flatly declared that 'education in the liberal arts for men is out for the duration.' Responding in print, Sir Robert thundered that to leave it at that showed that 'the "educators" were very muddled.' If the democracies were truly fighting for freedom, he argued, then they could not 'allow the way in which they conducted the war to do enduring damage to it.' Restating anew a long-favoured theme, he counselled Canadians to protect, as far as possible, the humanistic elements in higher education. Still a fervent idealist, he dreaded a peace in which mere quantity and simple efficiency would be the measure of well-being. 'Intellect,' he warned, 'when developed without moral purpose and a supreme human end, is destructive of what is most distinctive and worthy in man.'[27]

Given his feelings on this score, it was impossible for him to refuse an invitation from Emmanuel College to lecture on the New Testament that fall. An affiliate of the University of Toronto, the college was also the chief seminary of his beloved United Church. The combination proved irresistible. Doctors had warned him that he was in for a very hard winter. His reserves had been draining away rapidly throughout the year. But he agreed to deliver four lectures, 'perhaps,' as he told Murray, 'without good judgment.' Making light of the situation, he quipped, 'a reformed drunkard sometimes goes on a spree even in old age.'[28] Undertaken in this boyish spirit, the burden nevertheless became a taxing one as his strength ebbed rapidly in August.[29] When September came Falconer staggered to the podium, but not under the influence of strong drink. As he scanned his audience, however, the presence of scores of former students, many even from Pine Hill, buoyed him up. For three days, at least, the years melted away as Falconer held forth on *The Heart of the New Testament*.[30] Ranging broadly over the schools of biblical interpretation that had flourished in his day, he was in his natural element and among his friends. When the final applause faded away, he remarked to Sophie that his writings were now complete and he could go as slowly as he pleased.[31]

At the time he probably meant what he said. However, there was one cause that could always rouse him to action, whatever his condition. Even before the war broke out Falconer had been moved by the cries of the homeless and the persecuted. Surveying an already broken world, in January 1939 he wrote to Walter Murray observing that 'Chinese, Mid-European refugees and now Barcelona exiles – all these are appealing to us for help.' In conscience, he said, Canadians could not stand aside while so many suffered. 'Out of gratitude even for our own safety,' he argued, 'one must try to do a little for each.'[32] Certain that Hitler meant to crush Christianity as well as Judaism, Falconer came to feel a particular sympathy for the tortured children of Zion. Thus, as Canada closed its frontiers to victims of a new diaspora, he raised his voice in protest. In June 1939, for example, he joined George Wrong and a few others in begging Mackenzie King to admit the 900 German Jews aboard the *St Louis* who had wandered the Atlantic in a desperate search for sanctuary.[33] Unsuccessful in this bid, he continued to plead the cause of the dispossessed as honorary chairman of the National Committee on Refugees. Indeed, in the last days of October 1943 he took to the airwaves, calling for signatures to a petition that asked that Canada be opened to all those fleeing Hitler's persecution.[34] It was a heartfelt, but final, public act.

On the evening of 4 November a weary Falconer sat poring over his hefty stamp collection, now bound in handsome Morocco leather.[35] How it had blossomed since he had scavanged for cast-offs in the shops of far-off Trinidad! Aware of it or not, he was sinking, even as he turned the pages that colourfully recorded his many travels. Fortunate to the end, he had no need of blurred and momentary flashes to recall the joys and passions of a remarkable life. It was all there before him, plain as day and bright as new.

CHAPTER XIII

Some Thoughts on Robert Falconer

Complex individuals, especially intellectuals, we are told, have the disconcerting habit of confounding those who delight in rigid classification.[1] Robert Alexander Falconer is a good case in point. Throughout a long and crowded life he donned a wide variety of hats and none of them seemed out of place. Indeed, each helped highlight a different aspect of his many-sided character and thought. Unfortunately, the depths of his personal life are hidden from view. However, as a thinker, a public figure, and a university leader, Falconer is open to assessment. The question is, what are we to make of him?

Although seldom a truly systematic thinker, he can with justice be described as an idealist. After all, that broad, philosophical disposition suffused his thoughts on religion, national character, education, and scores of other themes. Even so, he fits uneasily into any interpretive scheme that posits an unforgiving struggle between idealism and empiricism in early twentieth-century Canada.[2] For some, perhaps, that conflict was definitive, but Falconer himself resisted strict polarization. Instead, in youth he acquired a flexible and eclectic cast of mind which left him hospitable to new ideas. To be sure, from first to last he maintained that the intellect had 'to pay homage to the spirit.' But he also firmly held that faith and intuition ignored reason only at their peril. Like his hero Harnack, he yearned for synthesis. Thus, while deploring 'untutored naturalism,' he quite easily reached an early accommodation with evolution and the higher citicism. Similarly, this devout humanist understood and helped promote the pure, applied, and social sciences at the University of Toronto. Ultimately he distinguished between empirical methods and empiricism itself. He could therefore embrace the former while eschewing the latter. Consequently, although recognizing a logical gulf between himself and a Harold Innis, in practice Falconer strove to de-emphasize and minimize the gap. As was evident in the debates over graduate studies, his mediating mind spurned extremes. In the intellectual tumult of his generation, Falconer tried to serve as an honest, if not wholly disinterested, broker. It was a stance that came naturally to one who finally assumed that all roads, when followed in a spirit of self-discipline and moral enthusiasm, led to a contemplation of the ideal.

In broader perspective, to identify his work as 'the apotheosis of nineteenth-century idealism in Canada' is not necessarily to limit its significance to a particular moment in time.[3] Here the pattern or tendency of his thought is more important than the mode of formal expression. Philosophical idealism might have waned, but the tradition of 'moral concern' flowed on. In ways appropriate to his own hour Falconer helped feed that continuing mainstream.[4] Similarly, it has been argued that, historically, English Canadians have employed philosophical reason as 'a device to explore alternatives, to suggest ways of combining apparently contradictory ideas, to discover new ways of passing from one idea to another.'[5] Intellectual 'federalism' of this sort, it is said, was the reflex of a people acutely aware of external dependence and internal social complexity.[6] Whatever its sources, Falconer clearly exhibited this eclectic trait of the Canadian *mentalité*.

A thinker of some significance, Sir Robert was also very much a man of action. Socially and politically he can be likened to a 'red Tory' or an American 'Progressive.' Neither unreservedly liberal nor uncompromisingly conservative, he was one of the prominent moderates of a turbulent age. Justice and harmony, he contended, were best fostered when a balance was struck between individual freedoms and the collective needs of the whole. As to how this end might be achieved, he offered no clear-cut formula. Indeed, he stood with Burke in distrusting the overly schematic designs of would-be social engineers. Spurning both liberalism and full-blown socialism, he urged the gradual reform of an organic society. In the end he hoped that the diffusion of essential Christianity and a 'higher conception of liberty' would lead to overall moral regeneration. To some extent, a penchant for voluntarism did battle in him with the urge to foster social amelioration. Accordingly, there was an unresolved tension in this man who championed broad reform but at times questioned the wisdom and efficacy of wholesale compulsion by the state. Similarly, for all that this Presbyterian divine wished to 'preach to the times,' he rejected the notion that churches should function as 'religio-political machines.' Thus, this intensely activist Protestant minister ultimately rejected the social gospel. Yet, flexible as always, Falconer was ready to take a cue from the left or to draw on tradition in working towards his goal. Not infrequently, therefore, he advised Canadians to be 'both conservative and progressive' in their search for social betterment.

On the wider stage, in many ways Falconer personified the emerging concept of the North Atlantic triangle. Born in Canada, he grew to maturity in other corners of the empire and in time came to know the United States as well. In him fervent nationalism came to blend with devout imperialism and a form of North American continentalism. The emphasis in his thought and action varied from time to time. There was always, for example, a measure of ambivalence in his attitude to the great republic. Equally, he disliked schemes for formal imperial integration that might undermine Canadian autonomy. Yet narrow nationalism was also unpalatable to his cosmopolitan mind. Increasingly, following the First World War, these tensions were resolved by Falconer's intensified spirit of internationalism. Indeed, he was one of those who laboured to keep that flame alight in the face of interwar isolationism. As such, he was in tune with an older tradition of overseas commitment which, spawned in the days of empire, would resurface after 1945.[7]

It was, however, as a university leader that Falconer made his foremost mark. Indeed, to most contemporaries he symbolized Canadian higher education as did no other in his day. A brilliant administrator, his greatest achievement was to make the constitution of 1906 work, when it could quite easily have failed. There were, inevitably, some failures and some serious errors of judgment, as in the medical dispute of the 1920s. Furthermore, the rejuvenation, expansion, and modernization of the University of Toronto was the work of many able hands. But for twenty-five crucial years it was Falconer who steadied the helm, providing continuity and coherence in an age of rapid growth and often fundamental change. On the whole his thoughts on the nature of the 'organic university' were appropriate for the period. Embracing the ideals of culture, scholarship, and service, he helped smooth the way as Varsity evolved into a 'multiversity.' Moreover, in stubbornly defending the University of Toronto against outside interference, Falconer played a vital part in enhancing some aspects of academic freedom. Nationally, with Walter Murray, H.M. Tory, Sir William Peterson, and others, he worked to develop closer bonds within, and a stronger collective voice for, the widely dispersed academic community. In conclusion, he who would plumb the official mind of Canadian academe in the early years of this century would be well advised to start with Robert Alexander Falconer, a complex man who mirrored the complexities of his age.

Notes

Abbreviations

DNB *Dictionary of National Biography*
FP Robert Alexander Falconer Papers. University of Toronto Archives.
FOR Fellowship of Reconciliation
MP Walter C. Murray Papers. University of Saskatchewan Archives
RLR R.A. Falconer *Religion on My Life's Road* Houston: Rice Institute 1938
WP Sir Byron Edmund Walker Papers. University of Toronto Rare Book Room
WIS Alexander Falconer *West Indian Sketches*. United Church of Canada Maritime Conference Archives, Atlantic School of Theology, Halifax

Chapter 1 Cold Baths and Classics

1 MacPhie *Pictonians at Home and Abroad* 11
2 McNeill *Presbyterian Church in Canada* 8. For a discussion of the complex history of Nova Scotian Presbyterianism with its Secessionists, Burghers, anti-Burghers, New and Old Lighters, Free Churchmen and Sons of the Kirk, see McNeill; Walsh *Christian Church in Canada;* Moir *Enduring Witness*; Grant *Canadian Experience of Church Union*; Silcox *Church Union in Canada*; and others.
3 On the history of the Pictou Academy and its offshoots see Falconer and Watson *Brief History of Pine Hill Divinity Hall* and Betts *Pine Hill Divinity Hall.*
4 Falconer and Watson *Pine Hill* 6
5 McNeill *Presbyterian Church* 72
6 E.A. McCurdy et al. 'Appreciations of the Late Rev. Alexander Falconer D.D.' *Presbyterian Witness* (29 July 1911) 4

7 'The Rev. Alexander Falconer: An Obituary' *The Westville Free Lance* (July 1911) clipping found in FP, Clipping File #137
8 Ibid.
9 MacLeod *History of Presbyterianism on Prince Edward Island* 144
10 Ibid. 145
11 For details see the *Presbyterian Witness* (25 Nov. 1865) 376.
12 Falconer *Religion on My Life's Road* 45, hereafter referred to as *RLR*. Unless otherwise indicated, all subsequent references here to the early family life of Robert Falconer are drawn from this source, 44–7.
13 For example see A. Falconer *West Indian Sketches, Letters and Clippings 1877–1886* (Halifax, 7 July 1877), hereafter referred to as *WIS*. This is a collection of his letters to various Presbyterian newspapers and journals written during his ten years as a missionary in Trinidad.
14 Robert Falconer 'Blaise Pascal' 353
15 Chown *The Story of Church Union in Canada* 80–2 and Silcox *Church Union* 199
16 Note, for example, his criticisms of church establishment among the Lutherans of St Thomas in the Virgin Islands and the Catholics around the world in his *WIS*, 6, 15–16.
17 Ibid. 14
18 Ibid. 15–16
19 McNeill *Presbyterian Church*, 70
20 For a discussion of Scottish attitudes to higher education see Davie *The Democratic Intellect: Scotland and Her Universities in the Nineteenth Century*.
21 Silcox *Church Union* 68
22 McNeill *Presbyterian Church*, 204
23 Forrest in McCurdy et al. 'Appreciations of A.F.' 4
24 For details see McNeill *Presbyterian Church* 204–8.
25 A. Falconer *Privilege and Responsibility* 30
26 Ibid. 34
27 A. Falconer 'The Fourth Professorship' *Theologue* 3 (1892) 15
28 Ibid. 16
29 Marble *Nova Scotians at Home and Abroad* 269
30 McNeill *Presbyterian Church* 48
31 Alex Falconer to G.M. Grant, 22 Dec. 1877, G.M. Grant Papers
32 K. Grant in McCurdy et al. 'Appreciations of A.F.' 4
33 *Minutes of the Presbytery of Trinidad 1845–1939*, Emmanuel College, United Church of Canada Archives. His candidacy was debated 24 Oct. 1876.
34 Happily his letters survive in the form of his memoir, *WIS*, which constitutes the only substantial body of direct evidence concerning the family sojourn in Trinidad.
35 Ibid. (17 Feb. 1877) 1. Note: the dates record the time of publication, not the days on which the letters were written.
36 For a close analysis of Trinidadian society in the nineteenth century see B. Brereton, *Race Relations in Colonial Trinidad 1870–1900*. Less detailed

but still helpful is D. Wood *Trinidad in Transition: The Years After Slavery.*

37 For details on the Chinese and Indian populations see Wood *Trinidad in Transition,* 160–7 and Ryan *Race and Nationalism in Trinidad and Tobago* 23–4.

38 For Alex's description of Greyfriars' manse see his *WIS* (4 Aug. 1877) 10–11.

39 *WIS* (4 July 1877) 9

40 Brereton *Race Relations* 52

41 *WIS* (7 July 1877) 8

42 Wood *Trinidad in Transition* 303

43 *WIS* 'The Trinidad Mission' (No. 2) 32

44 Brereton *Race Relations* 185

45 Ibid.

46 *WIS* 'Impressions of Trinidad' (4 Aug. 1877) 13

47 Wood *Trinidad in Transition* 163–7

48 Concerning social Darwinists see Semmel, *Imperialism and Social Reform.*

49 Brereton *Race Relations* 4

50 A. Falconer *Privilege and Responsibility* 20

51 *WIS*, 'Impressions of Trinidad' 12

52 *Minutes of Presbytery of Trinidad* (7 Oct. 1879)

53 Brereton *Race Relations* 186

54 For example, in the years just before 1914 he played an important role in efforts to build a western university in China. See his correspondence with Seth Low in FP.

55 Brereton *Race Relations* 73

56 Wood *Trinidad in Transition* 233

57 A Falconer to Grant, 8 April 1878, G.M. Grant Papers

58 Wood *Trinidad in Transition* 234

59 Ibid.

60 Brereton *Race Relations* 82

61 Robert Falconer to the boys of Queen's Royal College, 26 Oct. 1926, FP, Box 101

62 A. MacMechan 'The President of Toronto University' *The Canadian Magazine* (n.d.) FP Clippings File

63 R. Falconer 'The Biography of a Stamp Album' University of Toronto Archives Microfilm #B79-0065/1

64 Ibid.

65 For Alex's description of one such journey see *WIS*, 'Impressions of Trinidad' (1 Sept. 1877) 16.

66 For a description of the trip see *WIS* 'A Trip Up the Orinoco' (19 Aug. 1883) 42.

67 *WIS* 'Letters from Trinidad' (April 1880) 27

68 *Minutes of Presbytery of Trinidad* (11 April 1884); (14 Jan. 1885)

69 A. Falconer to Grant, 22 Dec. 1877, G.M. Grant Papers

70 *WIS* 'The Trinidad Mission' (No. 5) 38

71 Brereton *Race Relations* 118–23
72 A. Falconer to Grant, 8 April 1878, Grant Papers
73 *Minutes of Presbytery of Trinidad* (11 April 1884)
74 *Ibid.* (15 May 1885)
75 W.C. Murray 'President Falconer' *Dalhousie Gazette* (Sept. 1907) 4

Chapter II Of Tools and Their Wielders

1 Mackinnnon *Reminiscences* 80
2 *RLR* 49
3 Falconer 'In Edinburgh Fifty Years Ago' (1937) 441
4 *RLR* 49
5 Davie *Democratic Intellect* xvi
6 *RLR* 50
7 Turner *History of the University of Edinburgh 1883–1933* 168
8 Ibid. 171
9 'Studies in University Reform' *The Student* 2 (6 Feb. 1889) 90
10 *RLR* 49
11 Falconer 'Edinburgh Fifty Years Ago' 442
12 Ibid.
13 Turner *University of Edinburgh* xiv
14 Falconer 'Edinburgh Fifty Years Ago' 442–3
15 Ibid. 445
16 *University of Edinburgh Calendar* (1886–7) 233, 235
17 Ibid. (1887–8) 109; (1889–90) 103
18 See, for example, *Halifax Herald* (21 April 1905) 1 and 'Early Christian Art' *Queen's Quarterly* 11 (1904) 225–42
19 *The Student* 2 (23 Jan. 1889) 65
20 Falconer 'Edinburgh Fifty Years Ago' 448
21 Ibid. 449
22 Ibid. 450
23 *RLR* 49–50
24 Davie *Democratic Intellect* 85
25 Falconer 'Edinburgh Fifty Years Ago' 452
26 Mackinnnon *Reminiscences* 49
27 As J.M. Barrie recalled in his chatty book *An Edinburgh Eleven* (London 1908) 41
28 Falconer 'Edinburgh Fifty Years Ago' 452
29 Mackinnon *Reminiscences* 49
30 Mandelbaum *History, Man and Reason* 6
31 Tatarkiewicz *Nineteenth-Century Philosophy* 203
32 *RLR* 51
33 Richter *The Politics of Conscience* 183
34 Falconer 'A Study in Emerson' (1891)
35 W. Taylor 'In Memoriam, Sir Robert A. Falconer' *University of Toronto Quarterly* 13 (Jan. 1944) 159

36 *RLR* 51
37 Falconer 'Edinburgh Fifty Years Ago' 453; Barrie *Edinburgh Eleven* 46
38 *RLR* 50
39 Mackinnon *Reminiscences* 48–53
40 *RLR* 50
41 Ibid.
42 Falconer 'Edinburgh Fifty Years Ago' 445
43 *RLR* 52
44 Mackinnon *Reminiscences* 59
45 Chadwick *Victorian Church* 29
46 *RLR* 52
47 Chadwick *Victorian Church* 29
48 Falconer 'Edinburgh Fifty Years Ago' 454
49 *RLR* 53
50 Ibid. 52
51 Ibid. The italics are Falconer's.
52 Falconer 'Edinburgh Fifty Years Ago' 446
53 A. Falconer 'Cambridge & Its Colleges' *WIS* (July 1886) 48
54 Falconer 'Edinburgh Fifty Years Ago' 443
55 Falconer 'A Tramp Through Thuringia' (1889)
56 Falconer 'Reminiscences of Professor A.B. Davidson' (1918) 386
57 Bowen *Idea of the Victorian Church* 173–4
58 Ibid. 175
59 For a detailed discussion of the controversy, see Bowen *Idea* 174–84 and Chadwick *Victorian Church* 101–4.
60 For these assessments of Laidlaw, Blaikie, Duns, and Rainy see Mackinnon *Reminiscences* 56–8.
61 *RLR* 53
62 *Student* (7 June 1889) 74
63 'Studies in University Reform: The Theological Schools' *Student* 2 (6 Feb. 1889) 86–92
64 *RLR* 54
65 Mackinnon *Reminiscences* 54. For a recent discussion of the Robertson Smith case, see Riesen *Criticism and Faith in Victorian Scotland.*
66 Falconer 'Davidson' 387
67 Mackinnon *Reminiscences* 63
68 Falconer 'Davidson' 387
69 *RLR*, 55
70 Unless otherwise indicated, Falconer's impressions of Davidson are to be found in his brief biographical study of that professor. See Falconer 'Davidson' 385–400. A detailed analysis of Davidson's personality and thought is available in Riesen *Criticism and Faith.*
71 Mackinnon *Reminiscences* 54
72 This quotation from Davidson's lectures was recorded by Falconer in his 'Davidson' 395
73 Mackinnon *Reminiscences* 55

74 'Marcus Dods' *Student* 2 (7 June 1889) 74–5
75 Bowen *Idea* 169
76 Neill *Interpretation of the New Testament* 31
77 *DNB* (1901–11) 510–12
78 *DNB* xviii, W.R. Smith, 5–9. Riesen concurs in his *Criticism and Faith* xvii.
79 'Dods' 74
80 For a discussion of Baur's work and influence see Hasel *New Testament Theology* 30–5 and Neill *Interpretation* 19–28.
81 Bratton *History of the Bible* 318
82 Bowen *Idea* 169
83 *Ibid.* 168
84 Hasel *New Testament Theology* 35–8
85 Neill *Interpretation* 32; Chadwick *Victorian Church* 69
86 Chadwick *Victorian Church* 72
87 Hasel *New Testament Theology* 30
88 Chadwick *Victorian Church* 63
89 *Ibid.* 64
90 *RLR* 59
91 Bowen *Idea* 178
92 Chadwick *Victorian Church* 73
93 *Student* 2 (7 June 1889) 75
94 Mackinnon *Reminiscences* 56
95 'Professor Marcus Dods' *Student* 2 (11 Dec. 1889) 115
96 Dods *The Bible: Its Origins and Nature* 210
97 Ibid. 153
98 *RLR* 59
99 Falconer *Heart of New Testament* (1943) 3
100 Dods *Bible* 55
101 Ibid. 59
102 Bratton *History of the Bible* 316
103 *RLR* 59
104 'Professor Marcus Dods' 115
105 'Marcus Dods' *DNB* (1901–11) 511
106 *RLR* 59
107 Ibid. 63
108 Falconer 'My Memory of Harnack' (1930) 376
109 *RLR* 61
110 Ibid. 61–2
111 Ibid. 60
112 Falconer 'Harnack' 377
113 Ibid.
114 Falconer 'Davidson' 397–8
115 *RLR* 62
116 Ibid. 63
117 Ibid.

118 Wilhelm Pauck *Harnack and Troeltsch* 4
119 Ibid. 317. See also Falconer 'Harnack' 379 and H. Bauke 'The History of Christological Doctrine' in Pelikan ed. *Twentieth Century Theology* 137.
120 Mandelbaum *History, Man and Reason* 36
121 Ibid. 32
122 Ibid. 33
123 Taylor 'In Memoriam' 163. See also Bauke 'Christological Doctrine' 137.
124 Pauck *Harnack and Troeltsch* 34
125 Harnack *History of Dogma* 4
126 Pauck *Harnack and Troeltsch* 35
127 Neill *Interpretation* 133
128 Harnack *History of Dogma* 1
129 Harnack *What Is Christianity?* 14
130 This thumbnail methodological sketch can be found on page 15.
131 Harnack *History of Dogma* 2
132 On the growing consciousness of the subjective nature of history among men of Harnack's generation, see Hughes *Consciousness and Society*.
133 Harnack *What Is Christianity?* 18
134 Harnack *History of Dogma* 7
135 Ibid. 8
136 *RLR* 63
137 For a detailed account of these months with Harnack, see Falconer 'Harnack.'
138 Ibid. 378
139 Pauck, in his *Harnack and Troeltsch*, records the glowing descriptions of several of Harnack's students who, over the years, testified to his excellence as a lecturer. See 14–15.
140 Falconer 'Harnack' 378
141 Ibid.
142 *RLR* 64
143 Pauck *Harnack and Troeltsch* 37–8
144 Falconer *Heart of New Testament* 37–42
145 This was evident, for example, in his later attempt to rehabilitate Second Peter.
146 Falconer 'Harnack' 380
147 *RLR* 64

Chapter III Pine Hill

1 Falconer and Watson *Pine Hill* 14
2 Betts *Pine Hill Divinity Hall* 19
3 Minutes of the Board of Governors of Pine Hill, Archives of the United Church of Canada, Maritime Conference (2 Oct. 1890) 9
4 Ibid. (11 Aug. 1891) 18
5 Ibid. (23 April 1891) 16

6 Grant *George Pidgeon* 31–2
7 J.S. Sutherland 'Our Present Needs' *Theologue* 8 (1897) 123–8
8 Ibid. 128
9 Thomas Sedgwick 'The Fourth Professorship' *Theologue* 3 (1892) 111–17
10 *Halifax Herald* (27 Jan. 1892) 8
11 A. Falconer 'The Fourth Professorship' 12–18
12 Minutes of the Board of Pine Hill (6 Oct. 1892) 33–4
13 'The College Staff' *Theologue* 4 (1892) 28
14 Ibid.
15 MacMechan 'President of Toronto University'
16 Student interest in 'practical' training and contemporary issues was regularly displayed in the pages of the *Theologue* throughout the 1890s.
17 A. Pollok to G.M. Grant, 10 May 1898, Grant Papers
18 *Halifax Herald* (17 March 1896), 10
19 Ibid. (8 Oct. 1892) 1
20 For example, see ibid. (17 and 18 Jan. 1893).
21 Ibid. (19 Jan. 1893) 4
22 Ibid. (21 Jan. 1893) 4
23 Mackinnon *Reminiscences* 179
24 Ibid.
25 McNeill *Presbyterian Church* 203
26 *Halifax Herald* (23 April 1893) 8
27 McNeill *Presbyterian Church* 49
28 Pollock's address was reported in full in the *Halifax Herald* (3 Nov. 1892) 5.
29 *RLR* 67
30 Ibid. 68
31 Falconer *Heart of New Testament* 1
32 For complete versions of this speech see the *Theologue* 5 (1893) 1–16 and *Halifax Herald* (2 Nov. 1893) 8.
33 *Halifax Herald* (2 Nov. 1893) 8
34 *RLR* 81
35 Falconer 'An Historical Study.' This undated essay was clearly written before 1904, since it refers to 'Professor' rather than 'Principal' Falconer of Nova Scotia. See FP Miscellaneous Manuscripts and Pamphlets.
36 *RLR* 80
37 Falconer 'Prophet of New Israel' (1903) 263. See also 'Batch of Books on Paulinism' (1893).
38 *RLR* 81
39 Falconer 'Moral Standards in Primitive Christianity' (1919) 321
40 *RLR* 80
41 Falconer 'Sin as a Religious Concept' (1907) 65
42 Harnack *History of Dogma* 1–2
43 *RLR* 65
44 Ibid. 74. See also 'Holy Spirit in the Early Apostolic Age' (1900) 440.
45 Falconer 'The Ministry or the Priesthood – Which?' *Theologue* 9 (1897) 13

46 Ibid. 8–10
47 Ibid. 1–4
48 Falconer 'Holy Spirit' 452
49 Ibid.
50 *RLR* 87
51 Falconer 'Ministry or Priesthood?' 7
52 Falconer *Heart of New Testament,* 12.
53 Ibid. 2.
54 Falconer 'Prophet of New Israel' 259
55 *RLR* 84
56 Falconer 'Prophet of New Israel' 259
57 *RLR* 79
58 Falconer *Heart of New Testament* 26
59 Falconer 'Holy Spirit in Early Apostolic Age' 447
60 Ibid. 440
61 Falconer *Heart of New Testament* 26
62 *RLR* 86
63 Falconer *Heart of New Testament* 45
64 Ibid.
65 Falconer 'Book of Acts Once More' (1922) 112
66 Ibid. 113
67 Falconer 'Holy Spirit' 454
68 *RLR* 68
69 Ibid.
70 Falconer 'Holy Spirit' 439
71 *RLR* 69
72 Falconer 'Book of Acts' 120
73 Falconer 'Christ the Personal Source of Religion and Theology' (1893) 9
74 Falconer 'A Darwinian's Thoughts on Religion' (1895) 134–5
75 Falconer 'From College to University' *University of Toronto Quarterly* 5 (April 1936) 2
76 See, for example, his articles: 'Darwinian's Thoughts'; 'Science and Religion as Factors in Progress' (1913); 'The Difficulties of Religion in an Age of Science' (1928). It should also be remembered that he was an ardent champion of the Royal Society of Canada.
77 Falconer 'Darwinian's Thoughts' 137
78 J.D. Wood *The Interpretation of the Bible: An Historical Introduction* (London 1958) 145
79 Here the classic statement was penned by Schweitzer in his *The Quest for the Historical Jesus.*
80 This was the spirit that informed his early review article 'Batch of Books on Paulinism.'
81 Ibid. 56
82 Falconer 'Products from the New Testament Yield of 1898' (1899) 149–54
83 R. Falconer 'Some Noteworthy Books' *Theologue* 15 (1904) 47

84 Falconer 'Holy Spirit'
85 *RLR* 70
86 Falconer 'Sin as a Religious Concept' 63
87 The importance of 'congruity' was hinted at in an article entitled 'The Gospel According to Peter' (1893)
88 Ibid. 119
89 Falconer 'Holy Spirit'
90 Falconer 'Is Second Peter a Genuine Epistle?' (1901); (1902)
91 While not accepting Falconer's general thesis, Donald Guthrie in 1970 conceded that he was probably correct on this point about the compatibility of Second Peter with the teaching of the New Testament as a whole. See D. Guthrie *New Testament Introduction* (Downers Grove, IL: Inter-Varsity Press 1970) 843.
92 R. Falconer 'Peter, Second Epistle of' in J. Hastings ed. *Dictionary of the Bible* 718
93 See, for example, his several entries in ibid.; J. Hastings ed. *Dictionary of Christ and the Gospels*; M.W. Jacobus et al. eds. *New Standard Bible Dictionary*.
94 *Dictionary of the Bible*, for example, listed 105 authors, mostly from Britain and the United States. Of these only Falconer and J.F. McCurdy of Toronto represented Canada. Again, over a hundred writers contributed to *Dictionary of Christ and the Gospels*, but of these only five were resident in Canada. They included R.A. Falconer, J.W. Falconer, J.H. Farmer, T.B. Kilpatrick, and William Patrick.
95 'Pine Hill's Prosperity' *Halifax Herald* (27 April 1893) 2
96 *Theologue* 8 (1897) 94
97 Betts *Pine Hill* 21
98 *Halifax Herald* (27 April 1893) 8
99 'Our Fourth Professor' (1895) 153
100 Minutes of Board of Management (25 April 1895) 65
101 Subscription list for new library, Gordon Papers, Queen's University Archives, Box 3, File 4
102 Minutes of Board of Management (23 April 1891) 16. In 1898 the amount requested from congregations rose to $5,000. See ibid. (2 Nov. 1898) 94.
103 Ibid. (23 April 1891) 16; (1 Oct. 1891) 21
104 Sutherland 'Our Present Needs' 127
105 Ibid.
106 Minutes of Board of Management (2 Nov. 1898) 94
107 Ibid. (22 Aug. 1899) 105
108 Sutherland 'Our Present Needs' 128; *Halifax Herald* (7 Oct. 1904) 2
109 D.M. Gordon 'Our Summer School' *Theologue* 5 (1893) 82–6
110 J.A. MacGlashen 'Reminiscences of the Summer School' *Theologue* 6 (Nov. 1895–April 1896) 19
111 Ibid., 21
112 Betts *Pine Hill* 28
113 'The Guild of Theological Study' *Theologue* 9 (Dec. 1897–April 1898) 15

114 Ibid. 168–9
115 Shortt *Search for an Ideal* 44
116 Ibid. 41–57
117 Clarence Mackinnon, in his *Reminiscences*, draws a vivid picture of the proceedings of this club. See 105–8.
118 Ibid. 175
119 Robert Falconer to D.P. McColl (deputy commissioner, Dept of Education, Regina), 4 May 1908, FP, Box 2
120 See, for example, McKillop *A Disciplined Intelligence*.
121 Shortt *Search for an Ideal* 141 and passim
122 For a sketch of the work of Morton see Berger *Writing of Canadian History* 30, 163, 240–1.
123 Mackinnon *Reminiscences* 140
124 Ibid. 107
125 *Halifax Herald* (10 Sept. 1904) 2. Here Sophie's contributions to the foreign missions are noted.
126 Bladen *Bladen on Bladen* 50
127 Dorothy Falconer (their daughter-in-law) to H.G. Tuttle, 20 June 1968, letter found in Falconer biographical file, United Church Archives, Emmanuel College
128 In 1898, for example, he delivered a series of lectures on biblical history at the Halifax YMCA. See the report in the *Halifax Herald* (15 Jan. 1898) 8. The earliest mention of his participation in the activities of this group can be found in ibid. (26 April 1893) 2.
129 Falconer 'Great Western Country' (1898) 12
130 Ibid. 14
131 Ibid. 17
132 For a description of Gordon's rather stormy tenure at Queen's, see Neatby *Queen's University*.
133 They are listed as members of the board in its minutes of 28 April 1904, 2. For a recent study of Murray's life, see D.R. Murray and R.A. Murray, *The Prairie Builder: Walter Murray of Saskatchewan* (Edmonton, 1984). (The authors, incidentally, are not related to W.C. Murray.)

Chapter IV No Sabbath Droner

1 Minutes of Board of Pine Hill (29 April 1904) 4
2 Ibid. (28 April 1904) 3
3 'Principal Falconer' *Theologue* 16 (1904) 15
4 See, for example, assessments by MacMechan 'President of University of Toronto' and Murray 'President Falconer,' FP, Clipping File 1907.
5 *Halifax Herald* (21 Nov. 1904) 2
6 Minutes of Board of Pine Hill (25 Oct. 1904) 23
7 Ibid. (26 April 1906) 65
8 *Theologue* 13 (1902) 448

9 Ibid. 449
10 *Theologue* 15 (Jan. 1904) 53
11 Radall *Halifax: Warden of the North* 240–3
12 Mackinnon *Reminiscences* 141
13 Shortt *Search for an Ideal* 41–57
14 *Halifax Herald* (25 May 1905) 2. See also Mackinnon *Reminiscences* 141.
15 *Halifax Herald* (1 Feb. 1904) 1
16 R. Falconer 'Principal Pollok: An Appreciation' *Theologue* 15 (1904) 134
17 Ibid.
18 R. Falconer 'Preaching to the Times' *Theologue* 14 (1902) 459–67
19 Unidentified newspaper clipping found in FP, Clipping File, reflecting on his appointment as principal.
20 MacMechan 'President of University of Toronto'
21 *Halifax Herald* (7 Oct. 1904) 2
22 'President Falconer: An Organizing Genius' *Maclean's Magazine* (Nov. 1912) 40
23 Jeanneret *Contribution of Sir Robert Falconer* 16
24 'Sir Robert Falconer Long University of Toronto Head Dies' *Globe and Mail* (5 Nov. 1943) 4
25 *Halifax Herald* (26 Oct. 1904) 4. The speech was printed in full.
26 Ibid. (25 Oct. 1906) 2
27 On the growing disillusionment of socially conscious churchmen with competitive society see Allen *Social Passion*.
28 Shortt *Search for an Ideal*. See particularly his essays on Archibald MacMechan, Andrew Macphail, and Maurice Hutton, all of whom shared Falconer's diagnosis of the damaging effects of nationalism.
29 This particular element in his thought achieved its highest expression in Falconer's *Idealism in National Character*.
30 Falconer 'Science and Religion' 342
31 *Halifax Herald* (2 Jan. 1907) 2
32 *RLR* 76
33 Ibid 78
34 *Halifax Herald* (25 Oct. 1906) 2
35 Falconer 'Science and Religion' 342
36 *Halifax Herald* (2 Jan. 1907) 2
37 Falconer 'Science and Religion' 342–3. This statement, although written in 1913, reflected an earlier pronouncement in a speech entitled 'Man a Better Asset Than the Richest Wheat,' which he delivered in Halifax in December 1906. See *Halifax Herald* (1 Dec. 1906) 1.
38 The text of the address was printed in the *Halifax Herald* (3 Feb. 1905) 1–2.
39 Falconer 'Preaching to the Times' 466
40 This statement was made by Falconer in his opening address to a new session at Pine Hill on 24 October 1906. See *Halifax Herald* (25 Oct. 1906) 2.
41 Bratton *History of the Bible* 321

42 Ibid. 328
43 On the many roads that led to the birth of the social gospel see Allen *Social Passion* 1–8
44 Falconer recalled Dods's teaching on the point in his *Heart of New Testament* 6.
45 Dods *The Bible* 13
46 Harnack *What Is Christianity?* 7
47 Ibid. 7–8
48 Falconer 'Future of the Kingdom'
49 Falconer *Heart of New Testament* 7
50 Ibid. 46
51 See, for example, *Halifax Herald* (28 Nov. 1906) 1.
52 Ibid. (8 Dec. 1906) 8
53 Both the *Halifax Herald* and the *Chronicle* featured an increasing number of articles on the 'exodus' during the latter half of 1906.
54 See his speech on socialism in *Halifax Herald* (3 Feb. 1905) 1.
55 This comment was made at a meeting of the Halifax branch of the North British Society. See ibid. (1 Dec. 1906) 1.
56 This argument he advanced at a meeting of the Canadian Club. His address was printed in full in the *Halifax Herald* (19 July 1907) 1
57 Ibid. (1 Dec. 1906) 1
58 Ibid. (19 July 1907) 1
59 The speech was reprinted in full in *Halifax Herald* (2 Jan. 1907) 1–2.
60 This position was outlined in an address to a YMCA convention. See ibid. (21 Nov. 1904) 2. For the views of others who held a similar view of education see McKillop *Disciplined Intelligence* passim.
61 *Halifax Herald* (19 July 1907) 1
62 Ibid. (2 Jan. 1907) 2
63 Ibid. (19 July 1907) 1
64 Ibid. (26 Aug. 1905) 1
65 Ibid. (19 July 1907) 1
66 Falconer 'Age-Long Drama of Church and State' 167
67 *Halifax Herald* (2 Jan. 1907) 2
68 Ibid. (1 Dec. 1906) 1
69 The reference is to Cobden's favourite hobbyhorse, 'cumulative prosperity.'
70 Silcox *Church Union* 103; Grant *Canadian Experience of Church Union* 19
71 Grant *Canadian Experience of Church Union* 20
72 Ibid. 25–8. For more details on this informal co-operation see Silcox *Church Union* 77–100 and Walsh *Christian Church in Canada* 273.
73 *Theologue* 13 (1901) 329–31
74 Ibid. 15 (1904) 112
75 See, for example, 'The Great Dearth' ibid. 53–4.
76 Ibid. 112–14
77 *Halifax Herald* (10 March 1904) 3
78 Ibid.
79 Ibid. (2 April 1904) 2

80 Falconer 'Principal Pollok' 131
81 Falconer to Willison, 15 April 1904, Willison Papers, PAC
82 Falconer's letter to the *News* was reprinted in the *Halifax Herald* (30 April 1904) 4.
83 This at least was the impression of Dr Ephraim Scott, who later played a leading role in opposing union. See his *Church Union and The Presbyterian Church in Canada* 47.
84 He admitted this in an interview with a reporter from the *Herald* in December 1904. See *Halifax Herald* (26 Dec. 1904) 1.
85 For a discussion of the various grounds on which some Presbyterians objected to union at this early stage see Grant *Canadian Experience of Church Union* 54–6 and Silcox *Church Union* 199–206. A more recent analysis is available in Clifford *Resistance to Church Union*.
86 *Halifax Herald* (26 Dec. 1904) 1
87 General Assembly Minutes (1905) 280, cited in Scott *Church Union* 48.
88 Chown *Story of Church Union in Canada* 27
89 Silcox *Church Union* 133
90 *Proceedings of the Committee on Church Union Appointed by the Presbyterian Church in Canada* (21 Dec. 1905) United Church Archives, Emmanuel College
91 *Halifax Herald* (25 Dec. 1905) 1
92 Ibid.
93 Falconer 'Thoughts on Union' (1905)
94 *Halifax Herald* (13 June 1906) 1
95 Scott *Church Union* 47–51. Clifford, in his *Resistance*, argues that unionists were habitually high-handed towards critics like Scott.
96 He made this particular point clear in addressing the opening session at Pine Hill in 1906. See *Halifax Herald* (25 Oct. 1906) 2 for the text of this speech.
97 R. Falconer 'Alien from Nothing That Is Truly Human' (1905) 3
98 Ibid. 1
99 Ibid. 2
100 Ibid. 5
101 This point was driven home in the course of his address at the closing exercises of 1905. See *Halifax Herald* (27 April 1905) 1.
102 'Mutatis Mutandis' *Theologue* 16 (1905) 41
103 'Editorial' *Theologue* 18 (1907) 46
104 Ibid. 47
105 Ibid. (1907) 112
106 R. Falconer 'A Suggestion' *Theologue* 10 (1899) 85–7
107 Minutes of Board of Pine Hill (29 April 1904)
108 'Principal Falconer' *Theologue* 18 (1907) 133.
109 'The Post-Graduate School' *Theologue* 16 (1905) 111
110 *Theologue* 17 (1906) 111. See also *Halifax Herald* (21 April 1906) 1.
111 Ibid. (27 April 1906) 2

112 *Theologue* 17 (1906) 135
113 *Halifax Herald* (6 April 1905) 1
114 Ibid.
115 Ibid. (27 April 1905) 1 and *Theologue* 16 (1905) 132
116 *Theologue* 18 (1906) 19, 27
117 MacMechan 'President of University of Toronto'
118 On enrolment see *Theologue* 13 (1902) 448; 18 (Dec. 1906) 18; *Halifax Herald* (27 April 1905) 1.
119 *Theologue* 18 (Jan. 1907) 134

Chapter v Loudon's Ghost

1 Neatby *Queen's University* 250
2 E. Collard 'Sir William Peterson's Principalship 1895–1919' in H. MacLennan ed. *McGill* 79–81
3 This was Falconer's reaction when, at the Presbyterian General Assembly of 1904, he was asked to comment on the situation at Queen's. See *Halifax Herald* (4 June 1904) 1.
4 Bliss *Canadian Millionaire* 140
5 Bissell ed. *University College* 10
6 Bliss *Canadian Millionaire* 140
7 Ibid. 138–9
8 Wallace *History of University of Toronto* 164
9 Schull *Ontario since 1867* 76–7
10 J. Loudon to G. Wrong, 29 Aug. 1906, Wrong Papers, Box 2
11 For biographical information concerning Loudon see his unpublished auto-biography 'The Memoirs of James Loudon, President of the University of Toronto 1892–1906.' Loudon Papers
12 Ibid. 33
13 Schull *Ontario* 162
14 Wallace *University of Toronto* 149; Dawson *William Lyon Mackenzie King* Vol. 1 34; Sissons *History of Victoria University*, 216
15 Flavelle to J.P. Whitney, 3 March 1906, Flavelle Papers, Box 38
16 Bliss *Canadian Millionaire* 141
17 On the student strike of 1895 see Bissell *University College* 13; Sissons *Victoria* 216; Dawson *King* 33–6; Drummond *Political Economy at University of Toronto* 27.
18 For details concerning the promotion of Wrong see Meikle 'And Gladly Teach' 40–2
19 Dawson *King* 33
20 Meikle 'And Gladly Teach' 46
21 Loudon *Memoirs* 1902–3 1
22 Drummond *Political Economy* 27
23 For an excellent discussion of this affair see Bliss *Canadian Millionaire* 143.
24 Ibid. n. 13, 521

25 Ibid. 143–4
26 Sissons *Victoria* 229
27 For details see Schull *Ontario* 124–30.
28 Bliss *Canadian Millionaire*, 158
29 Schull *Ontario* 139
30 Bissell *University College* 93
31 Biographical sketches of Walker can be found in WP, Box 45.
32 Falconer 'Glimpses of the University at Work' 129
33 J.P. Sheraton (head of Wycliffe College) wrote to H.J. Cody to warn him of opposition on this point on 14 December 1905. See Cody Papers, Archives of Ontario.
34 Falconer 'University Federation in Toronto' 46
35 Goldwin Smith to H.J. Cody, 5 Jan. 1906, Cody Papers
36 Flavelle to Whitney, 3 March 1906, Flavelle Papers, Box 38
37 Hutton to Walker, 5 July 1906, WP, Box 16
38 Wrong to Walker, 15 May 1907, ibid.
39 Concerning Swanson's promotion of Cody's candidacy see the papers of the Presidential Search Committee, Office of the Secretary of the Board of Governors, Box 51
40 Swanson to Cody, 29 Oct. 1906, Cody Papers
41 Walker to Hutton, 6 July 1906, WP, Box 30
42 Walker to Wrong, 6 June 1907, ibid.
43 Walker to C.R. Van Hise, 8 Aug. 1906. ibid.
44 Smith to Walker, 8 March 1907, WP, Box 16
45 Smith to Walker, 19 March 1907, ibid.
46 Smith to Flavelle, 18 Aug. 1906, Flavelle Papers, Box 38
47 Flavelle to White, 17 Aug. 1906, copy in WP, Box 16
48 Flavelle to Smith, May 1906, Flavelle Papers, Box 38
49 Walker to Lord Grey, 19 July 1906, WP, Box 30
50 Grey to Walker, 14 July 1906; 27 Oct. 1906; 15 Dec. 1906, WP, Box 16.
51 Walker to Grey, 19 July 1906, WP, Box 30
52 Walker to Grey, 13 Dec. 1906, ibid.
53 Interim Report of Search Committee, 30 Jan. 1907, found in the papers of the Office of the Secretary of the Board of Governors, Box 51
54 J.G. Schurman to G. Smith, 18 Oct. 1906, ibid.
55 Osler to John Hoskin (Chairman of the Board of Governors), 31 Dec. 1906, ibid.
56 Walker to J.A. Macdonald, 21 Jan. 1907, WP, Box 30
57 Smith to Walker, 10 Jan. 1907, WP, Box 16
58 For the short list of four candidates see the Interim Report of the Search Committee, Office of the Secretary of the Board of Governors, 30 Jan. 1897, Box 51
59 M.E. Sadler to Walker, 15 March 1907, Box 51
60 Falconer recalled this prophetic statement in a letter to Murray, 30 Dec. 1907, MP.

61 Macdonald to Walker, 27 Jan. 1907, Office of the Secretary of the Board of Governors, Box 51
62 Smith wrote to Walker in March saying that 'there is a man whom I should prefer; but he is in orders, which I believe would be a bar.' While it is unclear whether he was referring to Falconer, Cody, or some other individual, there is no doubt that he and many others were reluctant to appoint any clergyman for fear of rousing sectarian jealousies on campus. Smith to Walker, 13 March 1907, WP, Box 16
63 Walker to Mackenzie Bowell, 26 April 1907, WP, Box 30
64 Letter of recommendation from Pine Hill, April 1907, FP, Box 1
65 G.H. Murray to Walker, 6 April 1907, Office of the Secretary of the Board of Governors, Box 51. See also W. Fielding to Walker, 6 April 1907, ibid.
66 D. Macgillivary to Walker, 6 April 1907, ibid.
67 Falconer 'Glimpses of the University at Work' 127
68 Jeanneret *Falconer* 11
69 A copy of the cable can be found in the papers of the search committee, Office of the Secretary of the Board of Governors, Box 51.
70 Walker to G.H. Murray, 15 April 1907, WP, Box 30
71 Falconer to Walker, 26 April 1907, Office of the Secretary of the Board of Governors, Box 51
72 *Halifax Herald* (29 May 1907) 1.
73 Minutes of Board of Pine Hill (30 May 1907) 89
74 Osler to Walker, 29 May 1907, Office of the Secretary of the Board of Governors, Box 51
75 Smith to Walker, 18 Aug. 1907, WP, Box 16
76 Neatby *Queen's University* 256
77 T. Callander to D.M. Gordon, 17 June 1907, Gordon Papers, Box 1
78 George Parkin to G.M. Wrong, 22 May 1907, Wrong Papers, Box 3.
79 Wrong to Walker, 15 May 1907, WP, Box 16.
80 Wrong to Walker, 28 May 1907, ibid.
81 Walker to Wrong, 16 May 1907; 6 June 1907, ibid.
82 Bowell to Walker, 30 April 1907, Office of the Secretary of the Board of Governors, Box 51
83 *Mail and Empire* (27 April 1907) 2
84 *News*, article reprinted in the *Halifax Herald* (4 June 1907) 1
85 Ibid. (30 April 1907) 1
86 *Presbyterian*, clipping found in FP, Clipping File.
87 Walker to Bowell, 26 April 1907, WP, Box 30
88 J.P. Whitney to E.C. Whitney, Sept. 1907, Whitney Papers, MU 3123
89 Falconer 'Glimpses of the University at Work' 128
90 See the numerous invitations and rejections recorded in FP (1907–8), Box 1
91 Falconer to the Rev. Robert Pogue (St Paul's Church, Peterborough) 7 March 1908, ibid., Box 2
92 See, for example, Walker to Falconer, 9 Dec. 1907, WP, Box 30
93 *News* (26 April 1907) 7

95 This from an item in FP, Clipping File, Item 72.
96 Ibid., Item 68
97 Ibid., Item 92
98 Ibid., Item 96
99 Ibid., Item 99
100 Ibid., Item 62
101 Ibid., Item 64
102 *Halifax Herald* (27 April 1907) 1
103 *Theologue* (18 April 1907) 136
104 Jeanneret *Falconer* 17
105 Falconer 'Glimpses of the University at Work' 389
106 Ibid.
107 Wrong to Walker, 28 May 1907, WP, Box 16
108 Wrong to W.L. Grant, 6 July 1907, Grant Papers, Box 10
109 Falconer to Murray, 29 June 1907, MP
110 Macgillivary to Walker, 3 June 1907, WP, Box 16
111 For a description of the event and transcripts of the speeches see the *Halifax Herald* and the Halifax *Morning Chronicle* (16 Aug. 1907) 1–2
112 G.H. Murray to Walker, 6 April 1907, Office of the Secretary of the Board of Governors, Box 51
113 Falconer to Murray, 28 Aug. 1907, MP
114 For a description of this demonstration of support see the *Globe* (27 Sept. 1907) 1–2
115 The text of the speech was printed in the *University of Toronto Monthly* 8 (1907) 6–14. It was also reported in most of the Toronto papers on 27 September 1907. For a discussion of the educational values and concept of a university Falconer outlined here, see chapter VI.
116 *Star* (28 Sept. 1907) 6
117 See these and other items in FP, Clipping File.
118 Flavelle to J.P. Whitney, 26 Sept. 1907, Whitney Papers, MU 3123
119 Falconer to John Hoskin, 27 Sept. 1907, FP, Box 1
120 Falconer to Murray, 9 March 1908, MP
121 Falconer 'Glimpses of the University at Work' 391
122 Jeanneret *Falconer* 16
123 This comment and the foregoing observations on Falconer's approach to soothing the university's factions are to be found in ibid., 16–17
124 Falconer to J.S. Robertson of the Canadian Temperance League, 12 Feb. 1908, FP, Box 2
125 For a sample of these Canadian Club speeches see the Ottawa *Free Press* (18 Nov. 1907); the Hamilton *Spectator* (21 Feb. 1908); the Collingwood *Bulletin* (8 April 1909), FP, Clipping File.
126 Falconer to Murray, 9 March 1908, MP
127 Bliss *Canadian Millionaire* 204
128 R. Falconer *President's Report 1907–1908* 13–14
129 Falconer to Flavelle, 16 May 1908, FP, Box 1

130 The compromise was engineered by Flavelle and described in Falconer's *President's Report 1908–1909* 10.

131 For the substance of this interview see the testimony of Elmore Harris and Falconer before the special committee of the Board of Governors set up to investigate the issue. Its proceedings can be found in WP, Box 40. See particularly 22 March 1909.

132 Johnston *McMaster University* (Vol. 1) 107

133 For this information I am indebted to Professor John Moir, who made early drafts of his book, *A Sense of Proportion,* available to me.

134 See Harris's statement to the special investigating committee of the Board of Governors, 22 March 1909, WP, Box 40.

135 S.H. Blake to Hoskin, 30 Nov. 1908, ibid.

136 Hoskin to Blake, 14 Dec. 1908, ibid.

137 Blake to Hoskin, 22 Dec. 1908, copy in Burwash Papers, Box 2

138 As late as 1909 Burwash was still lamenting Workman's fate and believed that he could have been saved if he had been less 'unfortunate in his way of putting things.' Burwash to Rev. Wm Philip, 6 Feb. 1909, Burwash Papers, Box 7

139 Burwash to Blake, 9 Jan. 1909, Burwash Papers, Box 2

140 Blake to J.P. Whitney, 28 Dec. 1908, Whitney Papers, MU 3126

141 Blake to Burwash, 11 Feb. 1909, Burwash Papers, Box 2

142 For details on the McMaster conflict see Johnston *McMaster* (Vol. 1) 91–106.

143 Bliss *Canadian Millionaire* 201–2

144 The records of the committee are preserved in WP, Box 40. All subsequent references to its deliberations, examination of witnesses and recommendations are based on this material unless otherwise noted below.

145 Blake *Teaching of Religious Knowledge;* copy in FP, Box 5

146 See Moir 'Mildewed with Discretion.'

147 Blake's views were printed in the *News* on 5 March, and on the following day most of the Toronto papers carried feature items on the dispute.

148 See, for example, the *Globe* (9 March 1909) 6 and (25 March 1909) 6; the *Star* (16 March 1909) 6, in which the editor condemned those who would stifle free inquiry at the University of Toronto.

149 Harris made great use of this editorial in his presentation to the committee on 22 March.

150 *Star* (12 March 1909) 1

151 The views of these ministers were published in the *Globe* (8 March 1909) 3.

152 Crummy's strictures levelled at Blake appeared in the *Star* (8 March 1909) 3.

153 Falconer to Murray, 10 March 1909, MP

154 Blake *The Orthodox Pupil Versus the Unorthodox Teacher; The Knife of the Higher Critic; What Is Truth?;* all were published by L.S. Haynes Press of Toronto in 1909. For copies see FP, Box 5.

155 Falconer to Z. Lash, 22 April 1909, FP, Box 6

Chapter VI The Organic University

1   Falconer to W.C. Murray, 30 Dec. 1907, MP
2   These remarks were made at a testimonial dinner sponsored by the Alumni Association in honour of Falconer and his immediate predecessor, Maurice Hutton. For details see the *University of Toronto Monthly* 8 (1908) 214–15.
3   L. Abbott 'William Rainey Harper' *Outlook* 82 (1906) 110–11, cited and penetratingly analysed in Rudolph *American College and University* 356
4   Thompson *University of Saskatchewan* 31–3
5   Heyck *Transformation of Intellectual Life* 186
6   Craig 'Compulsion of the National Life'
7   Rudolph *American College* 359–65. See also Veysey *Emergence of the American University* 60–5.
8   Newman *Idea of a University* 5
9   Ibid.
10 Bissell *Strength of a University* 83
11 Newman *Idea,* 5
12 Ibid. 8
13 Ibid. 12
14 Ibid. 13
15 Eric Ashby 'Reconciliation of Tradition and Modernity in Universities' in McMurrion ed. *Meaning of a University* 18
16 Newman *Idea* 10
17 The distinction between the virtues of civility and moral virtues in Newman's thought is nicely delineated by J.M. Cameron in his *On the Idea of a University* 17.
18 Heyck *Transformation* 166
19 Veysey *American University* 21–47
20 McKillop *Disciplined Intelligence* 13, 230–1
21 Rudolph *American College* 455
22 In fact over 9,000 Americans enrolled in German universities in the nineteenth century. See Hofstadter and Metzger *Development of Academic Freedom* 367.
23 Rudolph *American College* 338
24 Veysey *American University* 127. See also Hofstadter and Metzger *Academic Freedom* 373.
25 Rudolph *American College* 352
26 Brubacher *Philosophy of Higher Education* 6
27 Veblen *Higher Learning in America* 13, cited in Veysey *American University* 121
28 Bissell *Strength of a University* 83
29 Newman *Idea* 15
30 Brubacher *Higher Education* 6
31 Ibid. 3
32 Rudolph *American College* 363

33 On the influence of Green and his attitudes towards 'service' see Richter *Politics of Conscience* 267–323.
34 Nimocks *Milner's Young Men*
35 These observations on Peterson and McGill are drawn from E. Collard 'Peterson's Principalship' in MacLennan *McGill* 77–86.
36 Thompson *University of Saskatchewan* 31–3
37 On the 'Queen's spirit' and its influence see McKillop *Disciplined Intelligence* 218–19; Neatby *Queen's University* 269; Allen *Social Passion* passim; Granatstein *The Ottawa Men*, in all of which the influence of Queen's graduates in the federal civil service is assessed.
38 Heyck *Transformation* 176–8. For a full analysis of Pattison's views see Sparrow *Mark Pattison*.
39 C. Kerr *The Uses of a University* (1963), cited and analysed in Brubacher *Higher Education* 3
40 C.T. Bissell 'Characteristics of a Great University' speech delivered in Vancouver in February 1965 and reprinted in Bissell *Strength of a University* 153–62
41 Falconer to Beatty, 18 Dec. 1926, FP, Box 99
42 R. Falconer 'The Universities and the Balance of Studies' in Alex Hill ed. *The Second Congress of the Universities of the Empire 1921: Report of Proceedings* (London 1921) 19
43 Falconer *Idealism and National Character* 81
44 Ibid. 23
45 Ibid. 194–5
46 Falconer 'Inaugural Address' (1907)
47 Falconer 'Functions of State and Church in Education'
48 R. Falconer 'The Power of Ideas in National Life' speech delivered to Canadian Club of Hamilton, 20 Feb. 1908. The text of the speech is recorded in unidentified newspaper cuttings found in FP, Clipping File.
49 Falconer 'Conflict of Educational Ideals' 237
50 Ibid. 238
51 Falconer 'Place of Authority in the University Spirit' (1908) 13–15
52 Falconer *Idealism and National Character* 30, 85
53 Falconer 'Conflict of Educational Ideals' 228
54 Ibid. 239
55 'Inaugural Address' 8
56 R. Falconer 'The Mission of Canada to the Nations' *Collingwood Bulletin* (8 April 1909) 4
57 Falconer 'Conflict of Educational Ideals' 239
58 Falconer 'Place of Authority' 15
59 Falconer 'Distinctive Feature of an English Speaking University' (1918) 25
60 'Address on the Training of Dental Students' copy in FP, Box 71, 8–9
61 Veysey *American University* 203
62 'Inaugural Address' 7
63 'Address on Dental Students' 11

64 Falconer 'Humanities in the War-Time University' 4
65 *President's Report 1907–1908* 10
66 Falconer to Whitney, 9 July 1908, FP, Box 3. He made the same point about the need to induce students in the professional schools to take arts courses in his *President's Report 1907–1908* 8.
67 Rudolph *American College* 456 and Veysey *American University* 243, 250
68 For Falconer's version of the founding of Hart House, see his 'Glimpses of the University at Work' 131–2.
69 See, for example, his assertions on this point in his *President's Report 1907–1908*, 10 and *1908–1909*, 6, and *1911–1912*, 9.
70 Meikle 'And Gladly Teach' 98, 118
71 Falconer *United States as a Neighbour* 236
72 Rudolph *American College* 350–2.
73 Falconer 'Probably there is no country' untitled address dated 19 Feb. 1929, FP, Miscellaneous Manuscripts and Pamphlets
74 Falconer 'Functions of State and Church' 554
75 G.M. Wrong, J.S. Willison, Z.A. Lash, and R.A. Falconer *The Federation of Canada 1867–1917* (Toronto: Ryerson 1917) 133
76 'Inaugural Address' 8. He made precisely the same point in a speech to the Congress of the Universities of the Empire in 1921. See its *Report of Proceedings* 19
77 *President's Report 1907–1908* 11
78 Falconer 'Canada's Mission to the Nations' 4
79 *President's Report 1907–1908* 11–12
80 Ibid. *1910–1911* 12
81 Most of this paragraph is based on observations that Falconer made in ibid. *1907–1908* 11–12.
82 Falconer 'Place of Authority' 21
83 'Inaugural Address' 10
84 Ibid. 11
85 Falconer 'Address on Dental Students' 10
86 *Edmonton Daily Bulletin* (5 May 1913), copy in FP, Clipping File
87 Falconer *Idealism and National Character* 86
88 'Inaugural Address' 12
89 Resumé of speech by Falconer at alumni dinner in honour of Maurice Hutton, 25 Feb. 1908. See *University of Toronto Monthly* 8 (1908) 215.
90 'Inaugural Address' 10–11
91 R. Falconer 'Students and City Life' article contributed to Toronto *Star* (13 March 1909) 6
92 For the views of Cappon, Shortt, and Hutton on this point see Shortt *Search for an Ideal* 61, 62, 71, 88, 111.
93 This view was put forth by Falconer in an address to the Canadian Club of Hamilton on 20 February 1908. See clipping in FP, Clipping File.
94 These remarks on the value of the university as a unifying force in the nation are drawn from a speech to the Canadian Club of Ottawa, delivered on 17

November 1907. See a cutting from the Ottawa *Free Press* (18 Nov. 1907) in
FP, Clipping File. Similar statements can be found in his 'Inaugural Address.'
95 *President's Report 1909–1910* 7
96 Falconer 'Universities and Balance of Studies' 18
97 Falconer to the governor-general, Earl Grey, 27 April 1910, FP, Box 9
98 *President's Report 1913–1914* 10
99 Falconer to Walter Murray, 5 Sept. 1908, MP
100 See, for example, Loudon's address on technical education delivered to the
convocation of 1899 and a similar paper entitled 'High Schools,' both of
which can be found in the Loudon Papers, Box 1.

Chapter VII The Larger Context

1 Falconer to Flavelle, 23 Oct. 1913, Borden Papers, 77491
2 Queen's, for example, had put in a similar bid through J.S. Willison, and
McGill had urged its own cause. Willison to Borden, 28 Oct. 1913, Borden
Papers, 77488.
3 Falconer *Idealism and National Character* 12
4 Ibid. 14
5 The quotation is drawn from an address by Falconer to the English-Speaking
Union in New York in 1926. See a copy of the address in FP, Miscellaneous
Manuscripts and Pamphlets.
6 See, for example, his *President's Report 1913–1914* 5.
7 W.L. Grant to A.J. Glazebrook, 17 Dec. 1910, W.L. Grant Papers, Box 4
8 Glazebrook to Lord Milner, 12 Dec. 1916, Glazebrook Papers, Box 1
9 Falconer to Walter Murray, 15 May 1908, MP
10 Falconer 'Universities and Balance of Studies' 23–4
11 The clearest expression of his views on the matter are to be found in his
United States as a Neighbour.
12 For a discussion of the continentalist outlook in Falconer's generation see
Berger *Writing of Canadian History* 138–59.
13 Falconer *United States as a Neighbour* 174.
14 Ibid. 180–3
15 Ibid. 178
16 Ibid. 180
17 Falconer 'New Imperial Allegiance' 24
18 'Undergraduate Preparation for Post Graduate Study,' FP, Miscellaneous
Manuscripts and Pamphlets (7 May 1929), 4
19 Falconer *United States as a Neighbour* 236
20 'Undergraduate Preparation' 9
21 This was the title of his address to the Ottawa Canadian Club in November
1907; FP, Clipping File.
22 Falconer 'Unification of Canada' (1908). 'The Power of Ideas in Our
National Life' was a later version of the same work delivered as a speech in
Hamilton, 20 February 1908. See cutting in ibid.

23 Ibid.
24 Falconer 'Individuality of the Canadian People' (1910) which was an adaptation of an address delivered in February of that year at Johns Hopkins University.
25 Falconer 'Unification of Canada' 4–5
26 Ibid. 8–9
27 *President's Report 1907–1908* 5–6
28 Ibid. *1908–1909* 1
29 Ibid. *1907–1908* 7–8
30 Falconer 'Needs of the University of Toronto II' (1908) 54–6
31 *President's Report 1908–1909* 6
32 Falconer 'Needs of U. of T. II' 56. See also his *President's Report 1907–1908* 8.
33 He told Falconer as much in a letter of July 1908. J.P. Whitney to Falconer, 10 July 1908, FP, Box 3
34 Bliss *Canadian Millionaire* 205
35 Board of Governors Papers (9 July 1908)
36 J.P. Whitney to Falconer, 10 July 1908, FP, Box 3
37 Falconer to Murray, 4 April 1910, MP
38 Falconer to Murray, 21 May 1910, MP
39 Falconer to Murray, 4 April 1910, MP
40 *President's Report 1910–1911* 7–9
41 Ibid. *1911–1912* 11
42 The original letter has not survived. It was written before 6 Feb. 1913, when Falconer replied. Its contents, however, are easily inferred from another letter that expanded on Chown's first blast. See G.Y. Chown to Walker, 13 Feb. 1913, WP, Box 20.
43 Falconer to Walker, 6 Feb. 1913, ibid.
44 Falconer to Chown, 22 Feb. 1913, ibid.
45 Falconer to Murray, 6 Feb. 1910, MP
46 The substance of this meeting is recorded in *The Journal of B.E. Walker* 1 (18 Oct. 1910) 281. These papers are available in the University of Toronto Rare Book room.
47 *President's Report 1911–1912* 13
48 Falconer to Walker, 28 June 1913, WP, Box 20
49 Board of Governors Papers (11 June 1914)
50 J.P. Whitney to Walker, 2 July 1914, WP, Box 21
51 Walker to Falconer, 29 July 1914, WP, Box 33.
52 Falconer 'Glimpses of the University at Work' 134
53 For a sample of Falconer's complaints see his *President's Report 1907–1908* 11.
54 See the figures in Falconer's *President's Reports* for the appropriate years.
55 Ibid. *1910–1911* 9
56 Ibid. *1908–1909* 9
57 Ibid. *1910–1911* 9–12
58 Ibid. *1911–1912* 8
59 Ibid.

60 Falconer to Murray, 10 Feb. 1912, MP
61 Falconer 'Glimpses of the University at Work' 395
62 *President's Report 1912–1913* 9
63 Falconer 'Glimpses of the University at Work' 394
64 Ibid. 395–6
65 Falconer to Murray, 10 July 1914, MP
66 MacLennan *McGill* 105
67 Neatby *Queen's University* 185
68 Falconer 'Unification of Canada' 8–9
69 *President's Report 1907–1908* 11
70 Falconer 'Glimpses of the University at Work' 399
71 Meikle 'And Gladly Teach' 63
72 Drummond *Political Economy* 39
73 Meikle 'And Gladly Teach' 61
74 Drummond *Political Economy* 41
75 For a discussion of this prewar debate on graduate studies see Falconer's 'Glimpses of the University at Work' 398–9 and his 'From College to University' 13–14.
76 *President's Report 1910–1911* 12
77 Berger *The Sense of Power* 264
78 The term 'Britannic Nationalism' was aptly coined by D. Cole in his 'Canada's Nationalistic Imperialists' and his 'The Problem of "Nationalism" and "Imperialism" in British Settlement Colonies.'
79 Falconer to Wrong, 4 Jan. 1911, FP, Box 16 and Falconer to Kylie, 12 March 1912, FP, Box 18
80 On the tactics and goals of the Round Table see Kendle *The Round Table Movement and Imperial Union.* For further clarification see Nimocks *Milner's Young Men* and J. Eayrs 'The Round Table Movement in Canada 1909–1920' *Canadian Historical Review* 38 (1957) 1–20.
81 Letter of reference supporting William Caldwell addressed by Falconer to Whom it May Concern, 14 May 1908, FP, Box 1
82 Falconer's lengthy letter to Willison on the subject of imperial preference was penned on 27 June 1910. See the Willison Papers, Box 13. His criticism of Chamberlain's scheme not only meshed with that of the contemporary British Liberals but also has been mirrored in the sober reflections of later historians who have questioned the short-range feasibility and saleability of the idea. See, for example, Kubicek *The Administration of Imperialism* and, more recently, Porter *Britain, Europe and the World.*
83 Falconer to Murray, 10 Feb. 1912, MP
84 Falconer to Murray, 20 March 1911, ibid.
85 Bliss *Canadian Millionaire* 214
86 Falconer to Borden, 22 Sept. 1911, Borden Papers, 77650
87 Falconer to Murray, 31 July 1912, MP
88 Falconer to Willison, Oct.-Nov. 1909, Willison Papers, Box 13
89 Falconer *Idealism in National Character* 51

90 Falconer 'British Universities' (1925) 11
91 Falconer to Willison, 20 July 1925, Willison Papers, Box 13
92 Falconer 'The Quality of Canadian Life' in G.M. Wrong et al. *Federation of Canada* 133
93 Meikle 'And Gladly Teach' **87**, 166
94 Drummond *Political Economy* 43–4
95 Falconer to S. Mackenzie, 3 May 1912, FP, Box 19
96 Drummond *Political Economy* 45
97 Falconer to J.G. Robertson (University of London), 10 May 1915, FP, Box 36
98 Falconer to Mackenzie, 28 Feb. 1918, FP, Box 48
99 A.D. Steel-Maitland to Falconer, 28 Jan. 1908, ibid.
100 For details on the career of this individual see Grier *Achievement in Education*.
101 Falconer to H.R. Macintosh (Edinburgh), 6 March 1909, FP, Box 6
102 See, for example, his letters to A.L. Smith, Sydney Ball, Kenneth Bell, H.W. Blunt, D.S. Cairns, and H.R. Macintosh in FP, Boxes 5–8.
103 Falconer to D.S. Cairns (Aberdeen), 25 Nov. 1908, FP, Box 5.
104 Falconer to Mavor, 6 July 1909, Mavor Papers, Box 5
105 Falconer to Walker, 20 Aug. 1909, WP, Box 17
106 Ibid. See also Falconer to Mavor, 4 Aug. 1909, Mavor Papers for further details. For biographical information concerning Lloyd see his letter of application to the University of Sheffield, 12 May 1909, in FP, Box 9. See also Drummond *Political Economy*, passim.
107 Drummond *Political Economy* 45
108 Falconer to Sadler, 15 April 1913 and 30 May 1913, FP, Box 25
109 Haldane *Universities and National Life* 68
110 Grier *Achievement in Education* 26
111 Falconer to Sadler, 21 Dec. 1909, FP, Box 10
112 See a flier describing this body and its membership in FP, Box 81.
113 For further details see Greenlee *Education and Imperial Unity*.
114 J.A. Hill to Falconer, 6 July 1910, FP, Box 16
115 H.M. Tory to Wm. Peterson, 17 Dec. 1910, Peterson Papers, Box 19
116 Falconer to Murray, 6 Feb. 1910, MP
117 For a history of the Association of Universities and Colleges of Canada see Pilkington 'History of the National Conference of Canadian Universities'.
118 R.D. Roberts *Report on Preliminary Conference of Canadian Universities*, copy in FP, Box 16.
119 Much of this paragraph concerning the PH D degree is based on a recent study by Renate Simpson entitled *How the Ph.D. Came To Britain* passim.
120 Falconer to R.D. Roberts, 30 Sept. 1911 and Falconer to Sir Henry Miers, 11 Dec. 1911, FP, Box 19.
121 'The Congress of the Universities of the Empire 1912' *University of Toronto Monthly* 13 (1912) 62
122 R.M. Meredith to J.P. Whitney, 9 July 1912, Whitney Papers, MU 3133
123 'The Congress' 62
124 Falconer to Murray, 31 July 1912, MP

125 'The Congress' 64

126 Simpson *How the Ph.D. Came to Britain* 145

127 For the text of Parkin's speech and reactions to it see the *Report of the Congress of the Universities of the Empire*, excerpt of the afternoon session (5 July 1912), 1–5, copy in FP, Box 26.

128 Falconer to W.P. Ker (Shanghai), 20 April 1908, FP, Box 2

129 See, for example, a letter from W.E. Taylor to Falconer, 6 Oct. 1909, FP, Box 55. Taylor was associate secretary of the Central Chinese YMCA at Shanghai and had met Falconer at Northfield in 1905.

130 J.H. Wallace (associate secretary of the Central Chinese YMCA at Shanghai) to Falconer, 8 Sept. 1908, ibid. In this letter Wallace included a copy of a letter addressed to him by Ker, British acting consul general at Tientsin. Written on 8 May 1908, it outlined several of the arguments that Wallace put to Falconer.

131 Falconer to Ker, 20 April 1908, FP, Box 2

132 Minutes of the Board of Governors (28 Jan. 1909)

133 He mentioned this 'slight' prejudice in a letter to Mackenzie King, 10 May 1909, King Papers, Series J1.

134 For a discussion of the Laurier government's and especially Mackenzie King's attitude to this issue see Dawson *William Lyon Mackenzie King* Vol. 1, 146–96.

135 Falconer to Laurier, 26 Feb. 1909, FP, Box 6

136 Laurier to Falconer, 27 Feb. 1909, ibid.

137 Resolution of a meeting held in Montreal, 3 May 1909. The resolution was then communicated to Laurier. See a copy in ibid.

138 Falconer to Mackenzie King, 10 May 1909, ibid.

139 King to Falconer, 11 May 1909, King Papers, Series J1

140 Falconer to Wallace, 11 June 1909, FP, Box 7

141 Pilkington 'A History' 57–67. For details on the process of lobbying by Falconer and others, consult the Borden Papers, 100641, 100652–6, 100675–7, 100695–6, 100700–7, which cover the period 6 June 1914 to 16 May 1917.

142 *A University for China: The United Universities Scheme* 2. A copy of this brochure can be found in FP, Box 16.

143 Ibid. 3–4

144 Rev. Ld. Wm. Gascoyne-Cecil to Wrong, 16 Dec. 1910, Wrong Papers, Box 1

145 *A University for China* 2, 5

146 Cecil to Wrong, 16 Dec. 1910, Wrong Papers, Box 1

147 The involvement of Sadler and Miers was made plain to Falconer in a letter from the scheme's organizing secretary. See J. Leslie Johnston to Falconer, 7 June 1910, FP, Box 9.

148 Memorandum by Falconer on the China University Scheme, FP, Box 16

149 Falconer to Walker, 8 Jan. 1911, ibid. and Falconer to Seth Low, 12 Jan. 1912, FP, Box 18

150 Kurland *Seth Low* 220, 330

151 Cecil to Wrong, 11 March 1911, Wrong Papers, Box 1
152 Falconer to Wrong, 17 April 1911, FP, Box 16
153 Low to Ronald Hodgkin (secretary of the English Committee), 9 Jan. 1912, copy in ibid.
154 Low to Falconer, 1 May 1912, ibid.
155 Cecil to Wrong, 16 Dec. 1910, Wrong Papers, Box 1
156 Cecil to Wrong, 11 March 1911, ibid.
157 Low to W.E. Soothill, 10 Jan. 1912, copy in FP, Box 16. See also Low to Falconer, 1 May 1912, ibid.
158 See, for example, the exchange of letters between Falconer and Low on this problem, FP, Box 18 and specifically Low to Falconer, 18 Dec. 1912, FP, Box 24.
159 Falconer to Hon. H.E. Young (minister of education for British Columbia), 21 Dec. 1911, F.F. Wesbrook Papers, University of British Columbia Archives, Box 1
160 Falconer to Murray, 5 Aug. 1911, MP
161 Falconer 'Science and Religion' 340–4

Chapter VIII The Glorious Days of Our Race: 1914–18

1 Falconer recounted the events of the voyage in the *Calgarian* to Murray in a letter; 8 Sept. 1914, FP, Box 35.
2 Falconer to Murray, 1 April 1914, MP
3 Falconer to Murray, 10 July 1914, ibid.
4 'President Falconer Home From War Zone' *Globe* (8 Sept. 1914) 6
5 Falconer relayed his experiences in Norway and England to the press the day after his return. See, for example, the *Globe* (8 Sept. 1914) 6.
6 Falconer to Murray, 8 Sept. 1914, FP, Box 35
7 Falconer to Sir Henry Miers, 12 Sept. 1914, ibid.
8 Mueller, in the midst of his row with Hagarty, published a profile of himself in several Toronto newspapers. For example, see the *Star* (25 Sept. 1914) 8.
9 'German-Canadians and the War' *Globe* (6 Aug. 1914) 4
10 Mueller to Falconer, 14 Sept. 1914, FP, Box 35
11 'Critics are Censured, Hagarty Commended' *Star* (25 Sept. 1914) 3
12 All the Toronto papers covered the Board of Education meeting of 2 October, but the fullest and most balanced account was carried in the *Star* (3 Oct. 1914) 12.
13 W.H. Hearst to Falconer, 9 Oct. 1914, FP, Box 34
14 Falconer to Hearst, 10 Oct. 1914; Hearst to Falconer, 15 Oct. 1914, ibid.
15 'German Case Complete' *Star* (14 Oct. 1914) 2
16 J.S. Campbell to R.W. Leonard, 15 Oct. 1914, copy in FP, Box 34
17 This statement was recalled in Leonard's obituary. See the *Globe* (18 Dec. 1930) 4. It was perfectly typical of a man who throughout his life showered lavish gifts on imperial foundations such as Chatham House.

18 Leonard to Falconer, 16 Oct. 1914, FP, Box 34
19 Falconer to Leonard, 17 Oct. 1914, ibid.
20 *Star* (21 Oct. 1914) 8
21 Falconer to B.E. Walker, 23 Dec. 1913, WP, Box 20
22 Flavelle revealed the full details of these Conservative suspicions to Falconer in a letter of 17 Dec. 1914. See copy in FP, Box 37.
23 Falconer to Flavelle, 18 Dec. 1914, FP, Box. 34.
24 Falconer to George Coyne, 23 Dec. 1914, FP, Box 33.
25 Wilson ed. *Ontario and the First World War* xxv
26 *Star* (26 Oct. 1914) 6
27 *Globe* (14 Nov. 1914) 6
28 Ibid. (12 Dec. 1914) 9
29 Walker made this clear in a letter to the editor of the *Star* (5 Dec. 1914) 2.
30 I am indebted to Professor John Moir of Scarborough College for this information on Benzinger's background.
31 *Globe* (2 Sept. 1914) 6
32 A. Langmesser to Falconer, 9 Sept. 1914, FP, Box 33
33 This approach he later explained to Falconer, who in turn reported to the Board of Governors. See Minutes of the Board of Governors (3 Dec. 1914).
34 Macdonald testified to this suppression at a meeting of the Board of Governors on 4 Dec. 1914. See Board Minutes for that date. Falconer also referred to this in his report to the Board written the previous day. See *Report Regarding Native Born Germans*, 3 Dec. 1914, copy in FP, Box 33.
35 John Squair to Falconer, 28 Oct. 1914, FP, Box 36
36 Walker later disclosed that Falconer's letter to the press was prompted by an interview with Hearst. Walker to Sir Edmund Osler, 19 Nov. 1914, WP, Box 33.
37 A copy of the original letter, dated 14 Nov. 1914, can be found in FP, Box 37. The letter was published in the Toronto newspapers on 16 November.
38 Osler to Walker, 18 Nov. 1914, WP, Box 21. A copy of Osler's protest to Falconer can be found in the same box.
39 In his reply to Osler, Walker was conciliatory in tone but stated quite clearly his own view that there was no reason to fire the professors. Walker to Osler, 19 Nov. 1914, WP, Box 33.
40 Wilkie's letter and a description of the circumstances under which it was written appeared in the newspapers on 2 December 1914. See the *Globe* 4.
41 The *Varsity* article was reprinted by the *Star* (2 Dec. 1914) 3.
42 'President Inspires Entire University' *Star* (3 Dec. 1914) 5. The precise number of Toronto men who flocked to the colours in the wake of Falconer's opening address is recorded in Wilson *Ontario and First World War* civ.
43 Walker to Falconer, 2 Dec. 1914, WP, Box 33
44 Minutes of the Board of Governors (3 Dec. 1914)
45 Walker to Osler, 19 Nov. 1914, WP, Box 33

46 Falconer expressed many of the fears that haunted Walker in a letter to
Archibald MacMechan, 7 Jan. 1915, MacMechan Papers.

47 Falconer discussed this subject with Murray in a letter, 18 Jan. 1915, MP. He
stated that the German professors issue had raised for the first time the
question of the dismissal of the president. The *Star* also commented on the
issue (7 Dec. 1915) 1.

48 Ibid.

49 Orr was cited in the *Star* (7 Dec. 1914) 1.

50 *Globe* (8 Dec. 1914) 9

51 Ibid.

52 *Star* (7 Dec. 1914) 1

53 *Globe* (8 Dec. 1914) 13

54 Ibid. (9 Dec. 1914) 9. On the following day the *Globe* noted that the Cedar-
vale Conservative Association also passed a resolution condemning the
leave of absence; see 8.

55 For a description of Hearst's meeting with the all-party delegation see *ibid.*
(16 Dec. 1914) 8.

56 Falconer to McCurdy, 25 March 1915, FP, Box 35

57 For a large sample of Falconer's letters to American heads on this point, see
'German File,' FP, Box 37.

58 McCurdy brought this point to Falconer's attention after visiting Benzinger
at Princeton. See McCurdy to Falconer, 21 March 1915, FP Box 35.

59 See *Globe* (25 Dec. 1914) 13 and (31 Dec. 1914) 6.

60 Falconer to Flavelle, 18 Dec. 1914, FP, Box 34

61 Falconer to Willison, 12 Dec. 1914, Willison Papers, Box 13

62 Falconer to MacMechan, 26 Dec. 1914, MacMechan Papers

63 Falconer to J.S. Bell, 14 Dec. 1914, FP, Box 33

64 Falconer *German Tragedy* (1915) 19

65 Mason 'Sins of Civilization'

66 *Star* (29 Sept. 1914) 3

67 Ibid.

68 Falconer *German Tragedy* 1

69 Ibid. 35

70 Ibid. 14

71 Ibid. 45

72 *Star* (29 Sept. 1914) 3

73 Falconer to W.H. Dickenson, 13 Sept. 1911, FP, Box 21

74 *Star* (29 Sept. 1914) 3

75 Falconer *German Tragedy* 83

76 Ibid. 90

77 *Star* (5 Oct. 1914) 11

78 Falconer, letter to the editor of the Halifax *Morning Chronicle*. A copy of this
dated 21 Dec. 1914 can be found in FP, Box 33.

79 Falconer to MacMechan, 18 April 1915, MacMechan Papers

80 R. Falconer 'What About Progress?' address delivered at the Drexel Institute

in Philadelphia in the spring of 1916. It was eventually published in his *Idealism and National Character* 113–15.

81 Falconer *German Tragedy* 5
82 Pearson *Mike* 17
83 Falconer 'New Imperial Allegiance' (1916) 16
84 Falconer to W.A. Bailey, 2 Oct. 1914, FP, Box 33
85 Falconer *German Tragedy* 7
86 Ibid. 8
87 Falconer '1776 and 1914' (1918) 242
88 Falconer 'New Imperial Allegiance' 17
89 Greenlee '"A Succession of Seeleys"'
90 Falconer '1776 and 1914' 242
91 Falconer *German Tragedy* 76
92 Falconer '1776 and 1914' 241
93 Falconer 'New Imperial Allegiance' 20
94 Ibid. 14
95 Ibid. 21
96 Ibid. 24
97 *Star* (21 Oct. 1914) 8
98 These figures on enrolment in the University of Toronto OTC are cited in Wilson *Ontario and First World War* civ.
99 *President's Report 1914–1915* 8
100 Ontario Department of Education circular #2142, copy in FP, Box 38
101 *President's Report 1914–1915* 9
102 Falconer to Borden, 13 April 1915, Borden Papers, 16895
103 Walker to Borden, 21 April 1915, ibid.
104 The reference here is to a speech delivered by Borden to the Empire and Canadian Clubs of Toronto in joint session in which he praised the loyalty of German-Canadians and called for restraint by those who questioned their allegiance. See a copy of this speech in the *Star* (5 Dec. 1914) 10.
105 For details concerning Toronto's war work during this period see Falconer's *President's Report 1914–1915*.
106 Ibid. 8
107 Ibid. 1915–1916 8
108 Ibid. 1916–1917 7
109 Falconer 'An Address to Commemorate Varsity's Work in the War,' copy in FP, Box 56
110 *President's Report 1914–1915* 10
111 Ibid. *1916–1917* 7
112 Falconer to Murray, 24 Dec. 1915, MP
113 Falconer to Wm. Peterson, 14 Oct. 1916, Peterson Papers, Box 20
114 Wilson *Ontario and First World War* xlix
115 Falconer to Borden, 27 Nov. 1916, Borden Papers, 116773
116 Borden to Falconer, 30 Nov. 1916, ibid., 116772

117 Falconer to Borden, 2 Dec. 1916, ibid., 116790
118 Falconer referred to this meeting in a letter to MacMechan but did not elaborate on the substance of the conversation. Falconer to MacMechan, 25 Dec. 1916, MacMechan Papers
119 The substance of Wilson's Christmas note is cited by R. Hofstadter in his *American Political Tradition* 268.
120 Falconer to MacMechan, 25 Dec. 1916, MacMechan Papers
121 Wilson *Ontario and First World War* liv
122 Minutes of the Board of Governors (11 Jan. 1917)
123 Ibid. (10 May 1917)
124 *Globe* (19 May 1917) 8. Here Falconer's views on conscription and his Convocation Hall address were noted.
125 The proceedings of the General Assembly were reported in ibid. (11 June 1917) 7.
126 Falconer to Murray, 24 July 1917, MP
127 Falconer to Borden, 12 Oct. 1917, Borden Papers, 73499
128 Ibid., 30 Oct. 1917, 40935–6
129 Borden to Falconer, 31 Oct. 1917, ibid., 40943
130 Ibid.
131 For reaction to the knighting of Falconer see, for example, *Globe* (4 June 1917) 1; *Varsity* (26 Sept. 1917) 1; *Trinity University Review* (1917) 34.
132 Falconer to Walker, 4 June 1917, WP, Box 22
133 For example, this rumour was stated clearly in *Trinity University Review* (1917) 34
134 Jeanneret *Falconer* 25–6
135 In 1979 Robert D. Falconer told the author of this present work that he had relayed the story to Jeanneret. See tape of this interview, conducted on 13 July 1979, in the University of Toronto Archives, Oral History Project.
136 Ibid.
137 Falconer to Murray, 8 Aug. 1917, MP
138 Falconer to the Hon. J.J. Jusserand (French ambassador to Washington), 21 March 1918, FP, Box 47
139 War Lectures Bureau flier, found in FP, Box 49
140 Ibid.
141 There are several official and unofficial historical summaries of the growth of the KUC in the Tory Papers in the National Archives. See in particular Box 3.
142 H.M. Tory to J. Nicholson (secretary of the Canadian Universities Conference), 2 May 1919, ibid.
143 Tory to Falconer, 3 April 1918, ibid.
144 Ibid.
145 Curiously Falconer never recorded his impressions of the trenches. His son, however, long remembered Sir Robert's harrowing description of conditions at the front. See taped interview between the author and Robert D. Falconer.
146 Murray to Falconer, 12 Nov. 1918, MP

147 Falconer to Murray, 27 Jan. 1916, FP, Box 39
148 A.J. Glazebrook to Lord Milner, 15 Feb. 1915, Glazebrook Papers
149 Glazebrook to Milner, 18 Jan. 1916, ibid.
150 Vincent Massey to Philip Kerr, 3 April 1916, Lionel Curtis Papers C796, Bodleian Library
151 Falconer to Tory, 27 Jan. 1916, FP, Box 40
152 Ibid., 27 Jan. 1917, Box 44
153 Falconer to Glazebrook, 20 Sept. 1916, ibid.
154 A copy of the memorandum can be found in FP, Box 45.
155 Glazebrook to Milner, 17 Aug. 1917, Glazebrook Papers
156 Ibid., 26 March and 21 May 1918
157 For more detail and a more thorough coverage of the general context of Round Table activities, see Kendle *Round Table Movement*.
158 *Record of the Proceedings of the Committee on Church Union appointed by the General Assembly of the Presbyterian Church in Canada, Vol. 1, 1904–1921* (4 June 1915), hereafter referred to as *PCCU*
159 Falconer to Murray, 24 Dec. 1915, MP
160 *PCCU* (12 April 1916)
161 Falconer to Murray, 28 June 1916, MP
162 *PCCU* (26 July, 23 Sept. 1916)
163 'A Message to Sessions' (Sept. 1916), copy of which can be found in the Church Union Collection of the Archives of the United Church of Canada, Box 8
164 *PCCU* (9–10 Nov. 1916)
165 Grant *Church Union* 46
166 *PCCU* (29 Dec. 1916)
167 Ibid. (2–3 Jan. 1917)
168 For a report of Falconer's presentation to the 1917 General Assembly, see the *Globe* (11 June 1917) 7.
169 For coverage of this episode see the *Globe* (13 June 1917) 1.
170 Falconer acknowledged the necessity of generally having to 'mark time' in his *President's Report 1913–1914* 12.
171 Ibid. 12–13
172 Falconer to MacMechan, 7 Jan. 1915, MacMechan Papers
173 *President's Report 1915–1916* 12–13. See also Meikle 'And Gladly Teach' 135–9.
174 Falconer to Flavelle, 6 Jan. 1916, Flavelle Papers, Box 38
175 Falconer to Murray, 18 March 1915, MP. See also Falconer to Wm Peterson, 18 March 1915, Peterson Papers, Box 20.
176 Falconer to R.A. Pyne, 31 May 1915, FP, Box 35
177 Pilkington 'A History' 46–50
178 Ibid. 56
179 Falconer to the vice-chancellor of the University of Liverpool, 6 March 1917. This sample of the letter can be found in FP, Box 45.
180 Most of the information and analysis in this paragraph was found in Simpson *How the Ph.D. Came to Britain* 111–45.

181 Falconer to Murray, 14 Feb. 1918, FP, Box 48
182 H.M. Tory to Falconer, 22 Feb. 1918, FP, Box 49
183 Shortt *Search for an Ideal* 91
184 For those who wish to delve in more detailed fashion into Falconer's thoughts on the hope for progress at this juncture, let them refer to his 'What About Progress?' The substance of his views has been integrated into the closing paragraph of this chapter.
185 J. English *The Decline of Politics: The Conservatives and the Party System 1901–20* (Toronto: University of Toronto Press 1977) 106–22

Chapter IX Service, Tact, and Diplomacy

1 Falconer *Idealism in National Character*, 22
2 R. Falconer 'The First Fruits of Victory' undated address probably from 1919, found in FP, Box 56
3 Falconer *Idealism in National Character* 25
4 Ibid. 27
5 Ibid. 23–7
6 Falconer to Ernest Chalmers, 16 Jan. 1919, FP, Box 51
7 On this point see his *Heart of the New Testament*, a published version of lectures delivered by Falconer shortly before his death in 1943.
8 Falconer 'Moral Standards in Primitive Christianity' 307–22 and 'Book of Acts Once More' 111–21
9 Falconer to Willison, 4 March 1922, Willison Papers, Box 13
10 Falconer 'Universities and Balance of Studies' 18
11 Ibid. 17
12 Ibid. 22–3
13 R. Falconer, 'The Progressiveness of a Modern University' (Sept. 1922), 1, FP, Miscellaneous Manuscripts and Pamphlets. The reference here is to a manuscript version which was later published by the University of Toronto Press (see bibliography).
14 Ibid. 5
15 Minutes of the Board of Governors (28 Feb. 1918)
16 Pilkington 'A History' 78
17 Taylor to Falconer, 13 Nov. 1918, FP, Box 54
18 Ibid., 11 Dec. 1918
19 Falconer to Taylor, 12 Nov. 1918, ibid.
20 A copy of the petition was enclosed in a letter from Vincent Massey, then a member of the Repatriation Committee, to Falconer on 21 Dec. 1918, FP, Box 53.
21 Falconer to J.A. Nicholson (Registrar of McGill), 31 Jan. 1919, FP, Box 54
22 Falconer to Sir James Lougheed, 18 Feb. 1918 and 24 Feb. 1919, FP, Box 53. In one of these letters Falconer mentions having written to Lougheed on the matter several times before.
23 Murray to Falconer, 5 March 1919, ibid.

24 Copies of these letters dated 17 March 1919 can be found in FP, Box 55.
25 J.A. Calder to Falconer, 31 March 1919, ibid.
26 Ibid., 15 April 1919
27 Taylor to Falconer, 27 March 1919, ibid.
28 Taylor *Memoirs* 324. This is a typescript draft held by the Queen's University Archives.
29 Falconer to Borden, 7 June 1919, Borden Papers, 60199–205
30 N.W. Rowell to Borden, 11 July 1919, ibid., 60226.
31 Borden to Falconer, 16 July 1919, ibid, 60230, copy in FP, Box 57
32 Borden to H.P. Widden, 1 Dec. 1919, Borden Papers, 60262
33 *President's Report 1921–1922* 11
34 Ibid. *1919–1920* 7
35 For a summary of the work of the settlement house see a report on 'The Work of the University Settlement,' FP, Box 54
36 J.A. Dale, 'The Social Service Department: What Is It?' report, FP, Box 69
37 E.J. Urwick, 'Report on the Present Needs of the Department of Social Service' (17 Jan. 1929), FP, Box 129
38 Urwick to Falconer, 29 April 1932, FP, Box 133
39 J.P. McMurrich to Falconer, 13 Nov. 1919, FP, Box 59
40 *President's Report 1921–1922*, 8
41 Ibid. *1920–1921* 4
42 Ibid. *1931–1932* 5
43 Ibid.
44 *Interim Report by a Committee of the Council of the School of Graduate Studies*, FP, Box 129
45 McMurrich to Falconer, 8 May 1930, FP, Box 121
46 *Interim Report on Graduate Studies.*
47 Murray to Falconer, 15 March 1927, FP, Box 102
48 Meikle 'And Gladly Teach' 182
49 Falconer to Murray, 21 March 1927, FP, Box 102
50 For details on the discovery of insulin and its impact on the University of Toronto, see M. Bliss *The Discovery of Insulin* (Toronto: McClelland and Stewart 1982) 137–68, 240.
51 W.J. Dunlop 'Memorandum on University Extension,' 7 (23 Nov. 1920), FP, Box 69
52 Glazebrook to Milner, 21 May 1918, Glazebrook Papers
53 See, for example, a circular letter drafted by Falconer advertising the founding meeting of the WEA in Toronto, 24 April 1918, FP, Box 50.
54 'Memorandum on Extension' 4
55 H.V.F. Jones (chairman of the Editorial Committee of the *Journal of the Canadian Banking Association*) to Falconer, 27 Aug. 1919, FP, Box 58
56 Ibid., 7 Oct. 1919
57 Bladen *Bladen on Bladen* 32–3
58 E.F. Burton *Report of the Sub-Committee on University Extension* (Spring 1920), 3, FP, Box 62

59 Dunlop to Falconer, 10 Nov. 1920, FP, Box 64
60 Burton 'Report on Extension' 1–5
61 Dunlop 'Memorandum on Extension'
62 Dunlop to Falconer, 5 March 1921, FP, Box 64
63 'The Provincial University's Service,' copy in FP, Box 77
64 Dunlop to Falconer, 5 March 1921, FP, Box 64
65 Ibid., 29 May 1923, Box 77
66 Ibid., 1 Nov. 1927, Box 107
67 Dunlop to W. Sherwood Fox, 6 Nov. 1928, FP, Box 114
68 Falconer to J.R. Bone, 22 Oct. 1921, FP, Box 70
69 Falconer to G.S. Henry, 17 May 1926, FP, Box 94
70 J.E. Atkinson to Falconer, 11 Jan. 1923, FP, Box 76 and Dunlop to Falconer, 9 Feb. 1932, FP, Box 131
71 Mansbridge to Falconer, 25 April 1929, FP, Box 116
72 *President's Report 1917–1918* 3; *1919–1920* 3. The increase, moreover, represented significantly more than a return to 'normal' conditions, since in 1914 the figure was only 4,234.
73 For a record of these financial projections see the Minutes of the Board of Governors (19 May 1918), (20 June 1919), and (24 June 1920), respectively.
74 Hearst to Falconer, 18 June 1919, FP, Box 64
75 'Worst-Paid Class in Whole Province' article contributed by Walker to the *Globe* and the *Star* (6 Aug. 1920), clipping available in FP, Box 68
76 Wrong to A.L. Smith, 30 Sept. 1919, Smith Papers
77 'Distress among Faculty,' clipping from the *Telegram*, found in FP, Box 68
78 For a discussion of this issue, see C.M. Johnston *E.C. Drury: Agrarian Idealist* (Toronto 1986).
79 Falconer to Walker, 27 July 1920, WP, Box 24
80 Falconer to Smith, 26 Aug. 1920, FP, Box 68
81 The impressions of Walker and Russell concerning this meeting were conveyed to Falconer in separate letters. See Walker to Falconer, 3 Sept. 1920 and Russell to Falconer, 3 Sept. 1920, ibid.
82 R.H. Grant to Falconer, 14 Sept. 1920, ibid.
83 Falconer to the Finance Committee of the Board of Governors, Minutes of the Board of Governors (17 Sept. 1920)
84 Falconer to Willison, 30 Oct. 1920, FP, Box 67
85 Ibid.
86 For the proceedings, correspondence and recommendations of the commission, see Royal Commission on University Finances, Archives of Ontario, RB18 B-52, Boxes I and II.
87 Flavelle to Falconer, 11 April 1921, Flavelle Papers, Box 38
88 Falconer 'Need of the Hour' (1922)
89 *President's Report 1928–1929* and *1931–1932*
90 Minutes of the Board of Governors (9 April 1931)
91 Falconer to J.C. Smith (Edinburgh), 1 May 1923, FP, Box 80
92 Falconer to Walker, 3 Aug. 1921, WP, Box 24

93 Walker to Falconer, 15 July 1921, WP 35
94 Ibid., 18 Jan. 1922
95 Falconer to Walker, 19 Jan. 1922, WP, Box 25
96 Duncan Graham 'The Department of Medicine, University of Toronto,' an article reprinted from the *University of Toronto Monthly* 22 (April 1921), FP, Box 81
97 Bliss *Canadian Millionaire* 204–5
98 See McPhedran's letter to the Select Committee of the Legislature to Inquire into the Organization and Administration of the University of Toronto (hereafter referred to as Select Committee), Archives of Ontario, RG18, D-I-28, Box I.
99 Falconer to Flavelle, 16 Nov. 1918, Flavelle Papers, Box 38
100 Taylor *Memoirs* 327
101 Ibid. 327–8
102 Minutes of the Board of Governors (28 March 1918)
103 Falconer to Flavelle, 16 Nov. 1918, Flavelle Papers, Box 38
104 F.W. Marlow to Falconer, 14 Nov. 1921, FP, Box 72
105 Ibid., McIlwraith to Falconer, 1 Dec. 1921; Falconer to McIlwraith, 2 Dec. 1921; McIlwraith to Falconer, 30 Jan. 1922
106 Falconer noted but dismissed this attack in a letter to Walker, 10 Jan. 1922, FP, Box 74.
107 *Globe* (17 Jan. 1922) 14
108 Murray to Falconer, 17 Jan. 1922, MP; copy can be found in FP, Box 73
109 Falconer to Murray, 27 Jan. 1922, FP, Box 73
110 J.R. Nicholson to Drury, 13 Feb. 1922, Drury Papers, Box 30
111 J.F. March to Dury, 2 Feb. 1922, ibid.
112 For this insight into Drury's views of the medical profession I am indebted to his most recent biographer, C.M. Johnston. Where the views of McIlwraith and Marlow are concerned, see their letters to Falconer cited above.
113 *Saturday Night* (6 May 1922) 1
114 Falconer to Murray, 2 May 1922, MP
115 Flavelle to Colquhoun, 7 June 1922, Flavelle Papers, Box 38
116 Colquhoun to Flavelle, 8 June 1922, ibid.
117 Falconer and Walker were equally disturbed by these events, as is evident in their correspondence on the matter. See, for example, Falconer to Walker, 7 July 1922, WP, Box 25.
118 The allegation was contained in McIlwraith's statement to the committee and recorded in its report of 2 May 1923. See Select Committee.
119 Ibid.
120 For a lengthy and detailed account of Gibson's presentation to the committee, see the *Globe* (17 Nov. 1922) 13.
121 Ibid. (13 Dec. 1922) 13.
122 John A. Young to Drury, 12 Feb. 1923, Drury Papers, Box 37
123 George F. Young to Drury, letter found in the report of Select Committee.

124 *Globe* (18 Nov. 1922) 6
125 For details of the recommendations of the Select Committee see a copy of its report in FP, Box 81.
126 Walker to R.W. Leonard, 10 Sept. 1923, WP, Box 35
127 Walker to C.A.C. Jennings (editor of the *Mail and Empire*), 4 May 1923, ibid.
128 Flavelle to Ferguson, 7 Jan. 1926, Flavelle Papers, Box 39
129 J.H. Sterling (Queen's University, Belfast) to Falconer, 6 Dec. 1923, FP, Box 85

Chapter x Skylarking on the Ragged Edge of Folly

1 Jeanneret *Falconer*, 34
2 Moir 'Mildewed with Discretion' 178. Moir quotes the opinion of religious scholar William A. Irwin, who registered this assessment in 1930.
3 Hofstadter and Metzger *Academic Freedom* ix
4 Neatby *Queen's University* 292–3
5 R.W. Leonard to Falconer, 28 Feb. 1920, FP, Box 59
6 Falconer outlined all this for Leonard in a letter dated 22 Jan. 1921, FP, Box 65.
7 Balden *Bladen on Bladen* 32
8 Falconer to Leonard, 18 Jan. 1921, FP, Box 65
9 Leonard to Falconer, 21 Jan. 1921, ibid
10 MacIver to Falconer, 27 Jan. 1921, ibid
11 Falconer to Leonard, 12 Dec. 1921, ibid, FP, Box 72
12 Leonard to Falconer, 9 Dec. 1921, ibid
13 Falconer to Leonard, 12 Dec. 1921, ibid.
14 Leonard to Walker, 15 Dec. 1921, WP, Box 24
15 In researching the issue of academic freedom, Falconer wrote to several contacts in Britain and America. Typical of his correspondence on the matter are his communications with J.L. Kandel of the Carnegie Foundation. See FP, Box 72.
16 Hofstadter and Metzger *Academic Freedom* 401
17 Shortt *Search for an Ideal* 87
18 Ibid. 110–12
19 For the full text of Falconer's speech see his *Academic Freedom*, which was printed as a sixteen-page pamphlet by the University of Toronto Press in 1922.
20 For a full discussion of the report see Hofstadter and Metzger *Academic Freedom* 407–12.
21 *Globe* (15 Feb. 1922) 11
22 Walker to Falconer, 2 March 1922, WP, Box 35
23 Leonard to Falconer, 24 April 1922, FP, Box 72
24 Falconer to the Board of Governors, 22 Feb. 1923, FP, Box 81. Leonard's objections to the nomination were noted by Falconer in a letter to that millionaire dated 28 Feb. 1923, FP, Box 78.

25 This synopsis of Ferguson's policy towards the university is based on Oliver G. *Howard Ferguson* 23–42.

26 C.R. McKeown to Ferguson, 4 March 1924, copy in FP, Box 83

27 See, for example, his lengthy letters to Ferguson on the McKeown case, ibid.

28 Ferguson to Falconer, 17 March 1924, ibid.

29 For a closer look at Ferguson's interventions on behalf of students see the 'Ferguson' file in FP, Box 88. For a discussion from the premier's point of view see Oliver *Ferguson* 243.

30 Oliver *Ferguson* 232, 325–7

31 Ferguson to Falconer, 2 June 1924, FP, Box 83

32 Falconer to Ferguson, 4 June 1924, ibid.

33 Ferguson to Cody, 8 Dec. 1925, Ferguson Papers, Box 77

34 Oliver *Ferguson* 327

35 Ferguson to Falconer, 17 Oct. 1928, FP, Box 114

36 Underhill to Falconer, 22 Oct. 1928, ibid.

37 Falconer to Ferguson, 23 Oct. 1928, ibid.

38 Ferguson to Falconer, 26 Oct. 1928, ibid.

39 Oliver *Ferguson* 327

40 Ibid. 328

41 Moir 'Mildewed with Discretion' 177

42 Ibid.

43 Horn 'Free Speech' 30

44 Ibid. 31

45 D.J.G. Wishart to Falconer, 16 Jan. 1931, FP, Box 128

46 *Globe* (8 Jan. 1931) 11

47 For a list of the FOR's chief members see an article on the organization by Salem Bland in ibid. (16 Jan. 1931) 4.

48 Ibid. (10 Jan. 1931) 4

49 Ibid. (12 Jan. 1931) 4

50 Ibid. (14 Jan. 1931) 13

51 Horn 'Free Speech' 33

52 A copy of the letter can be found in FP, Box 126.

53 Horn 'Free Speech' 33

54 Ibid. 42

55 Ibid. 30

56 *Globe* (16 Jan. 1931) 4

57 Ibid. (17 Jan. 1931) 1

58 Ibid. 4; and (19 Jan. 1931) 4

59 Ibid. (4 Feb. 1931) 1

60 Falconer to G. Norlin, 5 June 1930, FP, Box 122

61 Falconer to Annie Patterson (his secretary), 29 Aug. 1930, FP, Box 125

62 Falconer to Professor J.C. Fields, 9 Oct. 1929, FP, Box 126

63 Falconer to Rev. H. Herbert Gray (London), 28 Jan. 1931, FP

64 *Globe* (16 Jan. 1931) 13

65 D.M. Hickey to the Board of Governors, 22 Jan. 1930, copy in FP, Box 120
66 *Globe* (16 Jan. 1931) 13
67 Falconer to Wishart, 20 Jan. 1931, FP, Box 128
68 Falconer to R.H. Lloyd, 23 Jan. 1931, FP, Box 126
69 Flavelle to Wrong, 20 Jan. 1931, Flavelle Papers, Box 19
70 Falconer to Cody, 3 Feb. 1931, FP, Box 125
71 Horn 'Free Speech' 39
72 Falconer to MacMechan, 7 March 1931, MacMechan Papers
73 *Globe* (26 Feb. 1931) 4
74 *Telegram* (25 Feb. 1931), 3
75 *Globe* (27 Feb. 1931) 1
76 Minutes of the Board of Governors (26 Feb. 1931)
77 *Globe* (4 March 1931) 4 and (12 March 1931) 4
78 Horn 'Free Speech' 40
79 Henry to A.T. DeLury, 23 March 1931, Henry Papers, Box 149; copy in FP, Box 126
80 M. Price to DeLury, 21 March 1931, FP, Box 127
81 The address was reprinted or summarized by all the Toronto newspapers on 7–8 April 1931.
82 *Globe* (9 April 1931)
83 Falconer to Underhill, 26 June 1931, FP, Box 133
84 *Globe* (2 July 1931) 4
85 A copy of the *London Advertiser* article of 15 July 1931 is available in FP, Box 133.
86 Underhill to Falconer, 24 Sept. 1931, ibid.
87 Falconer to Underhill, 28 Sept. 1931, ibid.
88 Falconer *The Lawful Mind* (1931) 3. This was his presidential address delivered to students in the fall of 1931 and subsequently published as a pamphlet by the Department of Extension; copy available in MP.
89 Carleton Stanley to Falconer, 22 Dec. 1931, Stanley Papers, Dalhousie University Archives
90 Howe's memorandum to Falconer was transcribed and passed on to Millar. A copy, dated 24 May 1932, can be found in FP, Box 132.
91 For a discussion of Veblen's critique see Hofstadter and Metzger *Academic Freedom* 452–67.
92 Fairley's remarks were made to J.G. Greenlee during the course of an interview at the former's home on 27 July 1979. A copy of the notes taken at that time are on file in the University of Toronto Archives.
93 See Howe's memorandum to Falconer concerning Millar, FP, Box 132.
94 Falconer to Underhill, 28 Sept. 1931, FP, Box 133
95 See Fairley interview with J.G. Greenlee.

Chapter XI Beyond the Office Walls

1 S.W. Dyde to Falconer, 27 Jan. 1921, FP, Box 64

2 Falconer to Dyde, 28 Jan. 1921, ibid.
3 This threat was politely but clearly set out in a statement by the association's president, D.J. Fraser, issued on 23 June 1921; copy in FP, Box 86.
4 Falconer to Murray, 1 March 1924, MP
5 For example, see J.W. Anderson to Ferguson, 7 Feb. 1924, Ferguson Papers, Box 51. Pleas came from as far afield as Red Deer, Alberta. See, for example, W.G. Brown to Ferguson, 22 Feb. 1924, ibid.
6 Malcolm A. McKay to Ferguson, 15 March 1924, ibid.
7 A.W. Paton to Ferguson, 29 March 1924, ibid.
8 Falconer to Murray, 8 April 1924, MP
9 Falconer to Murray, 30 April 1924, ibid.
10 For details of this question and answer session of the Parliamentary Committee, see the *Church Union Collection: Committee on Law and Legislation*, Box 12, File 210.
11 Falconer to Murray, 30 April 1924, MP
12 Paton to Ferguson, 7 April 1925, Ferguson Papers, Box 58
13 Falconer to Murray, 5 March 1925, MP
14 Falconer to Leonard, 30 Nov. 1923, FP, Box 84
15 Falconer 'Reign of Law' (1917) 97
16 Falconer to A.L. Smith, 10 Oct. 1918, A.L. Smith Papers
17 Falconer to N.W. Rowell, 28 Nov. 1918, FP, Box 54
18 R. Falconer 'An International Council of Revision' (1919), FP, Box 56, Addresses and Reports
19 Percy Hurd to Falconer, 1 Oct. 1919, FP, Box 58
20 Falconer to Hurd, 8 Oct. 1919, ibid.
21 Rowell to Lord Robert Cecil, 10 May 1920, Rowell Papers, PAC, Box 11
22 W.L. Grant to Maurice Hankey, 26 April 1920, Grant Papers, PAC, Box 5
23 Rowell to W.F. Chipman, 22 March 1921, Rowell Papers, Box 11
24 Leonard to Sir Robert Borden, 20 July 1921, ibid.
25 *Annual Report of the Executive Committee of the League of Nations Society in Canada* (31 May 1922), copy in FP, Box 81
26 Falconer to Murray, 17 Feb. 1920, MP
27 Falconer to G.F. Peabody, 27 Oct. 1925, FP, Box 96
28 Falconer to the editor of the New York *Herald*, 3 Jan. 1921, clipping in FP, Box 69
29 Falconer to Rev. G.J. Bond, 8 Nov. 1921, FP, Box 70
30 Falconer to John Fredstrom, 27 April 1926, FP, Box 93
31 C.C. Morrison to Falconer, 1 Dec. 1926, FP, Box 102
32 Falconer to Morrison, 3 Dec. 1926, ibid.
33 Falconer to Murray, 9 Sept. 1925, MP
34 Falconer to Sir C.P. Lucas, 8 Jan. 1920, FP, Box 59
35 Lucas to Falconer, 28 Jan. 1920, ibid.
36 Falconer to Lucas, 13 Feb. 1920, ibid.
37 Alex Hill to Falconer, 8 Aug. 1919, FP, Box 58.
38 J.W. Cunliffe to H.M. Tory, 17 Aug. 1920, copy in FP, Box 67.

39 Falconer to Tory, 7 Sept. 1920, ibid.
40 Hill ed. *Report of the Proceedings of the Congress of the Universities of the Empire* (1921) xxi–xxiii
41 Sir Frank Heath (Hill's successor in 1930) to Falconer, 15 April 1930, FP, Box 120
42 Falconer to A.B. Macallum, 14 Jan. 1920, FP, Box 59.
43 Falconer to W.C. Noxon, 27 Jan. 1927, FP, Box 103.
44 Falconer, Memorandum on the Development of Postgraduate Facilities in London (25 Nov. 1929), copy in FP, Miscellaneous Manuscripts and Pamphlets
45 Berger *Writing of Canadian History* 143; Falconer Memo on Postgrad. Facilities, 2
46 Falconer Memorandum on Postgraduate Facilities 1–5
47 For further details see Greenlee *Education and Imperial Unity*.
48 Aubrey Symonds (English Board of Education) to Lord Willingdon, 20 Jan. 1930, copy in FP, Box 123
49 A copy of Falconer's letter to the *Times* (London), dated 9 June 1930, is available in ibid.
50 For a list of the members of the 'London House' Committee see Symonds to Willingdon, 20 Jan. 1930, ibid.
51 This was explained to Falconer by F.C. Goodenough, chairman of Barclay's Bank, in a letter dated 17 June 1930, FP, Box 126.
52 Falconer to Goodenough, 7 Oct. 1930, ibid.
53 Falconer to F.P. Keppel, 2 Oct. 1930, ibid.
54 Falconer to the editor of *Varsity*, 2 March 1920, FP, Box 61.
55 Falconer 'Universities and Balance of Studies' 16–24
56 H.S. Perris to Falconer, 11 July 1923, FP, Box 85
57 Falconer to Perris, 20 Aug. 1923, ibid.
58 Falconer to Murray, 9 Sept. 1925, MP
59 Falconer to Perris, 20 Aug. 1923, FP, Box 85
60 On the rise of this continental approach to Canadian and American history see Berger *Writing of Canadian History* 137–59.
61 Falconer *United States as a Neighbour* 1–138
62 Ibid. 138
63 Ibid. 243
64 Ibid. 247
65 Ibid. 4
66 Ibid. 179–89
67 Ibid. 236
68 On Baker's analysis of the cultural domination of Canada by American literature see Berger *Writing of Canadian History* 143.
69 Falconer *United States as a Neighbour* 241
70 Ibid. 1
71 Ibid. 250
72 Ibid. 251

73 Falconer to Murray, 9 Sept. 1925, MP
74 Falconer to J.S. Willison, 20 July 1925, Willison Papers, Box 13
75 *United States as a Neighbour* was reviewed in several journals in Canada, the United States and Great Britain. For example, see *Canadian Historical Review* 7 (1926) 60; *Canadian Forum* 6 (1926) 217; *Dalhousie Review* 6 (1926–7) 132; *Outlook* 142 (14 April 1926) 573; *Scottish Historical Review* 24 (1927) 69; *History* 9 (1926) 72; *New York Times* (24 Jan. 1926) 3; *American Political Science Review* 20 (1926) 894; *Forum and Century* 77 (1927) 473.
76 *New York Times Book Review* (24 Jan. 1926) 3
77 *American Political Science Review* 20 (1926) 894–6
78 H.M. Watts to Falconer, 10 Sept. 1926, FP, Box 104
79 Falconer to Watts, 15 Sept. 1926, ibid.
80 Falconer to J.A. Stewart, 26 Sept. 1925, FP, Box 97.
81 R. Falconer *What Is Distinctive in American Civilization?* (10 Dec. 1926), FP, Miscellaneous Papers and Addresses
82 Falconer 'Address to English-Speaking Union' (10 Dec. 1926), FP, Miscellaneous Manuscripts and Pamphlets
83 Ibid. 7
84 R. Falconer 'Canadians Are A Distinct Type' *Christian Science Monitor* (16 April 1926) 2
85 R. Falconer 'President's Address to Students' (6 Jan. 1931), FP, Miscellaneous Manuscripts and Pamphlets
86 Lloyd to Falconer, 17 March 1925, FP, Box 88
87 Falconer to President C.A. Richmond (Union College), 6 Dec. 1926, FP, Box 103
88 For details concerning Falconer's appointment to the US–Paraguay Joint Commission, see his correspondence with the American chargé d'affaires, B. Reath Riggs, 26 Dec.–10 Jan. 1930, FP, Box 122
89 Falconer to Flavelle, 4 April 1929, Flavelle Papers, Box 39
90 Falconer to Sir Alfred Ewing (principal, University of Edinburgh), 12 April 1929, FP, Box 124
91 Falconer to Wm Wilson (University of Edinburgh), 20 May 1929 and Falconer to J.W. Simpson (University of Edinburgh), 22 Nov. 1929, FP, Boxes 117 and 122, respectively
92 Falconer to Murray, 16 Sept. 1930, MP
93 Falconer to A.S. MacKenzie, 12 Dec. 1930, MacKenzie Papers, Dalhousie
94 Falconer to Murray, 22 Dec. 1930, MP
95 Minutes of the Board of Governors (26 May 1932)
96 Ibid. (25 June 1931)
97 Charles W. Flint to Falconer, 8 Nov. 1931, FP, Box 131
98 Quoted in Jeanneret *Falconer* 33
99 Falconer to Prof. W.A. Irwin, 20 Oct. 1931, FP, Box 131
100 *Globe* (16 Dec. 1931) 11
101 Falconer to MacMechan, 15 Nov. 1931, MacMechan Papers

Chapter XII Emeritus

1 For a discussion of the most prominent works concerning this question, including Falconer's, see C.F.D. Moule 'The Problem of the Pastoral Epistles: A Reappraisal' in his *Essays in New Testament Interpretation*.
2 Falconer *Pastoral Epistles* (1937)
3 Ibid. 30–9
4 Ibid. 39
5 Ibid.
6 The chief exponent of the 'fragments' theory was P.N. Harrison who first outlined this interpretation in his *Problem of the Pastoral Epistles*.
7 For his analysis of the authorship question see Falconer *Pastoral Epistles* 13–17, 19–30.
8 Ibid. Preface
9 Ibid. Preface and 15
10 'The Pastoral Epistles: Problems of Church Order' *Times Literary Supplement* (11 Sept. 1937) 648
11 E.F. Scott 'The Pastoral Epistles' *University of Toronto Quarterly* 7 (1937) 139–40
12 Moule *Essays in New Testament Interpretation* 113–32
13 Falconer to Murray, 20 April 1934, MP
14 Ibid. 12 July 1935
15 Ibid. 20 April 1934
16 Ibid. 17 May 1936
17 Ibid.
18 Falconer to Murray, 26 May 1936, MP. Typical of Falconer's speeches on behalf of the league at the time was his 'Can the League of Nations Survive?' a radio address delivered on CBC at Montreal, 31 October 1936. See Miscellaneous Manuscripts and Pamphlets, FP.
19 Falconer to Murray, 27 April 1937, MP
20 Ibid., 25 June 1937
21 Falconer commented on the unstable weather and the toll it exacted from him in a letter to Murray, 9 April 1938, MP.
22 For Falconer's observations on the problems of the world in 1938 see the published version of his Rockwell lectures, *RLR* 90–113.
23 Falconer to Murray, 20 Sept. 1939, MP
24 Ibid. 7 Nov. 1939
25 Ibid. 28 July 1940
26 Ibid. 10 Jan. 1942
27 Falconer 'The Humanities in the War-Time University'
28 Falconer to Murray, 8 June 1943, MP
29 Sophie later commented on his rapid decline in August in a letter to Murray, 7 Dec. 1943, MP.
30 His Emmanuel College lectures were published under this title later in 1943 by Ryerson Press in association with the United Church.

31 Lady Falconer to Murray, 7 Dec. 1943, MP
32 Falconer to Murray, 27 Jan. 1939, MP
33 Abella and Troper *None Is Too Many* 63–4
34 The radio address was noted in the *United Church Observer* (1 Dec. 1943). See a clipping in Falconer's biographical file in the United Church Archives, Emmanuel College.
35 Information conveyed to the author by Sir Robert's son, Robert D. Falconer; tape in University of Toronto Archives.

Chapter XIII Some Thoughts on Robert Falconer

1 This caveat was boldly underscored by Clarence Karr in his article 'What is Canadian Intellectual History?'
2 Shortt *Search For an Ideal* 7
3 McKillop *Disciplined Intelligence* 231
4 Ibid. 231–2
5 L. Armour and E. Trott *The Faces of Reason: An Essay on Philosophy and Culture in English Canada 1850–1950* (Waterloo: Wilfrid Laurier University Press 1981) 4
6 Ibid. 4, 512
7 J.G. Greenlee 'Canadian External Affairs 1867–1957' *Historical Journal* 27 (1984) 503–11

Select Bibliography

PRIMARY SOURCES

UNPUBLISHED

Archives of Ontario
  Henry J. Cody Papers
  James P. Whitney Papers
  Ernest C. Drury Papers
  G. Howard Ferguson Papers
  George S. Henry Papers
Dalhousie University Archives
  A. Stanley MacKenzie Papers
  (Private and Presidential)
  Carleton Stanley Papers
  Archibald MacMechan Papers
McGill University Archives
  Sir Arthur Currie Papers
  Sir William Peterson Papers
Public Archives of Canada
  Sir Robert L. Borden Papers
  Sir Arthur Currie Papers
  Arthur J. Glazebrook Papers
  William L. Grant Papers
  W.L.M. King Papers
  Sir George Parkin Papers
  Newton W. Rowell Papers
  Charles B. Sissons Papers

Henry M. Tory Papers
Sir John S. Willison Papers
Queen's University Archives
  Sir Joseph W. Flavelle Papers
  Daniel M. Gordon Papers
  George M. Grant Papers
  R. Bruce Taylor Papers
United Church Archives (Emmanuel
College, University of Toronto)
  Nathaniel Burwash Papers
  Church Union Collection
  Minutes of the Presbytery of
  Trinidad (1845–1939)
  Record of Proceedings of the
  Committee on Church Union
  (Presbyterian Church of
  Canada)
  United Church of Canada Bio-
  graphical Files
United Church Archives: Maritime
Conference (Atlantic School of
Theology, Halifax)
  Alexander Falconer, West Indian

Sketches, Letters and Clippings
1877–1886.
Minutes of the Board: Presbyterian
College, Halifax (Pine Hill) 1892–
1907
University of British Columbia
Archives
  F.F. Wesbrook Papers
University of Oxford
  Lionel Curtis Papers (Bodleian
  Library)
  Arthur L. Smith Papers (Balliol
  College)
University of Saskatchewan Archives
  Walter C. Murray Papers
University of Toronto Archives and
Rare Book Room
  Biographical Files
  Minutes of the Board of Governors
  1901–1933
  Office of the Secretary to the Board
  of Governors: Presidential Search
  Committee 1906–1907, Box 51

Henry J. Cody Papers
Sir Robert A. Falconer Papers
Harold A. Innis Papers
James Loudon Papers
James Mavor Papers
Office of the Registrar (Falconer
Inaugural Material)
Sir B. Edmund Walker Papers
George M. Wrong Papers
Private Collections
  Sir Robert A. Falconer, Stamp
  Album with autobiography, courtesy
  of Robert D. Falconer, Toronto
Oral Evidence and Interviews (tapes
and notes deposited at the University
of Toronto Archives)
  Vincent W. Bladen (August 1979),
  two tapes
  Barker Fairley (August 1979),
  notes
  Robert D. Falconer (July–August
  1979), eight tapes

PUBLISHED

Newspapers

Toronto: particularly helpful among
many Toronto papers were
  Toronto Daily Star
  Globe
  Mail and Empire
  News
Halifax
  Chronicle
  Halifax Herald

Journals

Student (University of Edinburgh)

Theologue (Atlantic School of
Theology)
University of Toronto Monthly
University of Toronto Quarterly

Official Reports

A. Hill ed. *Report of Proceedings of the
Congress of the Universities of the Empire*
London: Hodder and Stoughton
1912
– ed. *Report of Proceedings of the Congress of the Universities of the Empire*
London: Bell 1921 and 1926

Books

Barrie, J.M. *An Edinburgh Eleven* London: Hodder and Stoughton 1908
Blake, S.H. *The Knife of the Higher Critic* Toronto: L.S. Haynes Press 1909
– *The Orthodox Pupil Versus the Unorthodox Teacher* Toronto: L.S. Haynes Press 1909

– *The Teaching of Religious Knowledge in the University of Toronto Ultra Vires* Toronto: L.S. Haynes Press 1909
– *What Is Truth?* Toronto: L.S. Haynes Press 1909
Chown, S.D. *The Story of Church Union in Canada* Toronto: Ryerson Press 1930
Dods, M. *The Bible: Its Origins and Interpretation* New York: Scribners 1905
Falconer, A. *Privilege and Responsibility* Edinburgh: Andrew Elliot 1885.
Haldane, R.B. *Universities and National Life* London: Murray 1910
Harnack, A. *Outlines of the History of Dogma* trans. E.K. Mitchell New York: Funk and Wagnalls 1893
– *What Is Christianity?* trans. E.B. Saunders London: Williams and Norgate 1901.
Harrison, P.N. *The Problem of the Pastoral Epistles* Oxford: 1921
Hastings, J. ed. *A Dictionary of Christ and the Gospels* New York: Scribners 1906
– *A Dictionary of the Bible* New York: Scribners 1909
Jacobus, M.W. ed. *A New Standard Bible Dictionary* New York: Funk and
– Wagnalls 1909
–*A New Standard Bible Dictionary* New York: Funk and Wagnalls 1909
Mackinnon, C. *Reminiscences* Toronto: Ryerson Press 1938
Newman, J.H. in I.T. Ker ed. *The Idea of a University* Oxford: Clarendon Press 1976
Schweitzer, A. *The Quest for the Historical Jesus* 1905
Scott, E. *Church Union and the Presbyterian Church in Canada* Montreal: Lovell and Sons 1928
Veblen, T. *The Higher Learning in America* New York: B.W. Huebsch 1918
Wallace, W.S. *A History of the University of Toronto 1827–1927* Toronto: University of Toronto Press 1927

Principal Published Works of Sir Robert Alexander Falconer
(arranged chronologically):

'A Tramp Through Thuringia' *Theologue* 1 (1889) 28–32
'A Study in Emerson' *Theologue* 2 (1891) 97–102
'A Batch of Books on Paulinism' *Theologue* 4 (1893) 56–61
'Christ the Personal Source of Religion and Theology' *Theologue* 5 (1893) 1–16
'The Gospel According to Peter' *Theologue* 4 (1893) 119–27
'A Darwinian's Thoughts on Religion' *Theologue* 6 (1895) 133-8
'The Prologue to the Gospel of St John' *Expositor* 5 (1897) 222–34
'The Great Western Country' *Theologue* 10 (1898) 12–17
'The Future of the Kingdom' *Expositor* 10 (1899) 339–50
'Products from the New Testament Yield of 1898' *Theologue* 10 (1899) 149–59
'The Holy Spirit in the Early Apostolic Age' *Presbyterian and Reformed Review* 11 (1900) 438–60
'Paul's Early Visits to Jerusalem' *Expository Times* 11 (1900) 487–90
'Apostolic Christianity in the Light of Criticism: A Study in Origins' *Westminster* (March 1901) 257–60
'The Gospels after a Century of Criticism: A Summary of Results' *Westminster* (Feb. 1901) 139–42

'Is Second Peter a Genuine Epistle to the Churches of Samaria?' *Expositor* 5
(1901) 459–72; 6 (1902) 47–56, 117–27, 218–27
'Jude 22, 23' *Expositor* 4 (1901) 200–7
'Prophet of the New Israel: A Study of the First Epistle of Peter' *Expository Times* 15
(1903) 259–63
'Early Christian Art' *Queen's Quarterly* 11 (1904) 225–42
The Truth of the Apostolic Gospel New York: YMCA 1904
'Alien from Nothing That Is Truly Human' *Theologue* 17 (1905) 1–6
'Some Thoughts on Union' *Theologue* 16 (1905) 59–63
'A New Method of New Testament Study' *Theologue* 18 (1906) 12–16
'Sin as a Religious Concept' *Theologue* 18 (1907) 63–7
'Inaugural Address' *University of Toronto Monthly* 8 (1907) 6–14
'University Spirit' *University of Toronto Monthly* 8 (1907) 65–71
'The Place of Authority in the University Spirit' *University of Toronto Monthly* 9
(1908) 12–22
'The Unification of Canada' *University Magazine* 7 (1908) 3–9
'The Needs of the University of Toronto' *University of Toronto Monthly* 9 (1908)
1–6, 52–6, 139–43, 177–81
'The Individuality of the Canadian People' *University of Toronto Monthly* 10 (1910)
437–48
'Blaise Pascal' *University Magazine* 10 (1911) 340–59
The Life and Times of Our Lord Jesus Christ with J. Ballantyne Toronto: Presbyter-
ian Publications 1912
'The Present Position of the Churches in Canada' *Constructive Quarterly* 1 (1913)
269–81
'Science and Religion as Factors in Progress' *Religious Education* 8 (1913) 340–4
The German Tragedy and Its Meaning for Canada Toronto: University of Toronto
Press 1915
'A New Imperial Allegiance' *University Magazine* 15 (1916) 12–24
What about Progress? Philadelphia: Drexel Institute Monographs 1916
'The Conflict of Educational Ideas Arising out of the Present War' *Royal Society
of Canada Transactions* 11 (1917) 227–40
'The Quality of Canadian Life' in G.M. Wrong et al. *The Federation of Canada
1867–1917* Toronto: Ryerson 1917
'The Reign of Law' *University of Toronto Monthly* 18 (1917) 94–7
'A Distinctive Feature of the English-Speaking University Suggested by George
Washington' *University Bulletins* 4 (1918) 11–27
'Reminiscences of Professor A.B. Davidson' *Constructive Quarterly* 6 (1918) 385–
400
'1776 and 1914: A Contrast in British Colonial Action' *Royal Society of Canada
Transactions* 12 (1918) 241–50
'To Commemorate the University's Work in the War' *University of Toronto
Monthly* 19 (1918) 6–8
'The Cultivation of National Virtue' *Religious Education* 14 (1919) 351–6
'The Moral Standards in Primitive Christianity' *Constructive Quarterly* 7 (1919) 307–22

Idealism in National Character: Essays and Addresses London: Hodder and Stoughton 1920

'The Mystery of Godliness' *Expositor* 19 (1920) 321–4

'Sir William Osler' *Canadian Medical Monthly* 4 (1920) 4–6

'John Henry Newman' *Constructive Quarterly* 9 (1921) 510–36

'The Need of the Hour' *University of Toronto Monthly* 22 (1921) 57–8

Academic Freedom Toronto: University of Toronto Press 1922

'The Book of Acts Once More' *Queen's Quarterly* 30 (1922) 111–21

The Progressiveness of a Modern University Toronto: University of Toronto Press 1922

'University Federation in Toronto' *Dalhousie Review* 3 (1923) 279-85

'Sir Edmund Walker' *University of Toronto Monthly* 24 (1924) 362-3

'The British Universities' *University of Toronto Monthly* 26 (1925) 8–11

'Humanism' *Hibbert Journal* 24 (1925) 123–35

The United States as a Neighbour, from a Canadian Point of View Cambridge: Cambridge University Press 1926

'What Is Implied in the Term Canadian?' *English Review* 41 (1925) 595–605

'The Mystery Religions' *Canadian Journal of Religious Thought* 3 (1926) 36–43

'The Opportunities of Teachers' *Advance* 4 (1926) 1

'The U.S. as Canada's Friend' *Current Histroy Magazine* 24 (1926) 181–8

'The Functions of State and Church in Education' *Religious Education* 22 (1927) 554–9

'Scottish Influence in the Higher Education of Canada' *Royal Society of Canada Transactions* 21 (1927) 7–20

Citizenship in an Enlarging World Sackville, NB: Mount Allison University 1928

'The Difficulties of Religion in an Age of Science' *Religious Education* 23 (1928) 278–84

'English Influence on the Higher Education of Canada ' *Royal Society of Canada Transactions* 22 (1928) 33–48

'American Influence on the Higher Education of Canada' *Royal Society of Canada Transactions* 24 (1930) 23-38

The Idea of Imortality and Western Civilization Cambridge: Harvard Univeristy Press 1930

'My Memory of Harnack' *Canadian Journal of Religious Thought* 7 (1930) 376–80

'The Pioneering Spirit' *Cambridge History of the British Empire* Vol. 6 Cambridge: Cambridge University Press 1930

'The Essential University as I Have Seen It' *University of Toronto Monthly* 32 (1931) 143–9

'The Intellectual Life of Canada as Reflected in its Royal Society' *Royal Society of Canada Transactions* 26 (1932) 37–55

'A Quarter of a Century at Varsity' *University of Toroto Monthly* 32 (1932) 342–8

'The University and the City' *University of Toronto Monthly* 32 (1932) 229–34

Some Factors in the Making of the Complete Citizen Houston: Rice Institute 1934

'From College to University' *University of Toronto Quarterly* 5 (1935) 1–20

'Irish Influence on the Higher Education in Canada' *Royal Society of Canada Transactions* 29 (1935) 131–43

'From College to University' *University of Toronto Quarterly* (April 1936) 1–20

'Can the League of Nations Survive?' Address delivered in Montreal 31 Oct. 1936

'St Paul at the Tomb of Virgil' *University of Toronto Quarterly* 6 (1936) 18–32

'Desiderius Erasmus: Humanist, Restorer of the New Testament in Greek' *Royal Society of Canada Transactions* 31 (1937) 13–23

'In Edinburgh Fifty Years Ago' *Queens's Quarterly* 44 (1937) 441–54

The Pastoral Epistles Introduction, Translation and Notes Oxford: Clarendon Press 1937

'Academic Canada Comes of Age' *Saturday Night* 53 (1938) 16–17

'Avenues of Approach to the English Bible' *University of Toronto Quarterly* 7 (1938) 56–68

'How Can We Ensure Peace?' *Saturday Night* 53 (1938) 3

Religion on My Life's Road Houston: Rice Institute 1938

'The Throne in Canada' *Queen's Quarterly* 46 (1939) 137–44

'The Age-Long Drama of Church and State' *University of Toronto Quarterly* 9 (1940) 152–69

'Maurice Hutton' *Royal Society of Canada Proceedings* 24 (1940) 111-14

'University Federation in Toronto' *Royal Society of Canada Transactions* 34 (1940) 43–54

'Ideals of Religion' *University of Toronto Quarterly* 10 (1941) 228–35

'Glimpses of the University at Work from 1907 until the First World War' *University of Toronto Quarterly* 11 (1942) 127–39, 389–402

The Heart of the New Testament Toronto: Ryerson Press 1943

'Jacques Maritain: A Prophet for Our Time' *University of Toronto Quarterly* 12 (1943) 133–45

'The Humanities in the War-Time University' *University of Toronto Quarterly* 13 (1943) 1–13

SECONDARY SOURCES

Books

Abella, I. and H. Troper *None Is Too Many: Canada and the Jews of Europe 1933–1948* Toronto: Lester and Orpen Dennys 1982

Allen, R. *The Social Passion: Religion and Social Reform in Canada 1914–1928* Toronto: University of Toronto Press 1971

Berger, C. *The Sense of Power: Studies in the Ideas of Canadian Imperialism 1867–1914* Toronto: University of Toronto Press 1970

– *The Writing of Canadian History* Toronto: Oxford University Press 1976

– *Science God and Nature in Victorian Canada* Toronto: University of Toronto Press 1983

Betts, E.A. *Pine Hill Divinity Hall 1820–1970* Truro, NS: Pine Hill 1970

Bissell, C.T. ed. *University College: A Portrait 1853–1953* Toronto: University of Toronto Press 1953
- *The Strength of a University* Toronto: University of Toronto Press 1968.
Bladen, V.W. *Bladen on Bladen: Memoirs of a Political Economist* Toronto: Scarborough College 1978.
Bliss, M. *A Canadian Millionaire: The Life and Business Times of Sir Joseph Flavelle, Bart. 1858–1939* Toronto: Macmillan 1978
Bowen, D. *The Idea of the Victorian Church* Montreal: McGill University Press 1970
Bratton, F.G. *A History of the Bible: An Introduction to the Historical Method* Boston: Beacon Press 1959
Brereton, B. *Race Relations in Colonial Trinidad 1870–1900* Cambridge: Cambridge University Press 1979
Brubacher, J.S. *On the Philosophy of Higher Education* San Francisco: Jossey-Bass 1977
Cage, R.A. ed. *The Scots Abroad: Labour, Capital and Enterprise 1750–1914* London: Croom Helm 1985
Cameron, J.M. *On the Idea of a University* Toronto: University of Toronto Press 1978
Chadwick, O. *An Ecclesiastical History of England: VIII The Victorian Church* London: Black 1970
Cheyne, A.C. *The Transformation of the Kirk: Victorian Scotland's Religious Revolution* Edinburgh: St Andrews 1983
Clifford, N.K. *The Resistance to Church Union in Canada 1904–1939* Vancouver: University of British Columbia Press 1985
Cook, R. *The Regenerators: Social Criticism in Late Victorian English Canada* Toronto: University of Toronto Press 1986
Dancocks, D. *Sir Arthur Currie: A Biography* Toronto: Methuen 1985
Davie, G.E. *The Democratic Intellect: Scotland and Her Universities in the Nineteenth Century* Edinburgh: Edinburgh University Press 1961
Dawson, R.M. *William Lyon Mackenzie King: A Political Biography* I Toronto: University of Toronto Press 1958
Drummond, I.M. *Political Economy at the University of Toronto: A History of the Department 1888–1982* Toronto: University of Toronto Faculty of Arts and Science 1983
Falconer, J.W. and W.G. Watson *A Brief History of Pine Hill Divinity Hall and the Theological Department at Mount Allison University* Halifax: Pine Hill 1946
Grant, J.W. *George Pidgeon* Toronto: Ryerson Press 1962
- *The Canadian Experience of Church Union* Richmond, VA: Knox Press 1967
Granatstein, J.S. *The Ottawa Men: The Civil Service Mandarins 1935–1957* Toronto: Oxford University Press 1982
Greenlee, J.G. *Education and Imperial Unity 1901–1926* New York: Garland Press forthcoming
Grier, L. *Achievement in Education: The Work of Michael Ernest Sadler* London: Constable 1952

Hasel, G. *New Testament Theology: Basic Issues in the Current Debate* Grand Rapids, MI: Erdmans 1978

Heyck, T.W. *The Transformation of Intellectual Life in Victorian England* London: Croom Helm 1982

Hofstadter, R. *The American Political Tradition* New York: Vintage 1948

Hofstadter, R. and W.P. Metzger *The Development of Academic Freedom in the United States* New York: Columbia University Press 1955

Hughes, H.S. *Consciousness and Society: The Reconstruction of European Social Thought 1890–1930* New York: Vintage 1961

Jeanneret, F.C.A. *The Contribution of Sir Robert Falconer to Higher Education* University of Toronto Archives, Miscellaneous Manuscripts and Pamphlets

Johnston, C.M. *McMaster University Vol. I: The Early Years* Toronto: University of Toronto Press 1976

Kendle, J. *The Round Table Movement and Imperial Union* Toronto: University of Toronto Press 1975

Kubicek, R.V. *The Administration of Imperialism: Joseph Chamberlain and the Colonial Office* Durham, NC: Duke University Press 1969

Kurland, G. *Seth Low: The Reformer in an Urban and Industrial Age* New York: Twayne n.d.

MacLennan, H. ed. *McGill: The Story of a University* London: Allen and Unwin 1960

MacLeod, J. *A History of Presbyterianism on Prince Edward Island* Chicago: Winona 1904

Mandelbaum, M. *History, Man and Reason: A Study in Nineteenth-Century Thought* Baltimore: Johns Hopkins 1971

MacPhie, J.P. *Pictonians at Home and Abroad* Boston: Pinkham Press 1914

Marble, A.E. *Nova Scotians at Home and Abroad* Windsor, NS: Lancelot Press 1977

McClelland, C.E. *State, Society and University in Germany 1700–1914* Cambridge: Cambridge University Press 1980

McKillop, A.B. *A Disciplined Intelligence: Critical Inquiry and Canadian Thought in the Victorian Era* Montreal: McGill-Queen's University Press 1979

McMurrion S.M. ed. *On the Meaning of a University* Salt Lake City: University of Utah Press 1976

McNeill, J.T. *The Presbyterian Church in Canada 1875–1925*. Toronto: Ryerson 1956

Moir, J. *Enduring Witness: A History of the Presbyterian Church in Canada* Toronto: Bryant Press 1974

Moule, C.F.D. *Essays in New Testament Interpretation* Cambridge: Cambridge University Press 1982

Murray, D.R. and R.A. Murray *The Prairie Builder: Walter Murray of Saskatchewan* Edmonton: NeWest Press 1984

Neatby, H. *Queen's University Vol. I 1841–1917* Montreal: McGill-Queen's University Press 1978

Neill, S. *The Interpretation of the New Testament 1861–1961* Oxford: Oxford University Press 1975

Nimocks, W. *Milner's Young Men* Durham, NC: Duke University Press 1968

Oliver, P. G. *Howard Ferguson: Ontario Tory* Toronto: University of Toronto Press 1977

Pauck, W. *Harnack and Troeltsch: Two Historical Theologians* New York: Oxford University Press 1968

Pearson, L.B. *Mike: The Memoirs of the Rt. Hon. Lester B. Pearson Vol. I 1897–1948* Toronto: University of Toronto Press 1972

Pelikan, J. ed. *Twentieth-Century Theology in the Making* (2 vols) London: Collins 1970

Porter, B. *Britain, Europe and the World: Delusions of Grandeur* London: Allen and Unwin 1983

Radall, T.H. *Halifax: Warden of the North* London: Dent 1948

Read, D. ed. *The Great War and Canadian Society* Toronto: New Hogtown Press 1978

Richter, M. *The Politics of Conscience: T.H. Green and His Age* London: Weidenfeld and Nicolson 1964

Riesen, R.A. *Criticism and Faith in Victorian Scotland: A.B. Davidson, William Robertson Smith and George Adam Smith* Lanham: University Press of America 1985

Rudolph, F. *The American College and University: A History* New York: Vintage 1962

Ryan, S.D. *Race and Nationalism in Trinidad and Tobago* Toronto: University of Toronto Press 1972

Schull, J. *Ontario since 1867* Toronto: McClelland and Stewart 1978

Semmel, B. *Imperialism and Social Reform* London: Allen and Unwin 1960

Shortt, S.E.D. *The Search for an Ideal: Six Canadian Intellectuals and Their Convictions in an Age of Transition 1890–1930* Toronto: University of Toronto Press 1976

Silcox, C.E. *Church Union in Canada* New York: Institute of Social and Religious Research 1933

Simpson, R. *How the Ph.D. Came to Britain* Guildford: Society for Research into Higher Education 1983

Sissons, C.B. *A History of Victoria University* Toronto: University of Toronto Press 1952

Sparrow, J. *Mark Pattison and the Idea of a University* Cambridge: Cambridge University Press 1967

Tatarkiewicz, W. *Nineteenth-Century Philosophy* Belmont, CA: Wadsworth Publishers 1973

Thompson, W.P. *The University of Saskatchewan: A Personal History* Toronto: University of Toronto Press 1970

Turner, A.L. *A History of the University of Edinburgh 1883–1933* London: Oliver and Boyd 1933

Veysey, L.R. *The Emergence of the American University* Chicago: University of Chicago Press 1965

Walsh, H.H. *The Christian Church in Canada* Toronto: Ryerson 1956

Wilson, B.M. ed. *Ontario and the First World 1914–1918* Toronto: University of Toronto Press 1977

Wood, D. *Trinidad in Transition: The Years After Slavery* London: Oxford University Press 1968

Wood, J.D. *The Interpretation of the Bible: An Historical Introduction* London: Duckworth 1958

Articles

Armour, L. 'Philosophy and Denominationalism in Ontario' *Journal of Canadian Studies* 20 (1985) 25–38

Bérard, R.N. 'Moral Education in Nova Scotia 1880–1920' *Acadiensis* 14 (1984) 49–63

Cole, D. 'Canada's Nationalistic Imperialists' *Journal of Canadian Studies* 5 (1970) 44–9

– 'The Problem of "Nationalism" and "Imperialism" in British Settlement Colonies' *Journal of British Studies* 10 (1971) 160–82

Cook, T. 'George Parkin and the Concept of Britannic Idealism' *Journal of Canadian Studies* 10 (1975) 15–31

Craig, G. 'The Compulsion of the National Life' Review of McClelland *State, Society and University* in *Times Literary Supplement* (7 Nov. 1980) 1267

Eayrs, J. 'The Round Table Movement in Canada 1909–20' *Canadian Historical Review* 38 (1957) 1–20

Francis, D. 'The Threatened Dismissal of Frank Underhill from the University of Toronto 1939–1941' *C.A.U.T. Bulletin* (supplement) 30 (Oct. 1983) 5–10

Gavereau, M. 'The Taming of History: Reflections on the Canadian Methodist Encounter with Biblical Criticism 1830–1900' *Canadian Historical Review* 65 (1984) 315–46

Greenlee, J.G. '"A Succession of Seeleys": The Old School Reconsidered' *Journal of Imperial and Commonwealth History* 4 (1976) 266–82

Horn, M. '"Free Speech Within the Law": The Letter of the Sixty-Eight Toronto Professors 1931' *Ontario History* 72 (1980) 27–48

– 'Academic Freedom in Canada; Retrospect and Prospect' *C.A.U.T. Bulletin* 28 (Feb. 1981) 13–14

– 'The History of Academic Freedom in Canada: A Comment' *C.A.U.T. Bulletin* (supplement) 30 (Oct. 1983) 3–4

Karr, C. 'What Is Canadian Intellectual History?' *Dalhousie Review* 55 (1975) 431–48

Mason, M. '"The Sins of Civilization": Bertrand Russell in Toronto' *Russell* (new series) (1983–4) 145–56

Miller, J.D.B. 'The Commonwealth and World Order: The Zimmern Vision and After' *Journal of Imperial and Commonwealth History* 8 (1979) 159–74

Moir, J. '"Mildewed with Discretion": Toronto's Higher Critics and Public Opinion in the 1920s' *Studies in Religion* 2 (1982) 173–9

Westfall, W. 'Order and Experience: Patterns of Religious Metaphor in Early

Nineteenth-Century Upper Canada' *Journal of Canadian Studies* 20 (1985) 5–23

Unpublished Dissertations

Meikle, W.D. 'And Gladly Teach: G.M. Wrong and the Department of History at the University of Toronto' PH D dissertation, Michigan State University 1977
Pilkington, G. 'A History of the National Conference of Canadian Universities 1911–1961' PH D dissertation, University of Toronto 1974

Index